2

# THE JEKYLL ISLAND CHRONICLES

## A DEVIL'S REACH

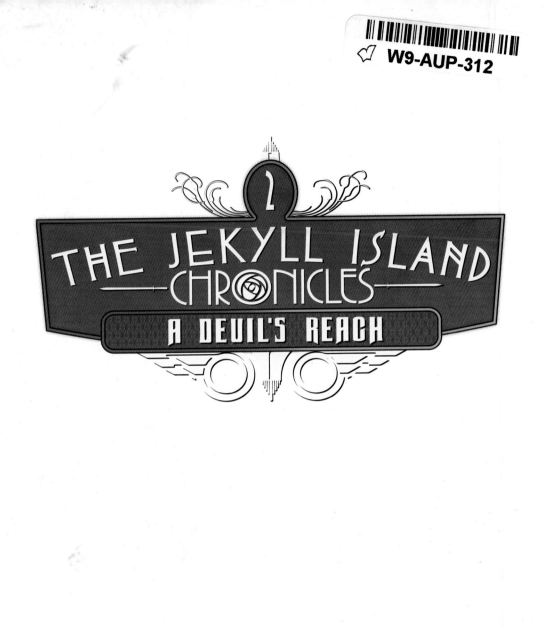

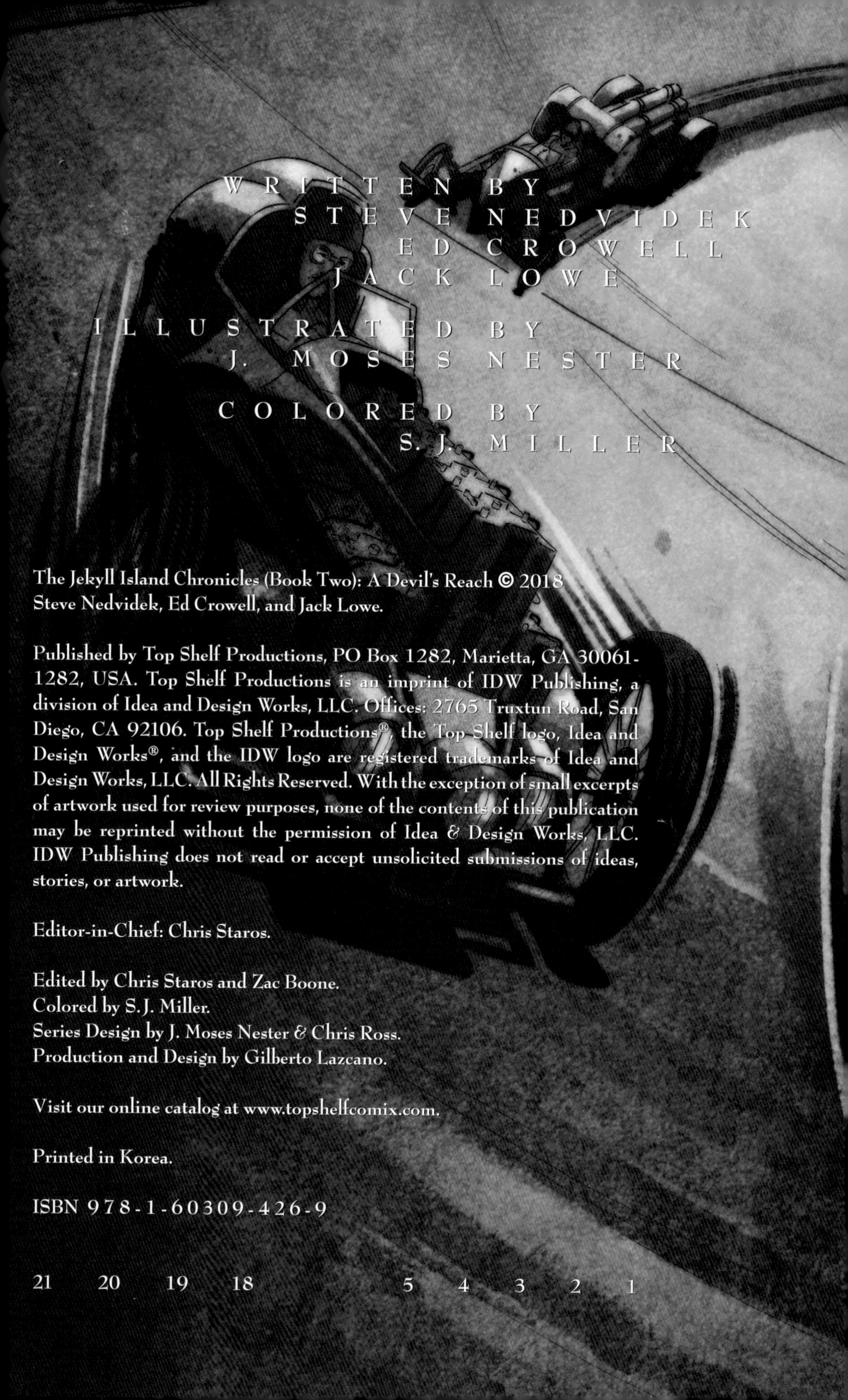

W R I T T E N  B Y
S T E V E  N E D V I D E K
E D  C R O W E L L
J A C K  L O W E

I L L U S T R A T E D  B Y
J. M O S E S  N E S T E R

C O L O R E D  B Y
S. J.  M I L L E R



Published by Top Shelf Productions, PO Box 1282, Marietta, GA 30061-1282, USA. Top Shelf Productions is an imprint of IDW Publishing, a division of Idea and Design Works, LLC. Offices: 2765 Truxtun Road, San Diego, CA 92106. Top Shelf Productions®, the Top Shelf logo, Idea and Design Works®, and the IDW logo are registered trademarks of Idea and Design Works, LLC. 

Editor-in-Chief: Chris Staros.

Edited by Chris Staros and Zac Boone.
Colored by S.J. Miller.
Series Design by J. Moses Nester & Chris Ross.
Production and Design by Gilberto Lazcano.

Visit our online catalog at www.topshelfcomix.com.

Printed in Korea.

ISBN 978-1-60309-426-9

21 20 19 18 5 4 3 2 1

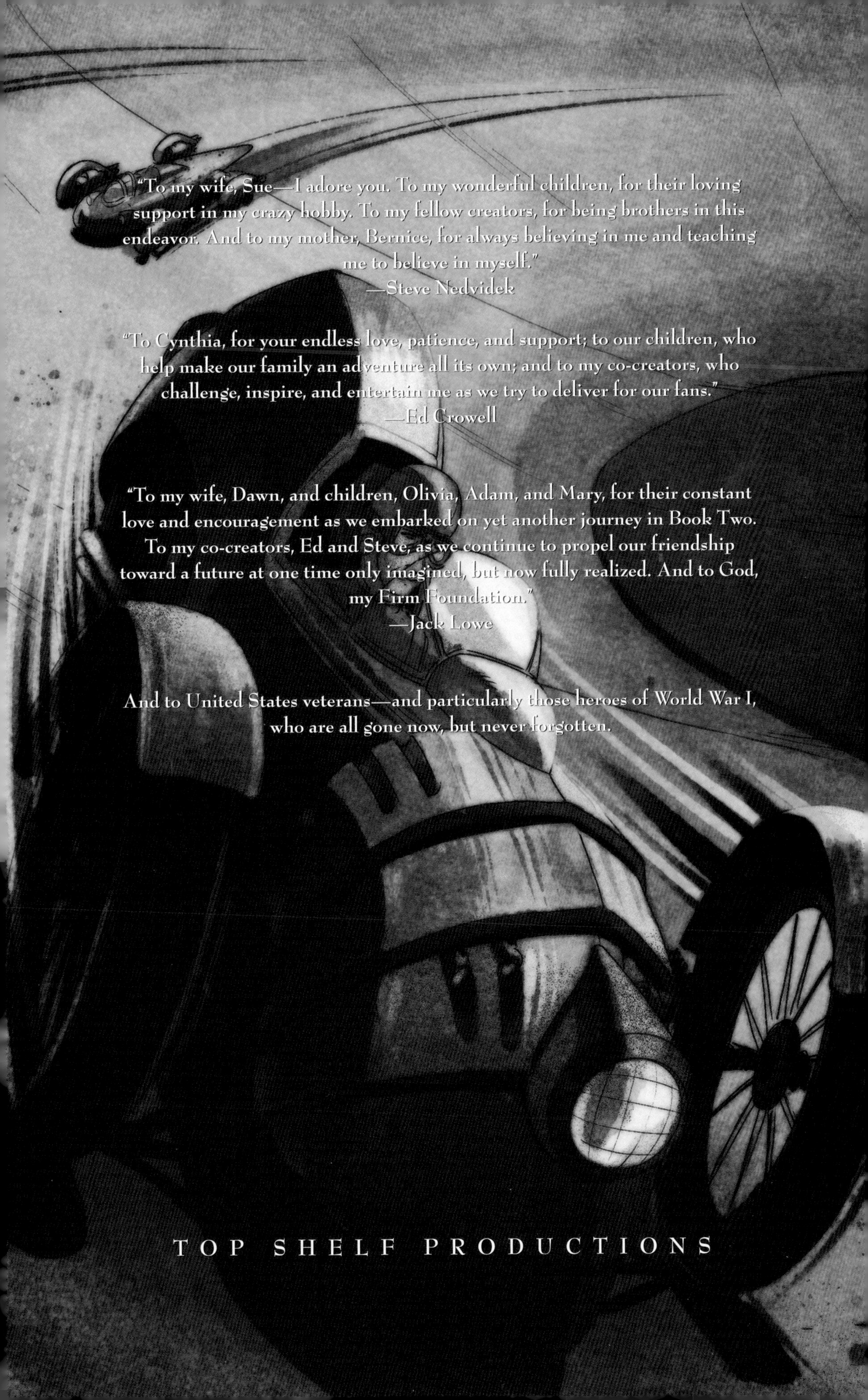

"To my wife, Sue—I adore you. To my wonderful children, for their loving support in my crazy hobby. To my fellow creators, for being brothers in this endeavor. And to my mother, Bernice, for always believing in me and teaching me to believe in myself."
—Steve Nedvidek

"To Cynthia, for your endless love, patience, and support; to our children, who help make our family an adventure all its own; and to my co-creators, who challenge, inspire, and entertain me as we try to deliver for our fans."
—Ed Crowell

"To my wife, Dawn, and children, Olivia, Adam, and Mary, for their constant love and encouragement as we embarked on yet another journey in Book Two. To my co-creators, Ed and Steve, as we continue to propel our friendship toward a future at one time only imagined, but now fully realized. And to God, my Firm Foundation."
—Jack Lowe

And to United States veterans—and particularly those heroes of World War I, who are all gone now, but never forgotten.

TOP SHELF PRODUCTIONS

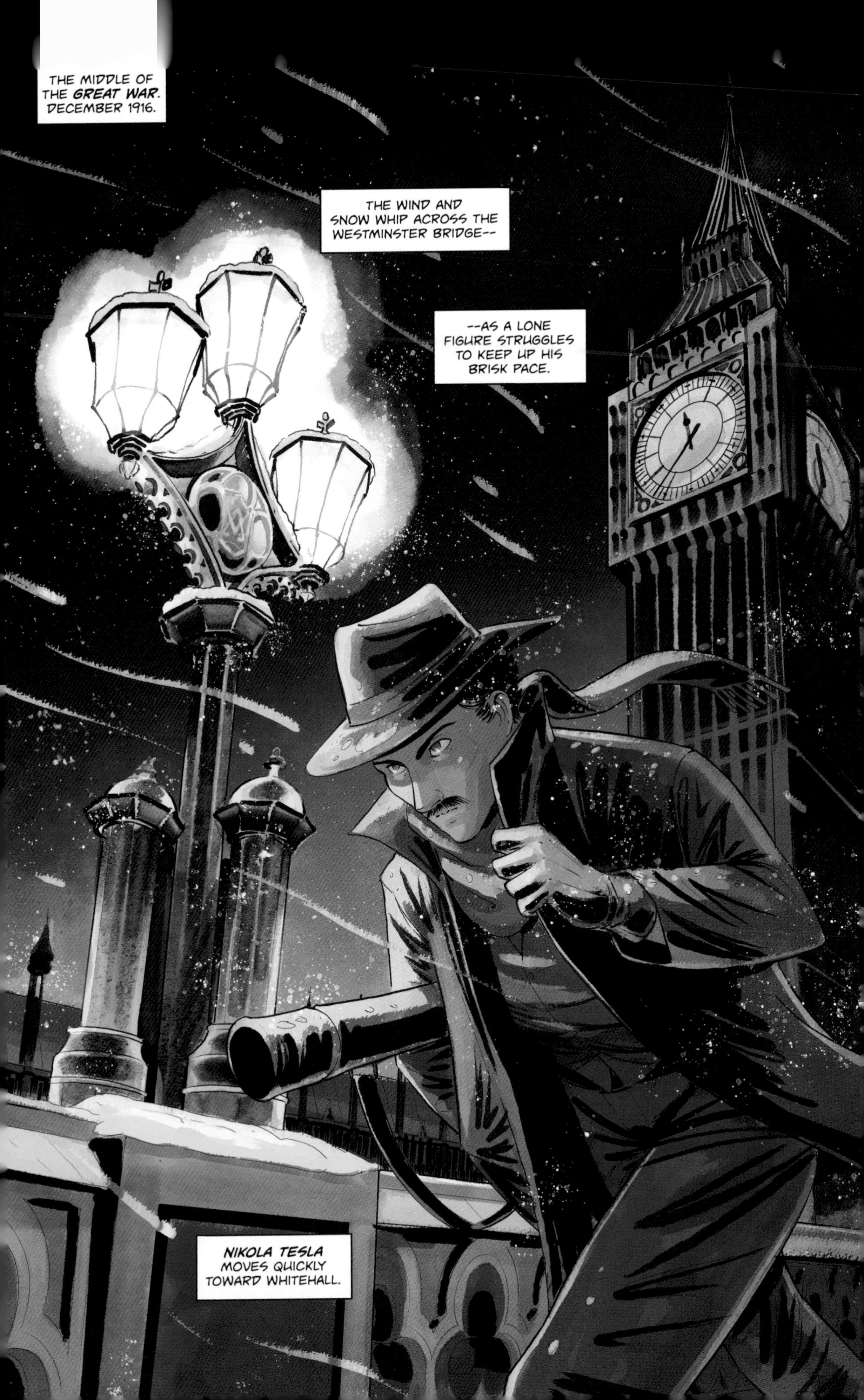
THE MIDDLE OF THE *GREAT WAR*. DECEMBER 1916.
THE WIND AND SNOW WHIP ACROSS THE WESTMINSTER BRIDGE--
--AS A LONE FIGURE STRUGGLES TO KEEP UP HIS BRISK PACE.
*NIKOLA TESLA* MOVES QUICKLY TOWARD WHITEHALL.

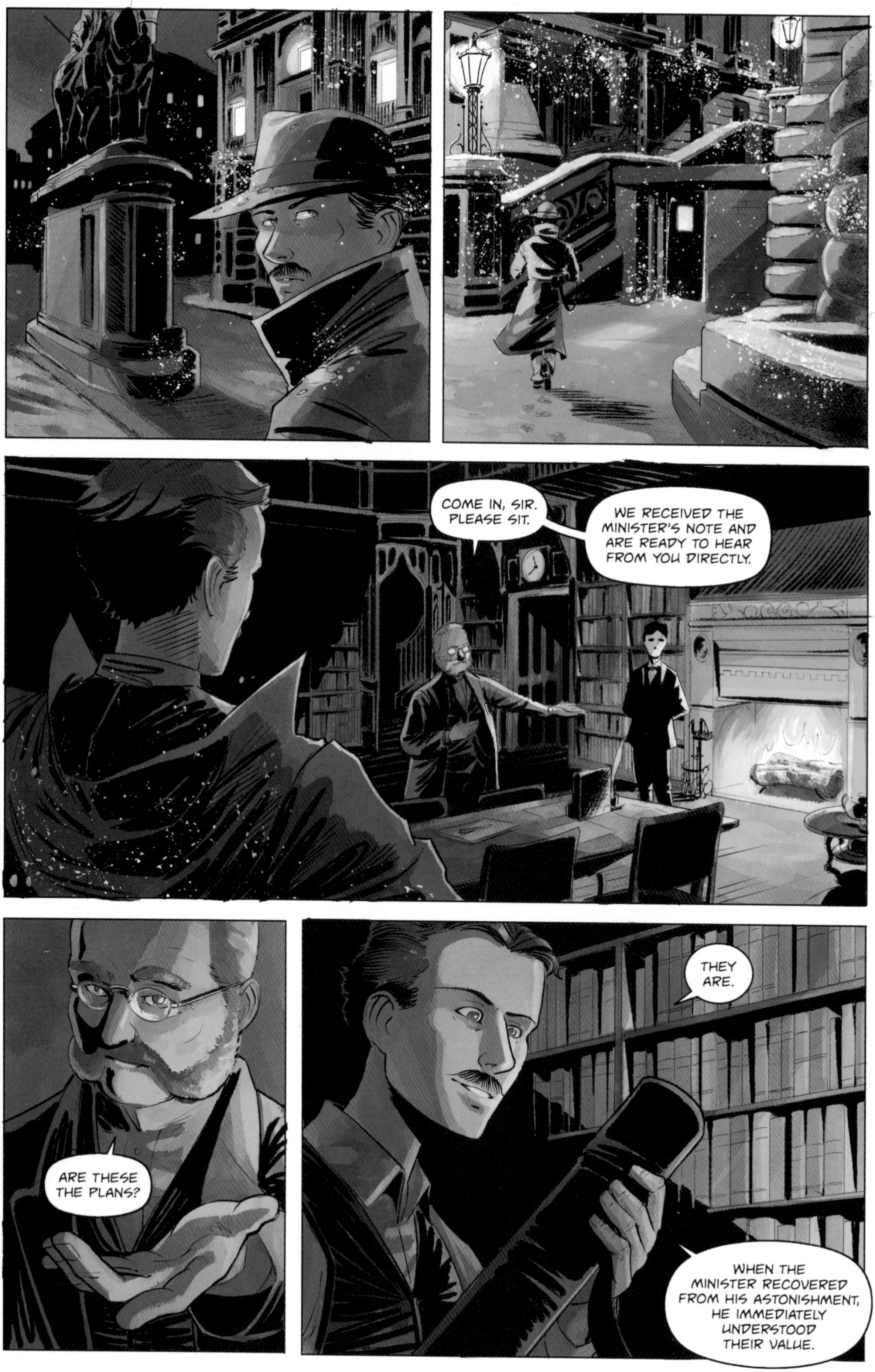
COME IN, SIR. PLEASE SIT.
WE RECEIVED THE MINISTER'S NOTE AND ARE READY TO HEAR FROM YOU DIRECTLY.
ARE THESE THE PLANS?
THEY ARE.
WHEN THE MINISTER RECOVERED FROM HIS ASTONISHMENT, HE IMMEDIATELY UNDERSTOOD THEIR VALUE.

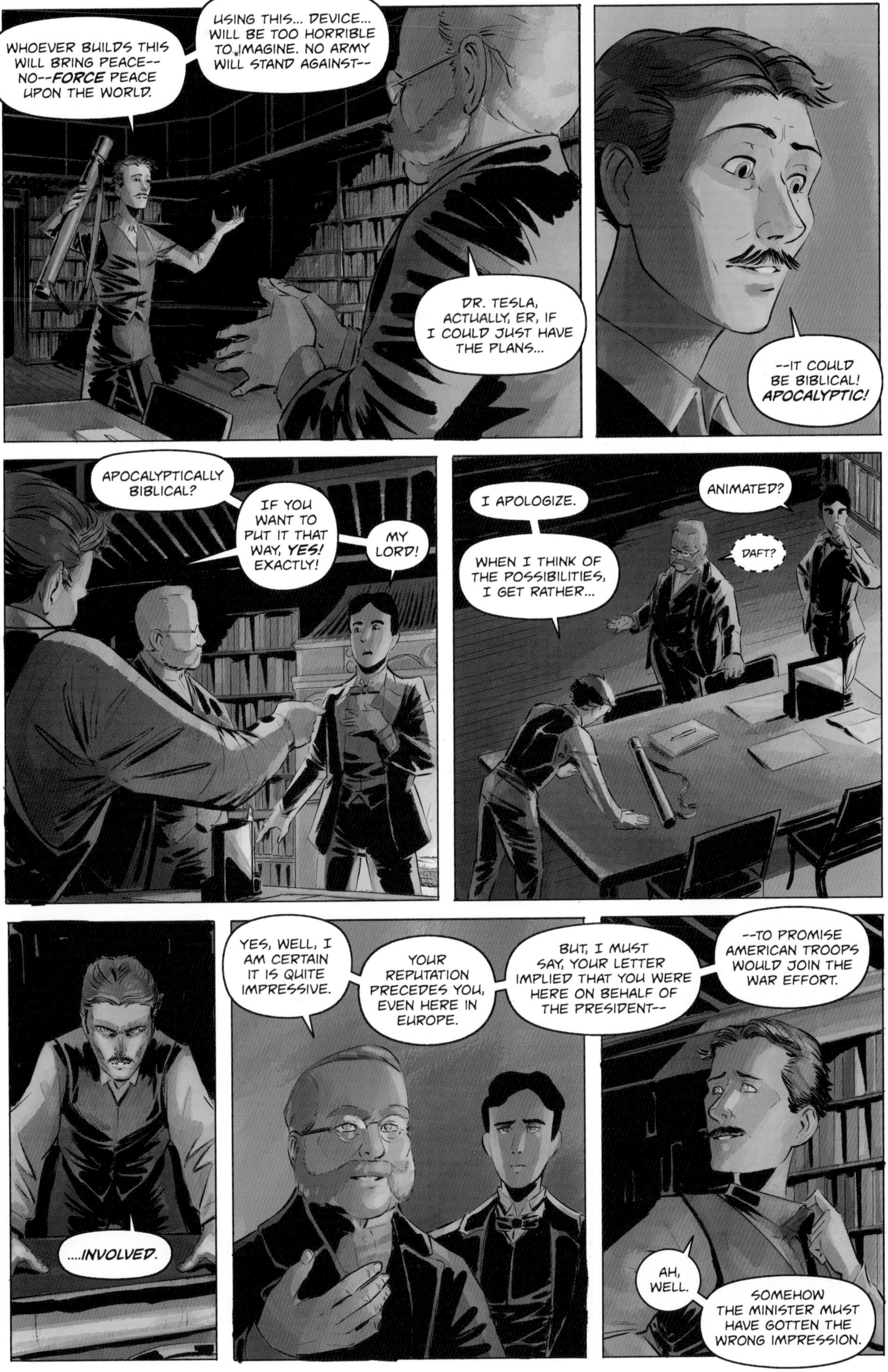
WHOEVER BUILDS THIS WILL BRING PEACE-- NO--*FORCE* PEACE UPON THE WORLD.
USING THIS... DEVICE... WILL BE TOO HORRIBLE TO IMAGINE. NO ARMY WILL STAND AGAINST--
DR. TESLA, ACTUALLY, ER, IF I COULD JUST HAVE THE PLANS...
--IT COULD BE BIBLICAL! *APOCALYPTIC!*
APOCALYPTICALLY BIBLICAL?
IF YOU WANT TO PUT IT THAT WAY, *YES!* EXACTLY!
MY LORD!
I APOLOGIZE.
WHEN I THINK OF THE POSSIBILITIES, I GET RATHER...
ANIMATED?
DAFT?
....*INVOLVED*.
YES, WELL, I AM CERTAIN IT IS QUITE IMPRESSIVE.
YOUR REPUTATION PRECEDES YOU, EVEN HERE IN EUROPE.
BUT, I MUST SAY, YOUR LETTER IMPLIED THAT YOU WERE HERE ON BEHALF OF THE PRESIDENT--
--TO PROMISE AMERICAN TROOPS WOULD JOIN THE WAR EFFORT.
AH, WELL.
SOMEHOW THE MINISTER MUST HAVE GOTTEN THE WRONG IMPRESSION.

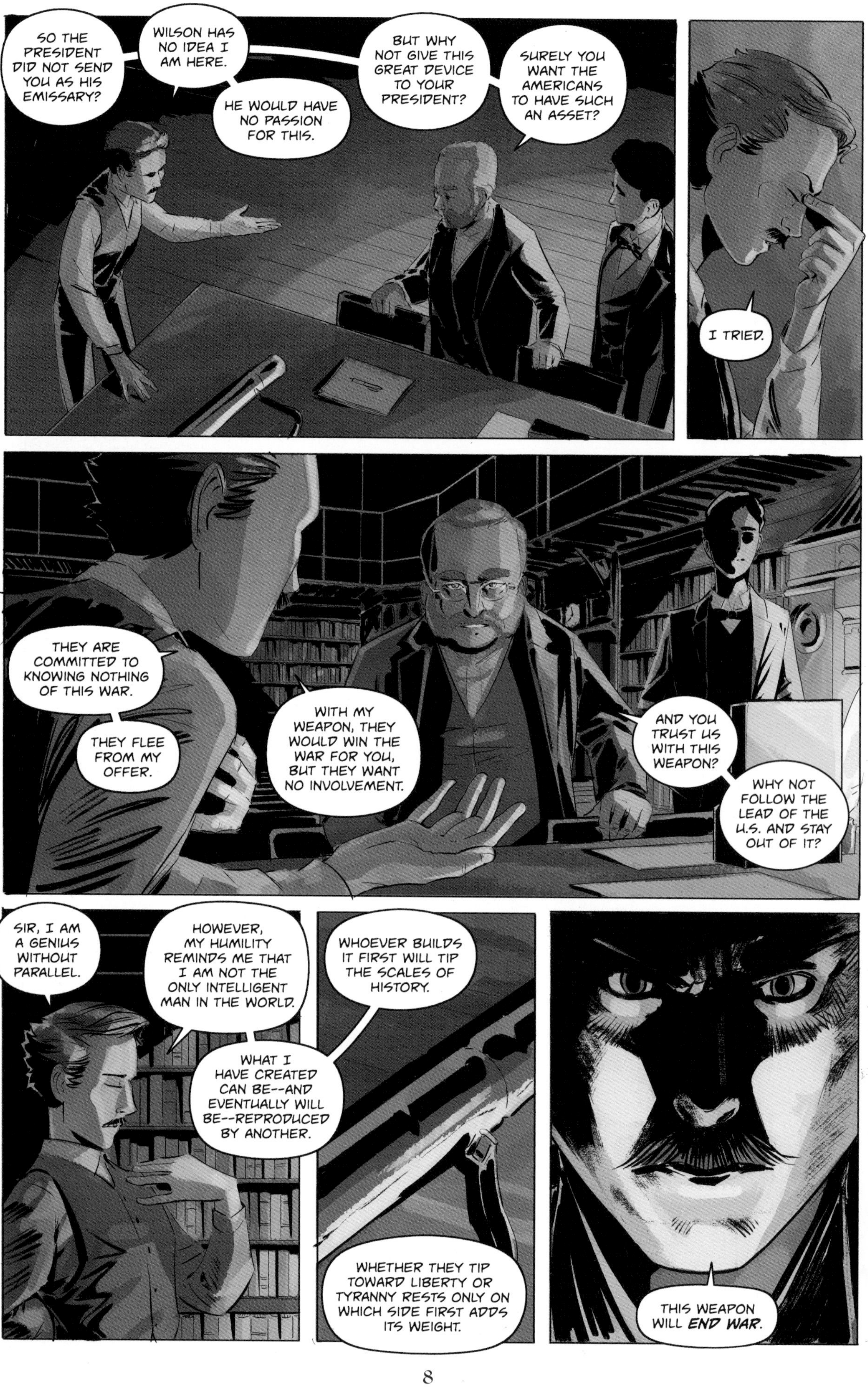
SO THE PRESIDENT DID NOT SEND YOU AS HIS EMISSARY?
WILSON HAS NO IDEA I AM HERE.
HE WOULD HAVE NO PASSION FOR THIS.
BUT WHY NOT GIVE THIS GREAT DEVICE TO YOUR PRESIDENT?
SURELY YOU WANT THE AMERICANS TO HAVE SUCH AN ASSET?
I TRIED.
THEY ARE COMMITTED TO KNOWING NOTHING OF THIS WAR.
THEY FLEE FROM MY OFFER.
WITH MY WEAPON, THEY WOULD WIN THE WAR FOR YOU, BUT THEY WANT NO INVOLVEMENT.
AND YOU TRUST US WITH THIS WEAPON?
WHY NOT FOLLOW THE LEAD OF THE U.S. AND STAY OUT OF IT?
SIR, I AM A GENIUS WITHOUT PARALLEL.
HOWEVER, MY HUMILITY REMINDS ME THAT I AM NOT THE ONLY INTELLIGENT MAN IN THE WORLD.
WHAT I HAVE CREATED CAN BE--AND EVENTUALLY WILL BE--REPRODUCED BY ANOTHER.
WHOEVER BUILDS IT FIRST WILL TIP THE SCALES OF HISTORY.
WHETHER THEY TIP TOWARD LIBERTY OR TYRANNY RESTS ONLY ON WHICH SIDE FIRST ADDS ITS WEIGHT.
THIS WEAPON WILL ***END WAR***.

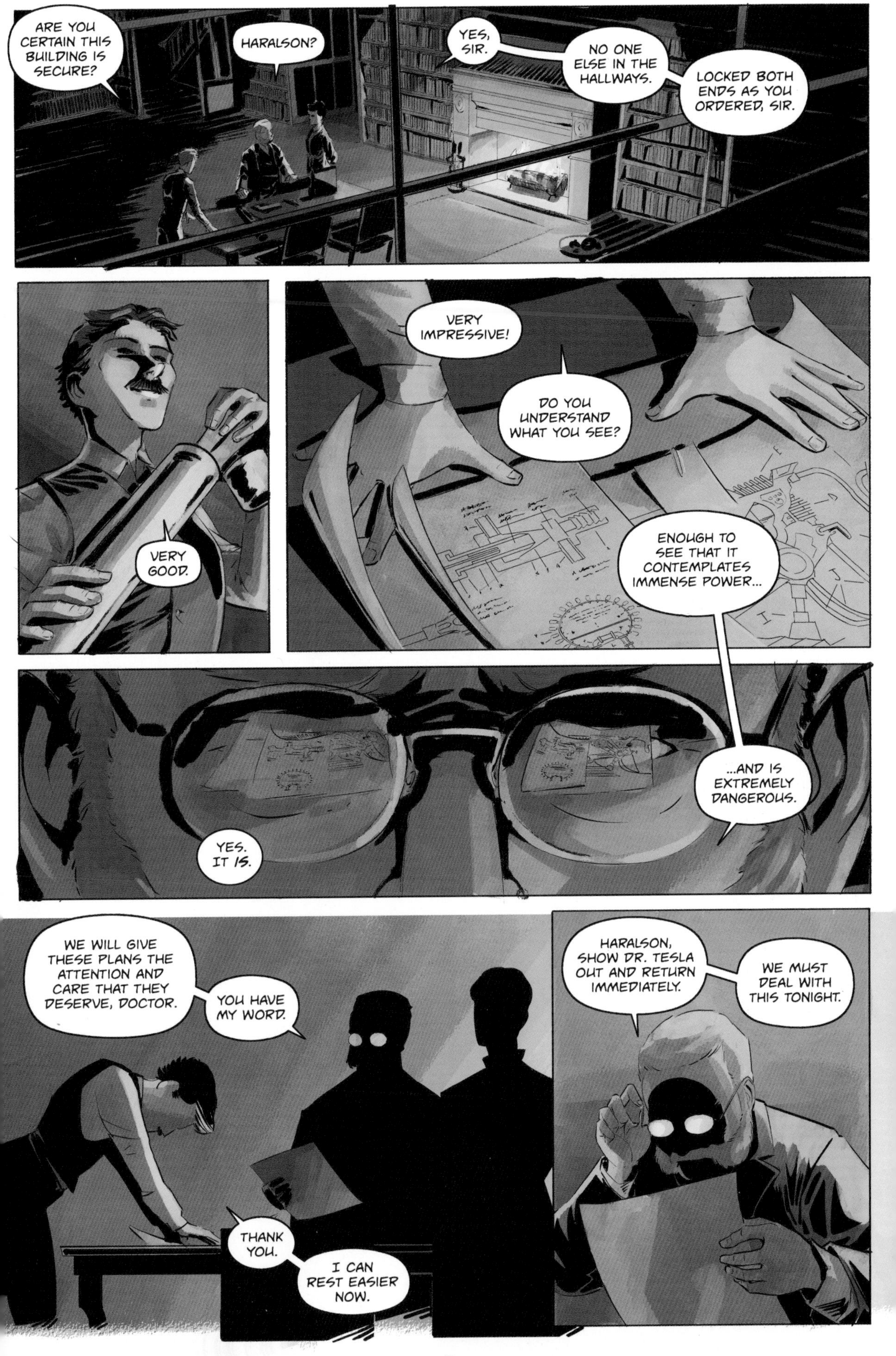
ARE YOU CERTAIN THIS BUILDING IS SECURE?
HARALSON?
YES, SIR.
NO ONE ELSE IN THE HALLWAYS.
LOCKED BOTH ENDS AS YOU ORDERED, SIR.
VERY GOOD.
VERY IMPRESSIVE!
DO YOU UNDERSTAND WHAT YOU SEE?
ENOUGH TO SEE THAT IT CONTEMPLATES IMMENSE POWER...
...AND IS EXTREMELY DANGEROUS.
YES. IT IS.
WE WILL GIVE THESE PLANS THE ATTENTION AND CARE THAT THEY DESERVE, DOCTOR.
YOU HAVE MY WORD.
THANK YOU.
I CAN REST EASIER NOW.
HARALSON, SHOW DR. TESLA OUT AND RETURN IMMEDIATELY.
WE MUST DEAL WITH THIS TONIGHT.

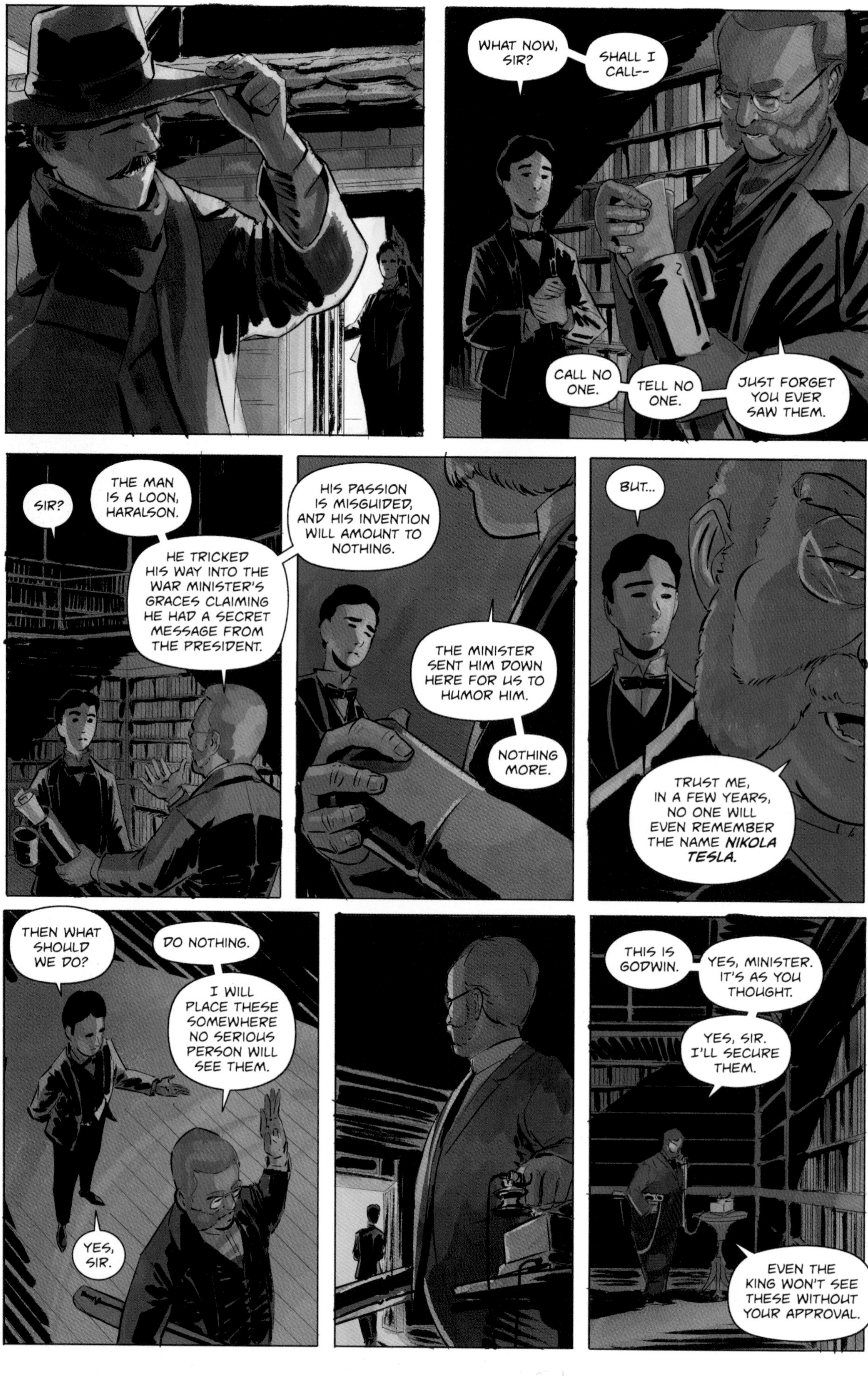
WHAT NOW, SIR?
SHALL I CALL--
CALL NO ONE.
TELL NO ONE.
JUST FORGET YOU EVER SAW THEM.
SIR?
THE MAN IS A LOON, HARALSON.
HE TRICKED HIS WAY INTO THE WAR MINISTER'S GRACES CLAIMING HE HAD A SECRET MESSAGE FROM THE PRESIDENT.
HIS PASSION IS MISGUIDED, AND HIS INVENTION WILL AMOUNT TO NOTHING.
THE MINISTER SENT HIM DOWN HERE FOR US TO HUMOR HIM.
NOTHING MORE.
BUT...
TRUST ME, IN A FEW YEARS, NO ONE WILL EVEN REMEMBER THE NAME NIKOLA TESLA.
THEN WHAT SHOULD WE DO?
DO NOTHING.
I WILL PLACE THESE SOMEWHERE NO SERIOUS PERSON WILL SEE THEM.
YES, SIR.
THIS IS GODWIN.
YES, MINISTER. IT'S AS YOU THOUGHT.
YES, SIR. I'LL SECURE THEM.
EVEN THE KING WON'T SEE THESE WITHOUT YOUR APPROVAL.

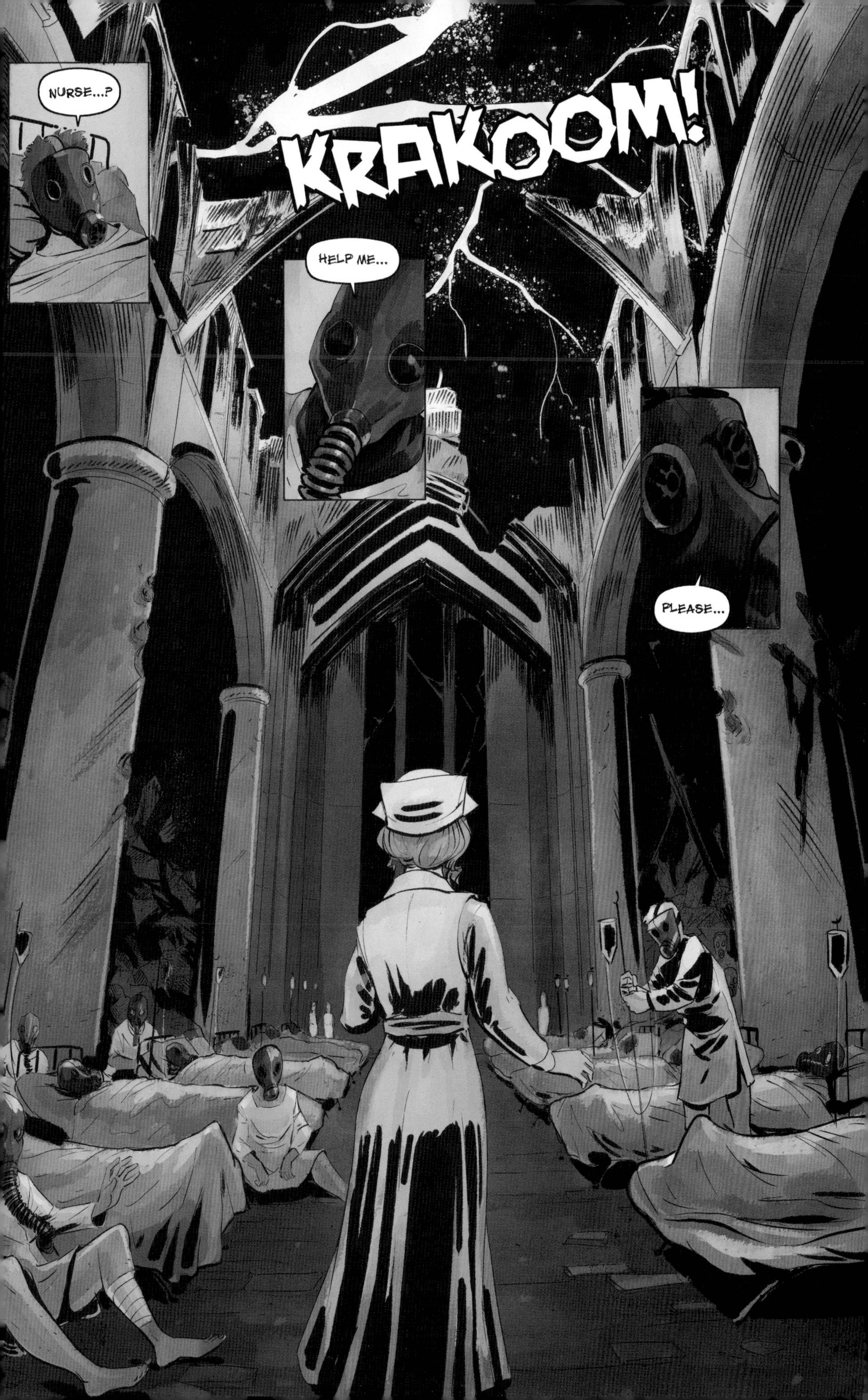
NURSE...?
KRAKOOM!
HELP ME...
PLEASE...

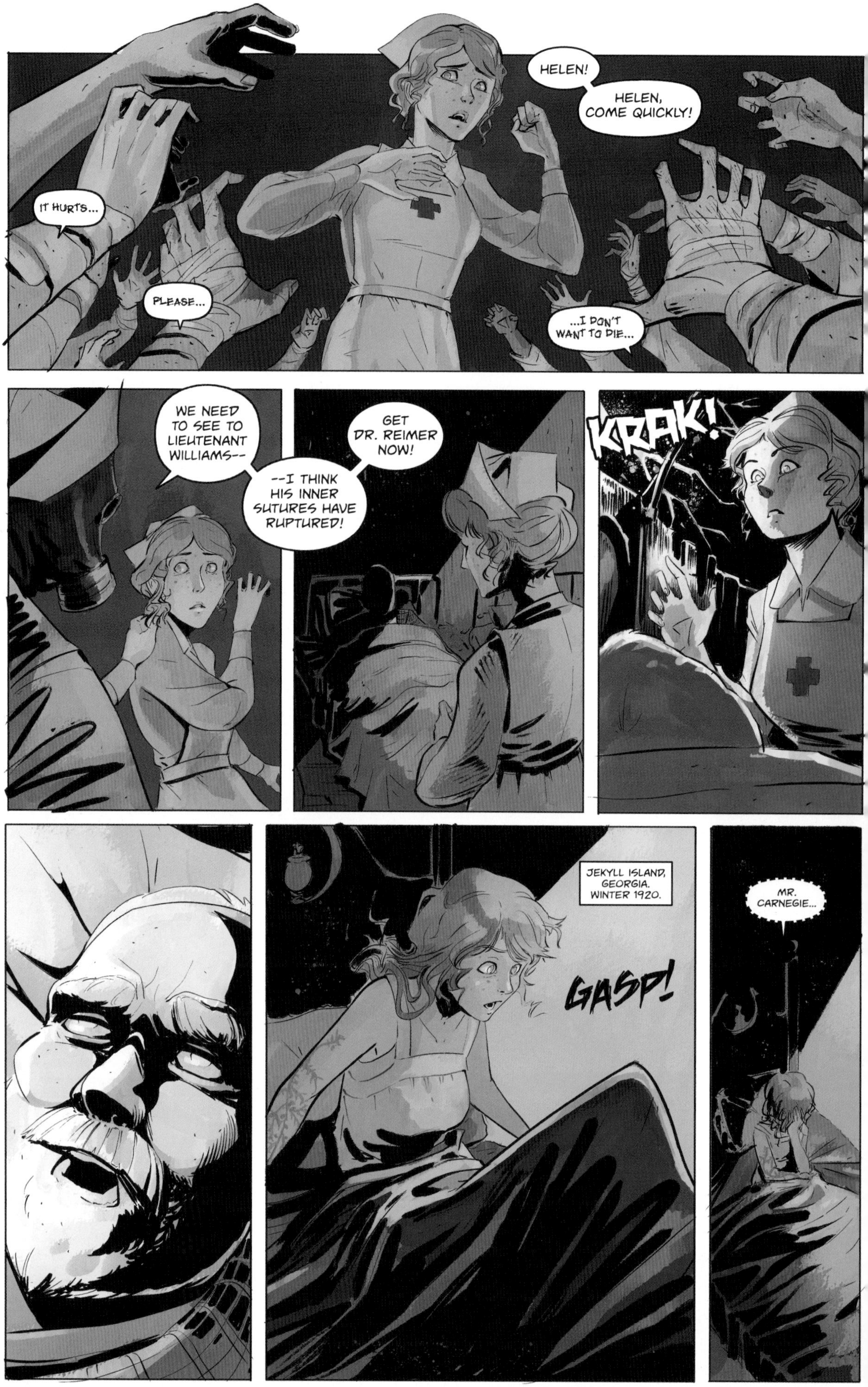
HELEN!
HELEN, COME QUICKLY!
IT HURTS...
PLEASE...
...I DON'T WANT TO DIE...
WE NEED TO SEE TO LIEUTENANT WILLIAMS--
--I THINK HIS INNER SUTURES HAVE RUPTURED!
GET DR. REIMER NOW!
KRAK!
JEKYLL ISLAND, GEORGIA. WINTER 1920.
GASP!
MR. CARNEGIE...

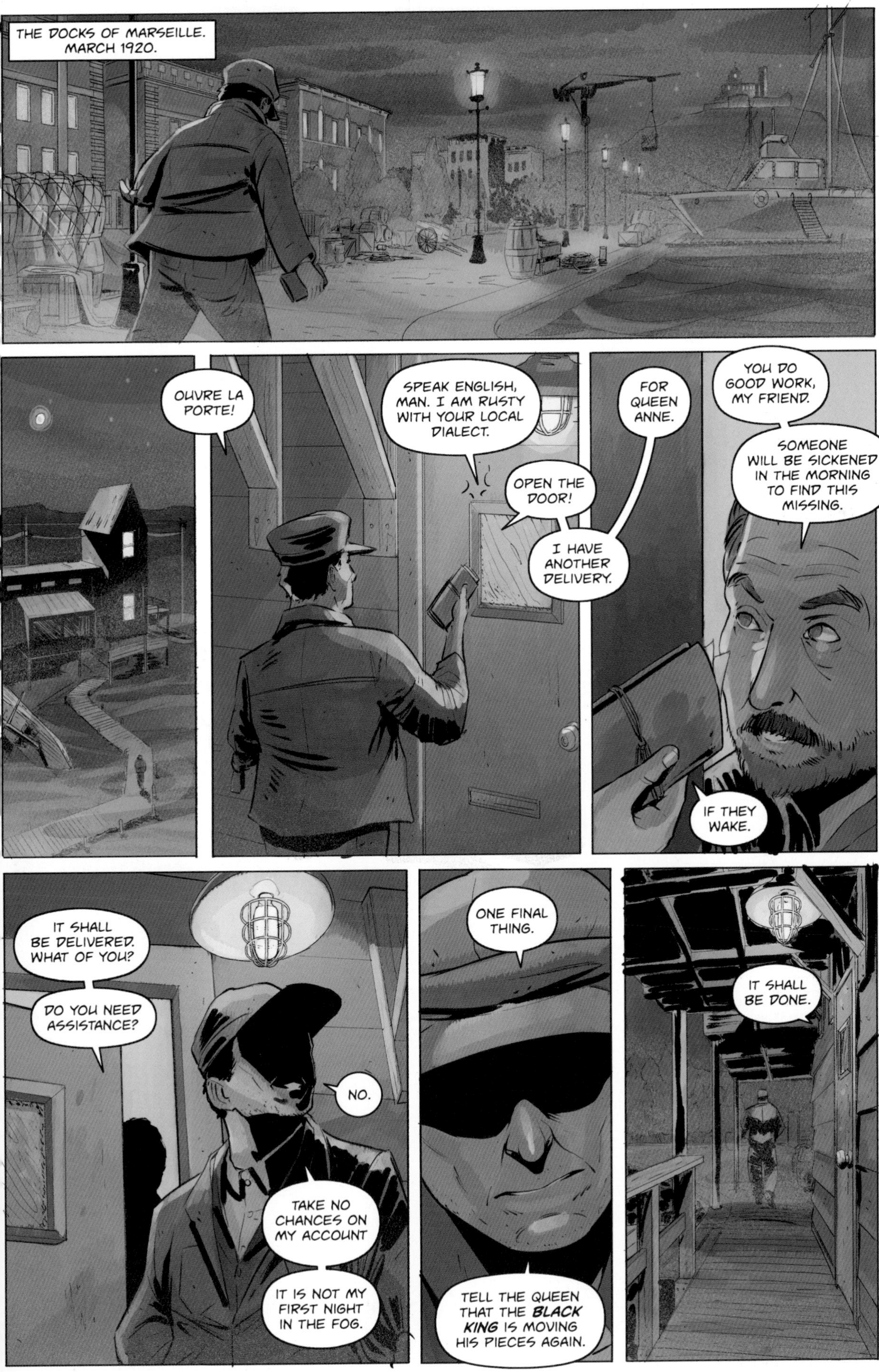
THE DOCKS OF MARSEILLE. MARCH 1920.
OUVRE LA PORTE!
SPEAK ENGLISH, MAN. I AM RUSTY WITH YOUR LOCAL DIALECT.
OPEN THE DOOR!
I HAVE ANOTHER DELIVERY.
FOR QUEEN ANNE.
YOU DO GOOD WORK, MY FRIEND.
SOMEONE WILL BE SICKENED IN THE MORNING TO FIND THIS MISSING.
IF THEY WAKE.
IT SHALL BE DELIVERED. WHAT OF YOU?
DO YOU NEED ASSISTANCE?
NO.
TAKE NO CHANCES ON MY ACCOUNT
IT IS NOT MY FIRST NIGHT IN THE FOG.
ONE FINAL THING.
TELL THE QUEEN THAT THE ***BLACK KING*** IS MOVING HIS PIECES AGAIN.
IT SHALL BE DONE.

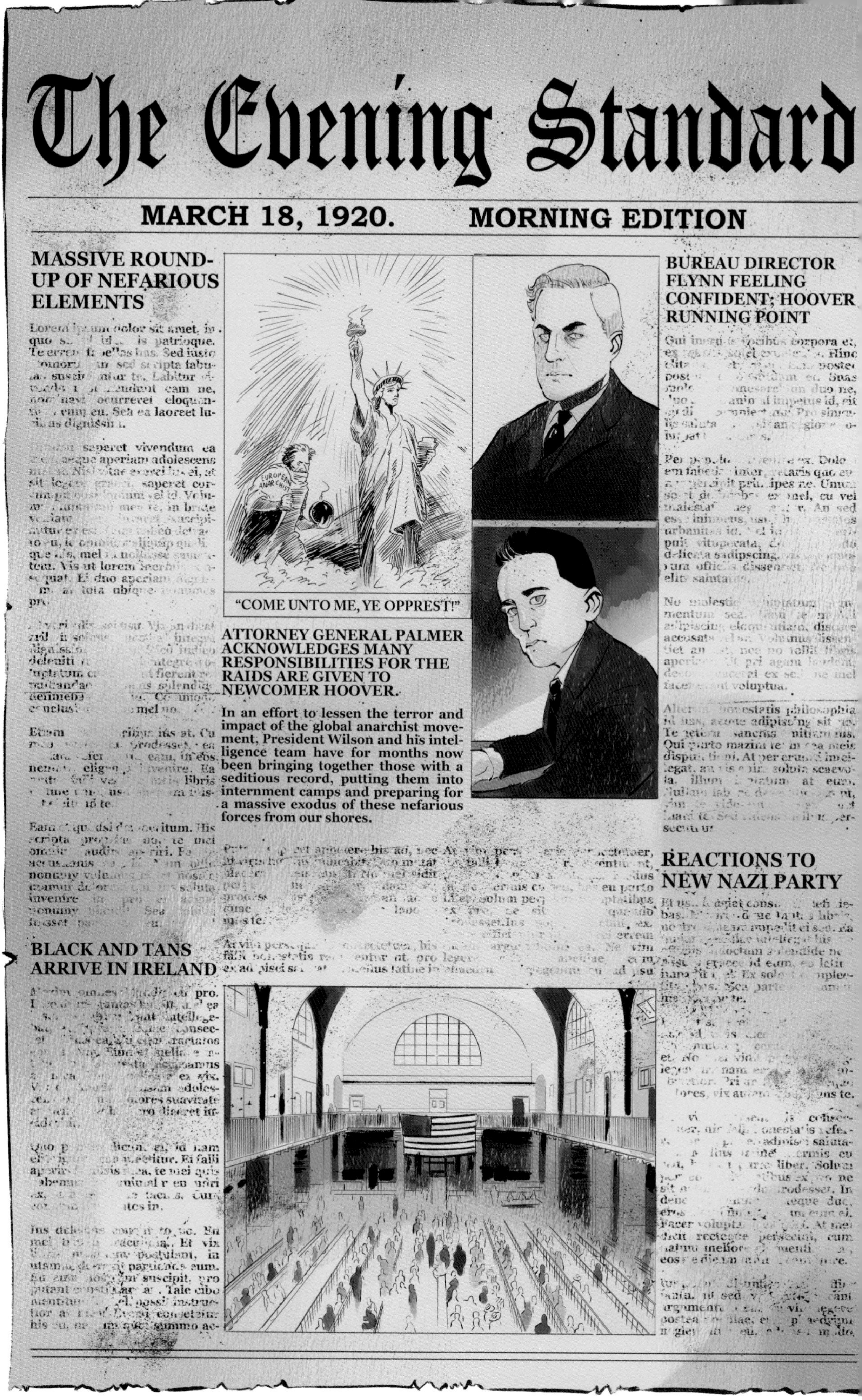
The Evening Standard
MARCH 18, 1920. MORNING EDITION
MASSIVE ROUND-UP OF NEFARIOUS ELEMENTS
EUROPEAN ANARCHIST
"COME UNTO ME, YE OPPREST!"
BUREAU DIRECTOR FLYNN FEELING CONFIDENT; HOOVER RUNNING POINT
ATTORNEY GENERAL PALMER ACKNOWLEDGES MANY RESPONSIBILITIES FOR THE RAIDS ARE GIVEN TO NEWCOMER HOOVER.
In an effort to lessen the terror and impact of the global anarchist movement, President Wilson and his intelligence team have for months now been bringing together those with a seditious record, putting them into internment camps and preparing for a massive exodus of these nefarious forces from our shores.
REACTIONS TO NEW NAZI PARTY
BLACK AND TANS ARRIVE IN IRELAND

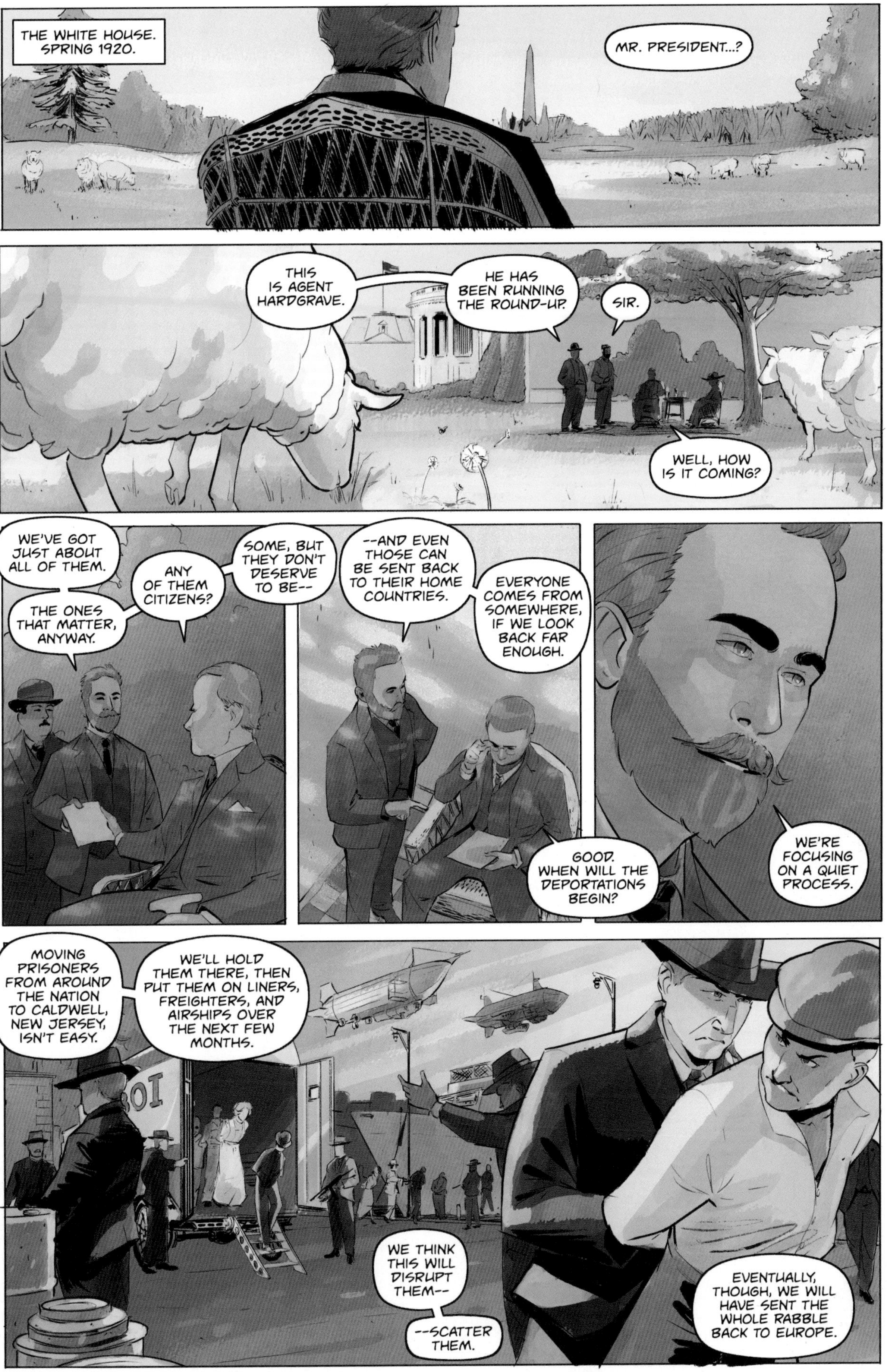
THE WHITE HOUSE. SPRING 1920.
MR. PRESIDENT...?
THIS IS AGENT HARDGRAVE.
HE HAS BEEN RUNNING THE ROUND-UP.
SIR.
WELL, HOW IS IT COMING?
WE'VE GOT JUST ABOUT ALL OF THEM.
THE ONES THAT MATTER, ANYWAY.
ANY OF THEM CITIZENS?
SOME, BUT THEY DON'T DESERVE TO BE--
--AND EVEN THOSE CAN BE SENT BACK TO THEIR HOME COUNTRIES.
EVERYONE COMES FROM SOMEWHERE, IF WE LOOK BACK FAR ENOUGH.
GOOD. WHEN WILL THE DEPORTATIONS BEGIN?
WE'RE FOCUSING ON A QUIET PROCESS.
MOVING PRISONERS FROM AROUND THE NATION TO CALDWELL, NEW JERSEY, ISN'T EASY.
WE'LL HOLD THEM THERE, THEN PUT THEM ON LINERS, FREIGHTERS, AND AIRSHIPS OVER THE NEXT FEW MONTHS.
WE THINK THIS WILL DISRUPT THEM--
--SCATTER THEM.
EVENTUALLY, THOUGH, WE WILL HAVE SENT THE WHOLE RABBLE BACK TO EUROPE.

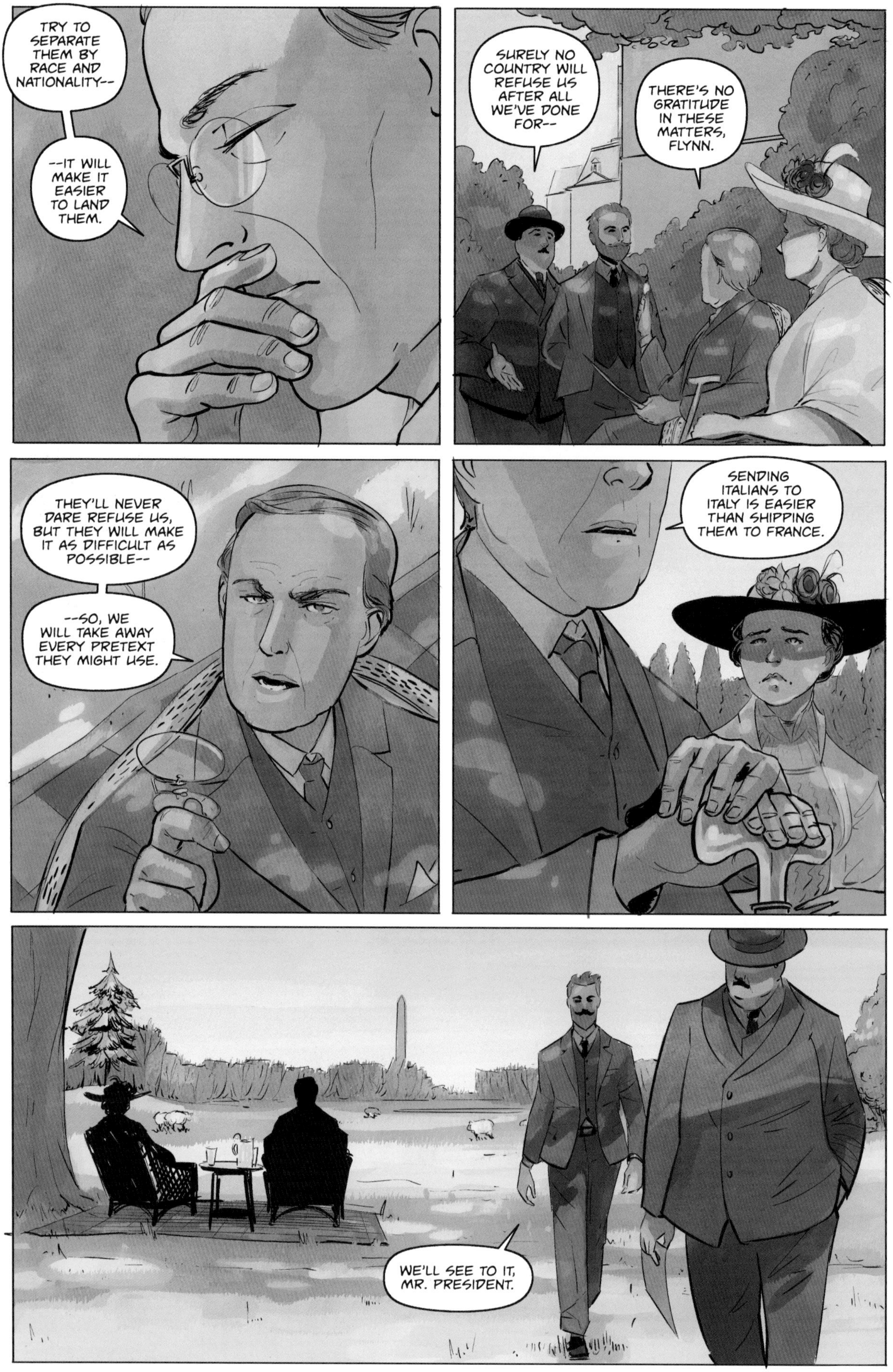
TRY TO SEPARATE THEM BY RACE AND NATIONALITY--
--IT WILL MAKE IT EASIER TO LAND THEM.
SURELY NO COUNTRY WILL REFUSE US AFTER ALL WE'VE DONE FOR--
THERE'S NO GRATITUDE IN THESE MATTERS, FLYNN.
THEY'LL NEVER DARE REFUSE US, BUT THEY WILL MAKE IT AS DIFFICULT AS POSSIBLE--
--SO, WE WILL TAKE AWAY EVERY PRETEXT THEY MIGHT USE.
SENDING ITALIANS TO ITALY IS EASIER THAN SHIPPING THEM TO FRANCE.
WE'LL SEE TO IT, MR. PRESIDENT.

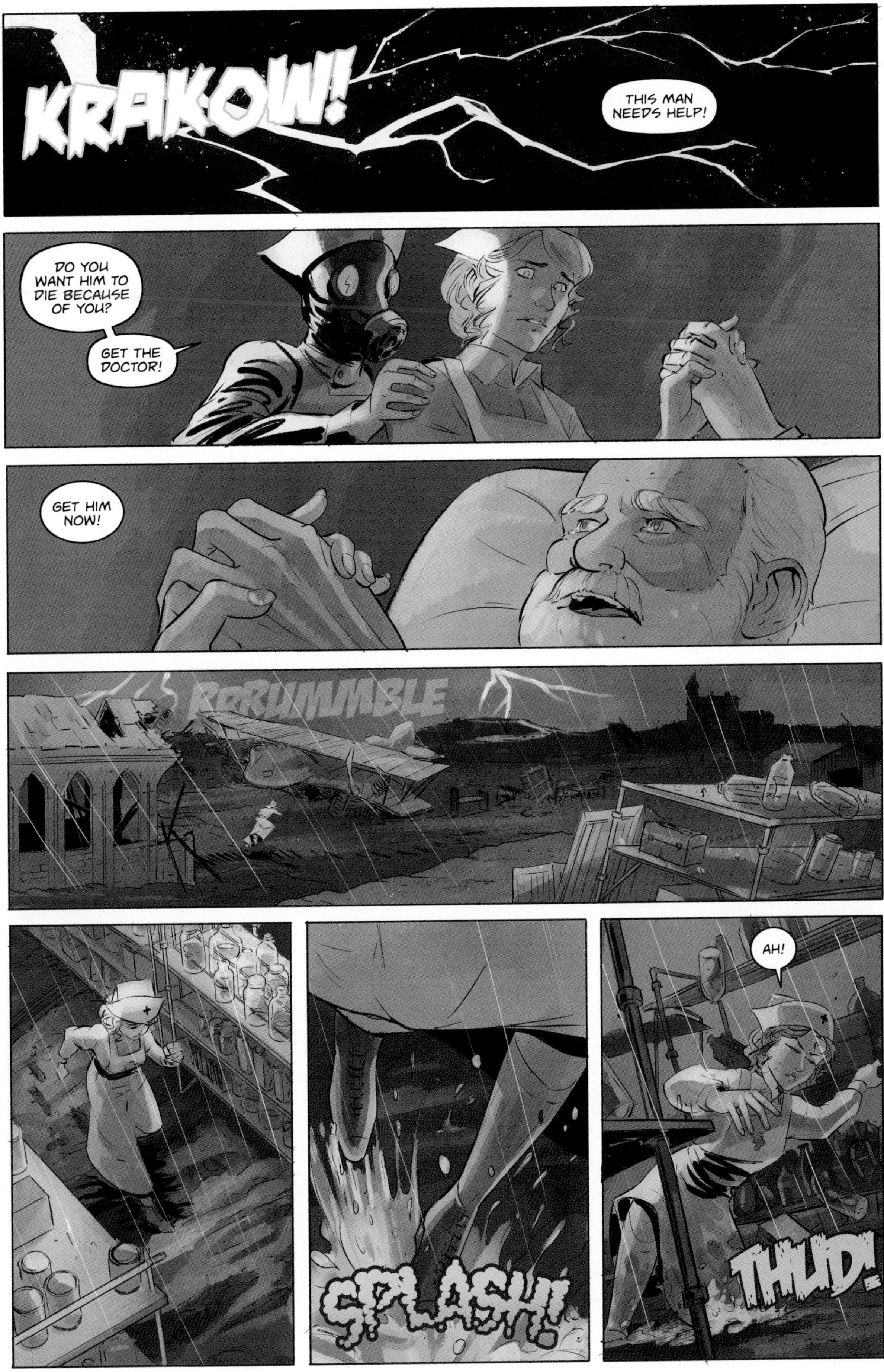
KRAKOW!
THIS MAN NEEDS HELP!
DO YOU WANT HIM TO DIE BECAUSE OF YOU?
GET THE DOCTOR!
GET HIM NOW!
RRRUMMBLE
AH!
SPLASH!
THUD!

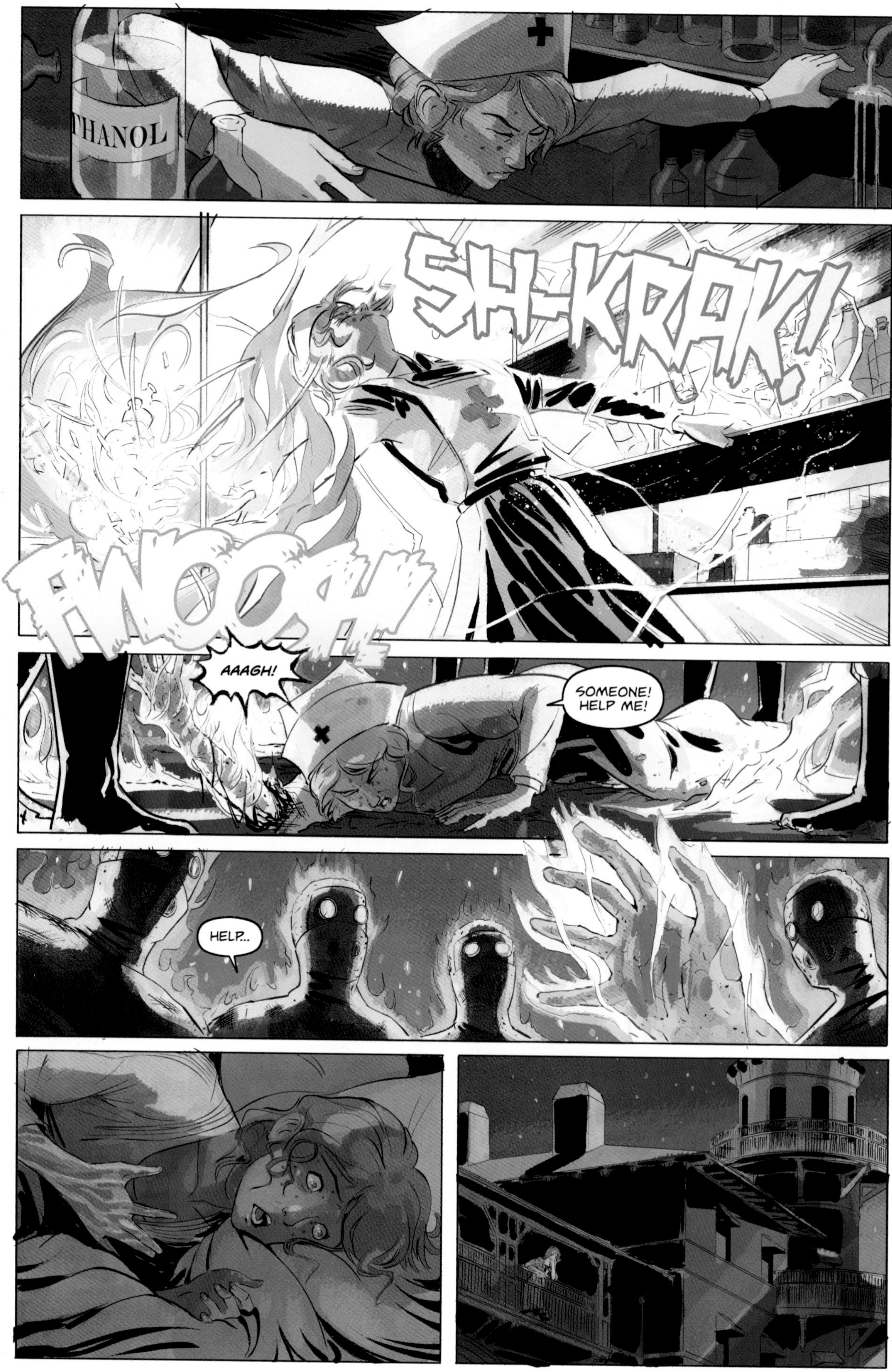
THANOL
SH-KRAK!!
FWOOSH
AAAGH!
SOMEONE! HELP ME!
HELP...

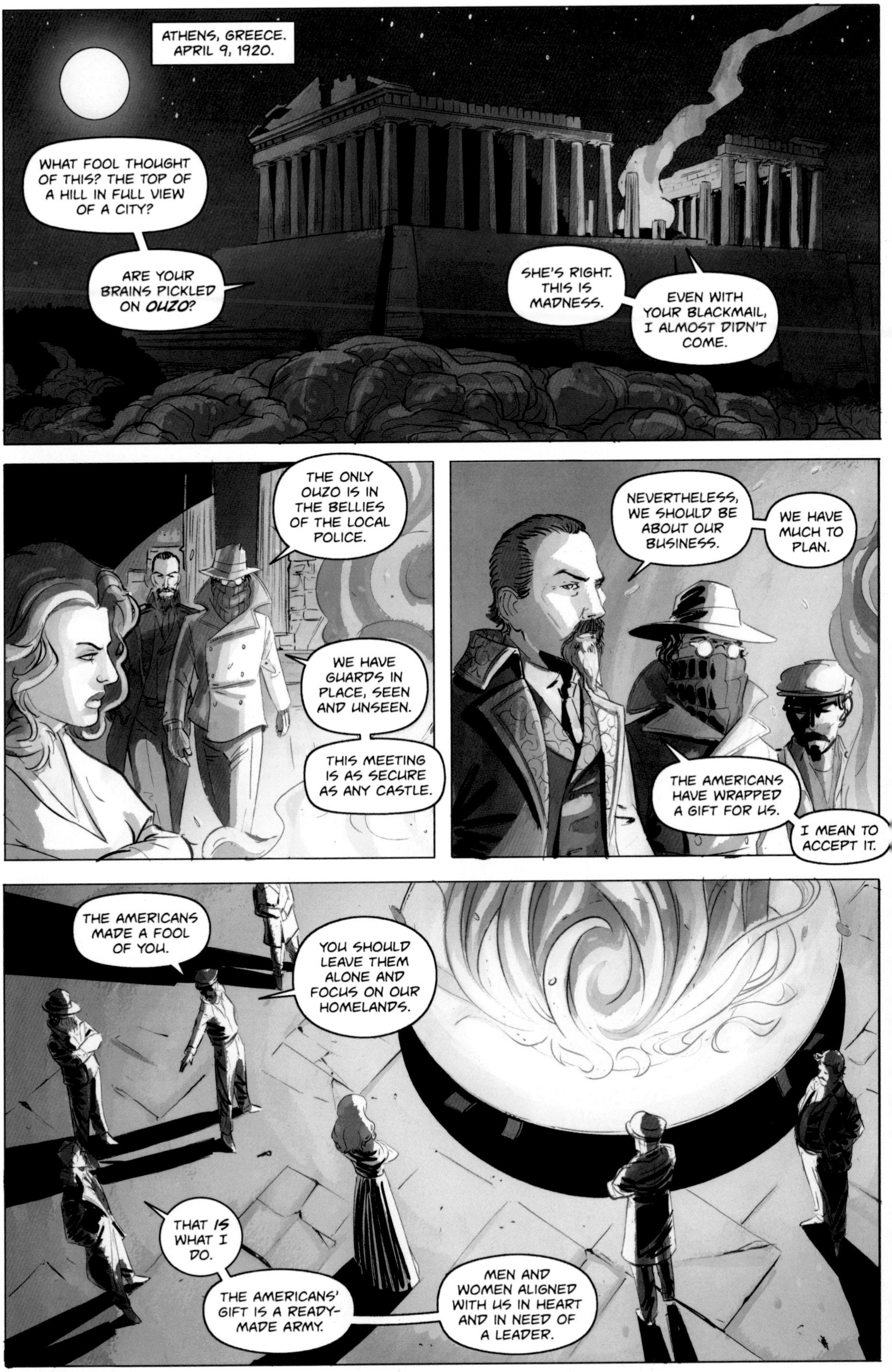
ATHENS, GREECE. APRIL 9, 1920.
WHAT FOOL THOUGHT OF THIS? THE TOP OF A HILL IN FULL VIEW OF A CITY?
ARE YOUR BRAINS PICKLED ON OUZO?
SHE'S RIGHT. THIS IS MADNESS.
EVEN WITH YOUR BLACKMAIL, I ALMOST DIDN'T COME.
THE ONLY OUZO IS IN THE BELLIES OF THE LOCAL POLICE.
WE HAVE GUARDS IN PLACE, SEEN AND UNSEEN.
THIS MEETING IS AS SECURE AS ANY CASTLE.
NEVERTHELESS, WE SHOULD BE ABOUT OUR BUSINESS.
WE HAVE MUCH TO PLAN.
THE AMERICANS HAVE WRAPPED A GIFT FOR US.
I MEAN TO ACCEPT IT.
THE AMERICANS MADE A FOOL OF YOU.
YOU SHOULD LEAVE THEM ALONE AND FOCUS ON OUR HOMELANDS.
THAT IS WHAT I DO.
THE AMERICANS' GIFT IS A READY-MADE ARMY.
MEN AND WOMEN ALIGNED WITH US IN HEART AND IN NEED OF A LEADER.

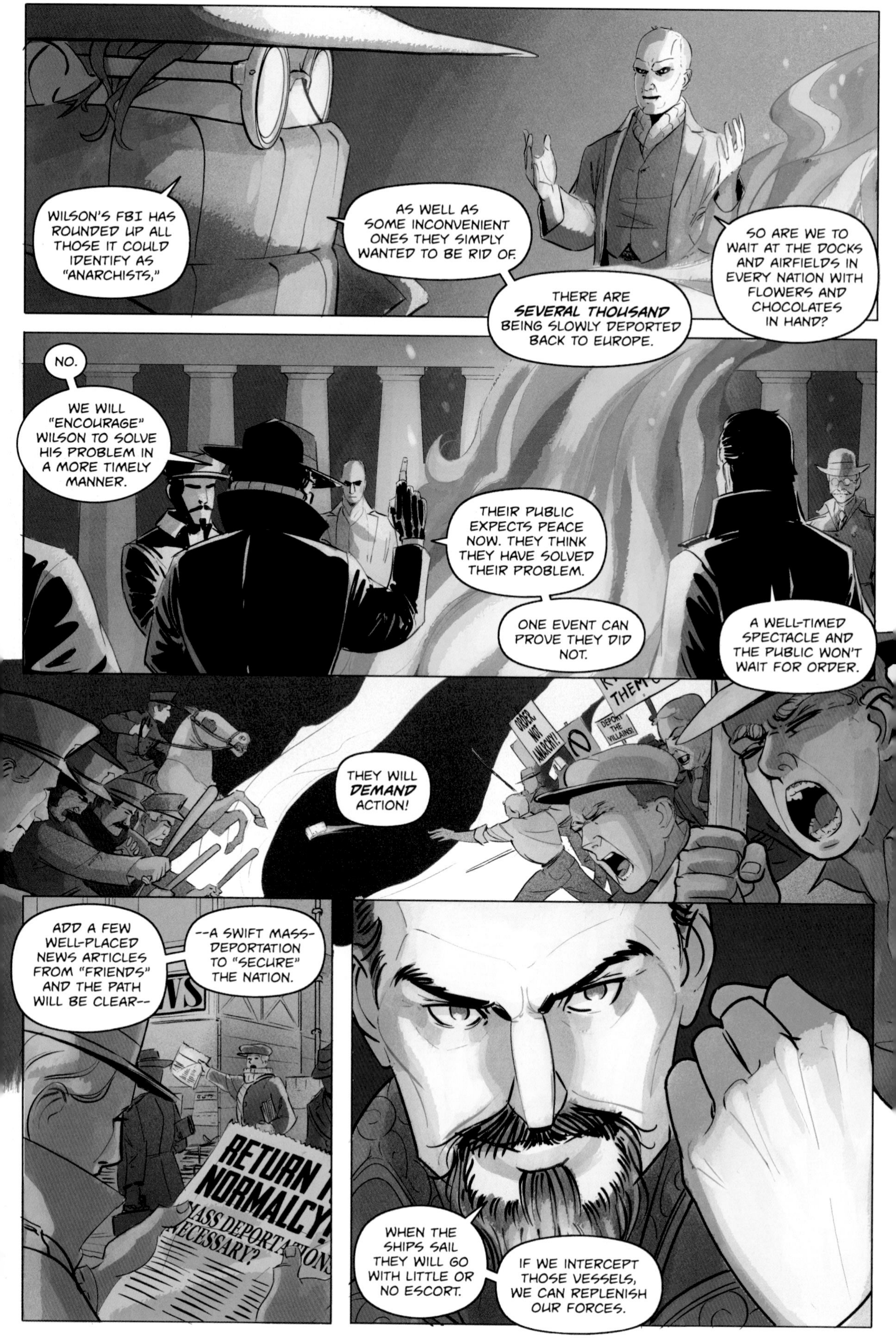

WILSON'S FBI HAS ROUNDED UP ALL THOSE IT COULD IDENTIFY AS "ANARCHISTS,"
AS WELL AS SOME INCONVENIENT ONES THEY SIMPLY WANTED TO BE RID OF.
THERE ARE **SEVERAL THOUSAND** BEING SLOWLY DEPORTED BACK TO EUROPE.
SO ARE WE TO WAIT AT THE DOCKS AND AIRFIELDS IN EVERY NATION WITH FLOWERS AND CHOCOLATES IN HAND?
NO.
WE WILL "ENCOURAGE" WILSON TO SOLVE HIS PROBLEM IN A MORE TIMELY MANNER.
THEIR PUBLIC EXPECTS PEACE NOW. THEY THINK THEY HAVE SOLVED THEIR PROBLEM.
ONE EVENT CAN PROVE THEY DID NOT.
A WELL-TIMED SPECTACLE AND THE PUBLIC WON'T WAIT FOR ORDER.
ORDER. NOT ANARCHY!
DEPORT THE VILLAINS!
THEY WILL **DEMAND** ACTION!
ADD A FEW WELL-PLACED NEWS ARTICLES FROM "FRIENDS" AND THE PATH WILL BE CLEAR--
--A SWIFT MASS-DEPORTATION TO "SECURE" THE NATION.
NORMALCY!
WHEN THE SHIPS SAIL THEY WILL GO WITH LITTLE OR NO ESCORT.
IF WE INTERCEPT THOSE VESSELS, WE CAN REPLENISH OUR FORCES.

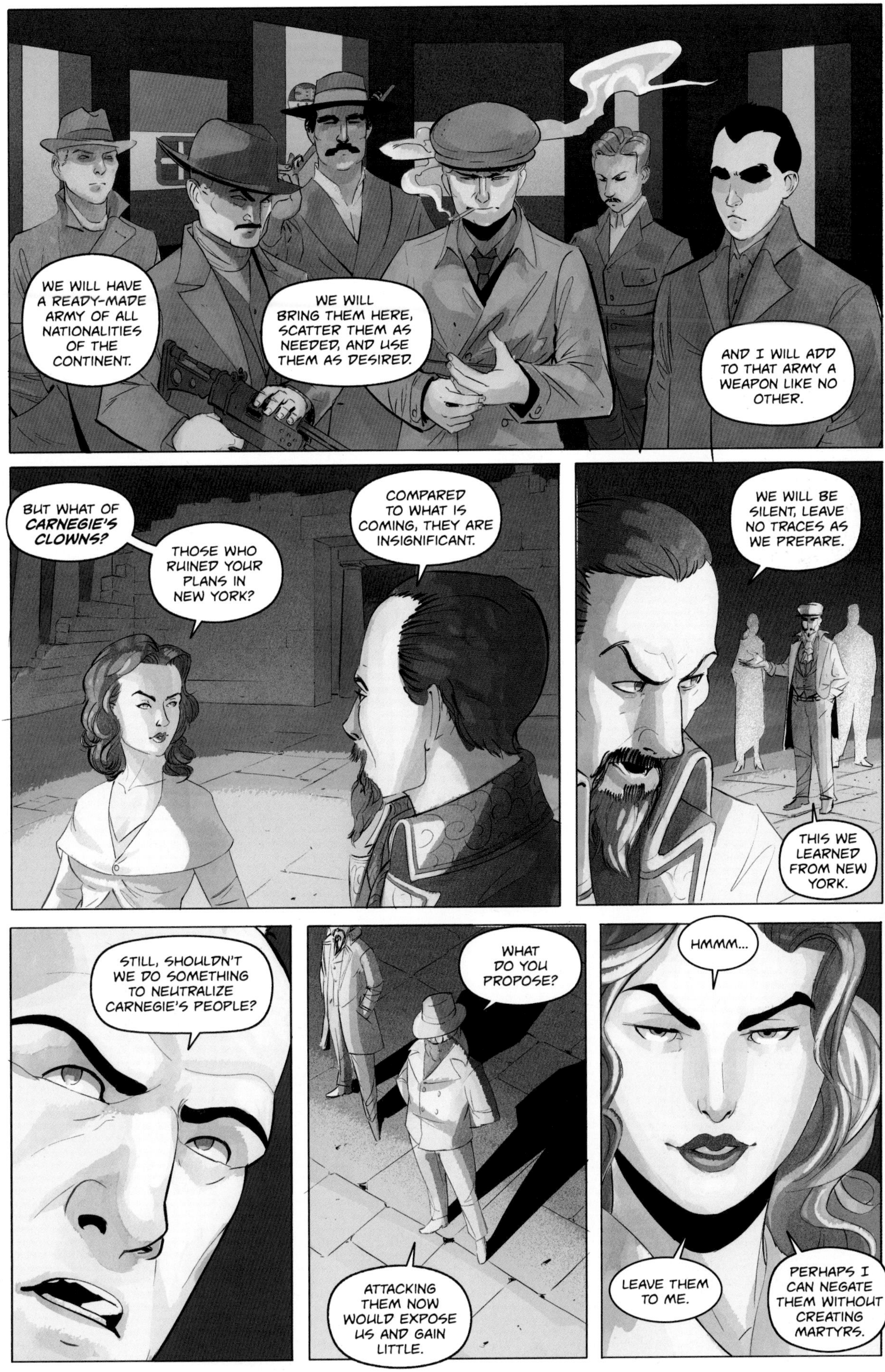
WE WILL HAVE A READY-MADE ARMY OF ALL NATIONALITIES OF THE CONTINENT.
WE WILL BRING THEM HERE, SCATTER THEM AS NEEDED, AND USE THEM AS DESIRED.
AND I WILL ADD TO THAT ARMY A WEAPON LIKE NO OTHER.
BUT WHAT OF *CARNEGIE'S CLOWNS?*
THOSE WHO RUINED YOUR PLANS IN NEW YORK?
COMPARED TO WHAT IS COMING, THEY ARE INSIGNIFICANT.
WE WILL BE SILENT, LEAVE NO TRACES AS WE PREPARE.
THIS WE LEARNED FROM NEW YORK.
STILL, SHOULDN'T WE DO SOMETHING TO NEUTRALIZE CARNEGIE'S PEOPLE?
WHAT DO YOU PROPOSE?
ATTACKING THEM NOW WOULD EXPOSE US AND GAIN LITTLE.
HMMM...
LEAVE THEM TO ME.
PERHAPS I CAN NEGATE THEM WITHOUT CREATING MARTYRS.

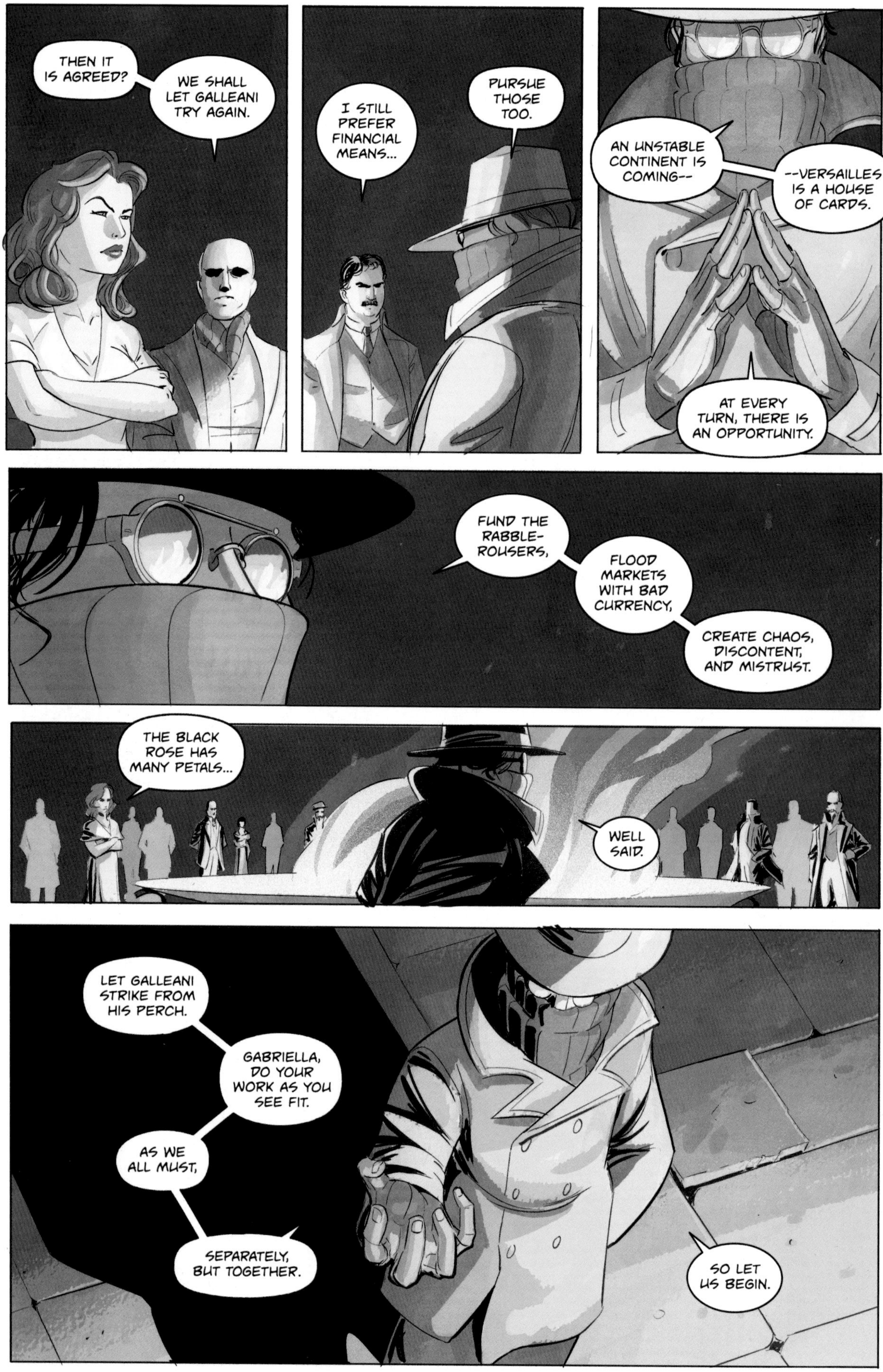
THEN IT IS AGREED?
WE SHALL LET GALLEANI TRY AGAIN.
I STILL PREFER FINANCIAL MEANS...
PURSUE THOSE TOO.
AN UNSTABLE CONTINENT IS COMING--
--VERSAILLES IS A HOUSE OF CARDS.
AT EVERY TURN, THERE IS AN OPPORTUNITY.
FUND THE RABBLE-ROUSERS,
FLOOD MARKETS WITH BAD CURRENCY,
CREATE CHAOS, DISCONTENT, AND MISTRUST.
THE BLACK ROSE HAS MANY PETALS...
WELL SAID.
LET GALLEANI STRIKE FROM HIS PERCH.
GABRIELLA, DO YOUR WORK AS YOU SEE FIT.
AS WE ALL MUST,
SEPARATELY, BUT TOGETHER.
SO LET US BEGIN.

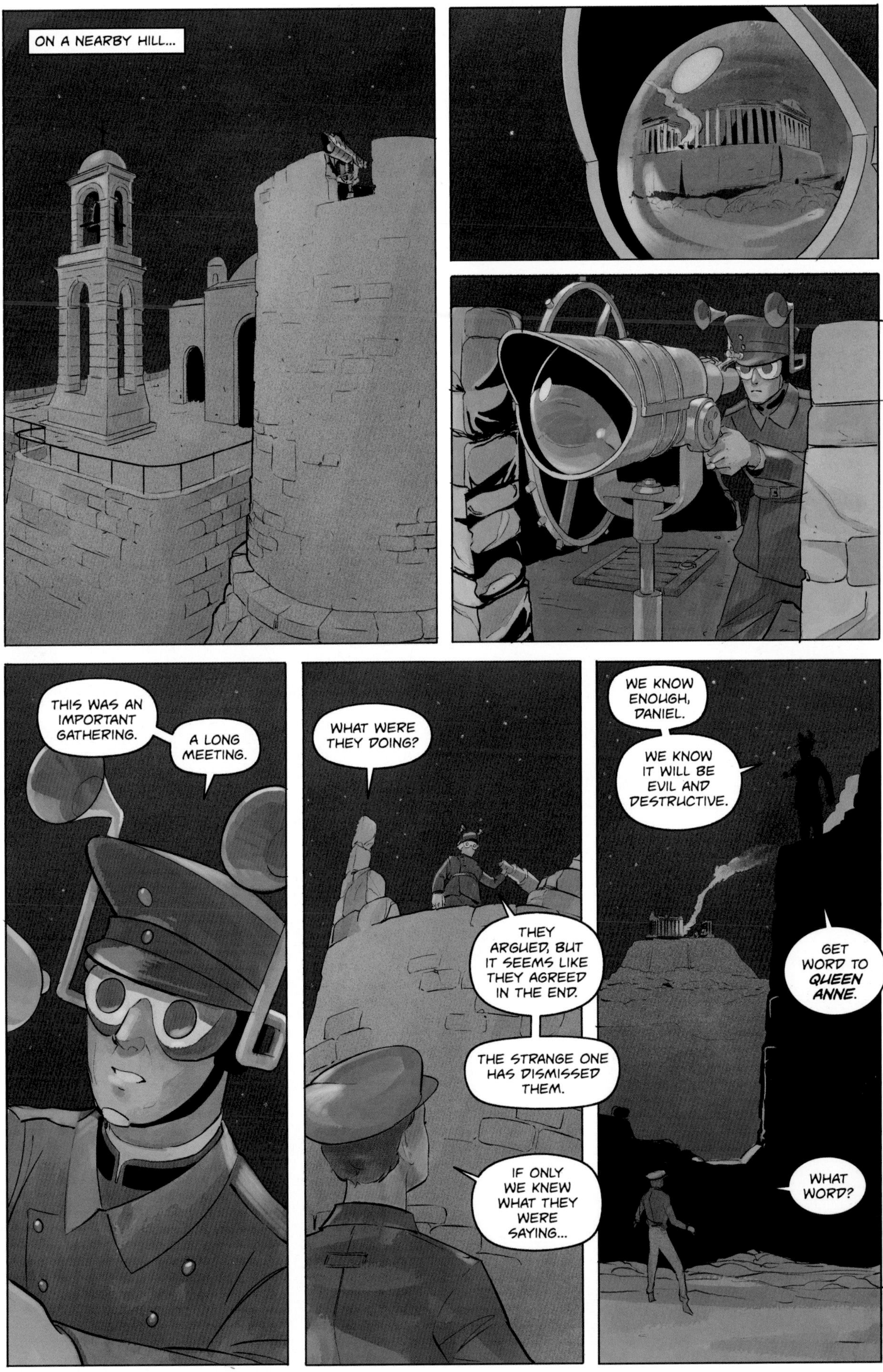
ON A NEARBY HILL...
THIS WAS AN IMPORTANT GATHERING.
A LONG MEETING.
WHAT WERE THEY DOING?
THEY ARGUED, BUT IT SEEMS LIKE THEY AGREED IN THE END.
THE STRANGE ONE HAS DISMISSED THEM.
IF ONLY WE KNEW WHAT THEY WERE SAYING...
WE KNOW ENOUGH, DANIEL.
WE KNOW IT WILL BE EVIL AND DESTRUCTIVE.
GET WORD TO QUEEN ANNE.
WHAT WORD?

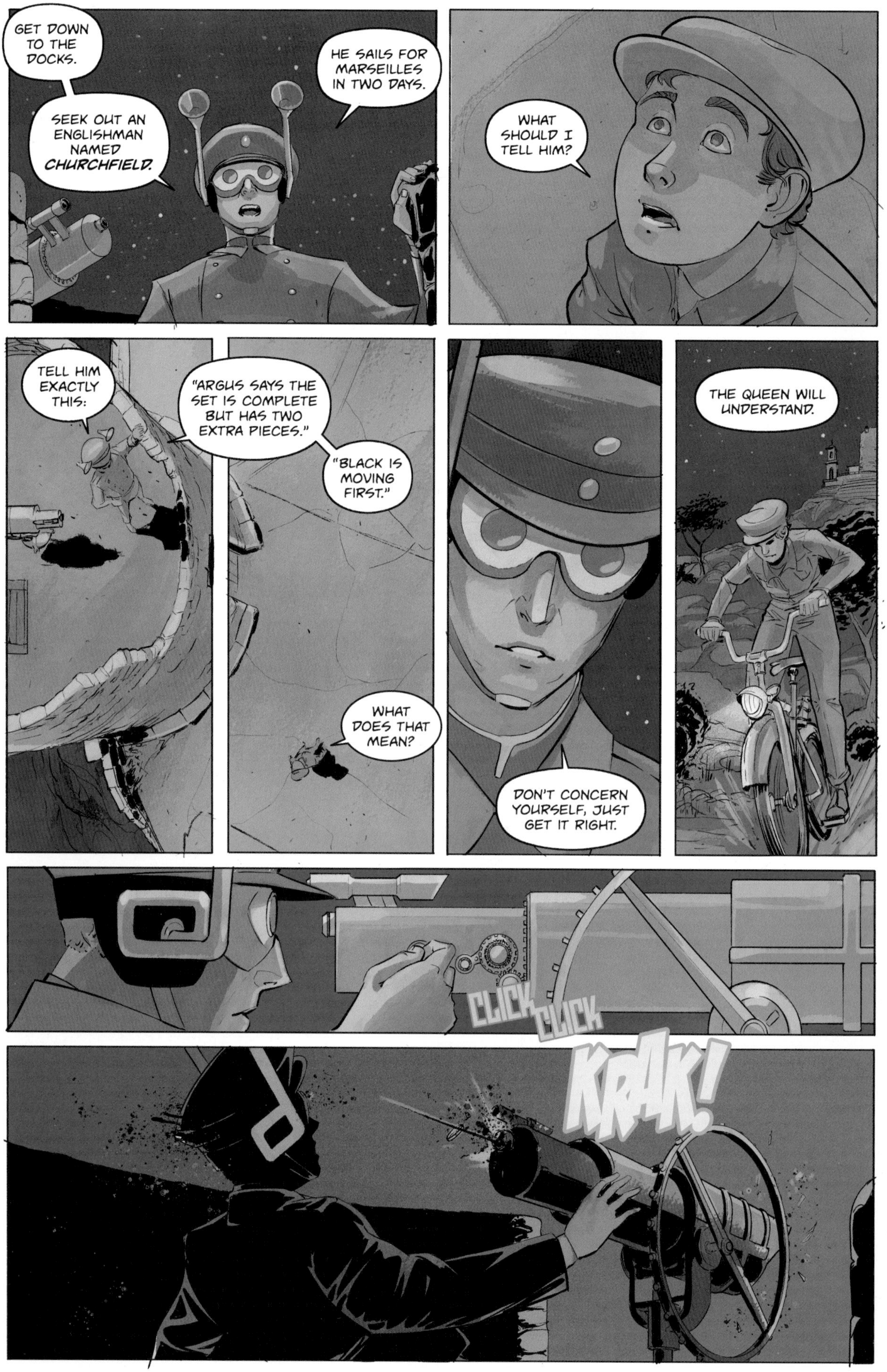
GET DOWN TO THE DOCKS.
SEEK OUT AN ENGLISHMAN NAMED CHURCHFIELD.
HE SAILS FOR MARSEILLES IN TWO DAYS.
WHAT SHOULD I TELL HIM?
TELL HIM EXACTLY THIS:
"ARGUS SAYS THE SET IS COMPLETE BUT HAS TWO EXTRA PIECES."
"BLACK IS MOVING FIRST."
WHAT DOES THAT MEAN?
DON'T CONCERN YOURSELF, JUST GET IT RIGHT.
THE QUEEN WILL UNDERSTAND.
CLICK CLICK
KRAK!

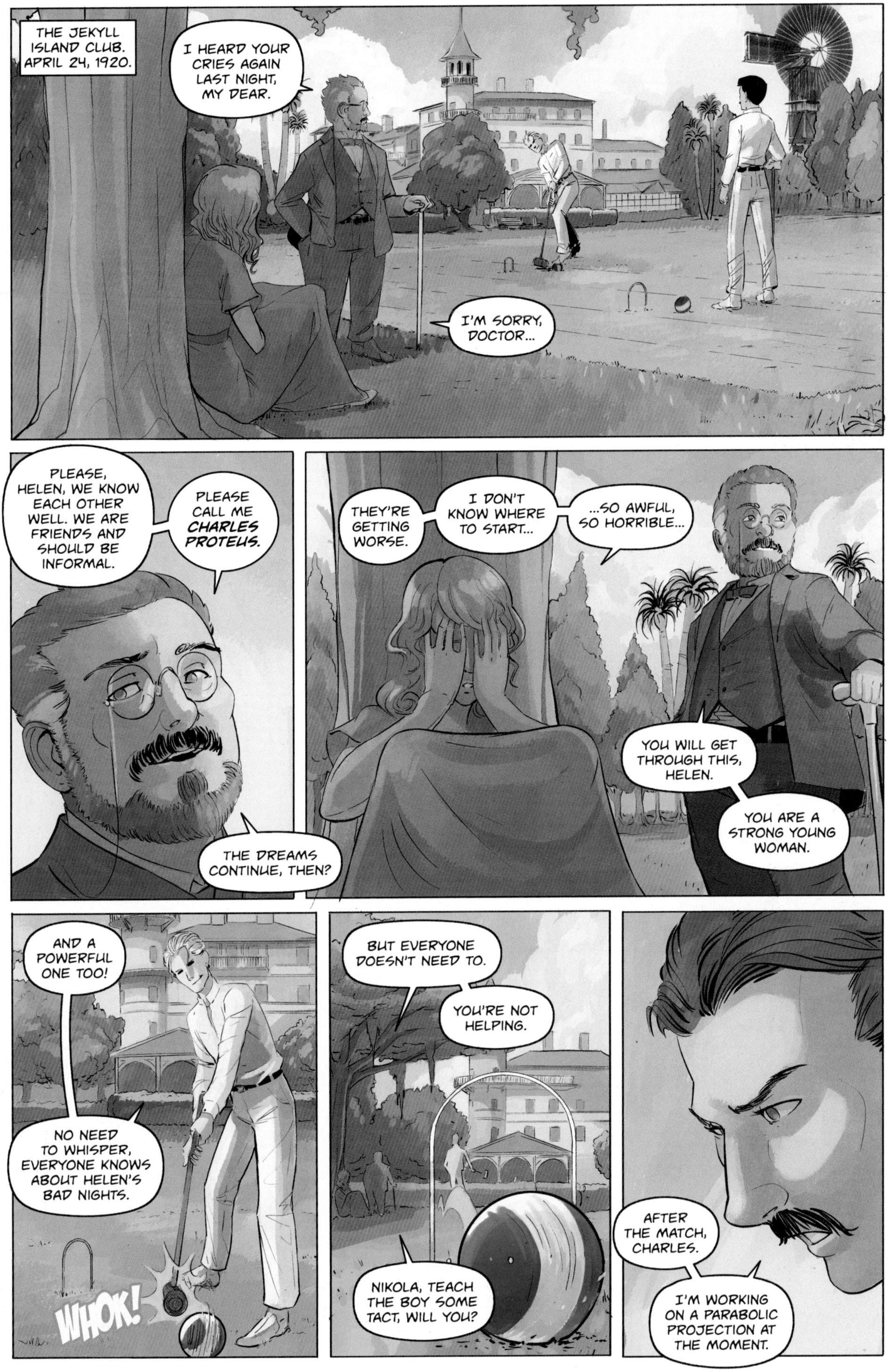
THE JEKYLL ISLAND CLUB. APRIL 24, 1920.
I HEARD YOUR CRIES AGAIN LAST NIGHT, MY DEAR.
I'M SORRY, DOCTOR...
PLEASE, HELEN, WE KNOW EACH OTHER WELL. WE ARE FRIENDS AND SHOULD BE INFORMAL.
PLEASE CALL ME CHARLES PROTEUS.
THE DREAMS CONTINUE, THEN?
THEY'RE GETTING WORSE.
I DON'T KNOW WHERE TO START...
...SO AWFUL, SO HORRIBLE...
YOU WILL GET THROUGH THIS, HELEN.
YOU ARE A STRONG YOUNG WOMAN.
AND A POWERFUL ONE TOO!
NO NEED TO WHISPER, EVERYONE KNOWS ABOUT HELEN'S BAD NIGHTS.
WHOK!
BUT EVERYONE DOESN'T NEED TO.
YOU'RE NOT HELPING.
NIKOLA, TEACH THE BOY SOME TACT, WILL YOU?
AFTER THE MATCH, CHARLES.
I'M WORKING ON A PARABOLIC PROJECTION AT THE MOMENT.

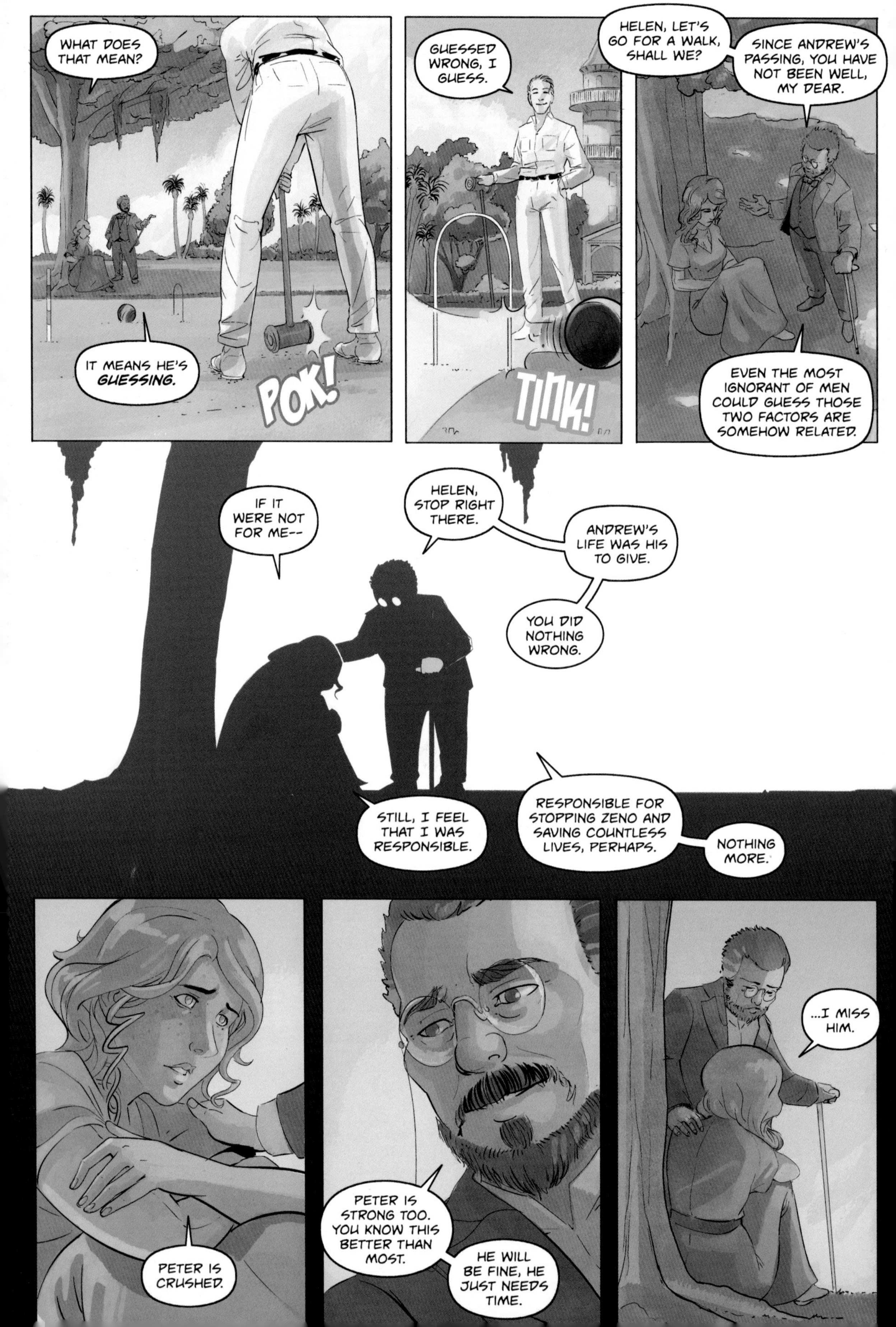
WHAT DOES THAT MEAN?
IT MEANS HE'S GUESSING.
POK!
GUESSED WRONG, I GUESS.
TINK!
HELEN, LET'S GO FOR A WALK, SHALL WE?
SINCE ANDREW'S PASSING, YOU HAVE NOT BEEN WELL, MY DEAR.
EVEN THE MOST IGNORANT OF MEN COULD GUESS THOSE TWO FACTORS ARE SOMEHOW RELATED.
IF IT WERE NOT FOR ME--
HELEN, STOP RIGHT THERE.
ANDREW'S LIFE WAS HIS TO GIVE.
YOU DID NOTHING WRONG.
STILL, I FEEL THAT I WAS RESPONSIBLE.
RESPONSIBLE FOR STOPPING ZENO AND SAVING COUNTLESS LIVES, PERHAPS.
NOTHING MORE.
PETER IS CRUSHED.
PETER IS STRONG TOO. YOU KNOW THIS BETTER THAN MOST.
HE WILL BE FINE, HE JUST NEEDS TIME.
...I MISS HIM.

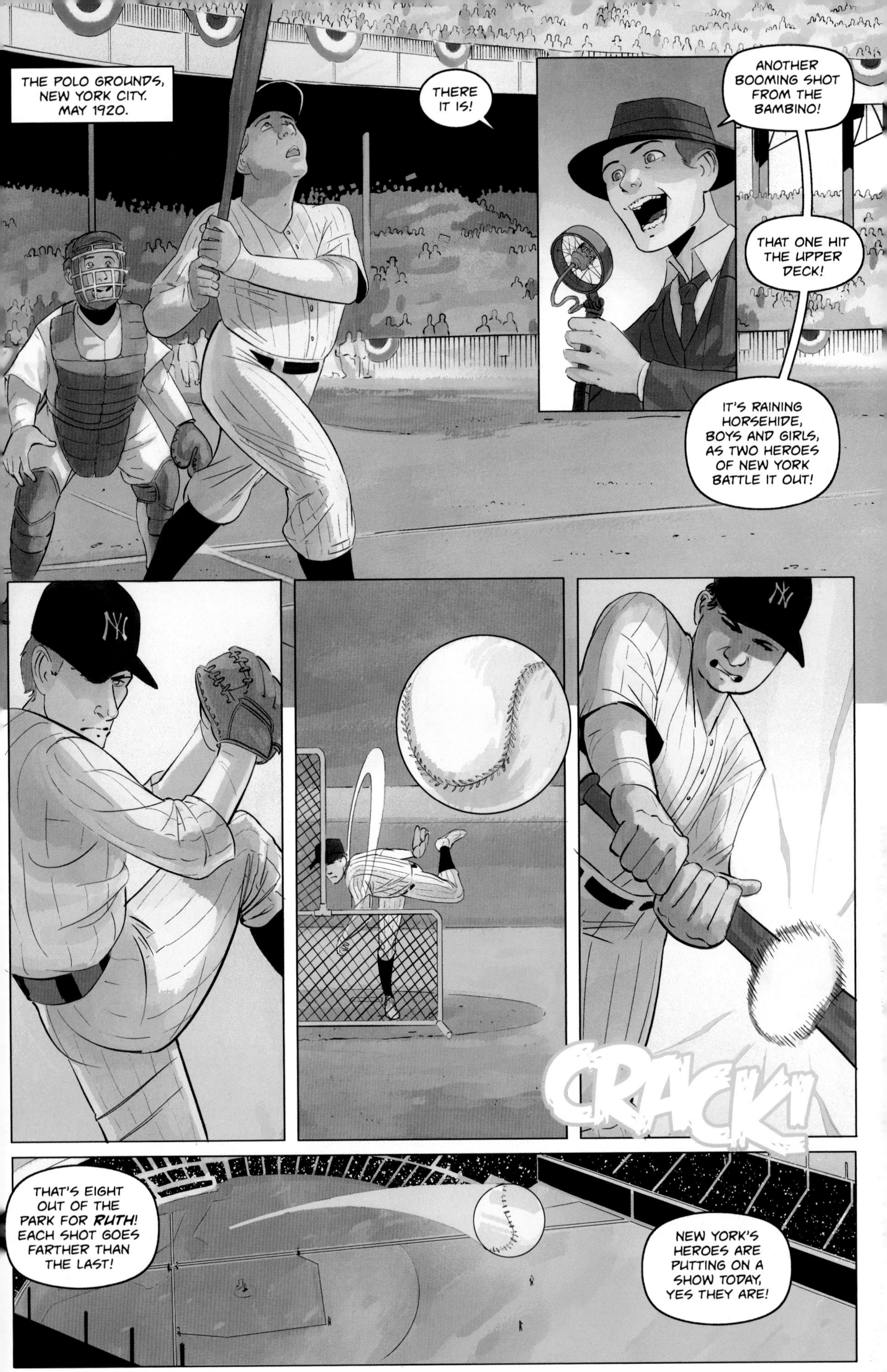
THE POLO GROUNDS, NEW YORK CITY. MAY 1920.
THERE IT IS!
ANOTHER BOOMING SHOT FROM THE BAMBINO!
THAT ONE HIT THE UPPER DECK!
IT'S RAINING HORSEHIDE, BOYS AND GIRLS, AS TWO HEROES OF NEW YORK BATTLE IT OUT!
CRACK!!
THAT'S EIGHT OUT OF THE PARK FOR *RUTH*! EACH SHOT GOES FARTHER THAN THE LAST!
NEW YORK'S HEROES ARE PUTTING ON A SHOW TODAY, YES THEY ARE!

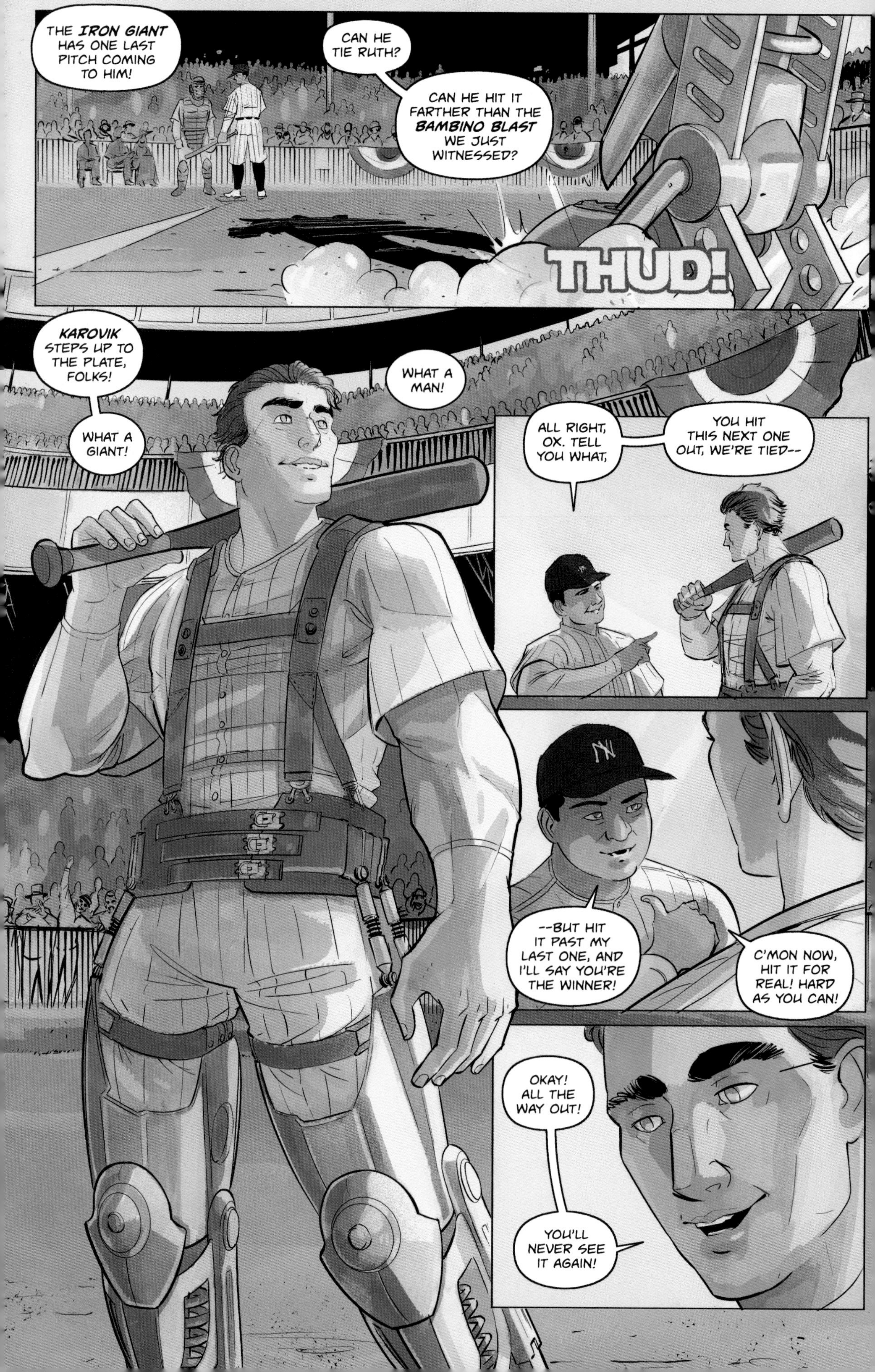

THE IRON GIANT HAS ONE LAST PITCH COMING TO HIM!
CAN HE TIE RUTH?
CAN HE HIT IT FARTHER THAN THE BAMBINO BLAST WE JUST WITNESSED?
THUD!
KAROVIK STEPS UP TO THE PLATE, FOLKS!
WHAT A GIANT!
WHAT A MAN!
ALL RIGHT, OX. TELL YOU WHAT,
YOU HIT THIS NEXT ONE OUT, WE'RE TIED--
--BUT HIT IT PAST MY LAST ONE, AND I'LL SAY YOU'RE THE WINNER!
C'MON NOW, HIT IT FOR REAL! HARD AS YOU CAN!
OKAY! ALL THE WAY OUT!
YOU'LL NEVER SEE IT AGAIN!

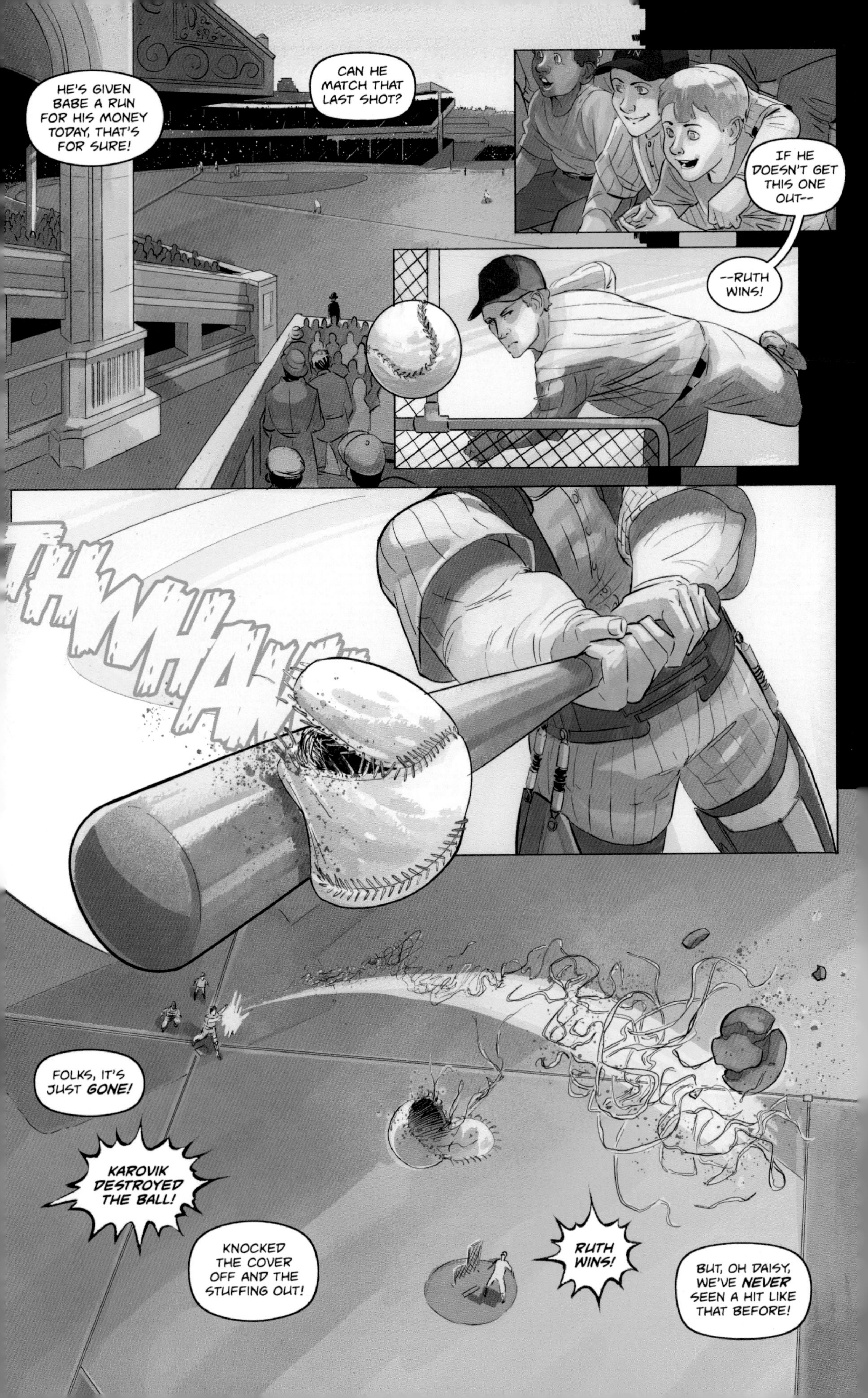
HE'S GIVEN BABE A RUN FOR HIS MONEY TODAY, THAT'S FOR SURE!
CAN HE MATCH THAT LAST SHOT?
IF HE DOESN'T GET THIS ONE OUT--
--RUTH WINS!
THWHAM
FOLKS, IT'S JUST GONE!
KAROVIK DESTROYED THE BALL!
KNOCKED THE COVER OFF AND THE STUFFING OUT!
RUTH WINS!
BUT, OH DAISY, WE'VE NEVER SEEN A HIT LIKE THAT BEFORE!

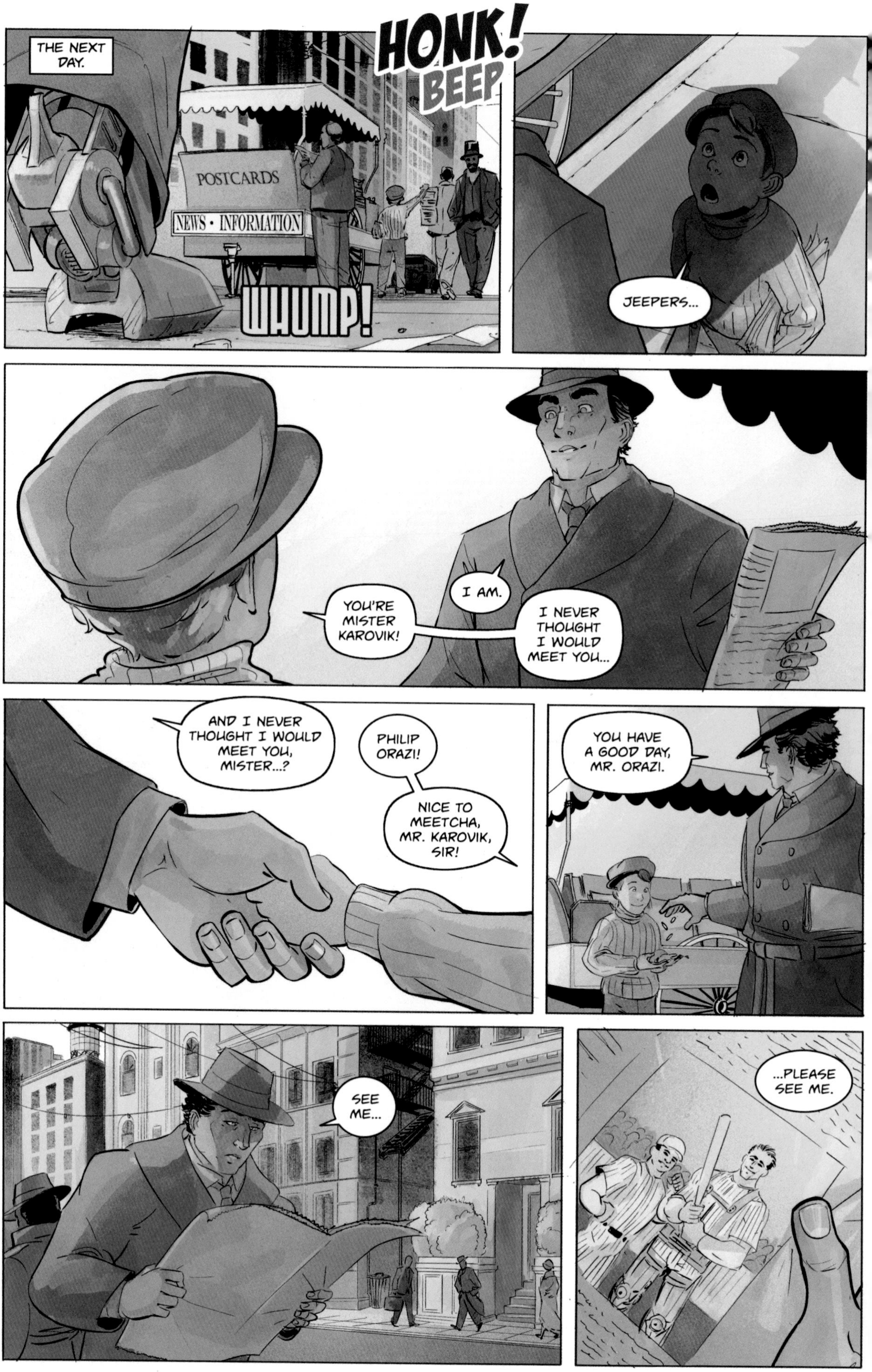
THE NEXT DAY.
HONK!
BEEP
POSTCARDS
NEWS • INFORMATION
WHUMP!
JEEPERS...
YOU'RE MISTER KAROVIK!
I AM.
I NEVER THOUGHT I WOULD MEET YOU...
AND I NEVER THOUGHT I WOULD MEET YOU, MISTER...?
PHILIP ORAZI!
NICE TO MEETCHA, MR. KAROVIK, SIR!
YOU HAVE A GOOD DAY, MR. ORAZI.
SEE ME...
...PLEASE SEE ME.

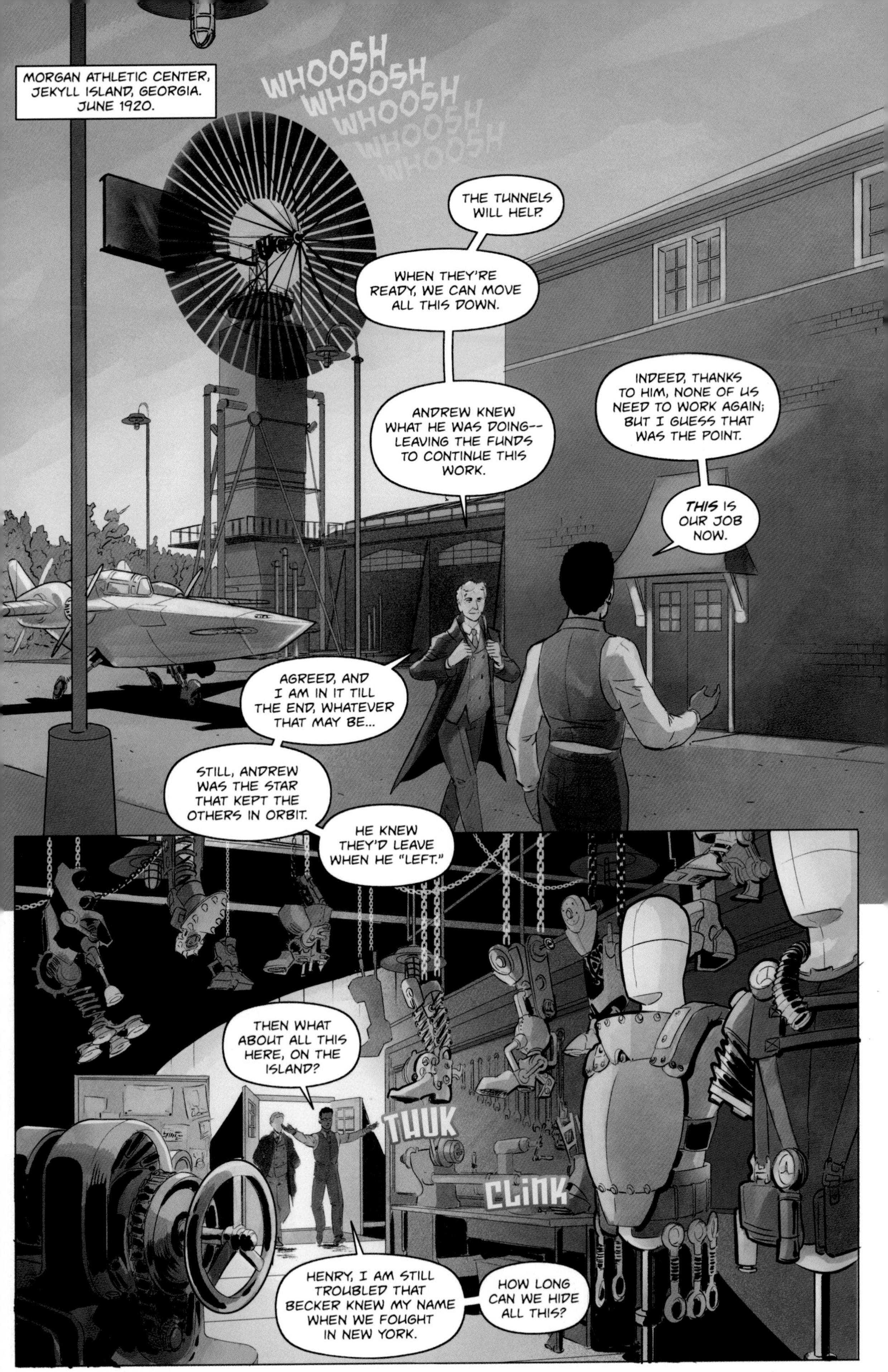
MORGAN ATHLETIC CENTER, JEKYLL ISLAND, GEORGIA. JUNE 1920.
WHOOSH WHOOSH WHOOSH WHOOSH WHOOSH
THE TUNNELS WILL HELP.
WHEN THEY'RE READY, WE CAN MOVE ALL THIS DOWN.
ANDREW KNEW WHAT HE WAS DOING-- LEAVING THE FUNDS TO CONTINUE THIS WORK.
INDEED, THANKS TO HIM, NONE OF US NEED TO WORK AGAIN; BUT I GUESS THAT WAS THE POINT.
THIS IS OUR JOB NOW.
AGREED, AND I AM IN IT TILL THE END, WHATEVER THAT MAY BE...
STILL, ANDREW WAS THE STAR THAT KEPT THE OTHERS IN ORBIT.
HE KNEW THEY'D LEAVE WHEN HE "LEFT."
THEN WHAT ABOUT ALL THIS HERE, ON THE ISLAND?
THUK
CLINK
HENRY, I AM STILL TROUBLED THAT BECKER KNEW MY NAME WHEN WE FOUGHT IN NEW YORK.
HOW LONG CAN WE HIDE ALL THIS?

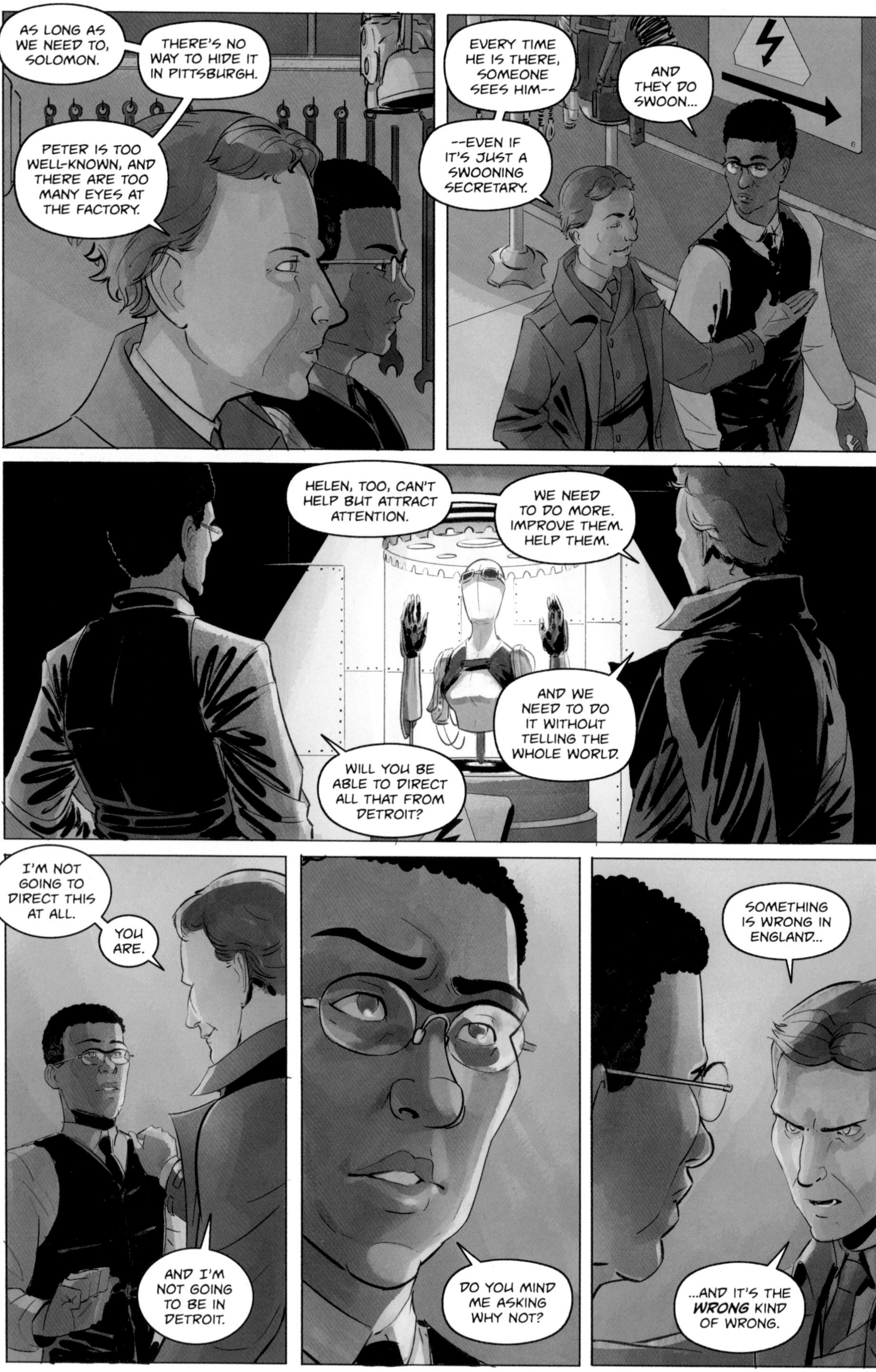
AS LONG AS WE NEED TO, SOLOMON.
THERE'S NO WAY TO HIDE IT IN PITTSBURGH.
PETER IS TOO WELL-KNOWN, AND THERE ARE TOO MANY EYES AT THE FACTORY.
EVERY TIME HE IS THERE, SOMEONE SEES HIM--
--EVEN IF IT'S JUST A SWOONING SECRETARY.
AND THEY DO SWOON...
HELEN, TOO, CAN'T HELP BUT ATTRACT ATTENTION.
WE NEED TO DO MORE. IMPROVE THEM. HELP THEM.
AND WE NEED TO DO IT WITHOUT TELLING THE WHOLE WORLD.
WILL YOU BE ABLE TO DIRECT ALL THAT FROM DETROIT?
I'M NOT GOING TO DIRECT THIS AT ALL.
YOU ARE.
AND I'M NOT GOING TO BE IN DETROIT.
DO YOU MIND ME ASKING WHY NOT?
SOMETHING IS WRONG IN ENGLAND...
...AND IT'S THE *WRONG* KIND OF WRONG.

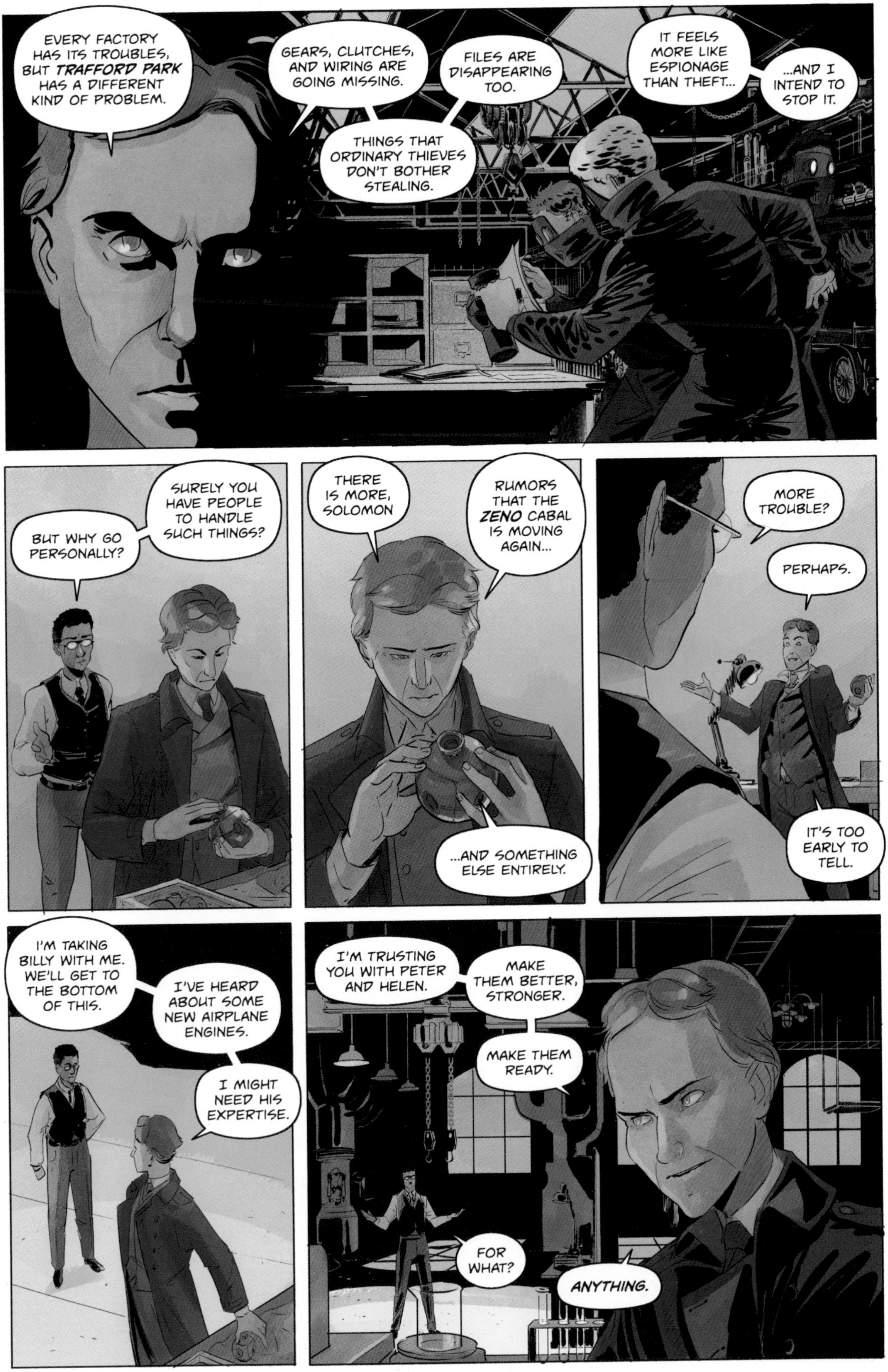
EVERY FACTORY HAS ITS TROUBLES, BUT TRAFFORD PARK HAS A DIFFERENT KIND OF PROBLEM.
GEARS, CLUTCHES, AND WIRING ARE GOING MISSING.
THINGS THAT ORDINARY THIEVES DON'T BOTHER STEALING.
FILES ARE DISAPPEARING TOO.
IT FEELS MORE LIKE ESPIONAGE THAN THEFT...
...AND I INTEND TO STOP IT.
BUT WHY GO PERSONALLY?
SURELY YOU HAVE PEOPLE TO HANDLE SUCH THINGS?
THERE IS MORE, SOLOMON
RUMORS THAT THE ZENO CABAL IS MOVING AGAIN...
...AND SOMETHING ELSE ENTIRELY.
MORE TROUBLE?
PERHAPS.
IT'S TOO EARLY TO TELL.
I'M TAKING BILLY WITH ME. WE'LL GET TO THE BOTTOM OF THIS.
I'VE HEARD ABOUT SOME NEW AIRPLANE ENGINES.
I MIGHT NEED HIS EXPERTISE.
I'M TRUSTING YOU WITH PETER AND HELEN.
MAKE THEM BETTER, STRONGER.
MAKE THEM READY.
FOR WHAT?
ANYTHING.

THE SLAUGHTERED LAMB PUB, HAMPSTEAD, ENGLAND. JULY 21, 1920.

DO YOU HAVE OUR PRIZE?

IF YOU HAVE MY PRICE.

YOU ASK A KING'S RANSOM.

AND I AM DELIVERING A KINGDOM.

SHOW ME PROOF.

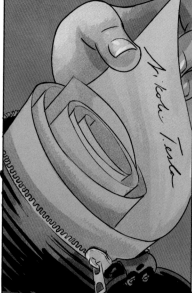

DONE AND DONE.

DIAMONDS, AS YOU ASKED.

AND THE REST OF MY TERMS?

AGREED. YOU ARE DONE.

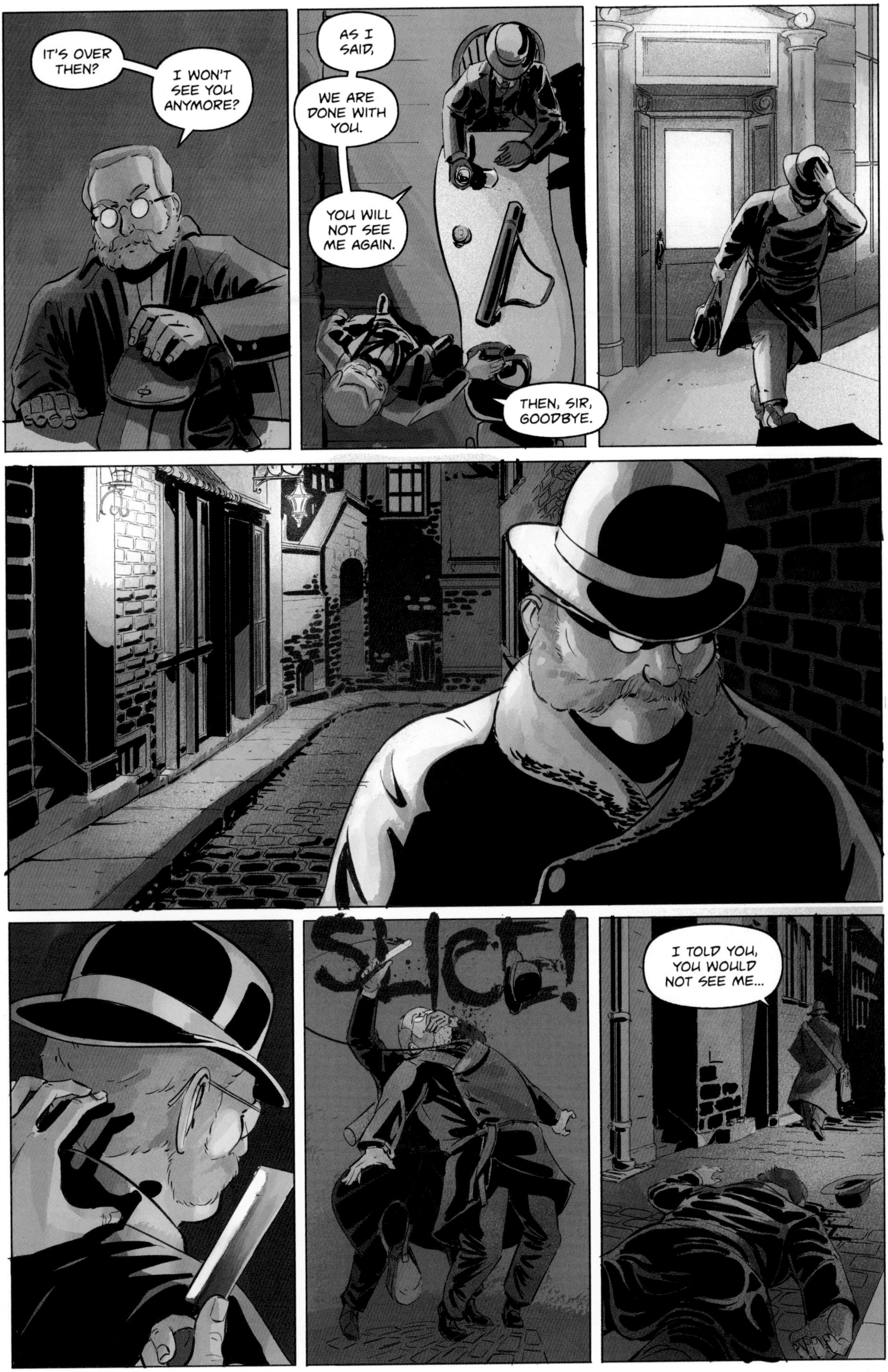
IT'S OVER THEN?
I WON'T SEE YOU ANYMORE?
AS I SAID,
WE ARE DONE WITH YOU.
YOU WILL NOT SEE ME AGAIN.
THEN, SIR, GOODBYE.
SLICE!
I TOLD YOU, YOU WOULD NOT SEE ME...

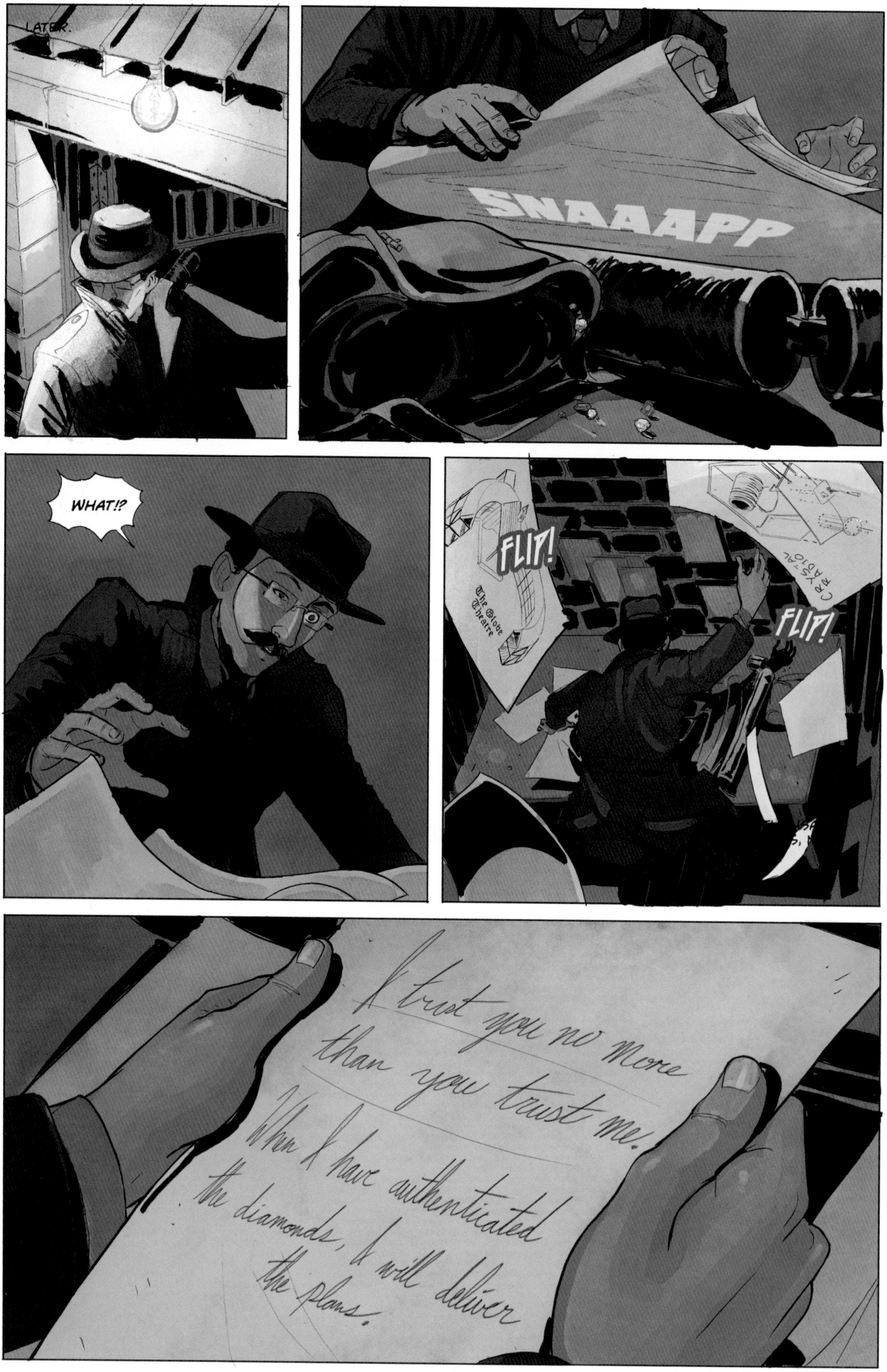
LATER.
SNAAAPP
WHAT!?
FLIP!
The Globe Theatre
CRYSTAL RADIO
FLIP!
I trust you no more
than you trust me.
When I have authenticated
the diamonds, I will deliver
the plans.

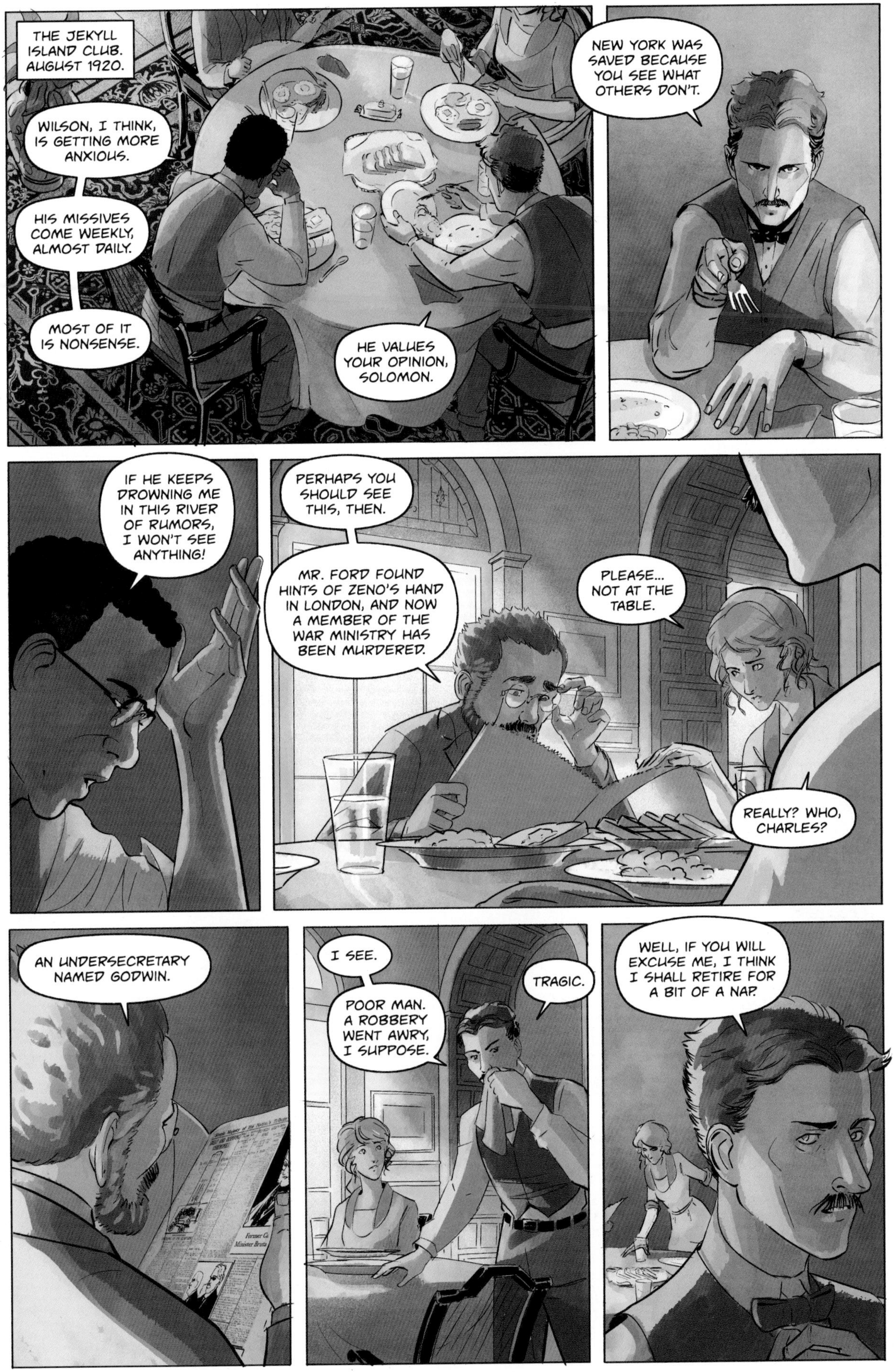
THE JEKYLL ISLAND CLUB. AUGUST 1920.
WILSON, I THINK, IS GETTING MORE ANXIOUS.
HIS MISSIVES COME WEEKLY, ALMOST DAILY.
MOST OF IT IS NONSENSE.
HE VALUES YOUR OPINION, SOLOMON.
NEW YORK WAS SAVED BECAUSE YOU SEE WHAT OTHERS DON'T.
IF HE KEEPS DROWNING ME IN THIS RIVER OF RUMORS, I WON'T SEE ANYTHING!
PERHAPS YOU SHOULD SEE THIS, THEN.
MR. FORD FOUND HINTS OF ZENO'S HAND IN LONDON, AND NOW A MEMBER OF THE WAR MINISTRY HAS BEEN MURDERED.
PLEASE... NOT AT THE TABLE.
REALLY? WHO, CHARLES?
AN UNDERSECRETARY NAMED GODWIN.
I SEE.
POOR MAN. A ROBBERY WENT AWRY, I SUPPOSE.
TRAGIC.
WELL, IF YOU WILL EXCUSE ME, I THINK I SHALL RETIRE FOR A BIT OF A NAP.

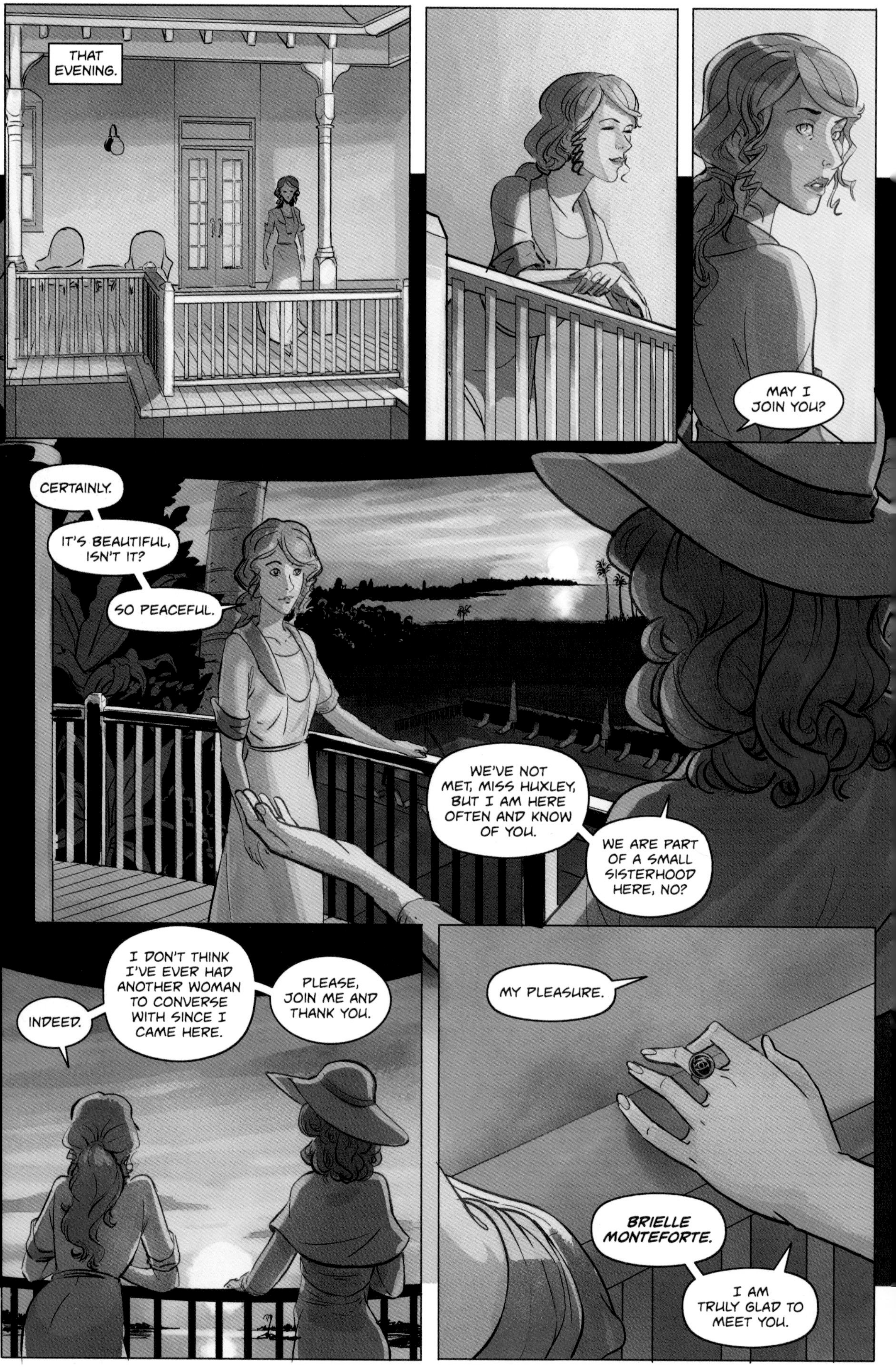
THAT EVENING.
MAY I JOIN YOU?
CERTAINLY.
IT'S BEAUTIFUL, ISN'T IT?
SO PEACEFUL.
WE'VE NOT MET, MISS HUXLEY, BUT I AM HERE OFTEN AND KNOW OF YOU.
WE ARE PART OF A SMALL SISTERHOOD HERE, NO?
INDEED.
I DON'T THINK I'VE EVER HAD ANOTHER WOMAN TO CONVERSE WITH SINCE I CAME HERE.
PLEASE, JOIN ME AND THANK YOU.
MY PLEASURE.
BRIELLE MONTEFORTE.
I AM TRULY GLAD TO MEET YOU.

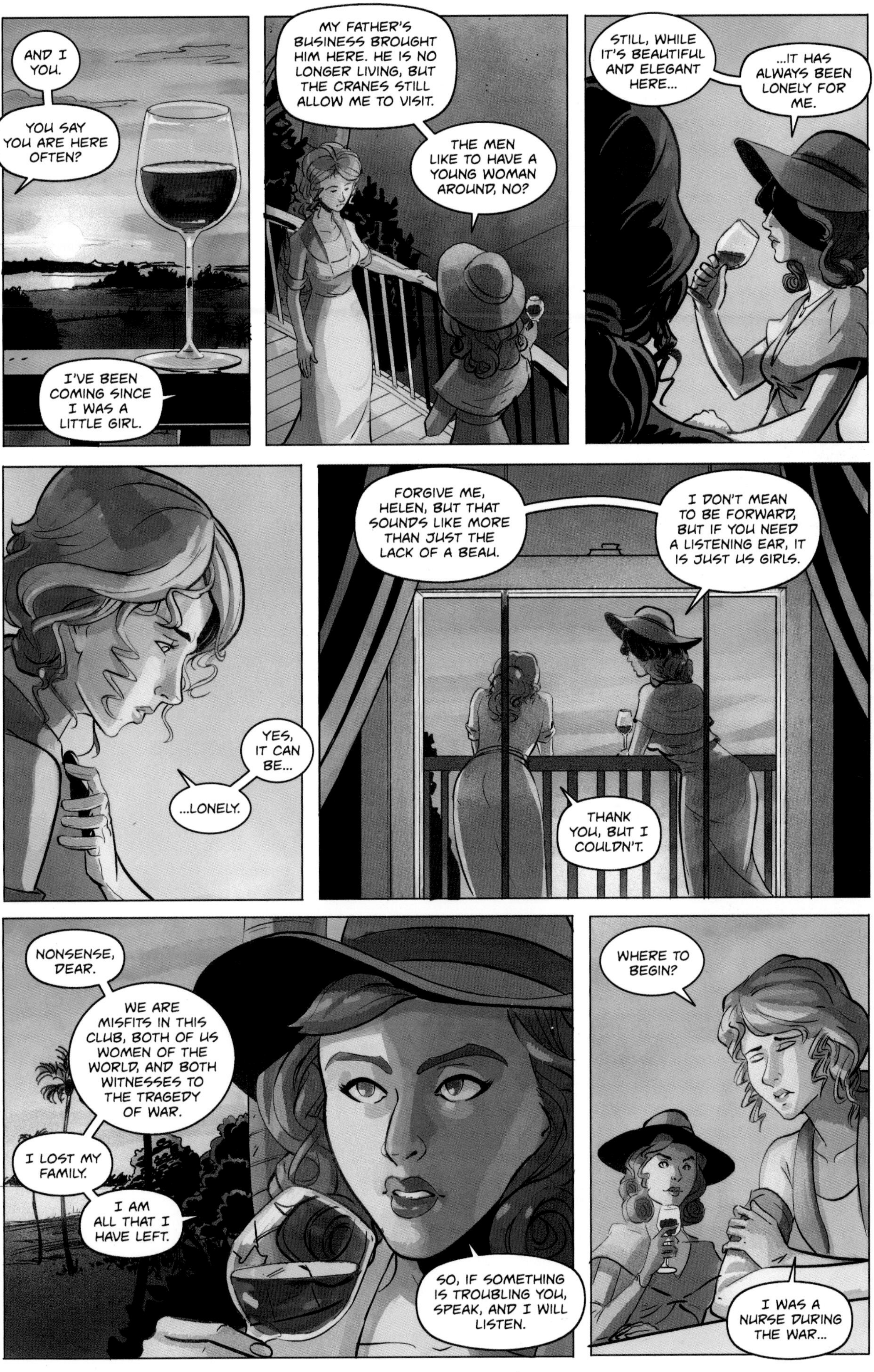
AND I YOU.
YOU SAY YOU ARE HERE OFTEN?
I'VE BEEN COMING SINCE I WAS A LITTLE GIRL.
MY FATHER'S BUSINESS BROUGHT HIM HERE. HE IS NO LONGER LIVING, BUT THE CRANES STILL ALLOW ME TO VISIT.
THE MEN LIKE TO HAVE A YOUNG WOMAN AROUND, NO?
STILL, WHILE IT'S BEAUTIFUL AND ELEGANT HERE...
...IT HAS ALWAYS BEEN LONELY FOR ME.
YES, IT CAN BE...
...LONELY.
FORGIVE ME, HELEN, BUT THAT SOUNDS LIKE MORE THAN JUST THE LACK OF A BEAU.
I DON'T MEAN TO BE FORWARD, BUT IF YOU NEED A LISTENING EAR, IT IS JUST US GIRLS.
THANK YOU, BUT I COULDN'T.
NONSENSE, DEAR.
WE ARE MISFITS IN THIS CLUB, BOTH OF US WOMEN OF THE WORLD, AND BOTH WITNESSES TO THE TRAGEDY OF WAR.
I LOST MY FAMILY.
I AM ALL THAT I HAVE LEFT.
SO, IF SOMETHING IS TROUBLING YOU, SPEAK, AND I WILL LISTEN.
WHERE TO BEGIN?
I WAS A NURSE DURING THE WAR...

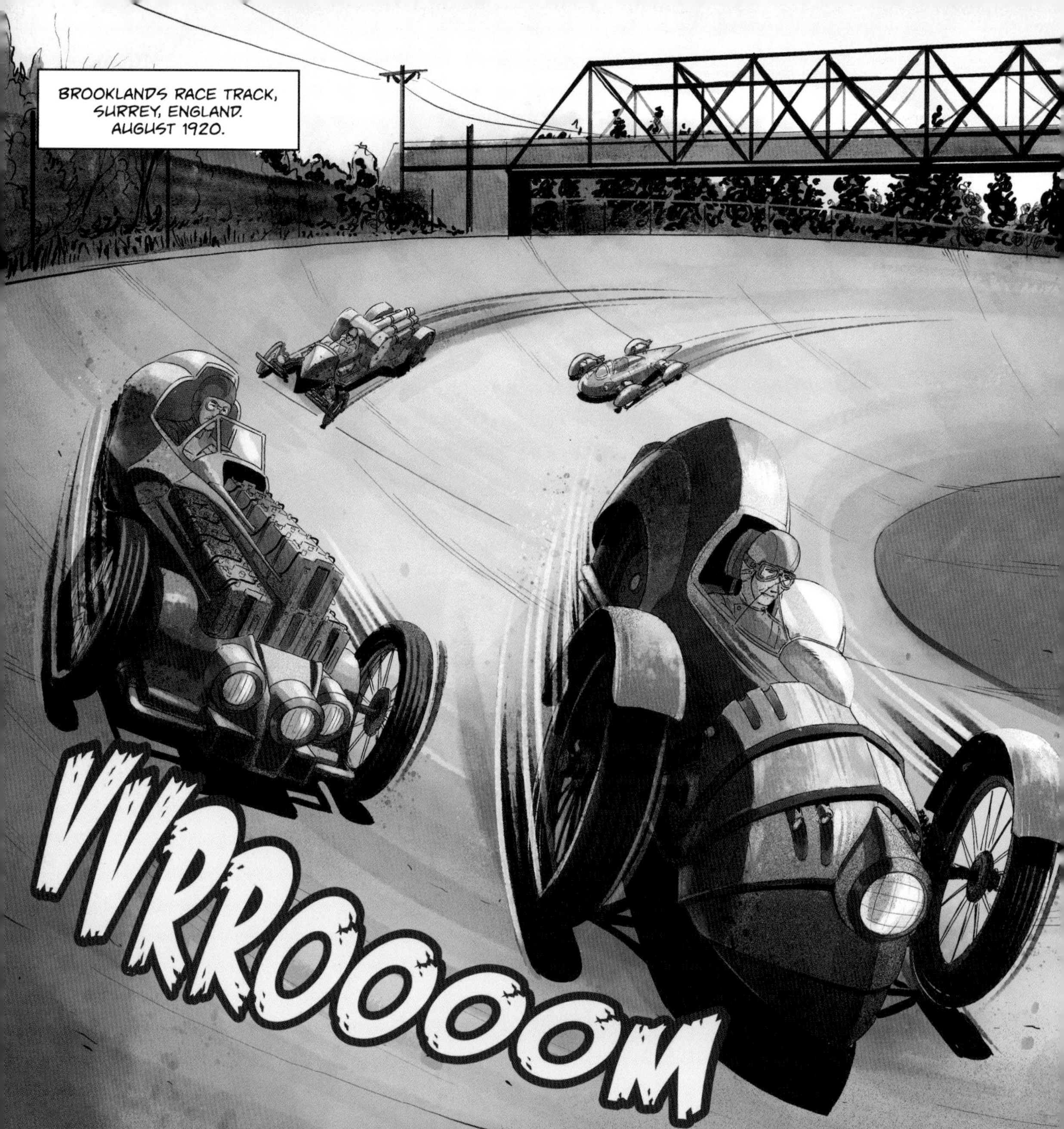
BROOKLANDS RACE TRACK, SURREY, ENGLAND. AUGUST 1920.
VVROOOOOM

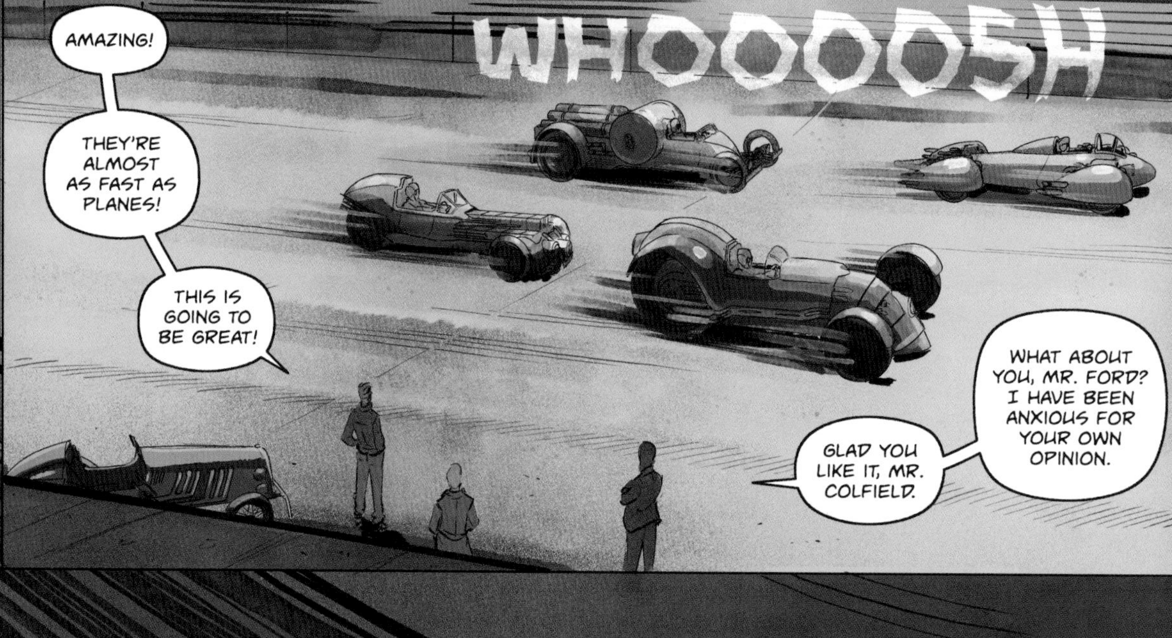
AMAZING!
WHOOOOOSH
THEY'RE ALMOST AS FAST AS PLANES!
THIS IS GOING TO BE GREAT!
GLAD YOU LIKE IT, MR. COLFIELD.
WHAT ABOUT YOU, MR. FORD? I HAVE BEEN ANXIOUS FOR YOUR OWN OPINION.

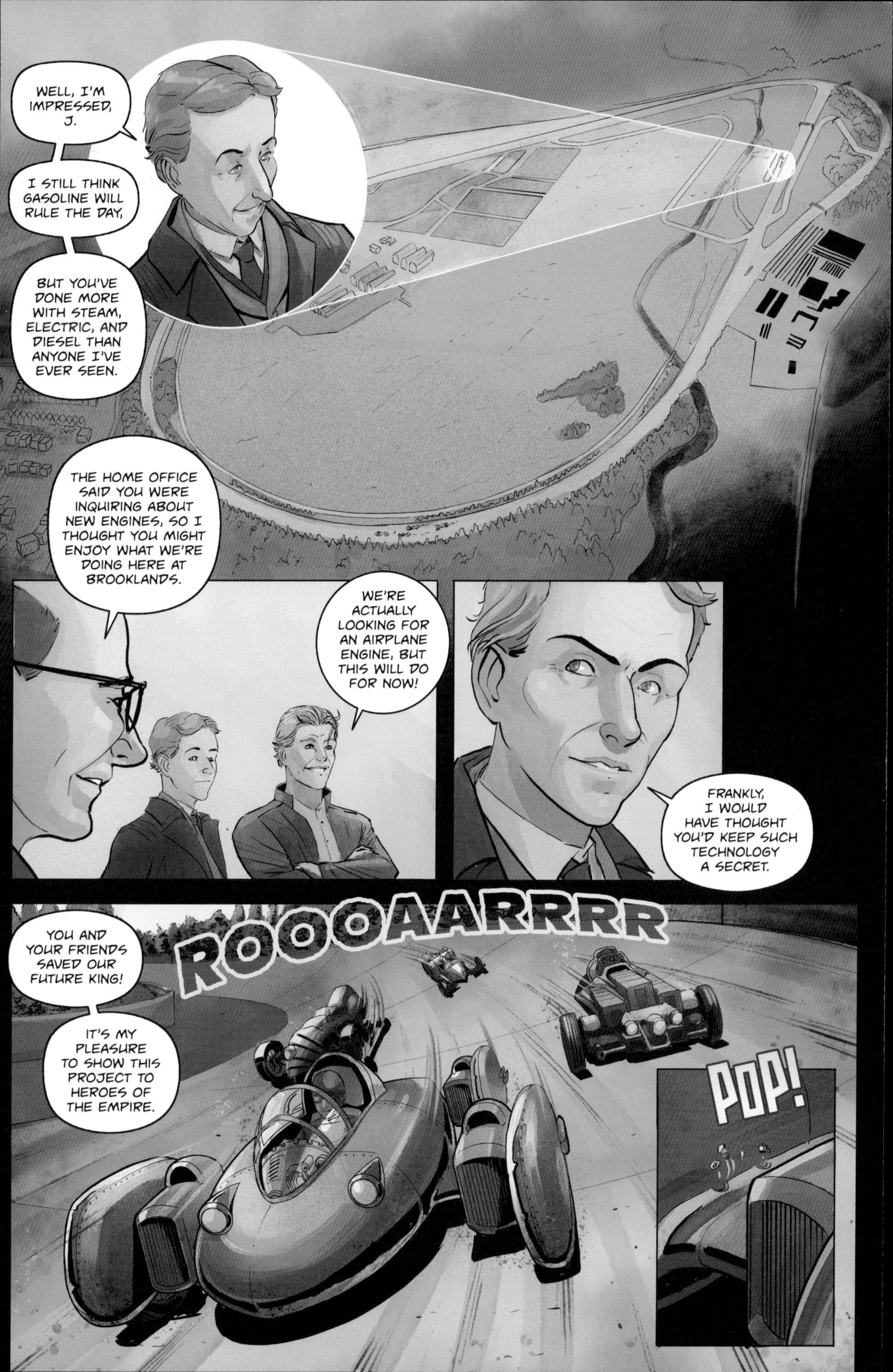
WELL, I'M IMPRESSED, J.
I STILL THINK GASOLINE WILL RULE THE DAY,
BUT YOU'VE DONE MORE WITH STEAM, ELECTRIC, AND DIESEL THAN ANYONE I'VE EVER SEEN.
THE HOME OFFICE SAID YOU WERE INQUIRING ABOUT NEW ENGINES, SO I THOUGHT YOU MIGHT ENJOY WHAT WE'RE DOING HERE AT BROOKLANDS.
WE'RE ACTUALLY LOOKING FOR AN AIRPLANE ENGINE, BUT THIS WILL DO FOR NOW!
FRANKLY, I WOULD HAVE THOUGHT YOU'D KEEP SUCH TECHNOLOGY A SECRET.
ROOOAARRRR
YOU AND YOUR FRIENDS SAVED OUR FUTURE KING!
IT'S MY PLEASURE TO SHOW THIS PROJECT TO HEROES OF THE EMPIRE.
POP!

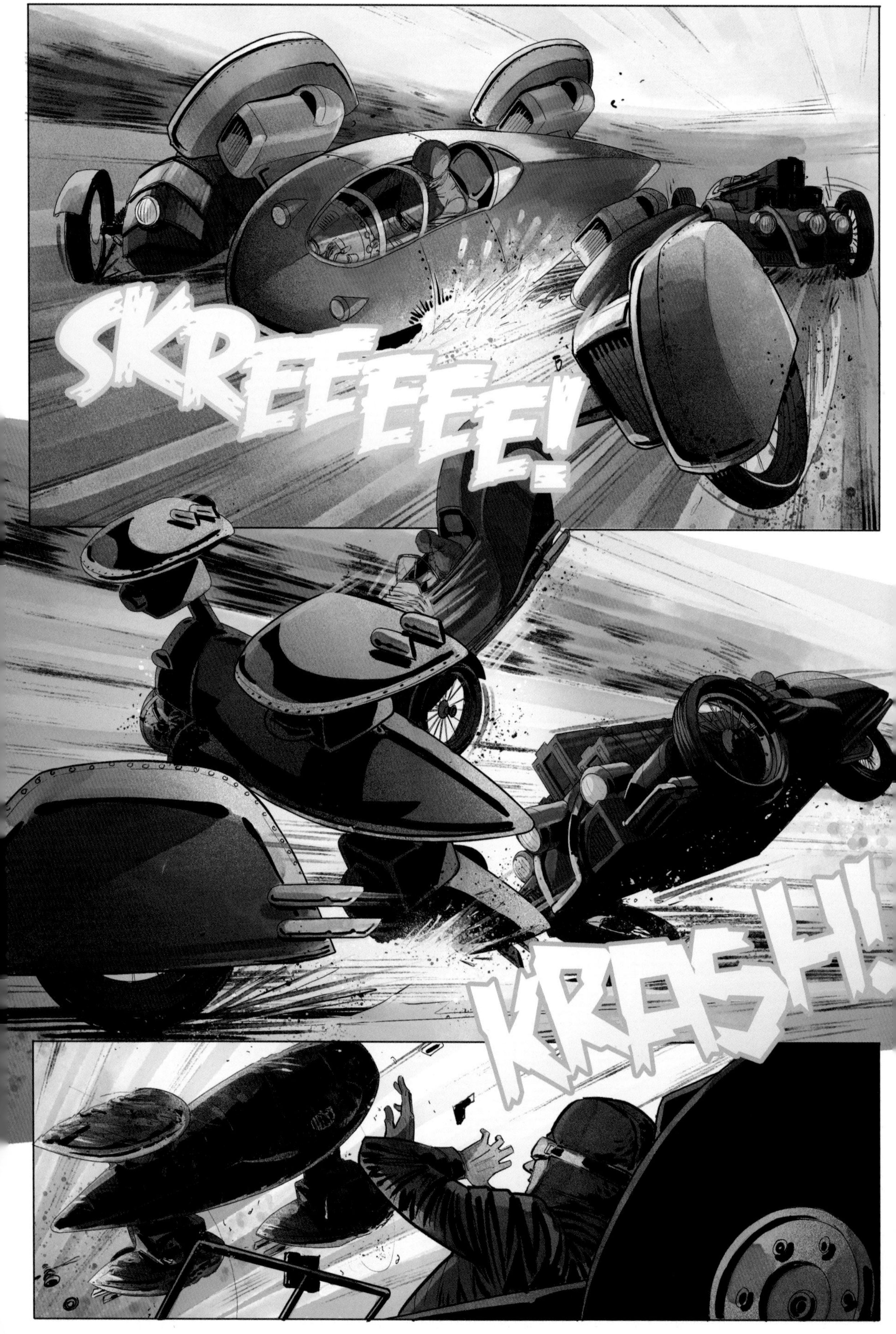
SKREEEEEE!
KRASH!

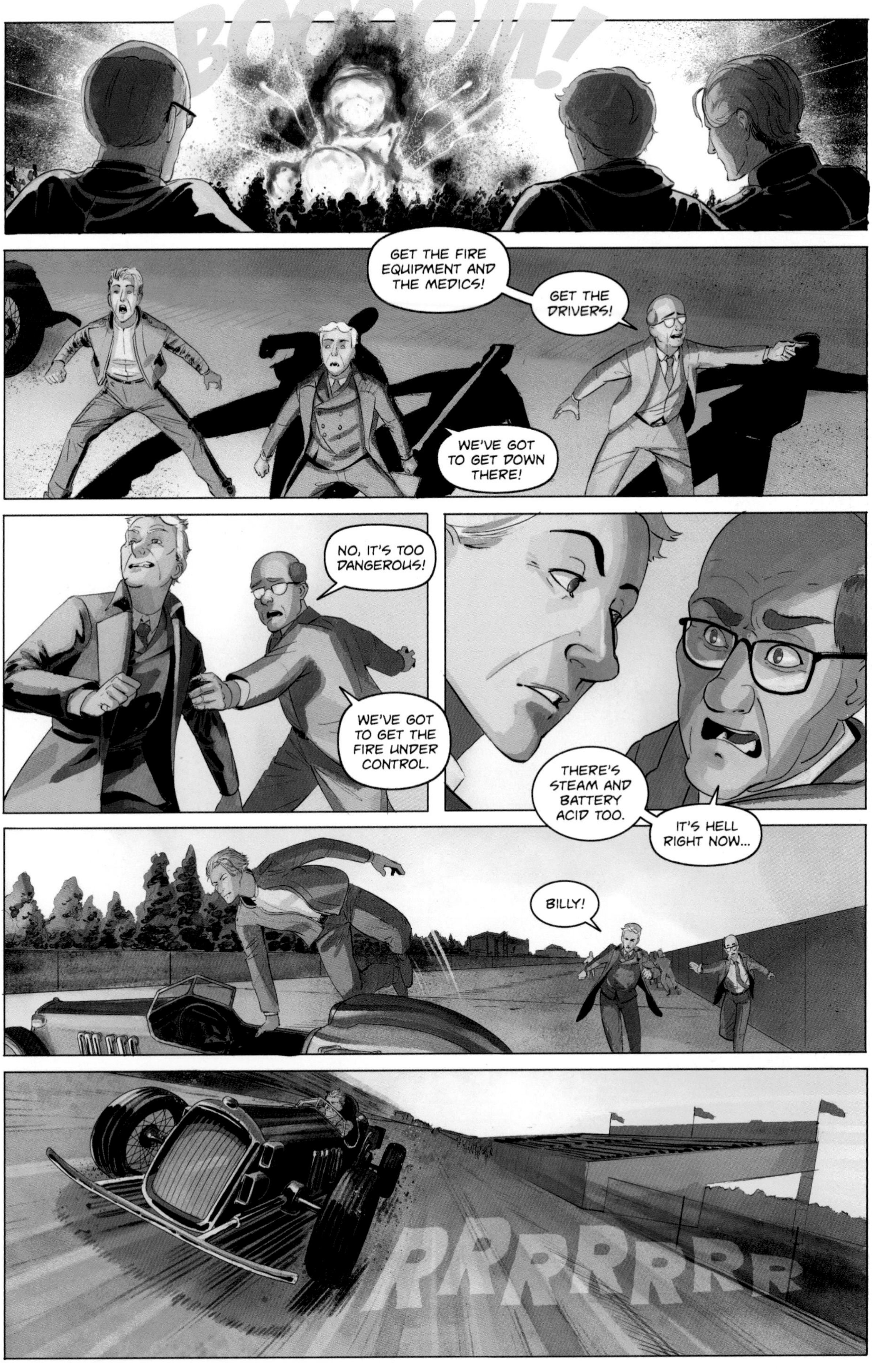
BOOOOOM!
GET THE FIRE EQUIPMENT AND THE MEDICS!
GET THE DRIVERS!
WE'VE GOT TO GET DOWN THERE!
NO, IT'S TOO DANGEROUS!
WE'VE GOT TO GET THE FIRE UNDER CONTROL.
THERE'S STEAM AND BATTERY ACID TOO.
IT'S HELL RIGHT NOW...
BILLY!
RRRRRRR

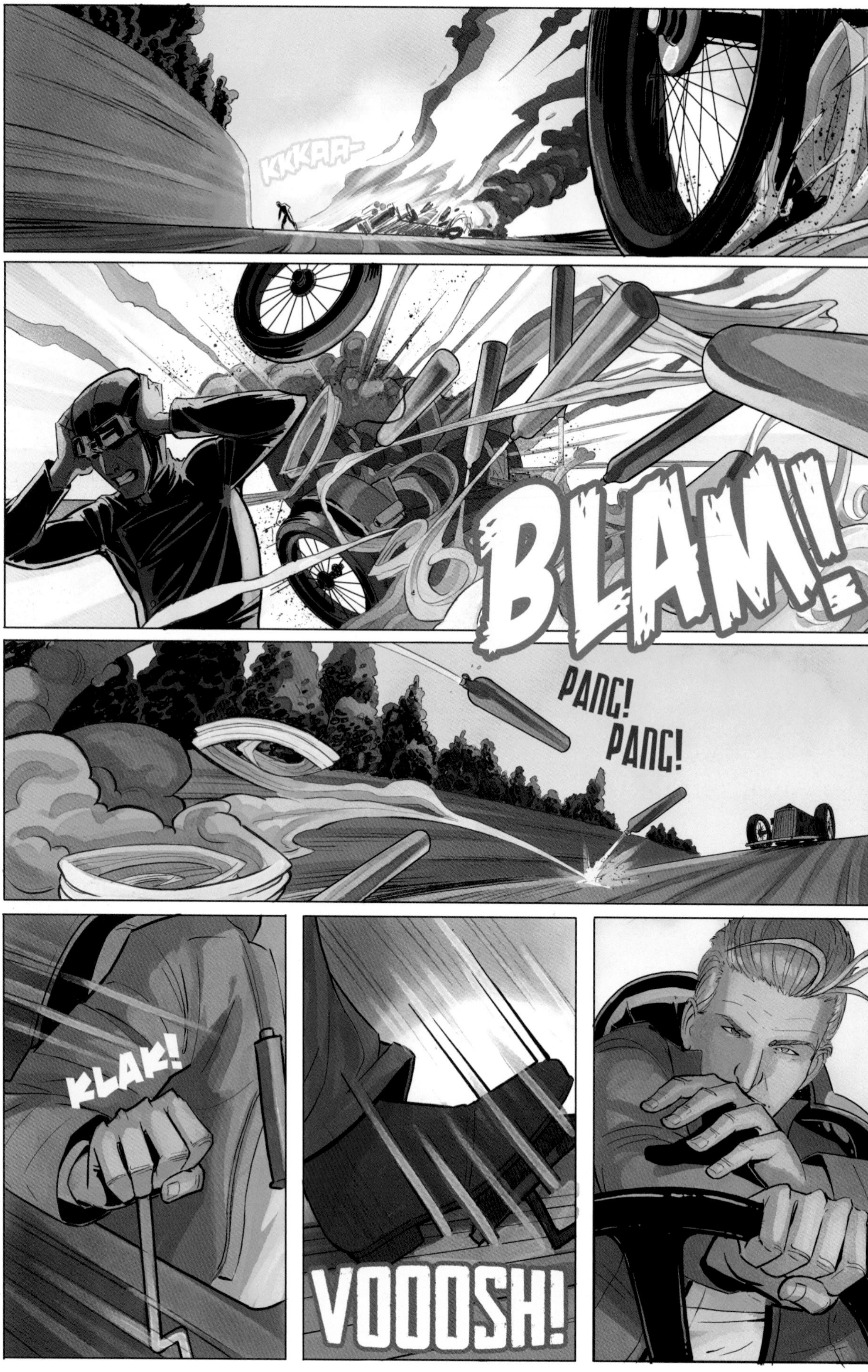

KKKAA-
BLAM!
PANG!
PANG!
KLAK!
VOOOSH!

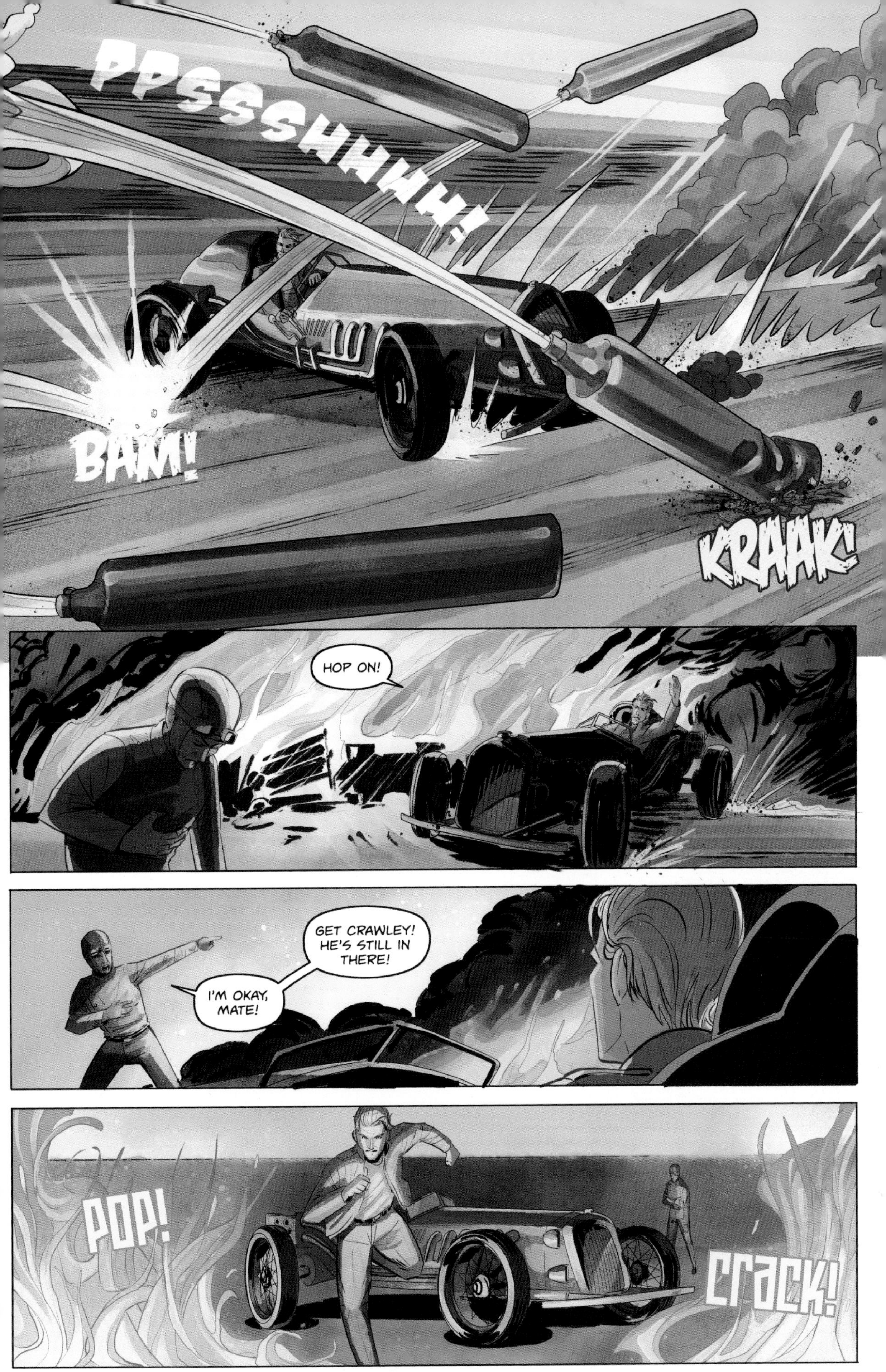
PPSSSHHHH!
BAM!
KRAAK!
HOP ON!
GET CRAWLEY! HE'S STILL IN THERE!
I'M OKAY, MATE!
POP!
CRACK!

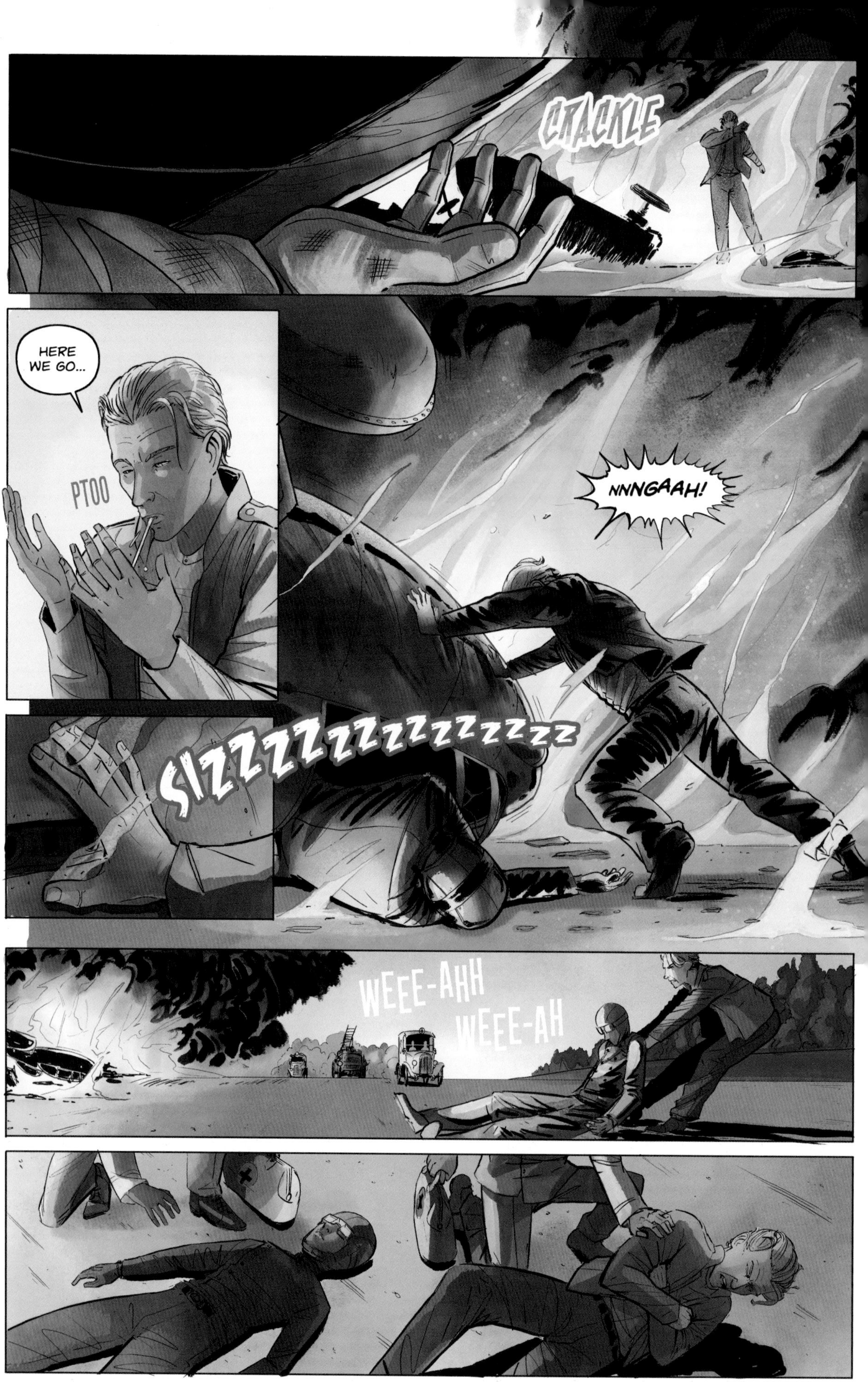
CRACKLE
HERE WE GO...
PTOO
NNNGAAH!
SIZZZZZZZZZZZZZZ
WEEE-AHH
WEEE-AH

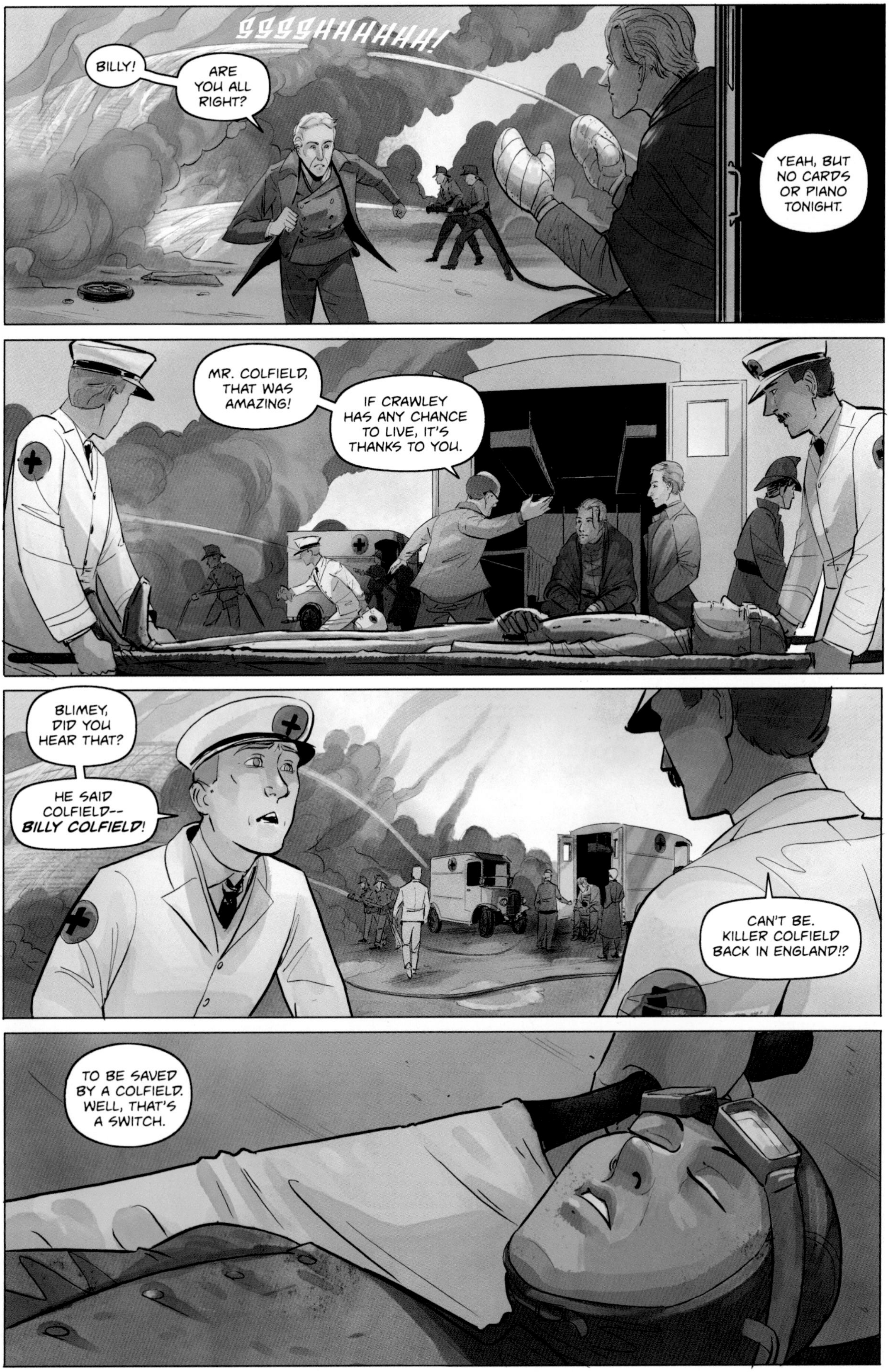
SSSSHHHHHH!
BILLY!
ARE YOU ALL RIGHT?
YEAH, BUT NO CARDS OR PIANO TONIGHT.
MR. COLFIELD, THAT WAS AMAZING!
IF CRAWLEY HAS ANY CHANCE TO LIVE, IT'S THANKS TO YOU.
BLIMEY, DID YOU HEAR THAT?
HE SAID COLFIELD-- ***BILLY COLFIELD!***
CAN'T BE. KILLER COLFIELD BACK IN ENGLAND!?
TO BE SAVED BY A COLFIELD. WELL, THAT'S A SWITCH.

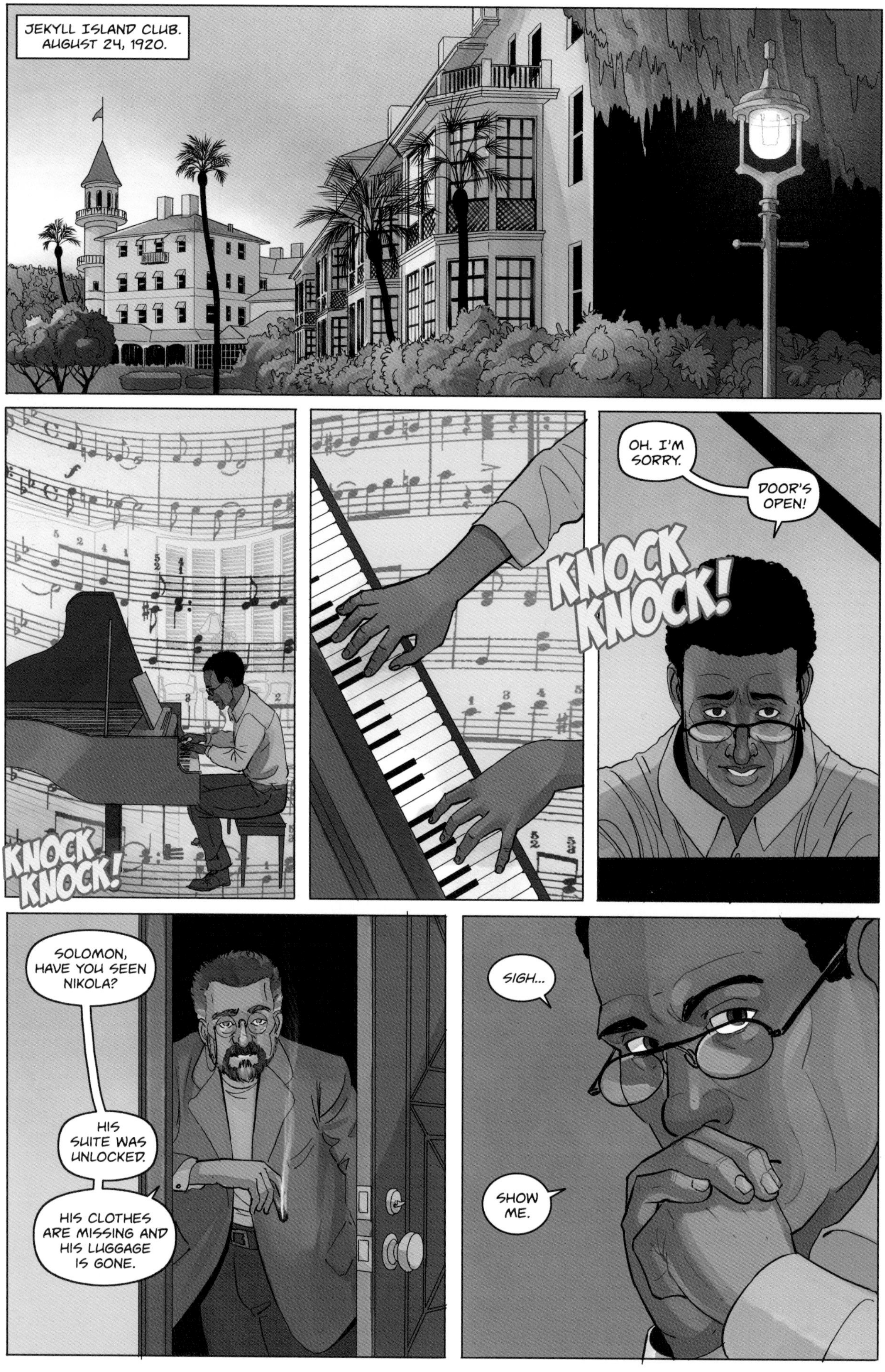
JEKYLL ISLAND CLUB. AUGUST 24, 1920.
KNOCK KNOCK!
OH. I'M SORRY.
DOOR'S OPEN!
KNOCK KNOCK!
SOLOMON, HAVE YOU SEEN NIKOLA?
HIS SUITE WAS UNLOCKED.
HIS CLOTHES ARE MISSING AND HIS LUGGAGE IS GONE.
SIGH...
SHOW ME.

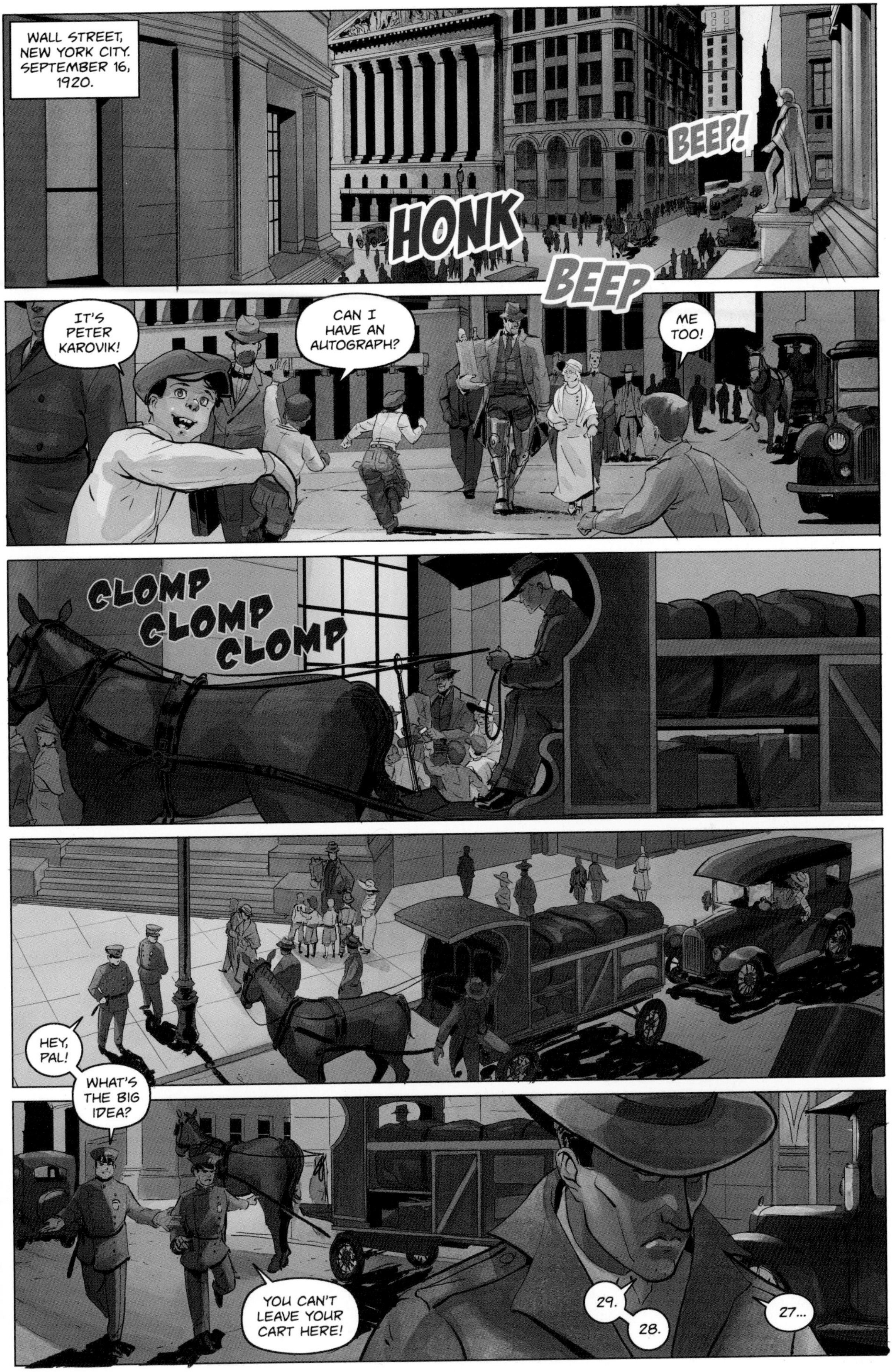
WALL STREET, NEW YORK CITY. SEPTEMBER 16, 1920.
HONK
BEEP!
BEEP
IT'S PETER KAROVIK!
CAN I HAVE AN AUTOGRAPH?
ME TOO!
CLOMP
CLOMP
CLOMP
HEY, PAL!
WHAT'S THE BIG IDEA?
YOU CAN'T LEAVE YOUR CART HERE!
29.
28.
27...

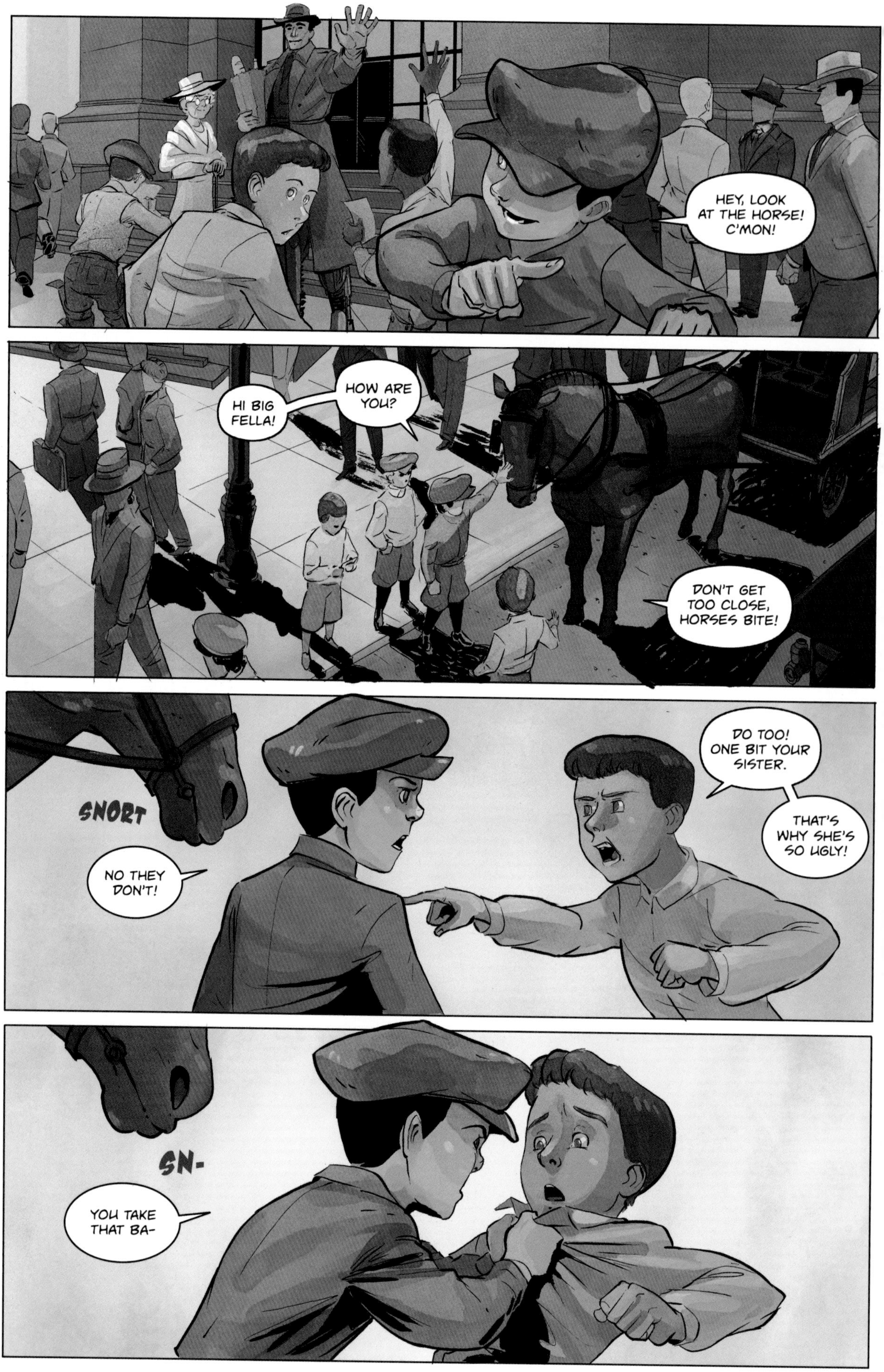
HEY, LOOK AT THE HORSE! C'MON!
HI BIG FELLA!
HOW ARE YOU?
DON'T GET TOO CLOSE, HORSES BITE!
SNORT
NO THEY DON'T!
DO TOO! ONE BIT YOUR SISTER.
THAT'S WHY SHE'S SO UGLY!
SN-
YOU TAKE THAT BA-

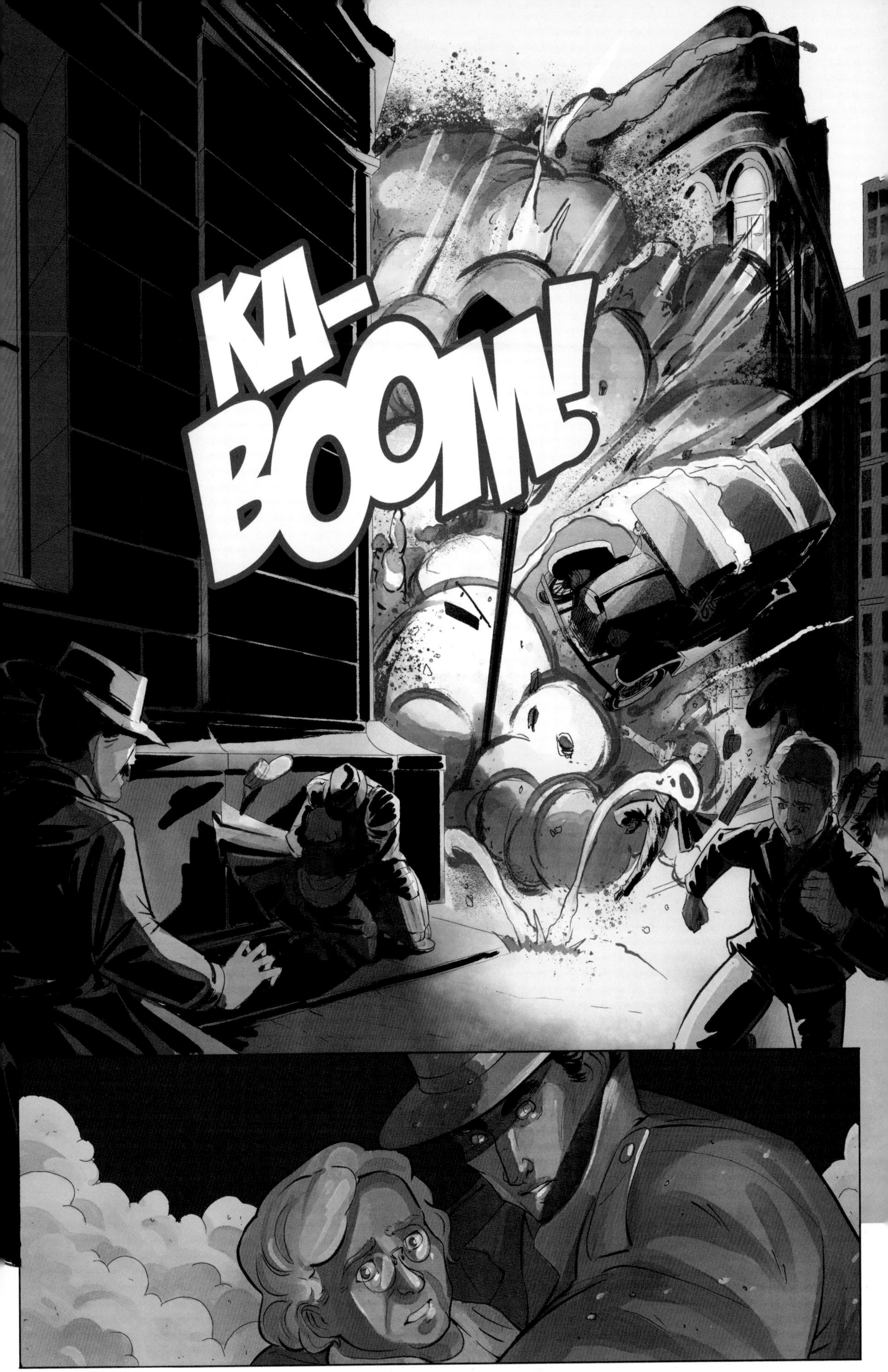
KA-
BOOM!

# The Daily Times

September 16, 1920     Three Cents     Evening Edition

# WALL STREET BOMBED!

## *DISASTER AT NOON*

### DOZENS PERISH, INCLUDING CHILDREN; ANARCHISTS CLAIM RESPONSIBILITY

Pellentesque et mei felis. Vestibulum vel vehicula ligula, duis semper ipsum. Nam fringilla, elit ac erat iaculis sodales, lorem lorem a mi, phasellus aliquet lorem sodales lobortis. Mauris risus lorem eleifend vitae risus eu varius lorem lund leo. Cras id libero odio. Ut sed sodales lacinia felis, eu malesuada ante scelerisque ut. Mauris tincidunt elit sit amet urna fermentum, consequat eget id ipsum. Aenean efficitur pulvinar viverra. Mauris vitae faucibus nunc. Donec porta quis nibh varius cibus. Aliquam tempus nisi risus, vitae rutrum odio malesuada eu. Aliquam gravida amet vitae lacus venenatis, eget vehicula tellus lacinia.

Pellentesque tristique a risus tellus a iaculis. Etiam et porta ligula vel turpis consectetur tempor. Praesent placerat, risus ac tristique convallis, dui urna lacinia, lacreet et ultrices enim dolor et augue. Donec fringilla tincidunt vehicula.

Today, at 12:01pm, a blast ripped through the Financial District of New York City, claiming 30 souls in its wake. Hundreds are injured, some critically. The event proves the continued presence among us of those who would terrorize our shores. NYPD has reported that a horse-drawn cart, filled with dynamite and shrapnel, was ignited, producing carnage of a great evil and damaging buildings in the process. Bodies were lined up, row upon row, covered, while holes could be seen in the J.P. Morgan bank building just above the grisly scene.

### PRESIDENT WILSON LIVID

**Despite the administration's best efforts to round up thousands of known anarchist and would-be trouble makers last year, evil still persists.**

Pellentesque faucibus posuere tincidunt. Phasellus bibendum velit sed magnis dictus egestas. Nunc maximus purus vitae sapien lobortis convallis. Integer volutpat odio non elit interdum, et fringilla velit posuere. Nullam finibus purus id. Aliquam nec accumsan augue, sit amet maximus lorem. Nullam massa eros, facilisis ut tortor eu, varius vestibulum dui. Curabitur enim mi, vulputate eget pulvinar id, gravida a tortor. Donec libero ex, sagittis ac bibendum et, vulputate sit amet dui. Aenean fermentum semper metus a lobortis. Fusce convallis efficitur vulputate egestas. Nullam est neque, luctus quis varius et, porttitor vitae elit.

### CANDIDATE HARDING PROMISES "RETURN TO NORMALCY"

Duis at dictum diam in varius odio. Donec mollis tellus vel ultricies fringilla. Integer nec tempor felis. In egestas aliquet tincidunt. Integer felis sem, feugiat eu scelerisque efficitur, interdum id libero. Mauris elit nulla, maximus ac gravida vel, feugiat id eros. Etiam eleifend id laoreet lectus ac consequat.

Pellentesque tincidunt posuere tincidunt. Phasellus bibendum velit sed magnis lorem egestas. Nunc maximus purus vitae sapien lobortis convallis. Integer volutpat odio non elit interdum, et fringilla velit posuere. Nullam finibus purus ut. Aliquam non malesuada neque, sit amet maximus lorem. Nullam massa sapien, facilisis id lacus eu, varius vestibulum dui. Curabitur enim mi, vulputate eget, pulvinar id, gravida a tortor. Donec libero ex, sagittis ac bibendum ut, vulputate sit amet dui. Aenean fermentum semper metus et lobortis. Fusce venenatis felis eu vulputate egestas. Nullam est neque, luctus quis varius et, porttitor vitae elit.

### GERMAN MARK HITS NEW LOW

Cras vestibulum orci nec lacus scelerisque, quis venenatis tortor commodo. Sed arcu dui, efficitur nec ligula vitae, tincidunt finibus orci. Donec blandit purus ut metus fringilla auctor, nec eget integer quam. In imperdiet dapibus risus nec sodales. Donec mollis accumsan lorem pretium. Sed ut nibh id ornare quisque ut pellentesque nisl. Maecenas gravida tortor a laoreet posuere. Aliquam et pharetra nibh. Curabitur blandit eros. Quisque sollicitudin dolor a egestas tincidunt. Nunc ultrices est vitae tellus maximus, euismod tristique. Maecenas blandit ex vitae enim tempus.

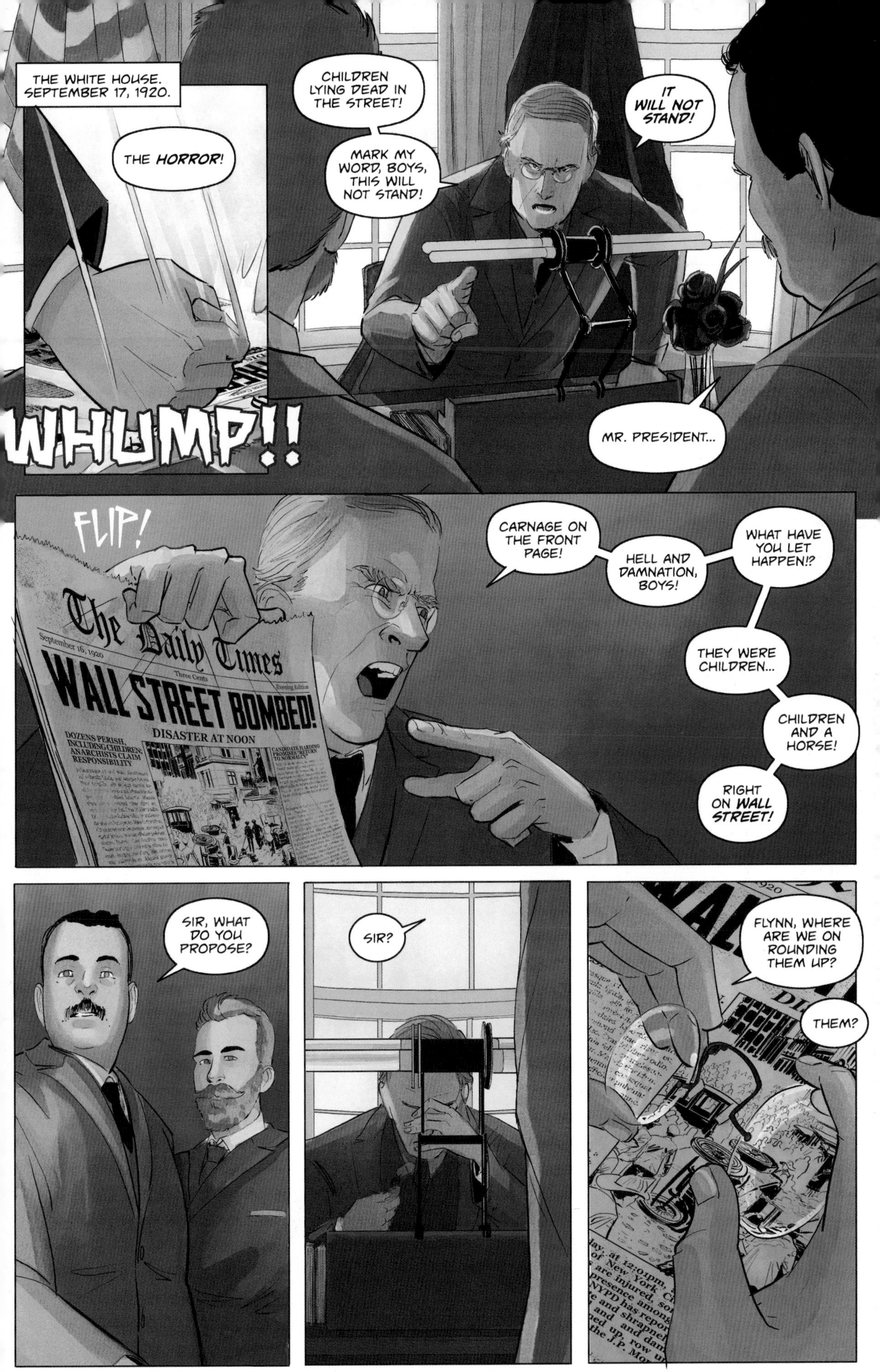
THE WHITE HOUSE. SEPTEMBER 17, 1920.
THE HORROR!
CHILDREN LYING DEAD IN THE STREET!
MARK MY WORD, BOYS, THIS WILL NOT STAND!
IT WILL NOT STAND!
WHUMP!!
MR. PRESIDENT...
FLIP!
The Daily Times
September 16, 1920
Three Cents
Evening Edition
WALL STREET BOMBED!
DISASTER AT NOON
DOZENS PERISH, INCLUDING CHILDREN; ANARCHISTS CLAIM RESPONSIBILITY
CANDIDATE HARDING PROMISES "RETURN TO NORMALCY"
CARNAGE ON THE FRONT PAGE!
HELL AND DAMNATION, BOYS!
WHAT HAVE YOU LET HAPPEN!?
THEY WERE CHILDREN...
CHILDREN AND A HORSE!
RIGHT ON WALL STREET!
SIR, WHAT DO YOU PROPOSE?
SIR?
FLYNN, WHERE ARE WE ON ROUNDING THEM UP?
THEM?

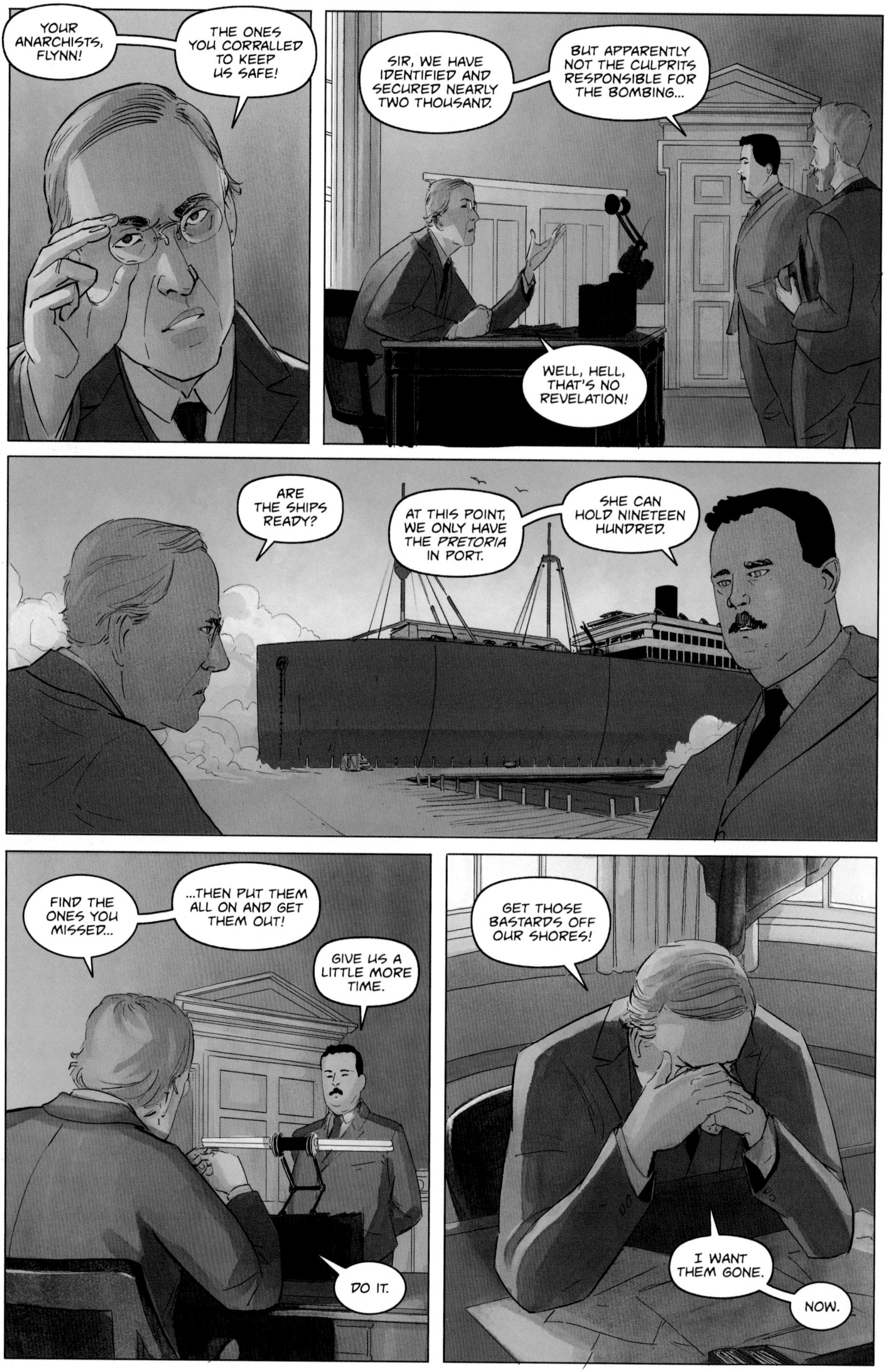
YOUR ANARCHISTS, FLYNN!
THE ONES YOU CORRALLED TO KEEP US SAFE!
SIR, WE HAVE IDENTIFIED AND SECURED NEARLY TWO THOUSAND.
BUT APPARENTLY NOT THE CULPRITS RESPONSIBLE FOR THE BOMBING...
WELL, HELL, THAT'S NO REVELATION!
ARE THE SHIPS READY?
AT THIS POINT, WE ONLY HAVE THE *PRETORIA* IN PORT.
SHE CAN HOLD NINETEEN HUNDRED.
FIND THE ONES YOU MISSED...
...THEN PUT THEM ALL ON AND GET THEM OUT!
GIVE US A LITTLE MORE TIME.
DO IT.
GET THOSE BASTARDS OFF OUR SHORES!
I WANT THEM GONE.
NOW.

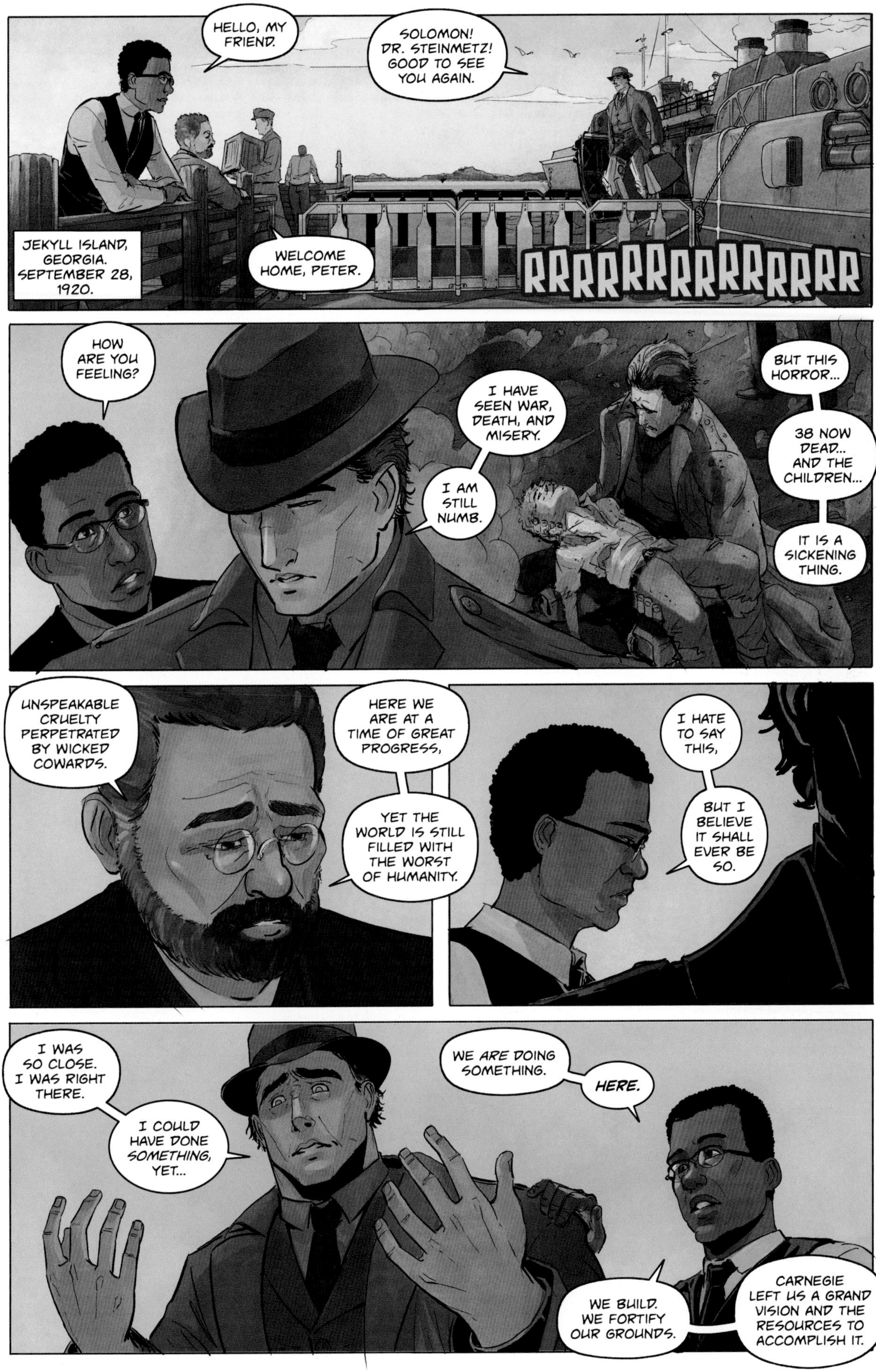
JEKYLL ISLAND, GEORGIA. SEPTEMBER 28, 1920.
HELLO, MY FRIEND.
SOLOMON! DR. STEINMETZ! GOOD TO SEE YOU AGAIN.
WELCOME HOME, PETER.
RRRRRRRRRRRRRR
HOW ARE YOU FEELING?
I HAVE SEEN WAR, DEATH, AND MISERY.
I AM STILL NUMB.
BUT THIS HORROR...
38 NOW DEAD... AND THE CHILDREN...
IT IS A SICKENING THING.
UNSPEAKABLE CRUELTY PERPETRATED BY WICKED COWARDS.
HERE WE ARE AT A TIME OF GREAT PROGRESS,
YET THE WORLD IS STILL FILLED WITH THE WORST OF HUMANITY.
I HATE TO SAY THIS,
BUT I BELIEVE IT SHALL EVER BE SO.
I WAS SO CLOSE. I WAS RIGHT THERE.
I COULD HAVE DONE SOMETHING, YET...
WE *ARE* DOING SOMETHING.
*HERE.*
WE BUILD. WE FORTIFY OUR GROUNDS.
CARNEGIE LEFT US A GRAND VISION AND THE RESOURCES TO ACCOMPLISH IT.

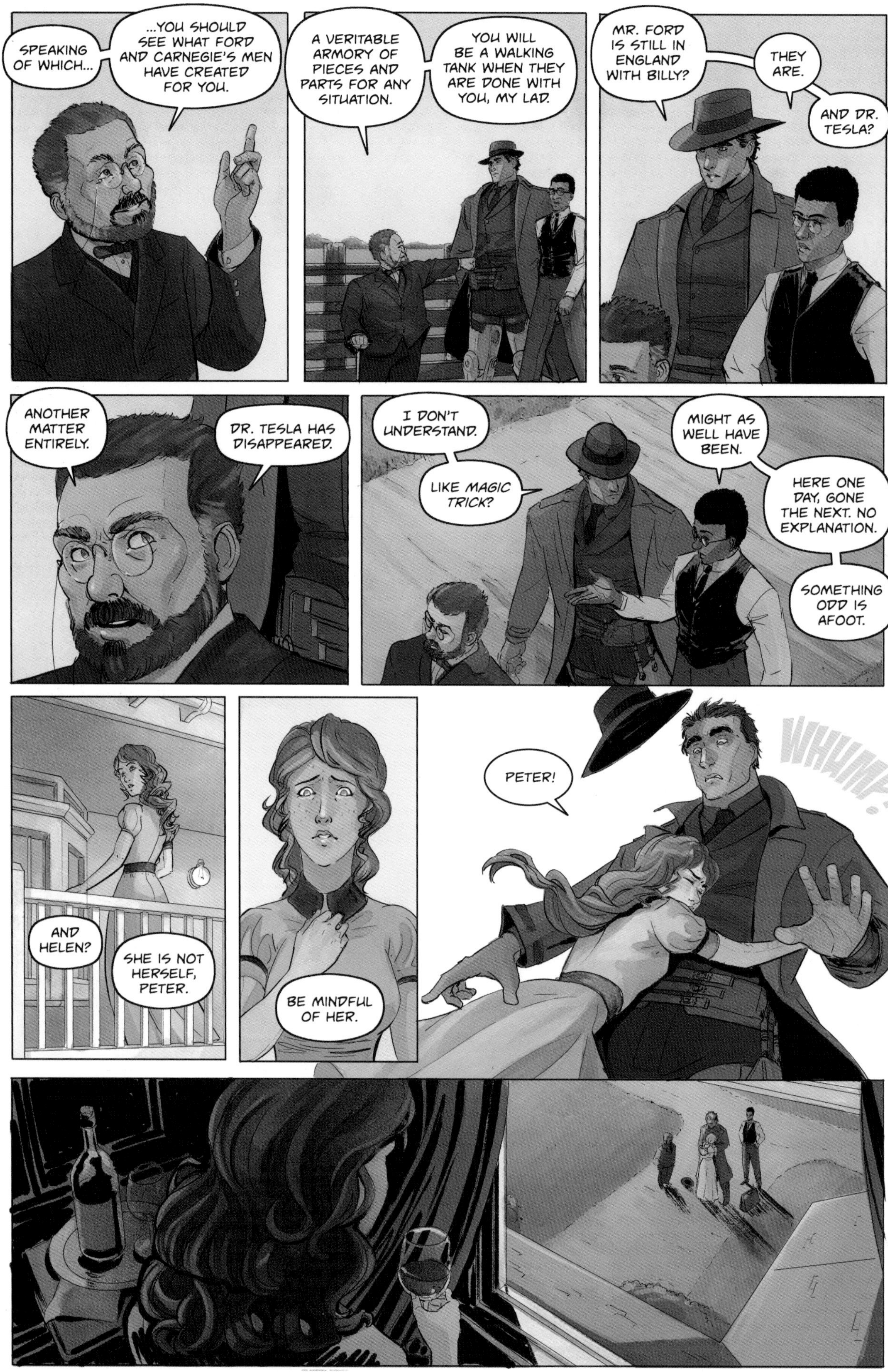
SPEAKING OF WHICH...
...YOU SHOULD SEE WHAT FORD AND CARNEGIE'S MEN HAVE CREATED FOR YOU.
A VERITABLE ARMORY OF PIECES AND PARTS FOR ANY SITUATION.
YOU WILL BE A WALKING TANK WHEN THEY ARE DONE WITH YOU, MY LAD.
MR. FORD IS STILL IN ENGLAND WITH BILLY?
THEY ARE.
AND DR. TESLA?
ANOTHER MATTER ENTIRELY.
DR. TESLA HAS DISAPPEARED.
I DON'T UNDERSTAND.
LIKE MAGIC TRICK?
MIGHT AS WELL HAVE BEEN.
HERE ONE DAY, GONE THE NEXT. NO EXPLANATION.
SOMETHING ODD IS AFOOT.
AND HELEN?
SHE IS NOT HERSELF, PETER.
BE MINDFUL OF HER.
PETER!
WHUMP!

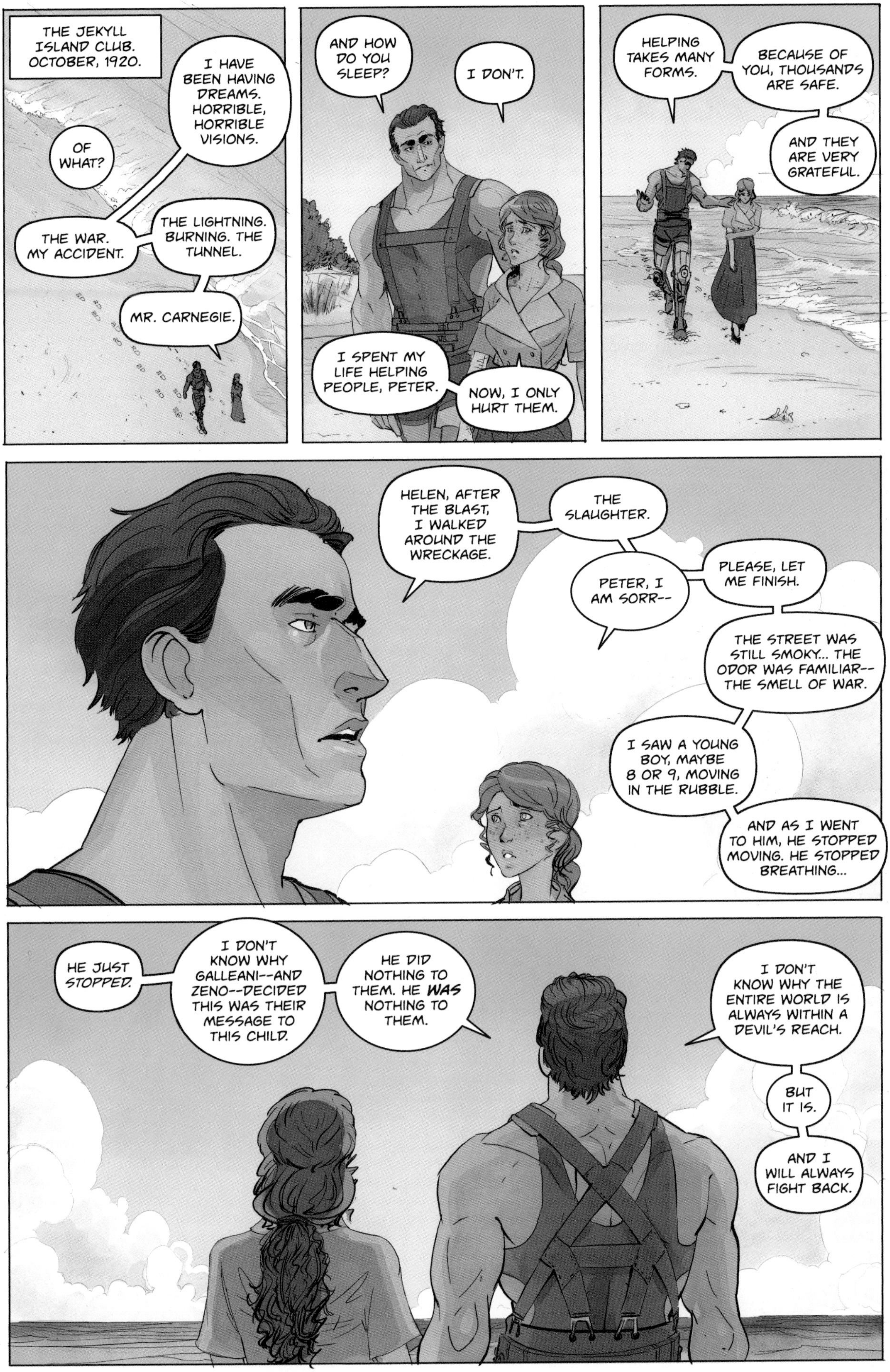
THE JEKYLL ISLAND CLUB. OCTOBER, 1920.
I HAVE BEEN HAVING DREAMS. HORRIBLE, HORRIBLE VISIONS.
OF WHAT?
THE WAR. MY ACCIDENT.
THE LIGHTNING. BURNING. THE TUNNEL.
MR. CARNEGIE.
AND HOW DO YOU SLEEP?
I DON'T.
I SPENT MY LIFE HELPING PEOPLE, PETER.
NOW, I ONLY HURT THEM.
HELPING TAKES MANY FORMS.
BECAUSE OF YOU, THOUSANDS ARE SAFE.
AND THEY ARE VERY GRATEFUL.
HELEN, AFTER THE BLAST, I WALKED AROUND THE WRECKAGE.
THE SLAUGHTER.
PETER, I AM SORR--
PLEASE, LET ME FINISH.
THE STREET WAS STILL SMOKY... THE ODOR WAS FAMILIAR-- THE SMELL OF WAR.
I SAW A YOUNG BOY, MAYBE 8 OR 9, MOVING IN THE RUBBLE.
AND AS I WENT TO HIM, HE STOPPED MOVING. HE STOPPED BREATHING...
HE JUST STOPPED.
I DON'T KNOW WHY GALLEANI--AND ZENO--DECIDED THIS WAS THEIR MESSAGE TO THIS CHILD.
HE DID NOTHING TO THEM. HE ***WAS*** NOTHING TO THEM.
I DON'T KNOW WHY THE ENTIRE WORLD IS ALWAYS WITHIN A DEVIL'S REACH.
BUT IT IS.
AND I WILL ALWAYS FIGHT BACK.

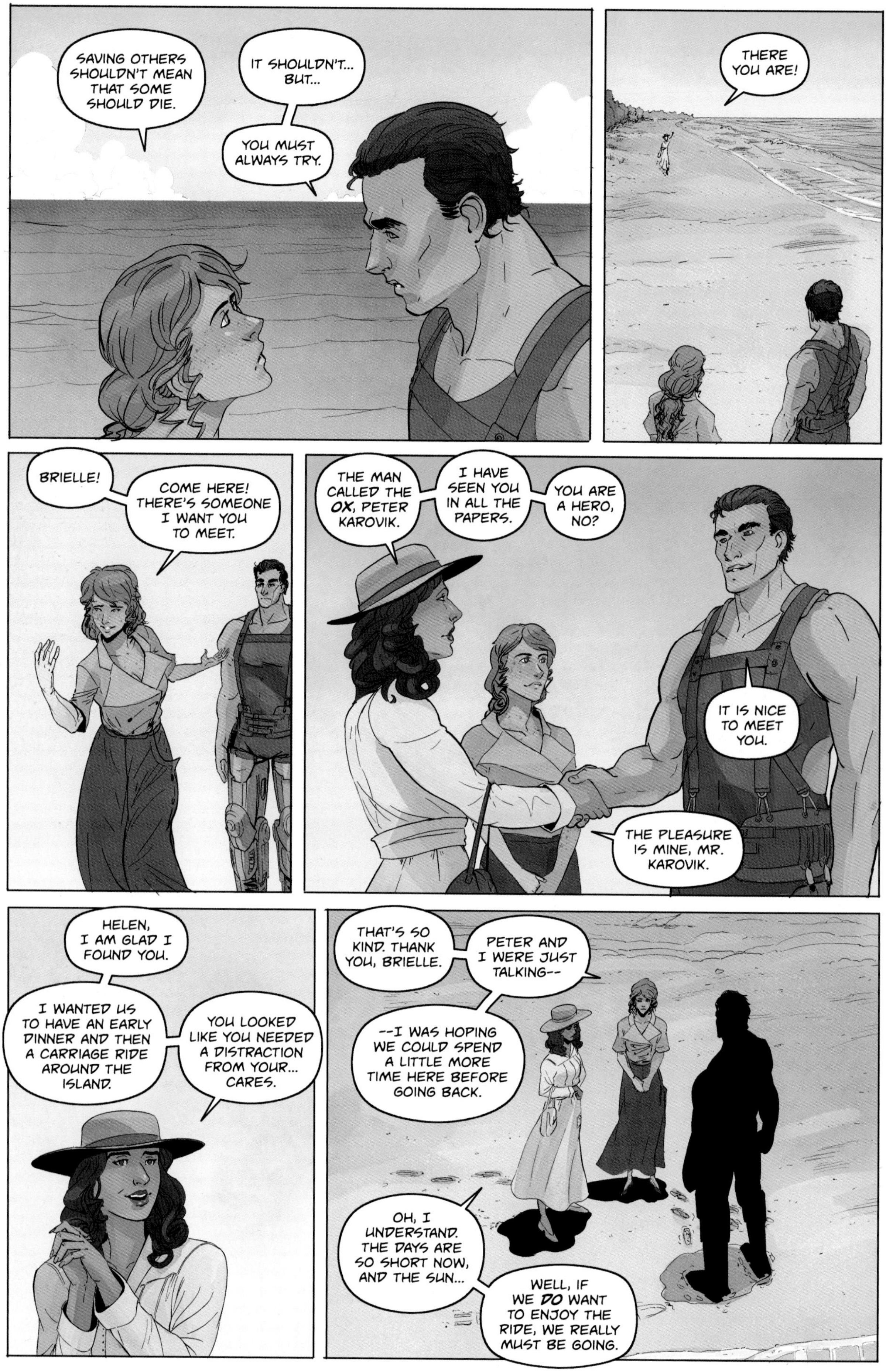
SAVING OTHERS SHOULDN'T MEAN THAT SOME SHOULD DIE.
IT SHOULDN'T... BUT...
YOU MUST ALWAYS TRY.
THERE YOU ARE!
BRIELLE!
COME HERE! THERE'S SOMEONE I WANT YOU TO MEET.
THE MAN CALLED THE OX, PETER KAROVIK.
I HAVE SEEN YOU IN ALL THE PAPERS.
YOU ARE A HERO, NO?
IT IS NICE TO MEET YOU.
THE PLEASURE IS MINE, MR. KAROVIK.
HELEN, I AM GLAD I FOUND YOU.
I WANTED US TO HAVE AN EARLY DINNER AND THEN A CARRIAGE RIDE AROUND THE ISLAND.
YOU LOOKED LIKE YOU NEEDED A DISTRACTION FROM YOUR... CARES.
THAT'S SO KIND. THANK YOU, BRIELLE.
PETER AND I WERE JUST TALKING--
--I WAS HOPING WE COULD SPEND A LITTLE MORE TIME HERE BEFORE GOING BACK.
OH, I UNDERSTAND. THE DAYS ARE SO SHORT NOW, AND THE SUN...
WELL, IF WE DO WANT TO ENJOY THE RIDE, WE REALLY MUST BE GOING.

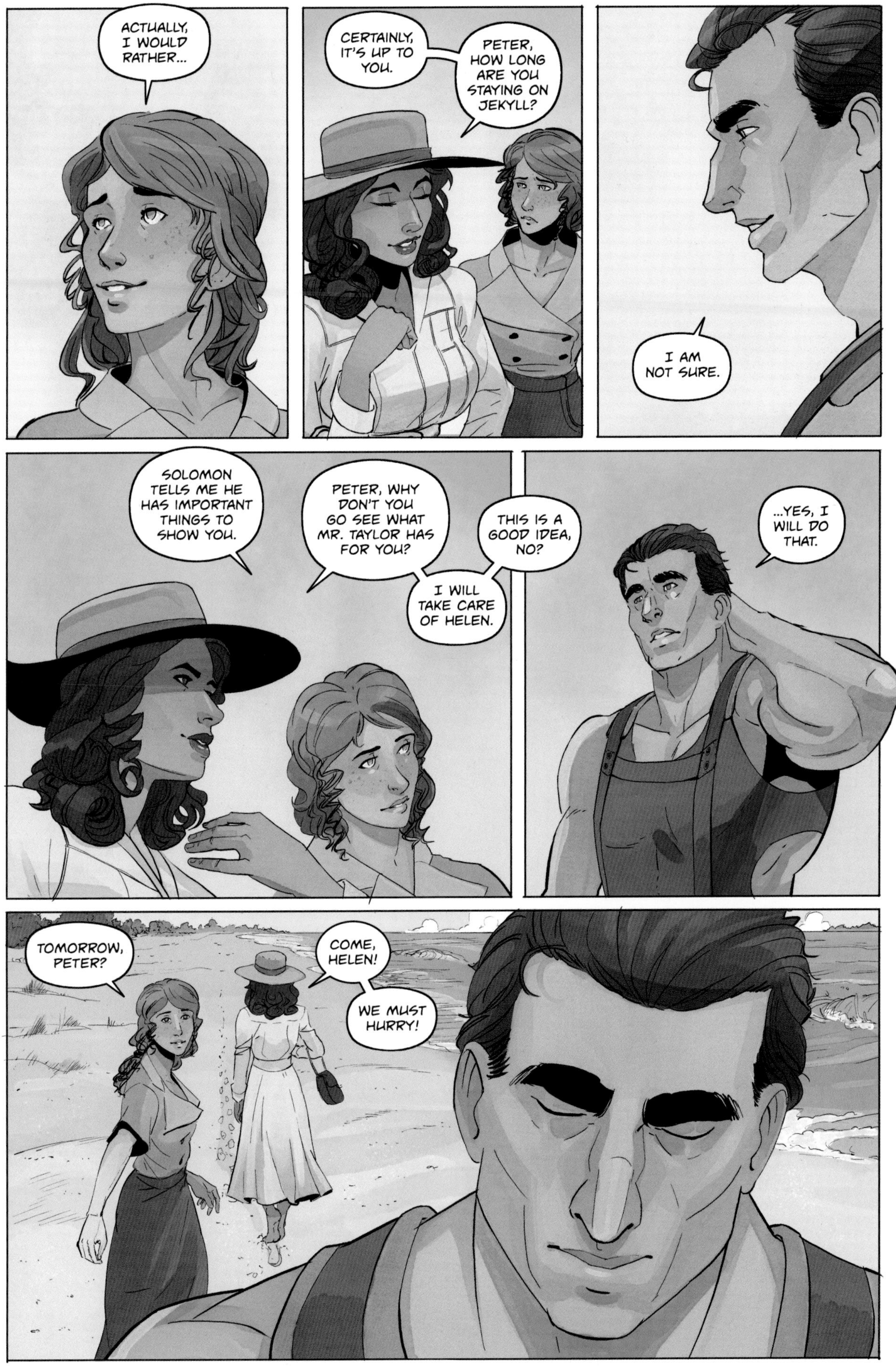
ACTUALLY, I WOULD RATHER...
CERTAINLY, IT'S UP TO YOU.
PETER, HOW LONG ARE YOU STAYING ON JEKYLL?
I AM NOT SURE.
SOLOMON TELLS ME HE HAS IMPORTANT THINGS TO SHOW YOU.
PETER, WHY DON'T YOU GO SEE WHAT MR. TAYLOR HAS FOR YOU?
THIS IS A GOOD IDEA, NO?
I WILL TAKE CARE OF HELEN.
...YES, I WILL DO THAT.
TOMORROW, PETER?
COME, HELEN!
WE MUST HURRY!

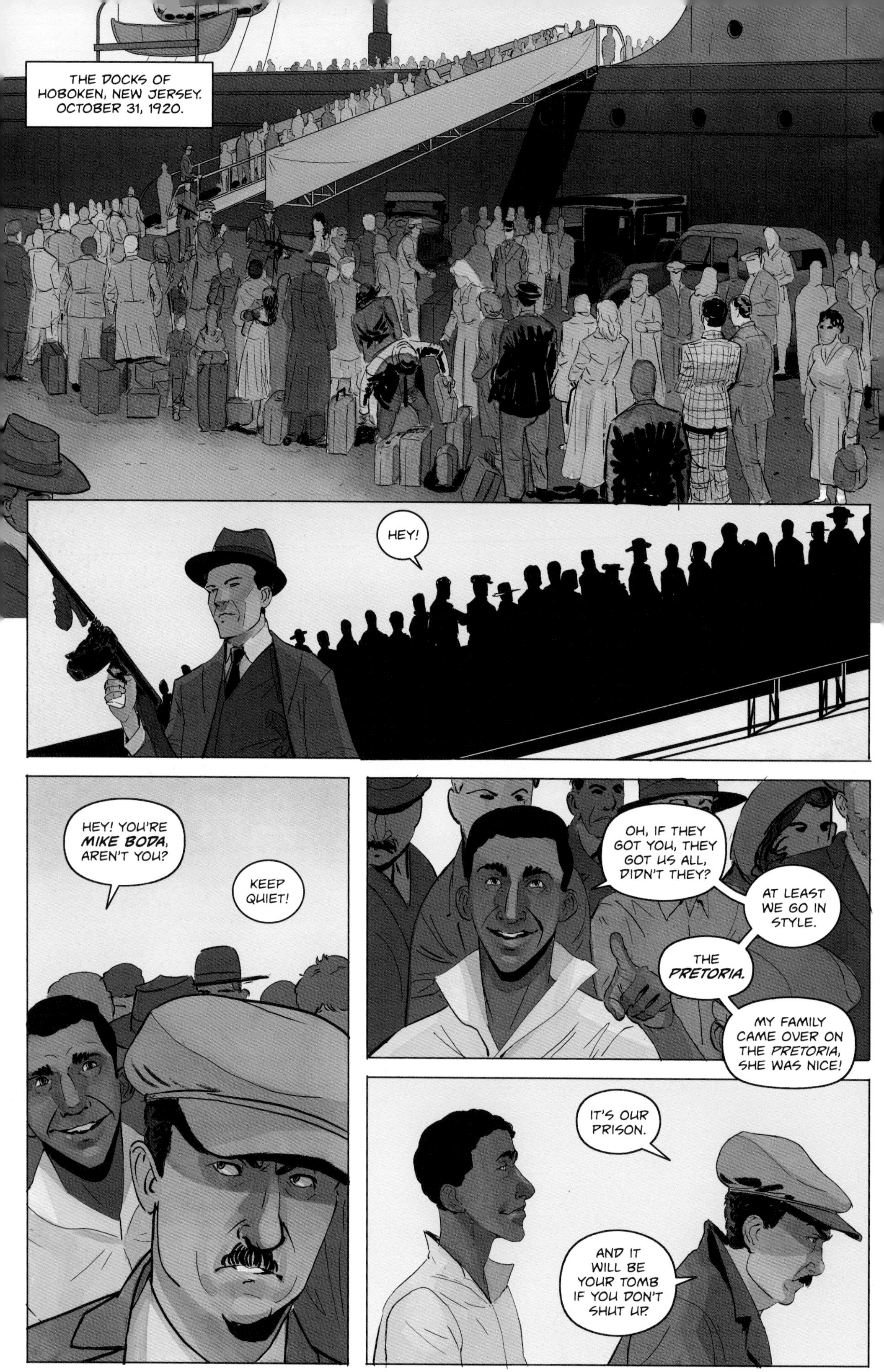
THE DOCKS OF HOBOKEN, NEW JERSEY. OCTOBER 31, 1920.
HEY!
HEY! YOU'RE *MIKE BODA*, AREN'T YOU?
KEEP QUIET!
OH, IF THEY GOT YOU, THEY GOT US ALL, DIDN'T THEY?
AT LEAST WE GO IN STYLE.
THE *PRETORIA.*
MY FAMILY CAME OVER ON THE *PRETORIA*, SHE WAS NICE!
IT'S OUR PRISON.
AND IT WILL BE YOUR TOMB IF YOU DON'T SHUT UP.

MOVE ALONG.

CRONACA SOWERSIV

SALVATION COMES AT DAWN ON THE THIRD DAY.

LOOK TO THE RISING SUN.

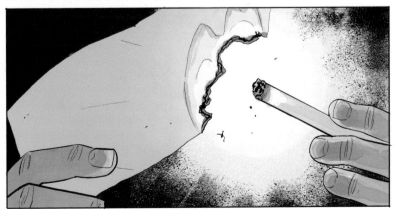

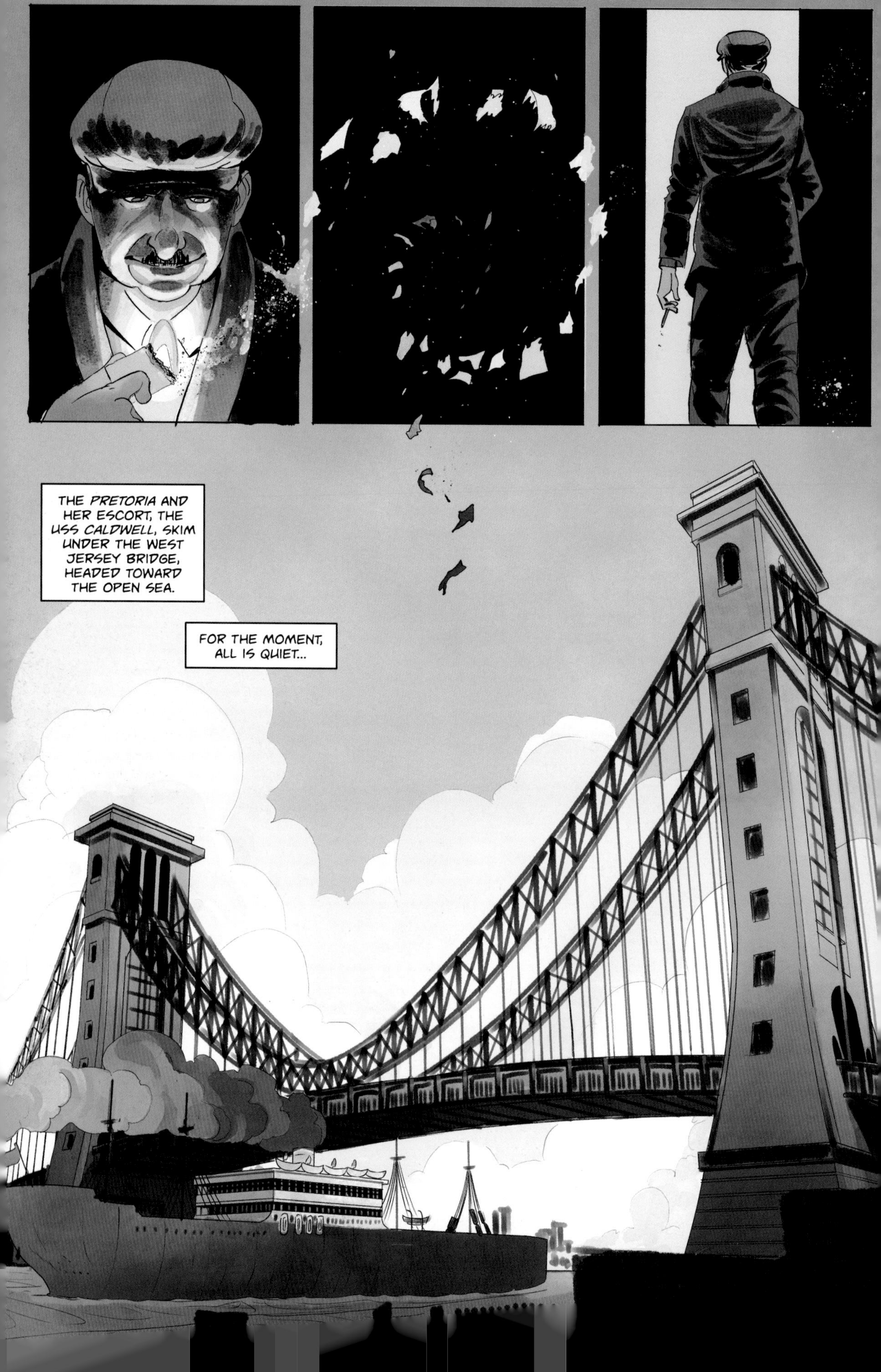
THE *PRETORIA* AND HER ESCORT, THE USS *CALDWELL*, SKIM UNDER THE WEST JERSEY BRIDGE, HEADED TOWARD THE OPEN SEA.
FOR THE MOMENT, ALL IS QUIET...

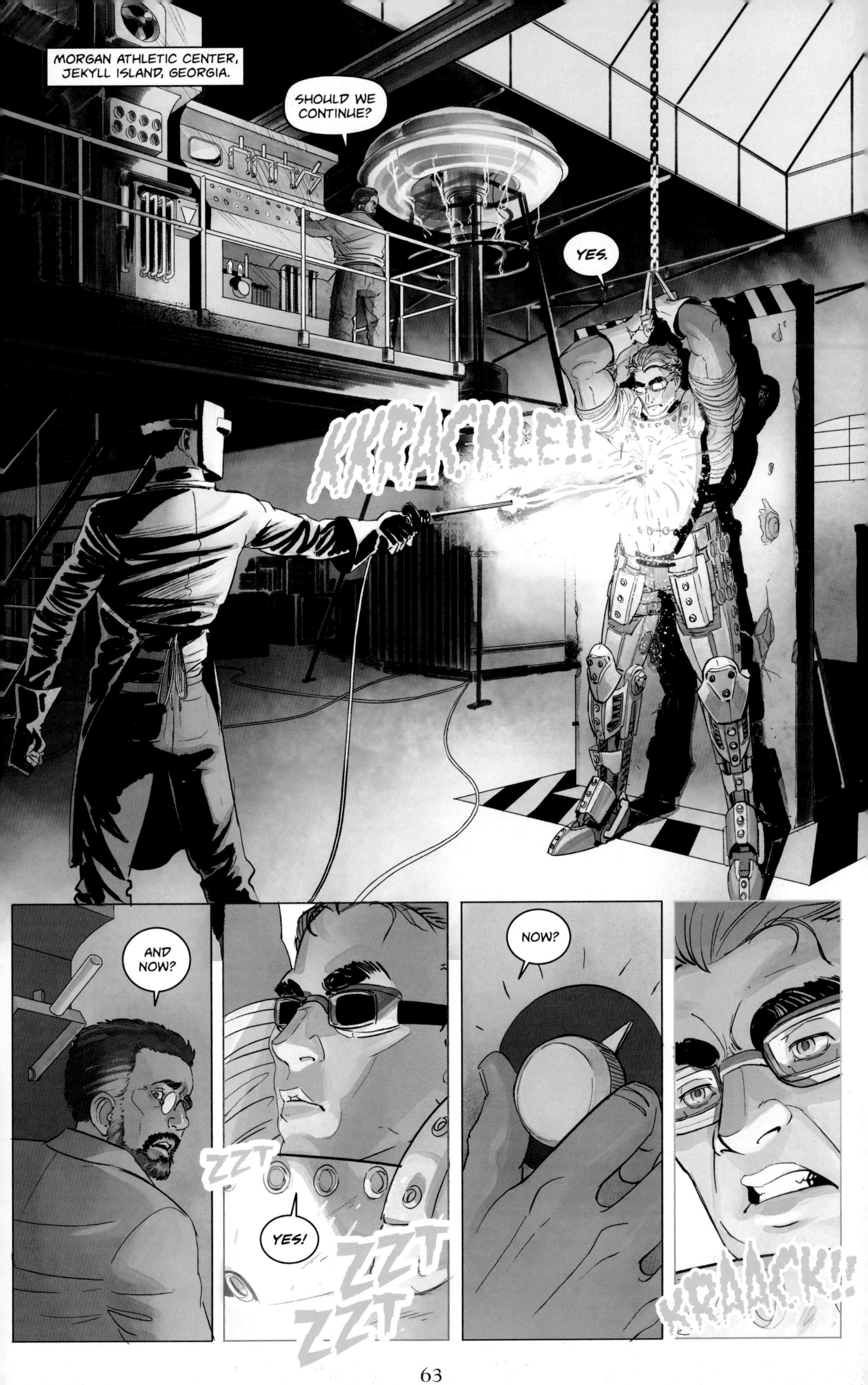
MORGAN ATHLETIC CENTER, JEKYLL ISLAND, GEORGIA.
SHOULD WE CONTINUE?
YES.
KKRACKLE!!
AND NOW?
ZZT
YES!
ZZZT
ZZZT
NOW?
KRAACK!!

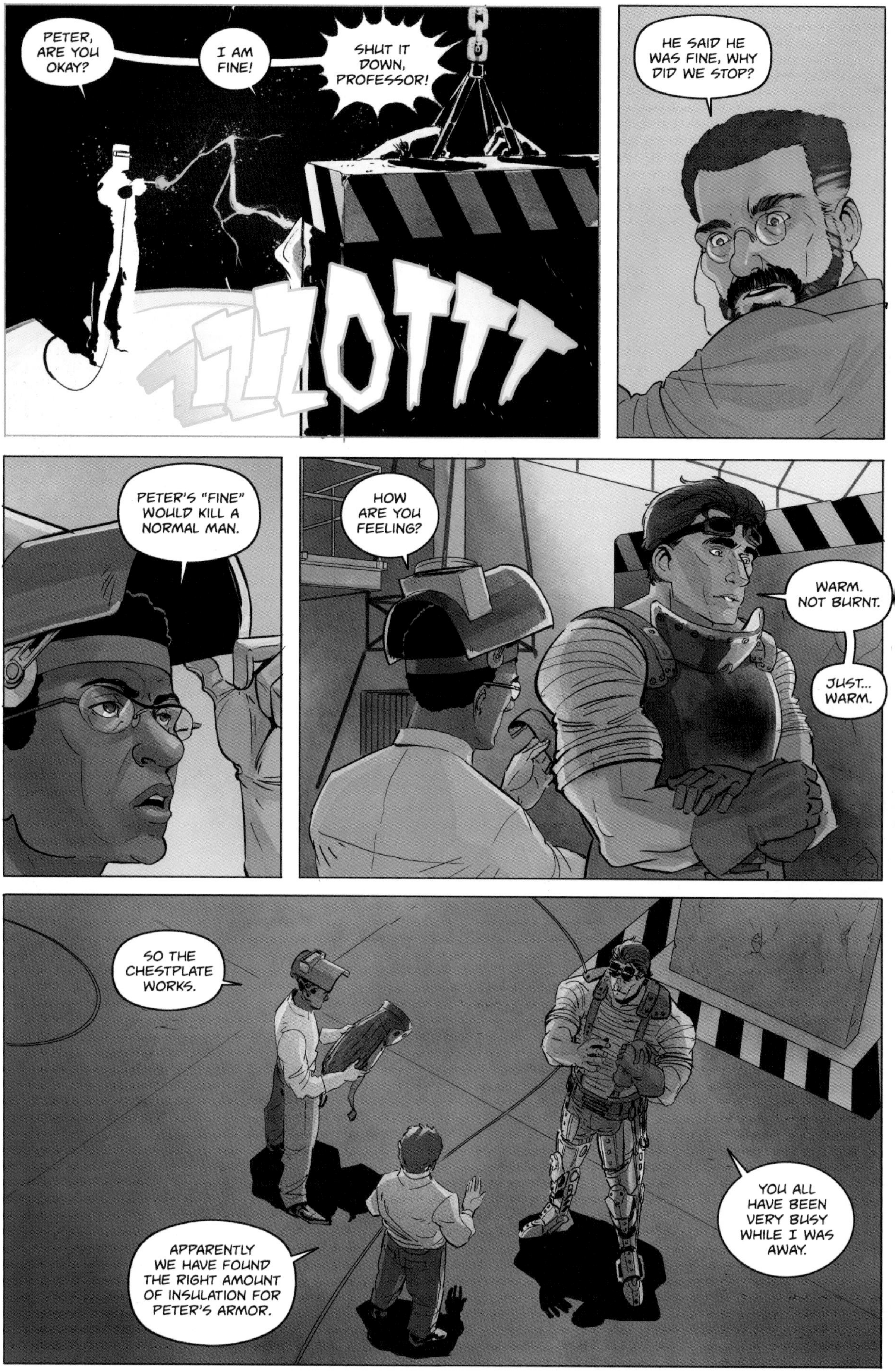
PETER, ARE YOU OKAY?
I AM FINE!
SHUT IT DOWN, PROFESSOR!
ZZZZOTTTT
HE SAID HE WAS FINE, WHY DID WE STOP?
PETER'S "FINE" WOULD KILL A NORMAL MAN.
HOW ARE YOU FEELING?
WARM. NOT BURNT.
JUST... WARM.
SO THE CHESTPLATE WORKS.
APPARENTLY WE HAVE FOUND THE RIGHT AMOUNT OF INSULATION FOR PETER'S ARMOR.
YOU ALL HAVE BEEN VERY BUSY WHILE I WAS AWAY.

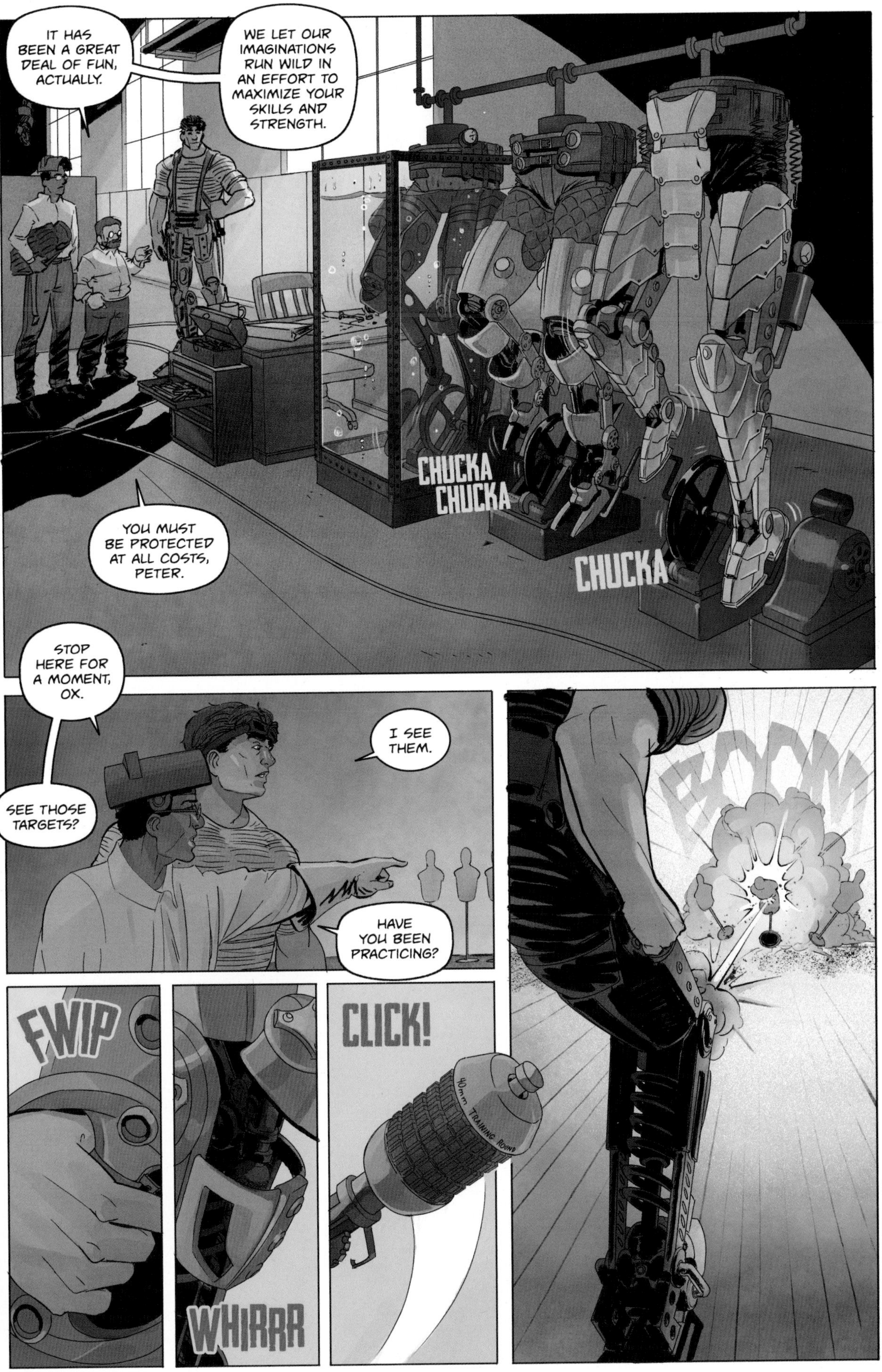
IT HAS BEEN A GREAT DEAL OF FUN, ACTUALLY.
WE LET OUR IMAGINATIONS RUN WILD IN AN EFFORT TO MAXIMIZE YOUR SKILLS AND STRENGTH.
YOU MUST BE PROTECTED AT ALL COSTS, PETER.
CHUCKA CHUCKA
CHUCKA
STOP HERE FOR A MOMENT, OX.
SEE THOSE TARGETS?
I SEE THEM.
HAVE YOU BEEN PRACTICING?
FWIP
WHIRRR
CLICK!
40mm TRAINING ROUND
BOOM

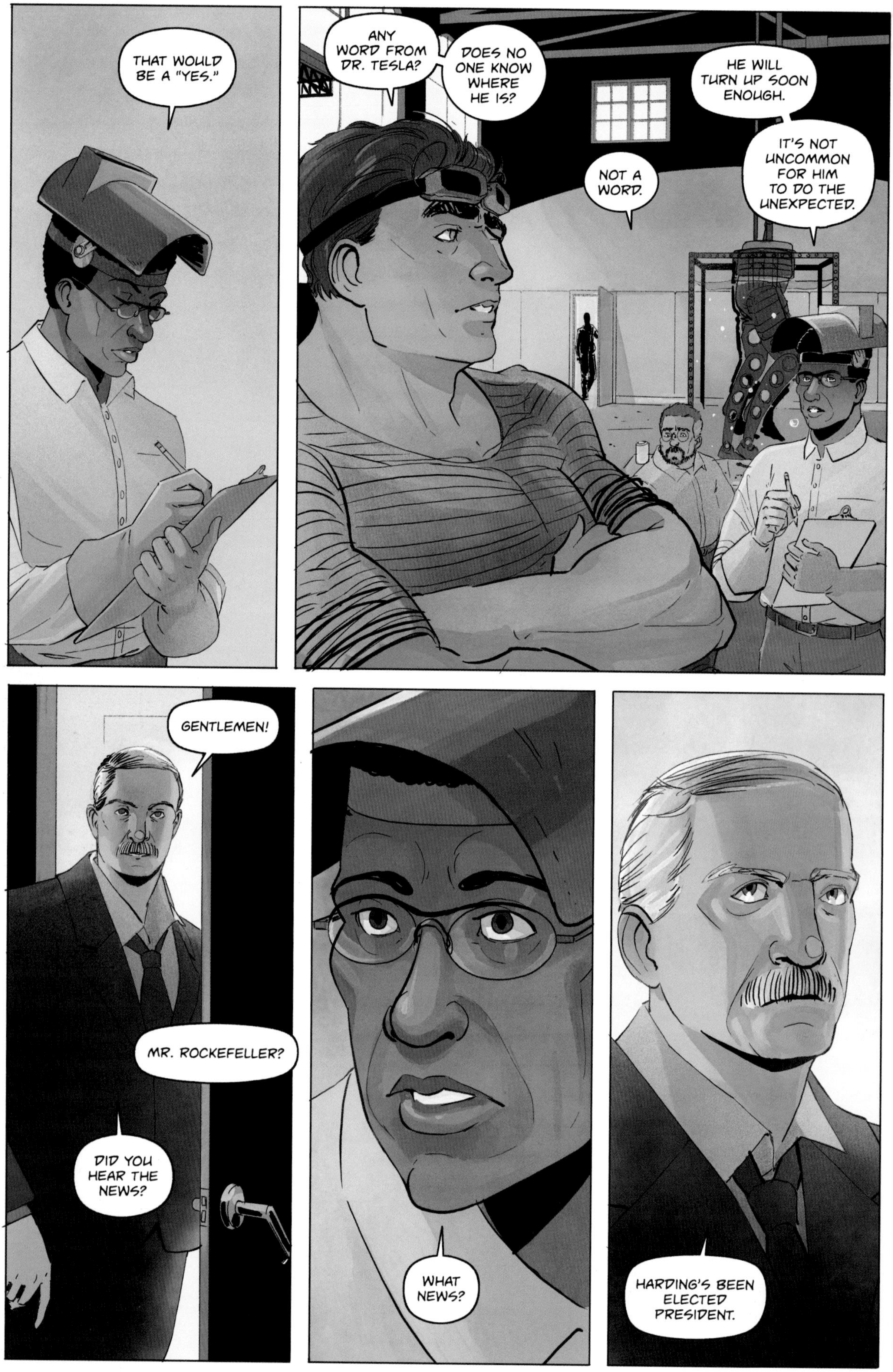
THAT WOULD BE A "YES."
ANY WORD FROM DR. TESLA?
DOES NO ONE KNOW WHERE HE IS?
HE WILL TURN UP SOON ENOUGH.
NOT A WORD.
IT'S NOT UNCOMMON FOR HIM TO DO THE UNEXPECTED.
GENTLEMEN!
MR. ROCKEFELLER?
DID YOU HEAR THE NEWS?
WHAT NEWS?
HARDING'S BEEN ELECTED PRESIDENT.

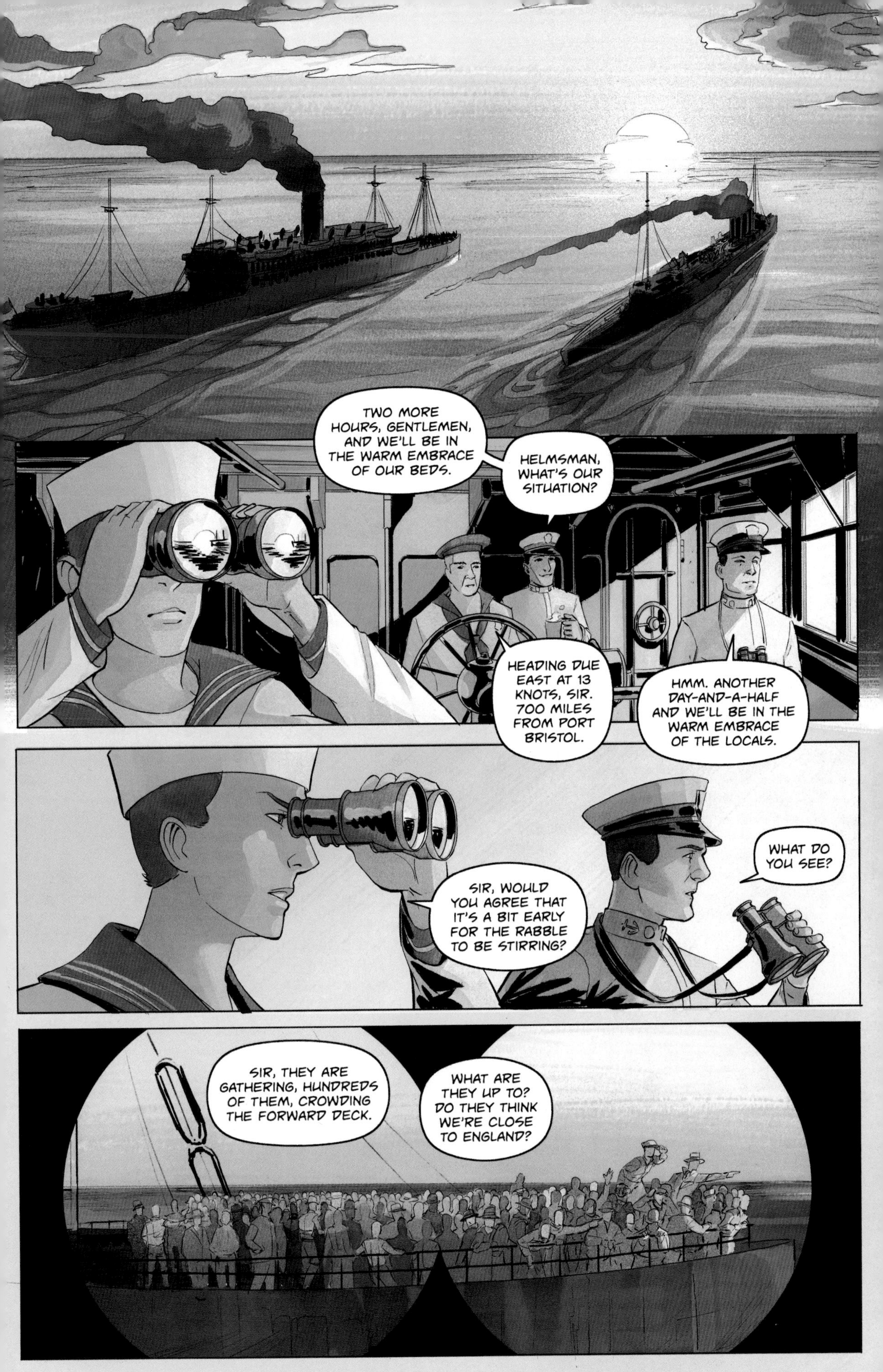
TWO MORE HOURS, GENTLEMEN, AND WE'LL BE IN THE WARM EMBRACE OF OUR BEDS.
HELMSMAN, WHAT'S OUR SITUATION?
HEADING DUE EAST AT 13 KNOTS, SIR. 700 MILES FROM PORT BRISTOL.
HMM. ANOTHER DAY-AND-A-HALF AND WE'LL BE IN THE WARM EMBRACE OF THE LOCALS.
WHAT DO YOU SEE?
SIR, WOULD YOU AGREE THAT IT'S A BIT EARLY FOR THE RABBLE TO BE STIRRING?
SIR, THEY ARE GATHERING, HUNDREDS OF THEM, CROWDING THE FORWARD DECK.
WHAT ARE THEY UP TO? DO THEY THINK WE'RE CLOSE TO ENGLAND?

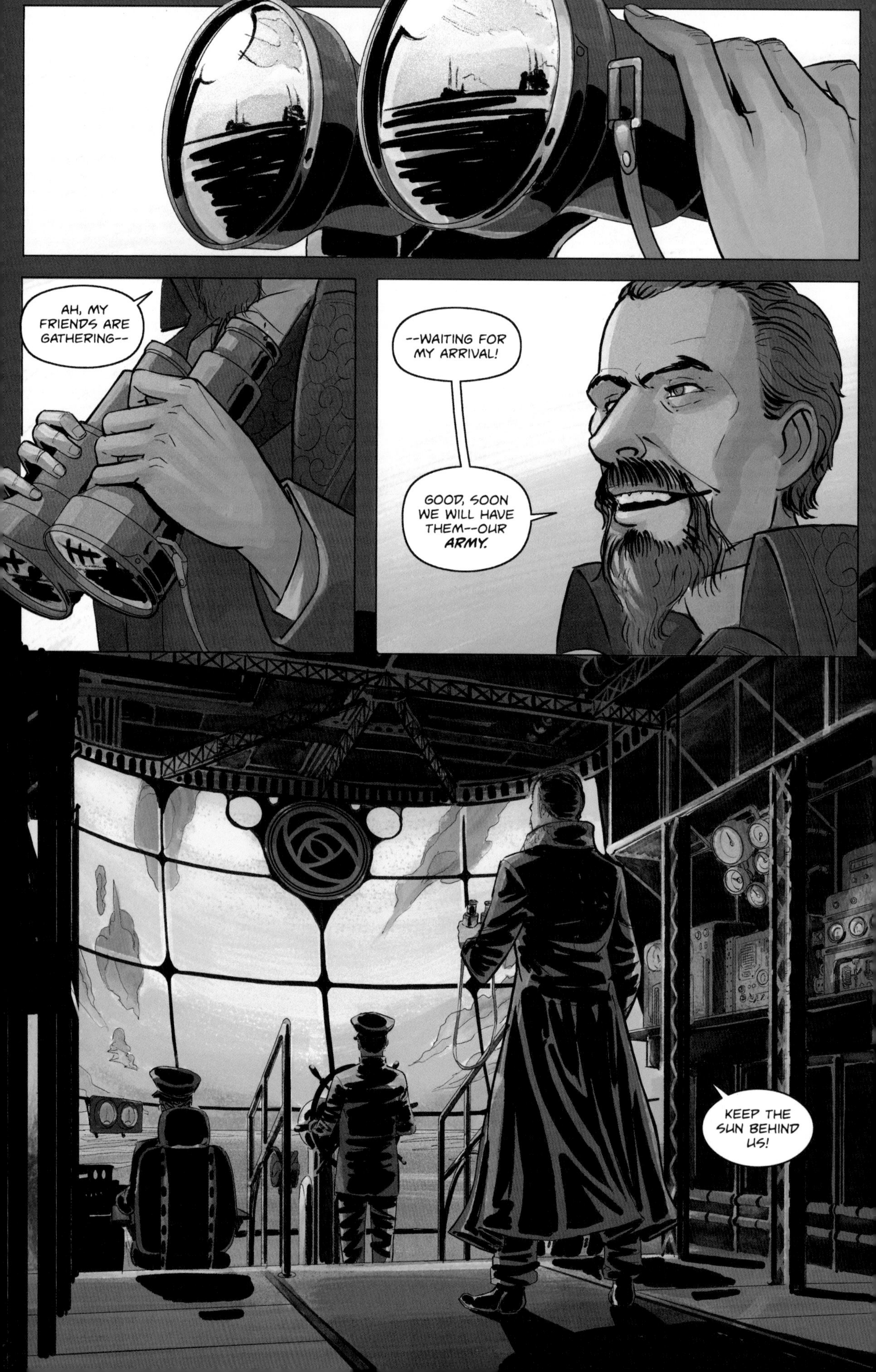
AH, MY FRIENDS ARE GATHERING--
--WAITING FOR MY ARRIVAL!
GOOD, SOON WE WILL HAVE THEM--OUR ARMY.
KEEP THE SUN BEHIND US!

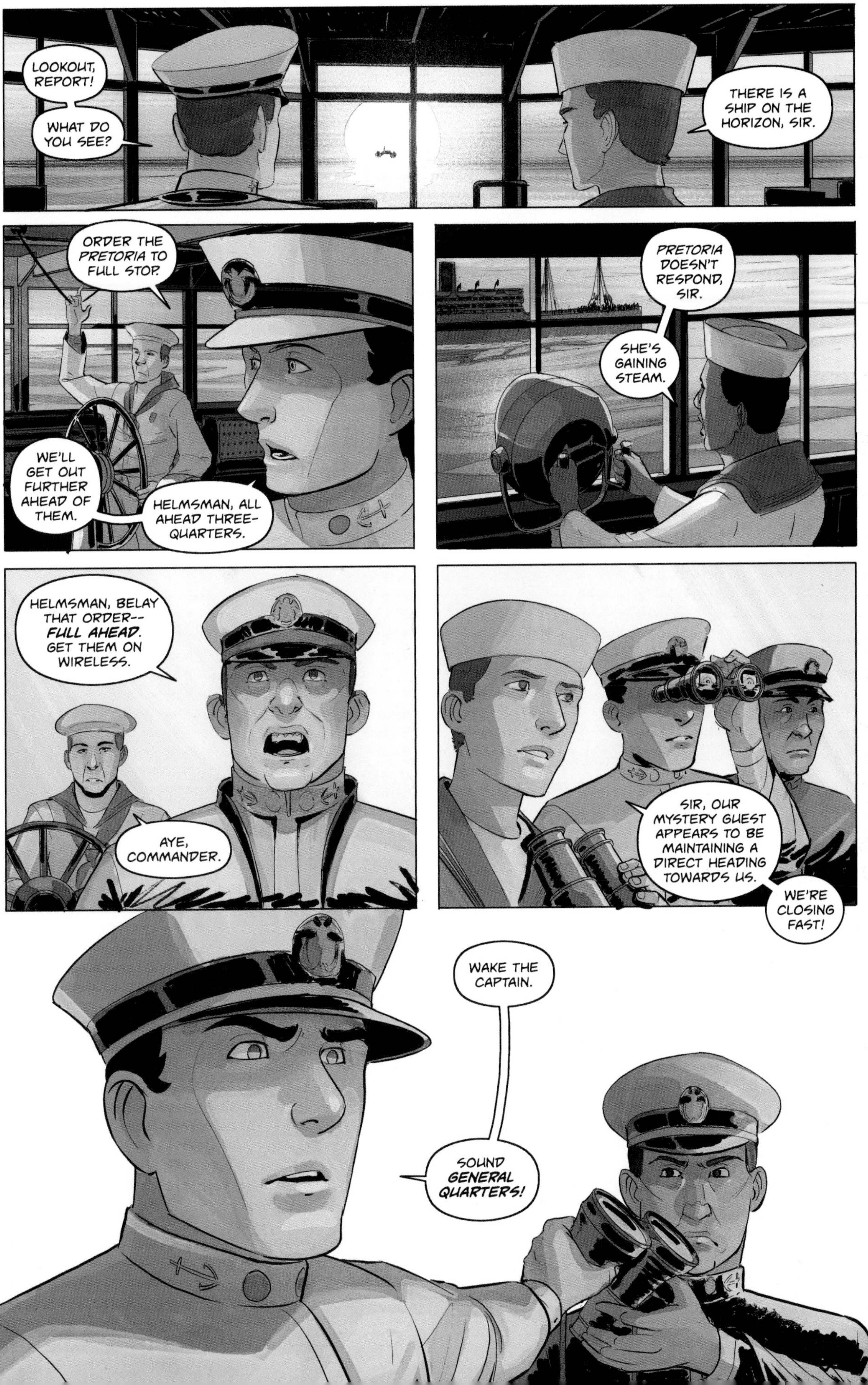
LOOKOUT, REPORT!
WHAT DO YOU SEE?
THERE IS A SHIP ON THE HORIZON, SIR.
ORDER THE PRETORIA TO FULL STOP.
WE'LL GET OUT FURTHER AHEAD OF THEM.
HELMSMAN, ALL AHEAD THREE-QUARTERS.
PRETORIA DOESN'T RESPOND, SIR.
SHE'S GAINING STEAM.
HELMSMAN, BELAY THAT ORDER-- FULL AHEAD. GET THEM ON WIRELESS.
AYE, COMMANDER.
SIR, OUR MYSTERY GUEST APPEARS TO BE MAINTAINING A DIRECT HEADING TOWARDS US.
WE'RE CLOSING FAST!
WAKE THE CAPTAIN.
SOUND GENERAL QUARTERS!

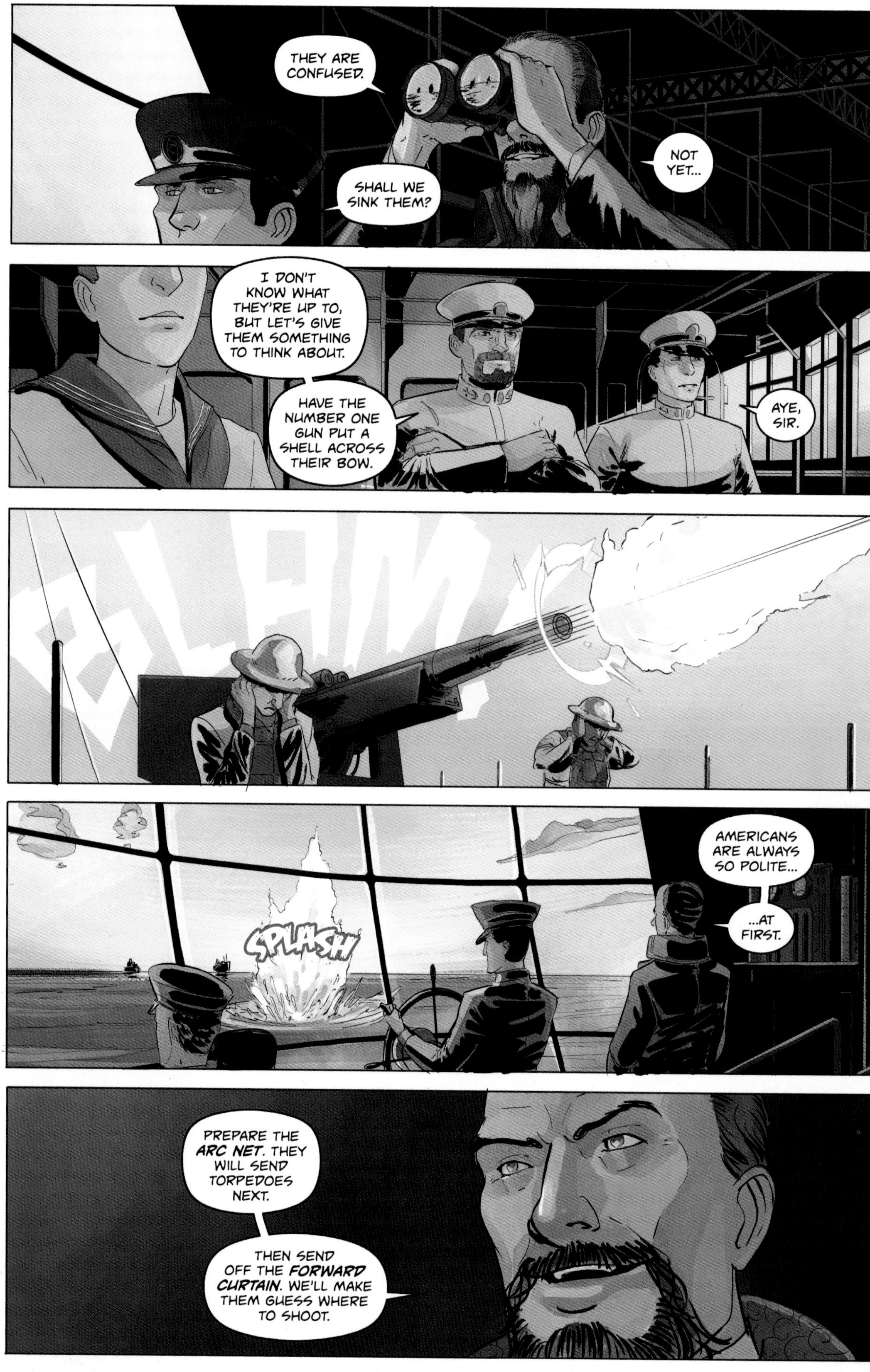
THEY ARE CONFUSED.
SHALL WE SINK THEM?
NOT YET...
I DON'T KNOW WHAT THEY'RE UP TO, BUT LET'S GIVE THEM SOMETHING TO THINK ABOUT.
HAVE THE NUMBER ONE GUN PUT A SHELL ACROSS THEIR BOW.
AYE, SIR.
BLAM
SPLASH
AMERICANS ARE ALWAYS SO POLITE...
...AT FIRST.
PREPARE THE ***ARC NET***. THEY WILL SEND TORPEDOES NEXT.
THEN SEND OFF THE ***FORWARD CURTAIN***. WE'LL MAKE THEM GUESS WHERE TO SHOOT.

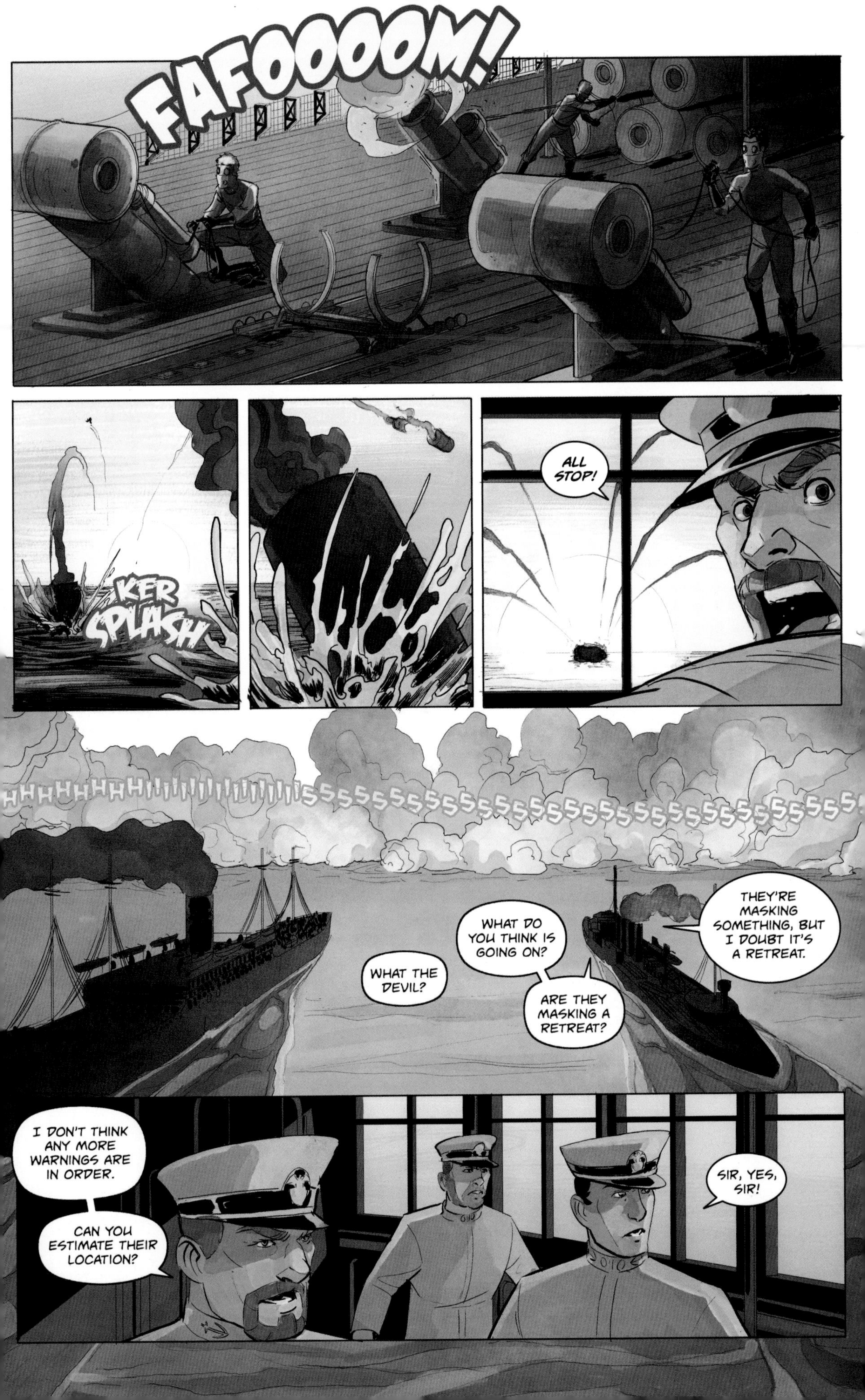
FAFOOOOM!
KER SPLASH
ALL STOP!
HHHHHHHHIIIIIIIIIIIIIIIISSSSSSSSSSSSSSSSSSSSSSSSSS!
WHAT THE DEVIL?
WHAT DO YOU THINK IS GOING ON?
ARE THEY MASKING A RETREAT?
THEY'RE MASKING SOMETHING, BUT I DOUBT IT'S A RETREAT.
I DON'T THINK ANY MORE WARNINGS ARE IN ORDER.
CAN YOU ESTIMATE THEIR LOCATION?
SIR, YES, SIR!

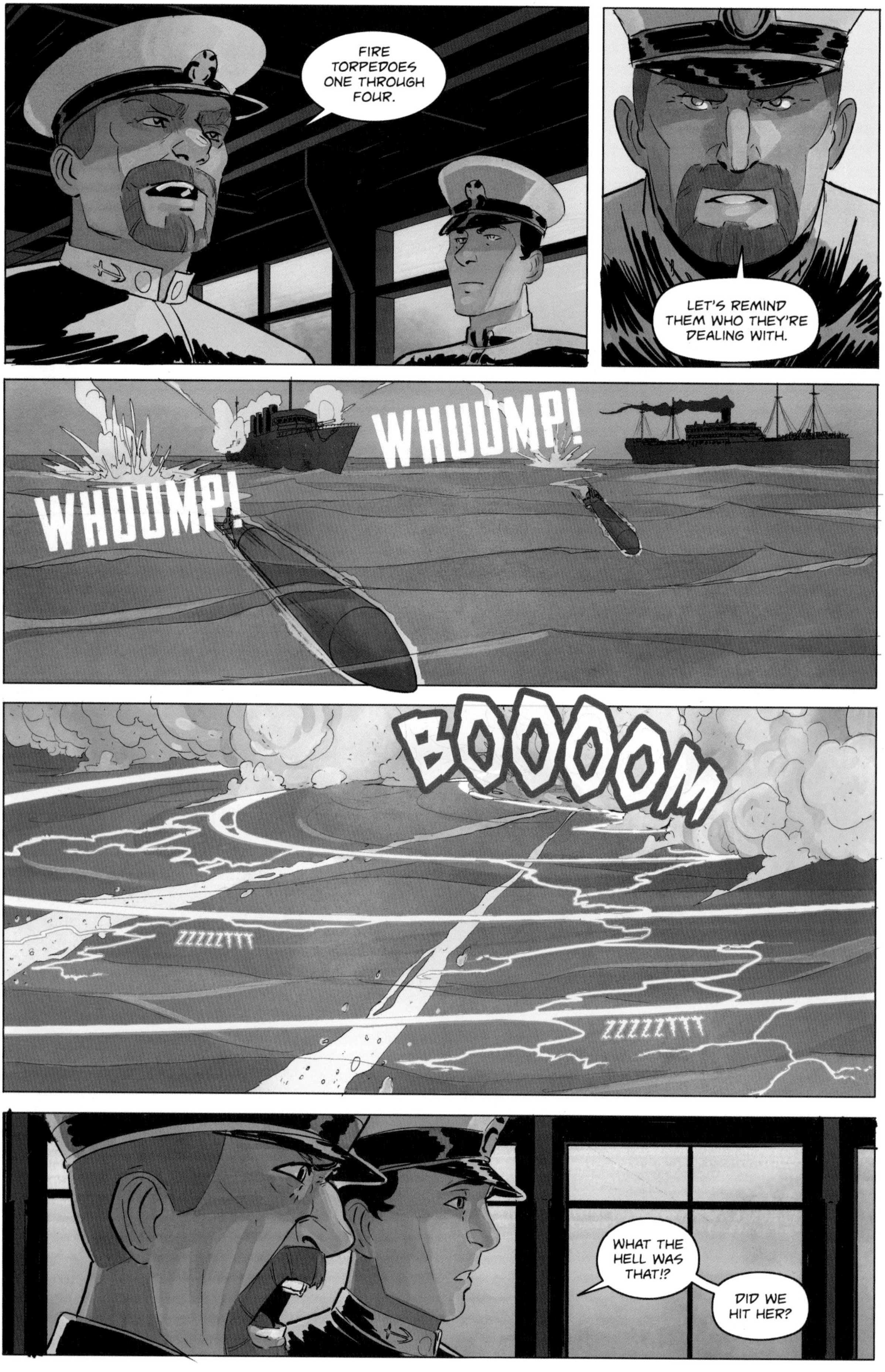
FIRE TORPEDOES ONE THROUGH FOUR.
LET'S REMIND THEM WHO THEY'RE DEALING WITH.
WHUUMP!
WHUUMP!
BOOOOM
ZZZZZTTT
ZZZZZTTT
WHAT THE HELL WAS THAT!?
DID WE HIT HER?

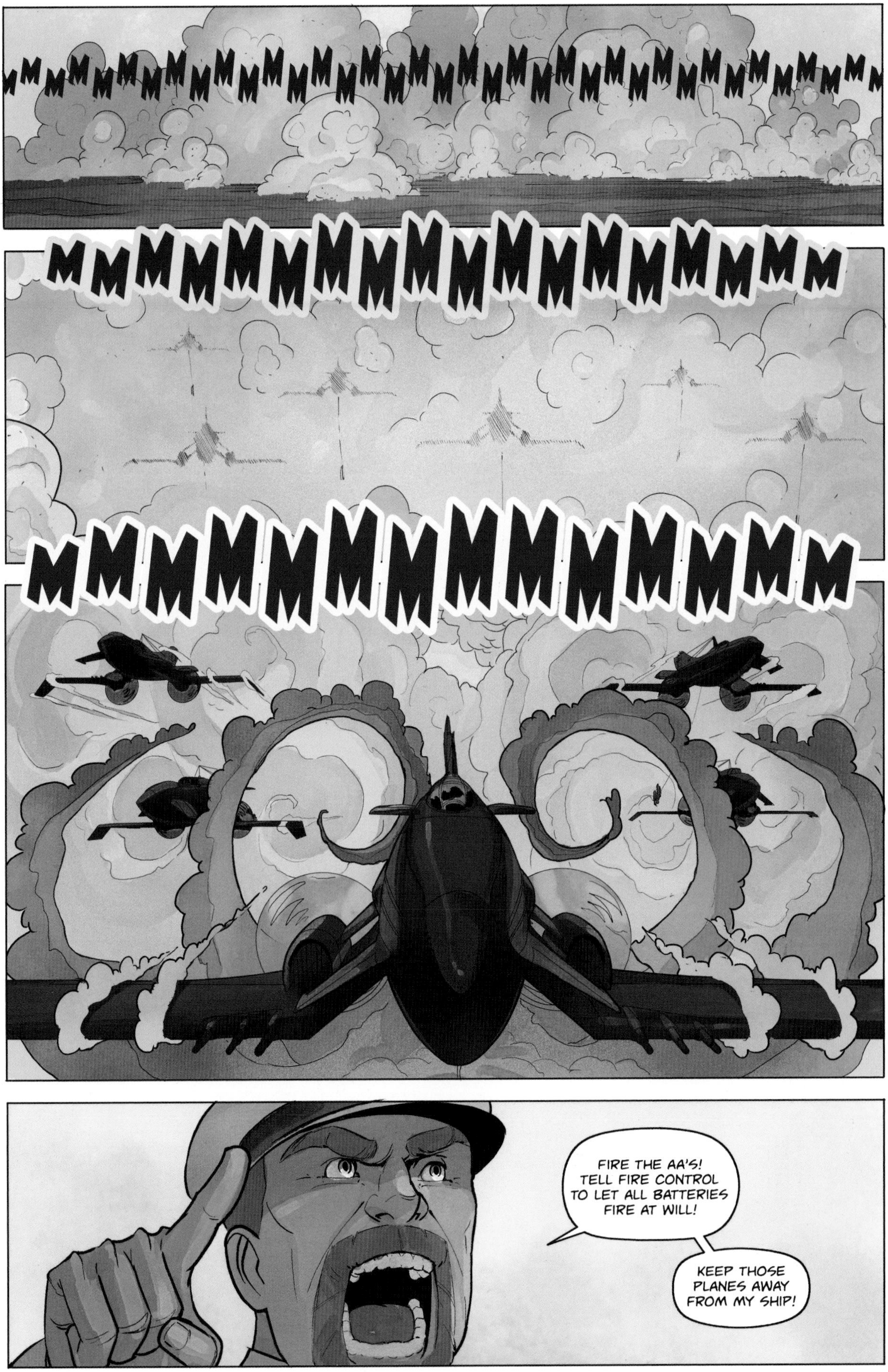
MMMMMMMMMMMMMMMMMMMMMMMMMMMMMMMMMMM
MMMMMMMMMMMMMMMMMM
MMMMMMMMMMMMMMMM
FIRE THE AA'S! TELL FIRE CONTROL TO LET ALL BATTERIES FIRE AT WILL!
KEEP THOSE PLANES AWAY FROM MY SHIP!

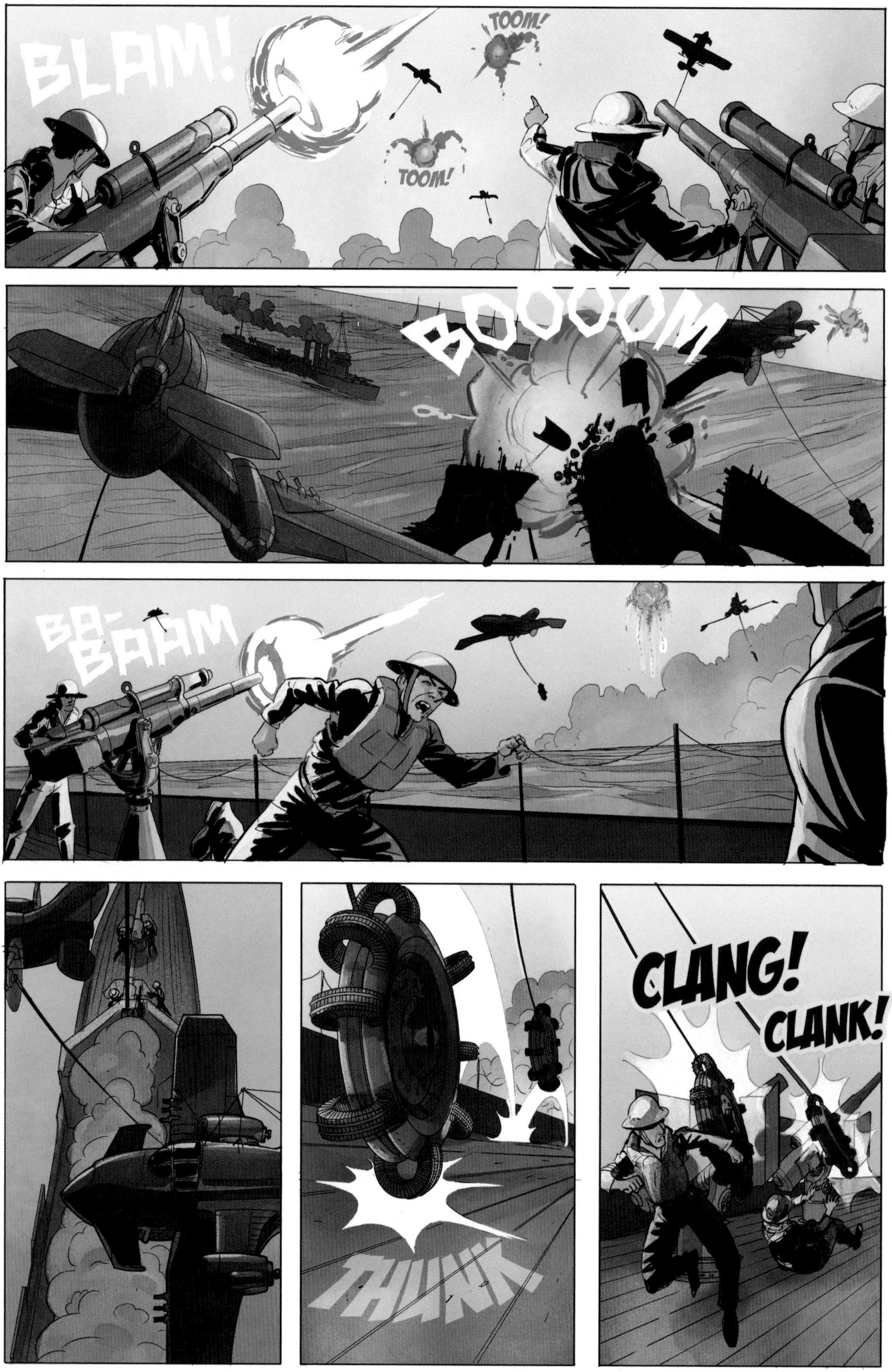
BLAM!
TOOM!
TOOM!
BOOOOM
BA-BAAM
THUNK
CLANG!
CLANK!

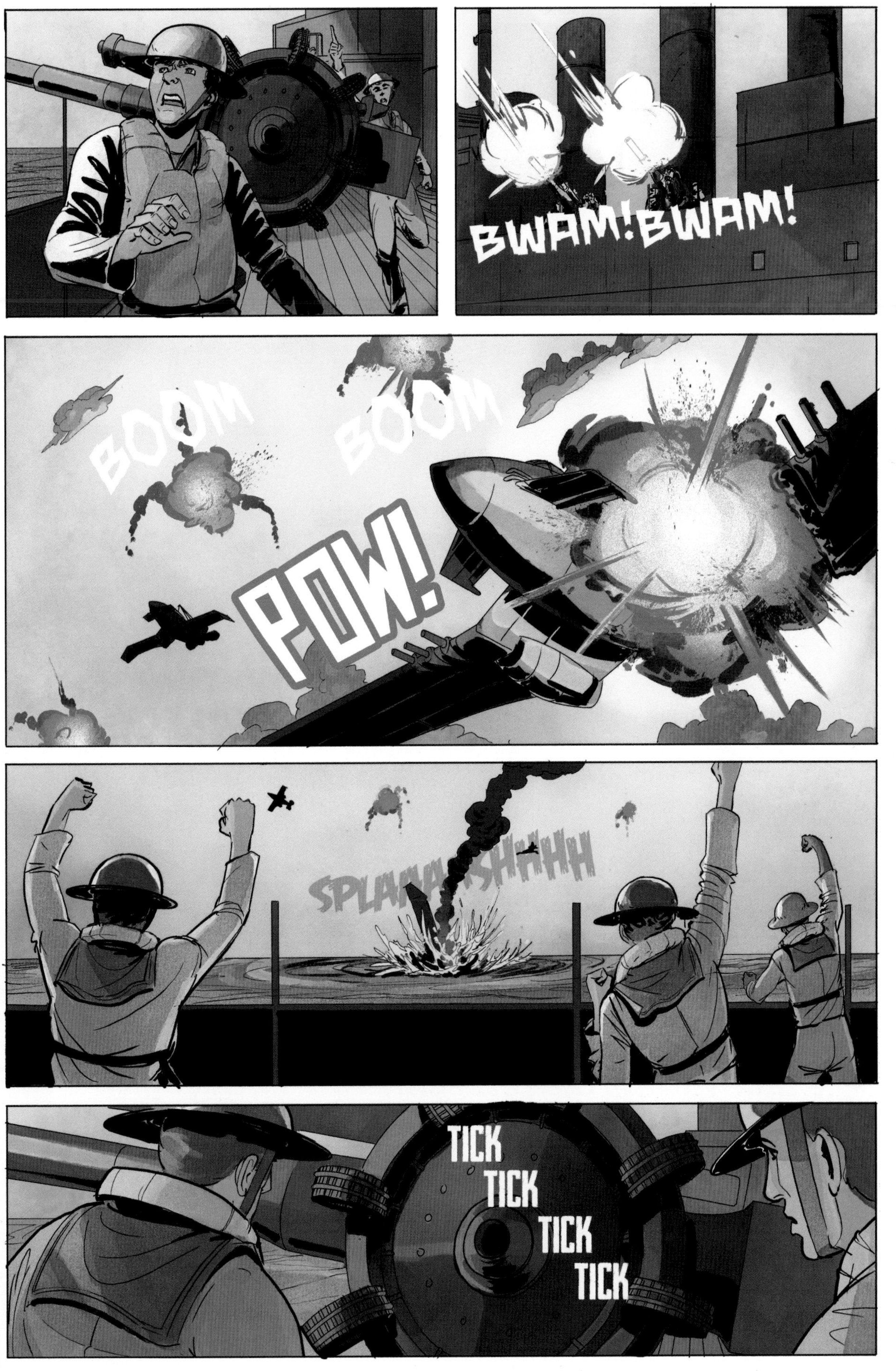
BWAM! BWAM!
BOOM
BOOM
POW!
SPLAAAASHHHH
TICK
TICK
TICK
TICK

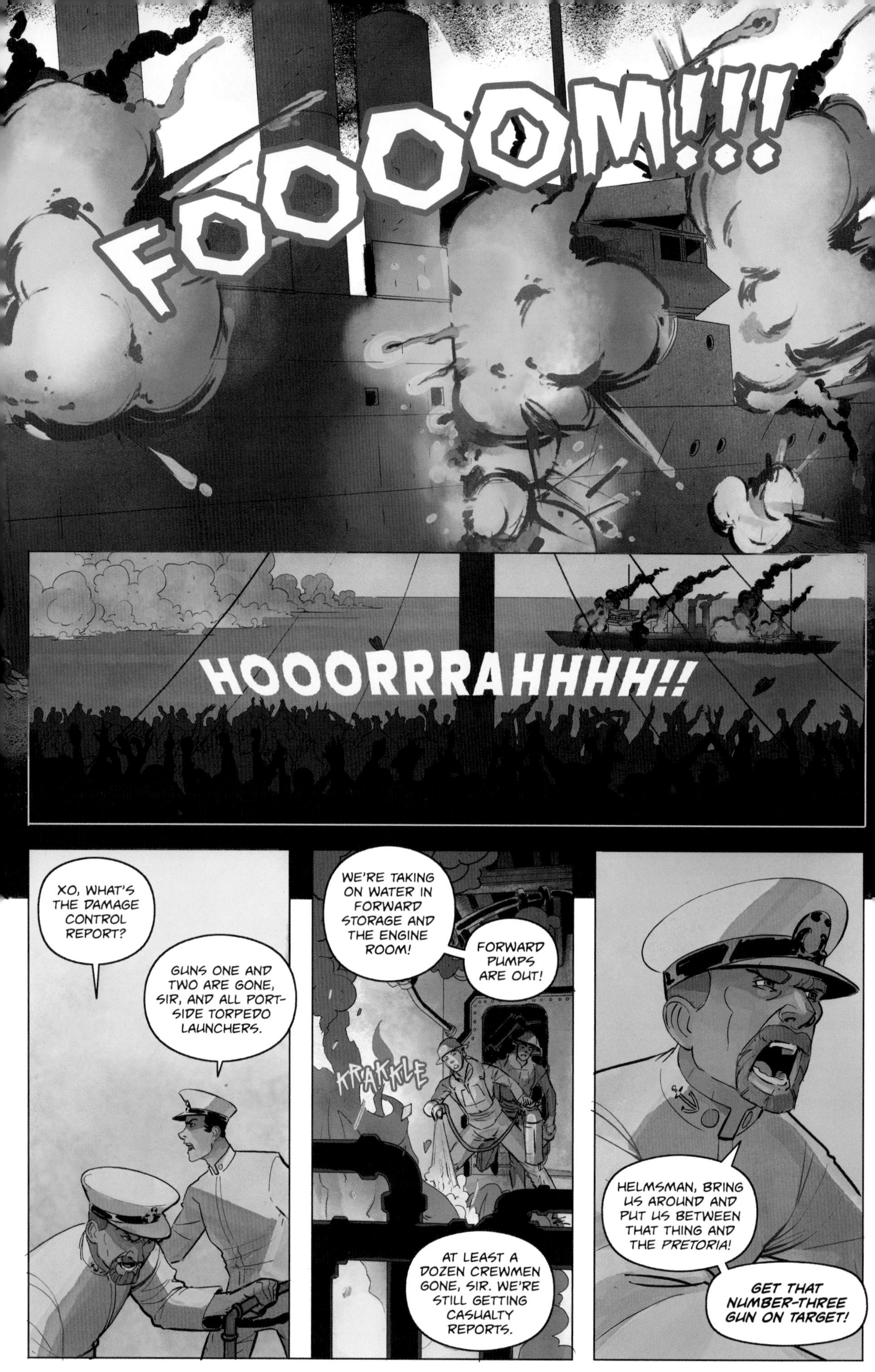
FOOOOOM!!!
HOOORRRAHHHH!!
XO, WHAT'S THE DAMAGE CONTROL REPORT?
GUNS ONE AND TWO ARE GONE, SIR, AND ALL PORT-SIDE TORPEDO LAUNCHERS.
WE'RE TAKING ON WATER IN FORWARD STORAGE AND THE ENGINE ROOM!
FORWARD PUMPS ARE OUT!
KRAKKLE
AT LEAST A DOZEN CREWMEN GONE, SIR. WE'RE STILL GETTING CASUALTY REPORTS.
HELMSMAN, BRING US AROUND AND PUT US BETWEEN THAT THING AND THE *PRETORIA*!
***GET THAT NUMBER-THREE GUN ON TARGET!***

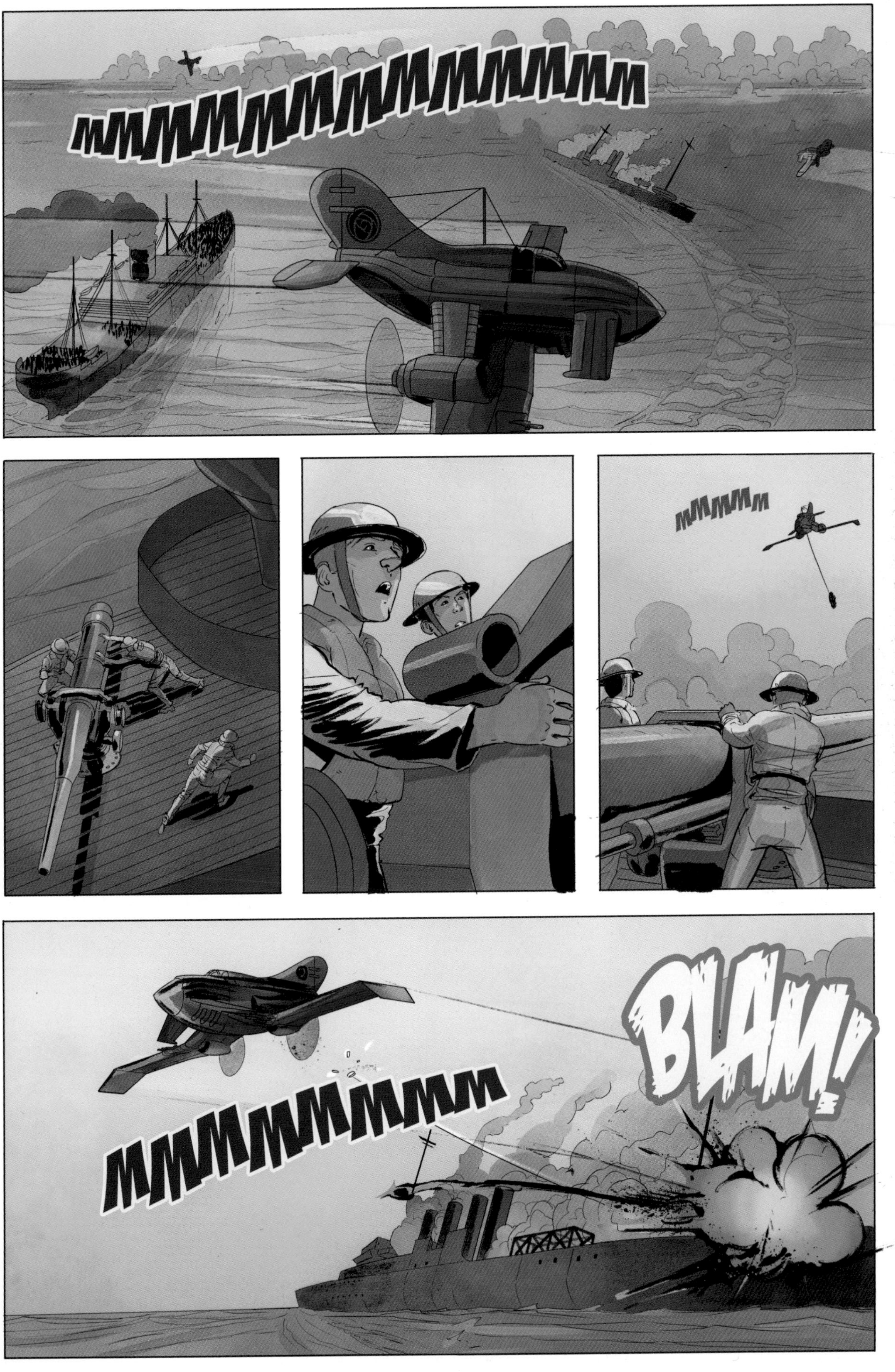
MMMMMMMMMMMMMMMM
MMMMMM
MMMMMMMMMM
BLAM!

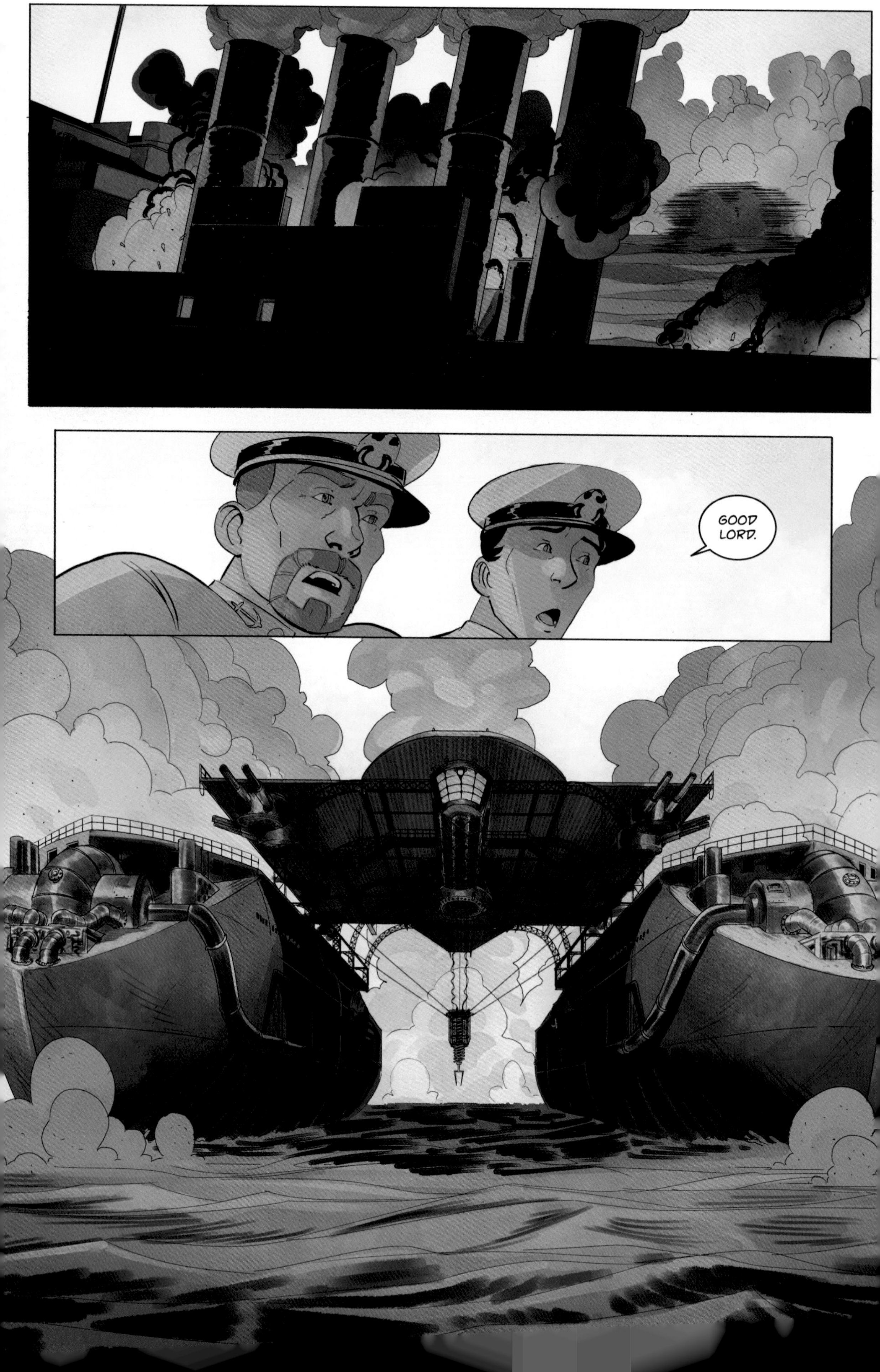
GOOD LORD.

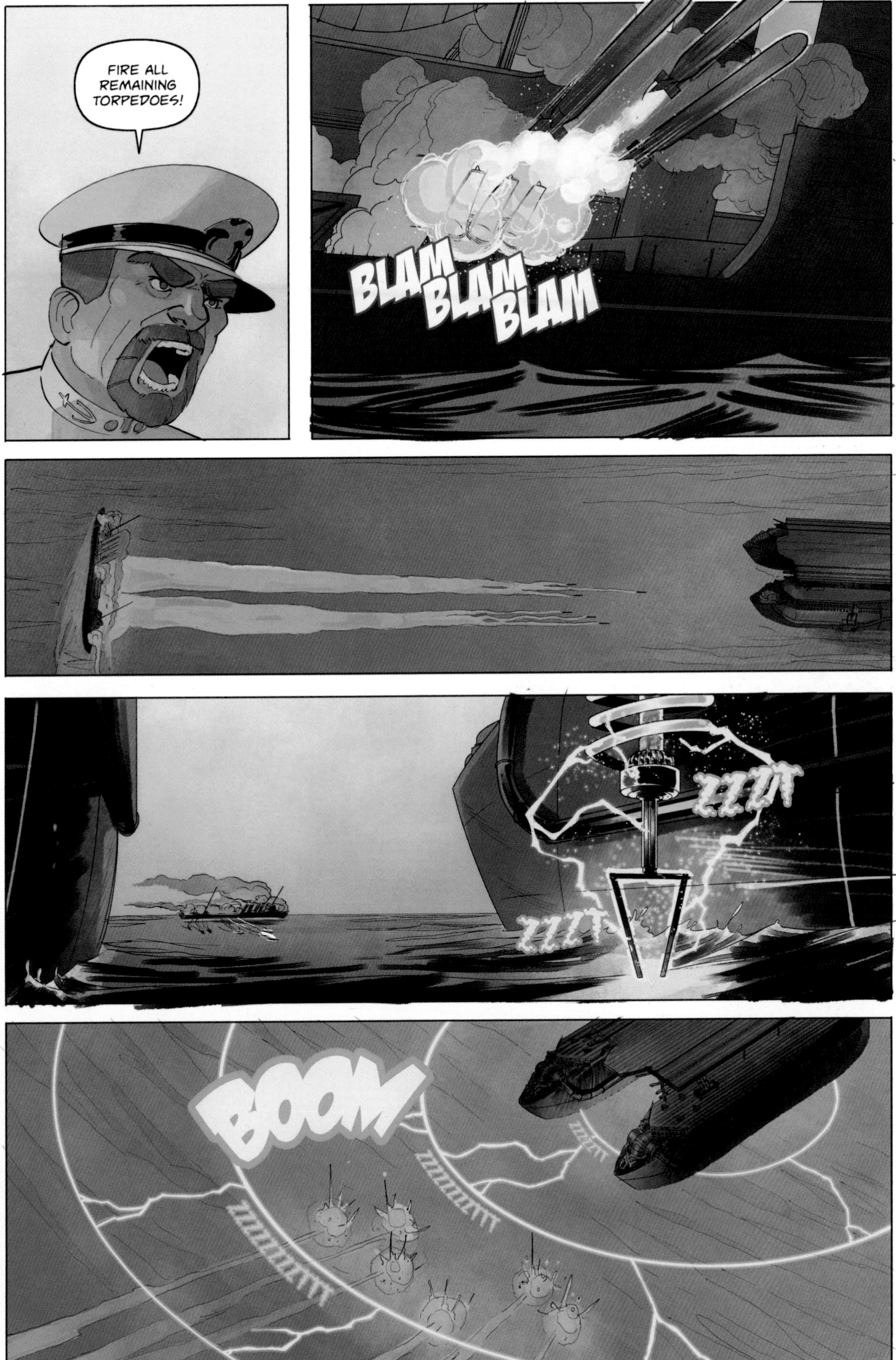
FIRE ALL REMAINING TORPEDOES!
BLAM
BLAM
BLAM
ZZZT
ZZZT
BOOM

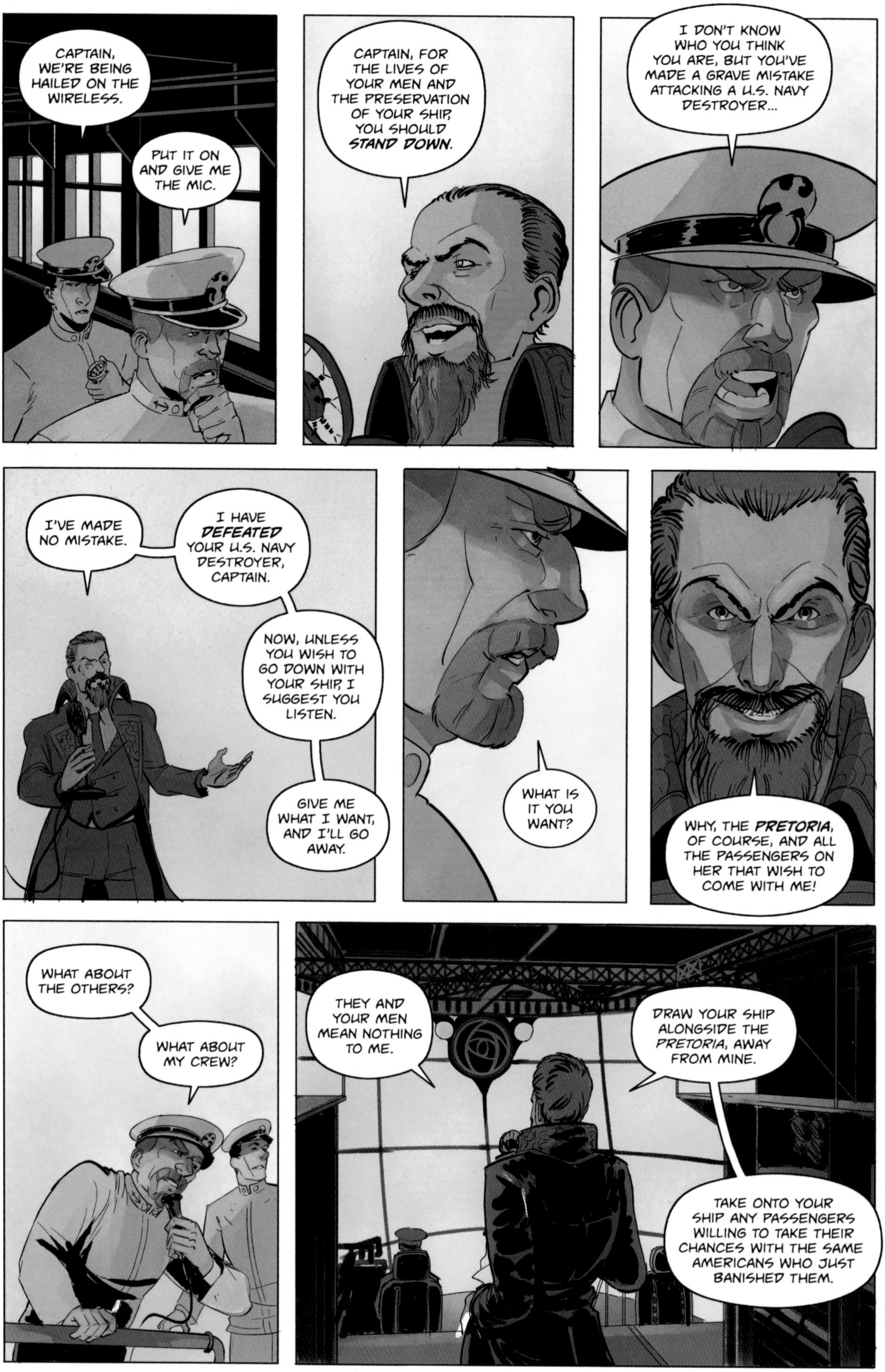
CAPTAIN, WE'RE BEING HAILED ON THE WIRELESS.
PUT IT ON AND GIVE ME THE MIC.
CAPTAIN, FOR THE LIVES OF YOUR MEN AND THE PRESERVATION OF YOUR SHIP, YOU SHOULD *STAND DOWN*.
I DON'T KNOW WHO YOU THINK YOU ARE, BUT YOU'VE MADE A GRAVE MISTAKE ATTACKING A U.S. NAVY DESTROYER...
I'VE MADE NO MISTAKE.
I HAVE *DEFEATED* YOUR U.S. NAVY DESTROYER, CAPTAIN.
NOW, UNLESS YOU WISH TO GO DOWN WITH YOUR SHIP, I SUGGEST YOU LISTEN.
GIVE ME WHAT I WANT, AND I'LL GO AWAY.
WHAT IS IT YOU WANT?
WHY, THE *PRETORIA*, OF COURSE, AND ALL THE PASSENGERS ON HER THAT WISH TO COME WITH ME!
WHAT ABOUT THE OTHERS?
WHAT ABOUT MY CREW?
THEY AND YOUR MEN MEAN NOTHING TO ME.
DRAW YOUR SHIP ALONGSIDE THE *PRETORIA*, AWAY FROM MINE.
TAKE ONTO YOUR SHIP ANY PASSENGERS WILLING TO TAKE THEIR CHANCES WITH THE SAME AMERICANS WHO JUST BANISHED THEM.

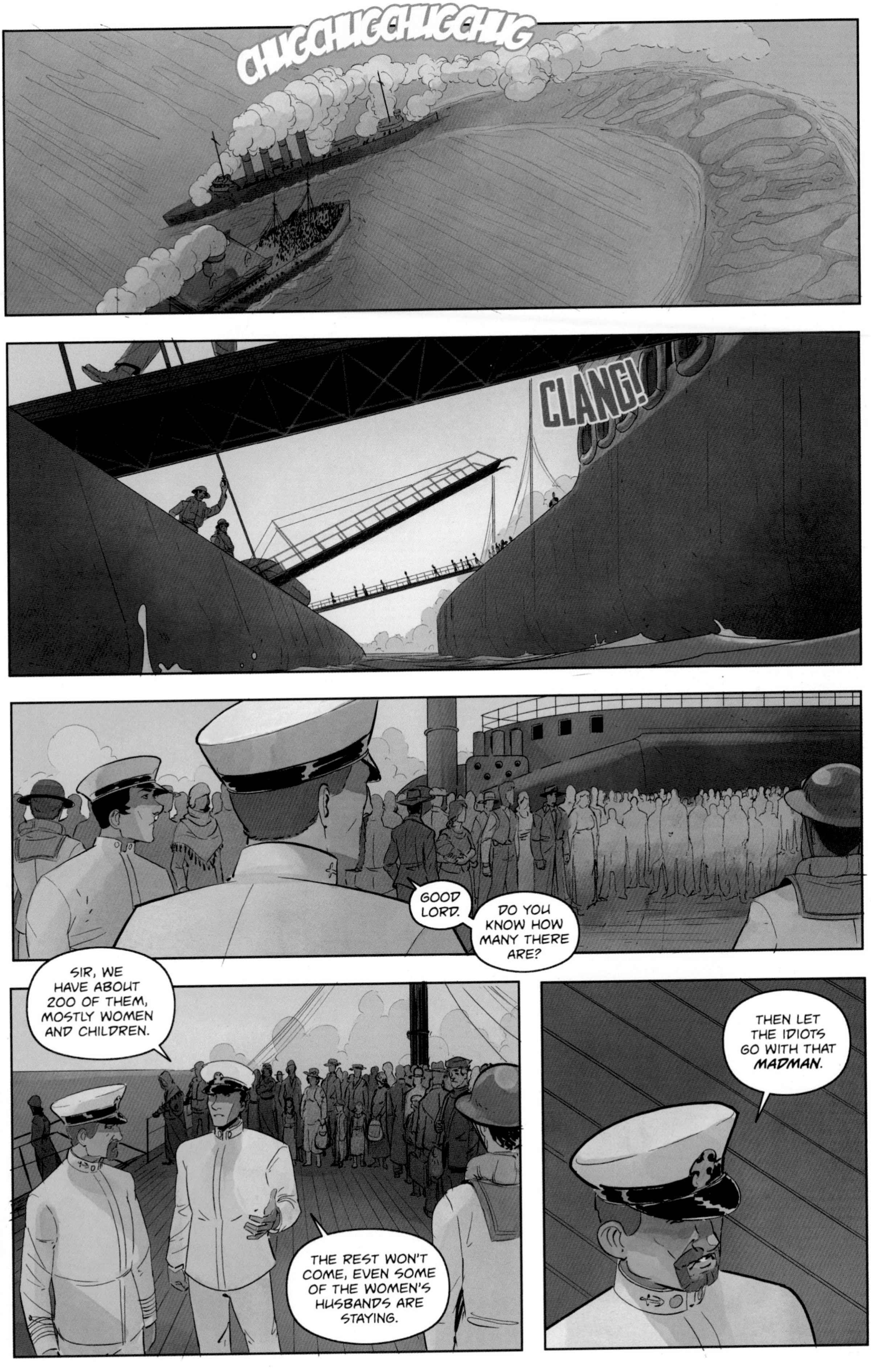
CHUGCHUGCHUGCHUG
CLANG!
GOOD LORD.
DO YOU KNOW HOW MANY THERE ARE?
SIR, WE HAVE ABOUT 200 OF THEM, MOSTLY WOMEN AND CHILDREN.
THE REST WON'T COME, EVEN SOME OF THE WOMEN'S HUSBANDS ARE STAYING.
THEN LET THE IDIOTS GO WITH THAT *MADMAN*.

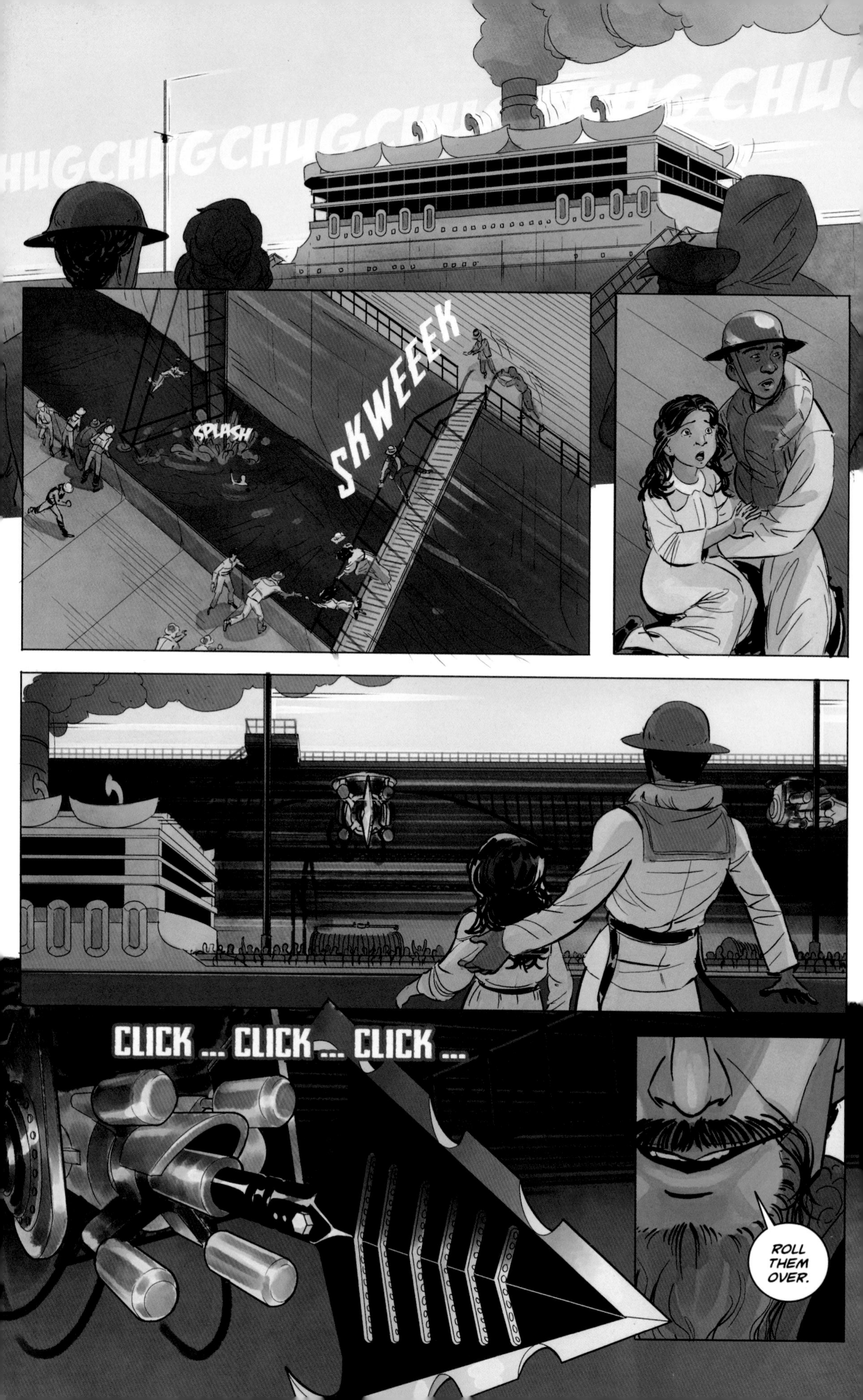
CHUGCHUGCHUGCHUGCHUG
SKWEEEK
SPLASH
CLICK ... CLICK ... CLICK ...
ROLL THEM OVER.

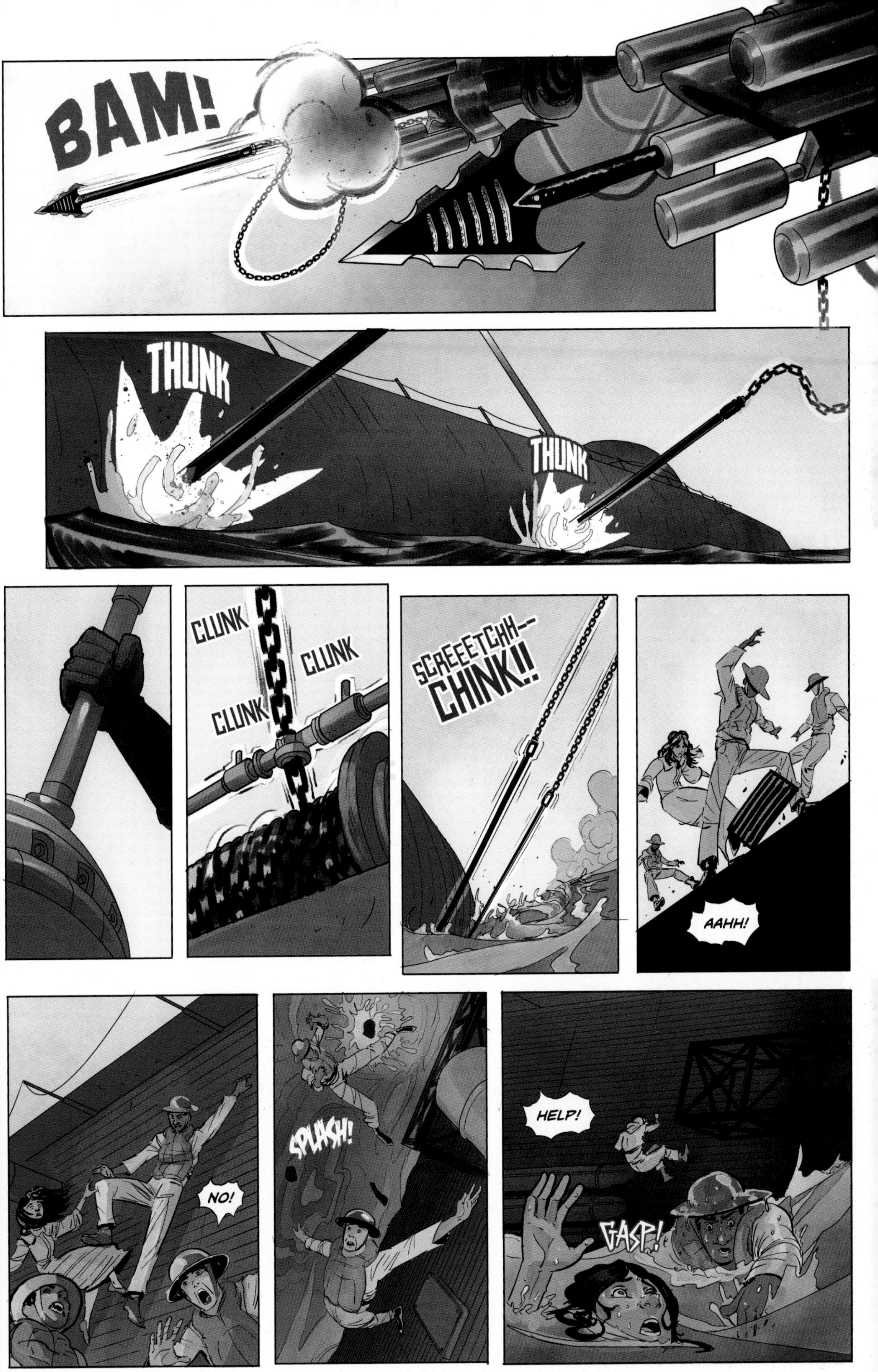
BAM!
THUNK
THUNK
CLUNK
CLUNK
CLUNK
SCREEETCHH--
CHINK!!
AAHH!
NO!
SPLASH!
HELP!
GASP!

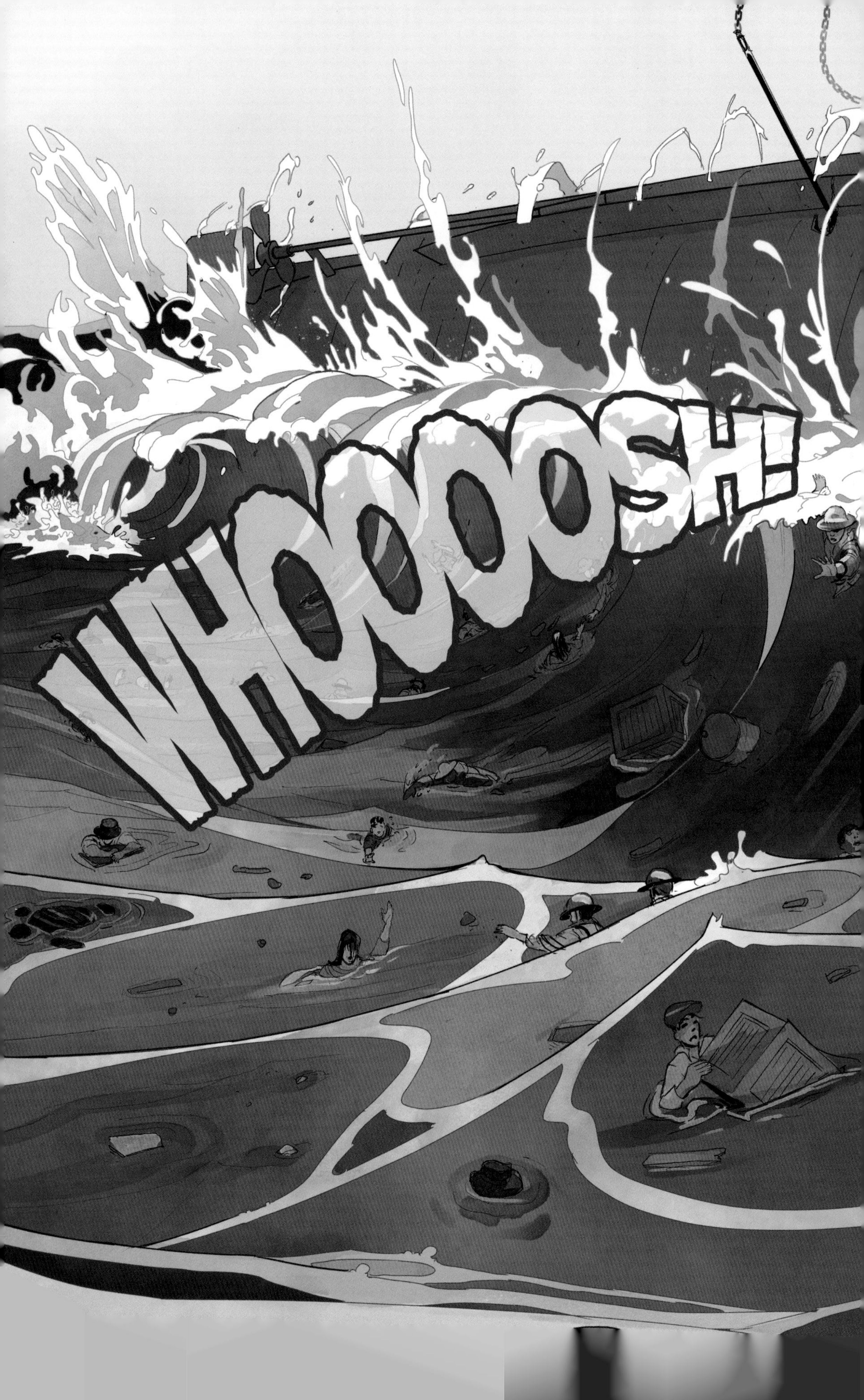
WHOOOOSH!

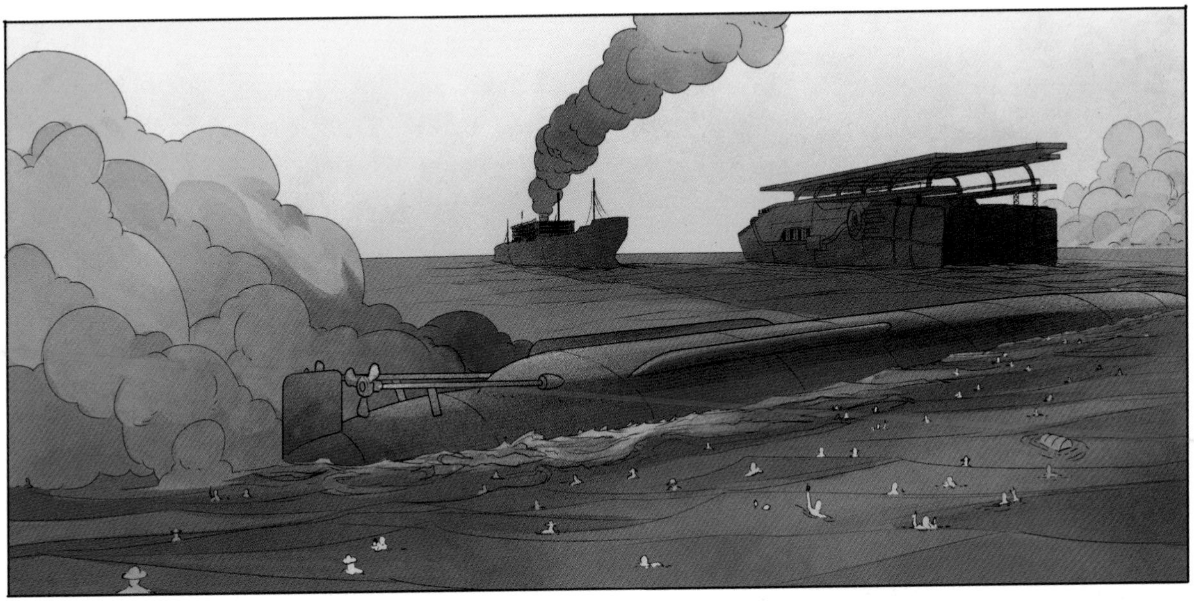

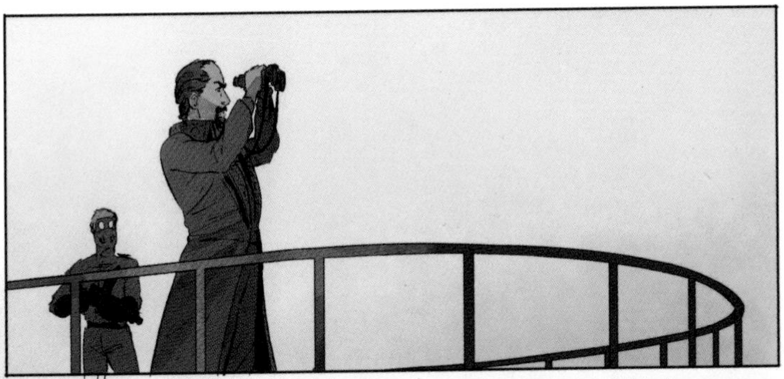

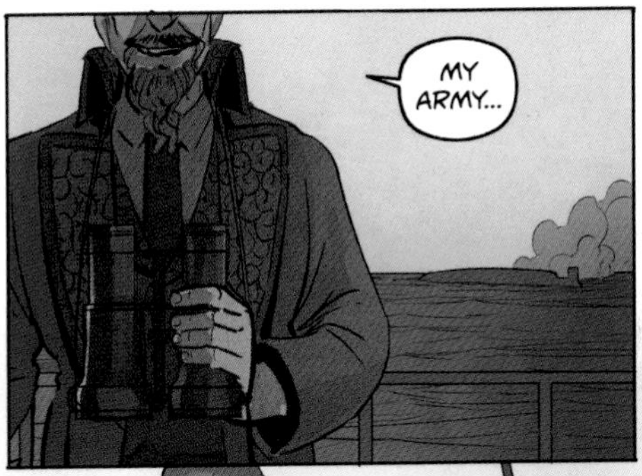
MY ARMY...

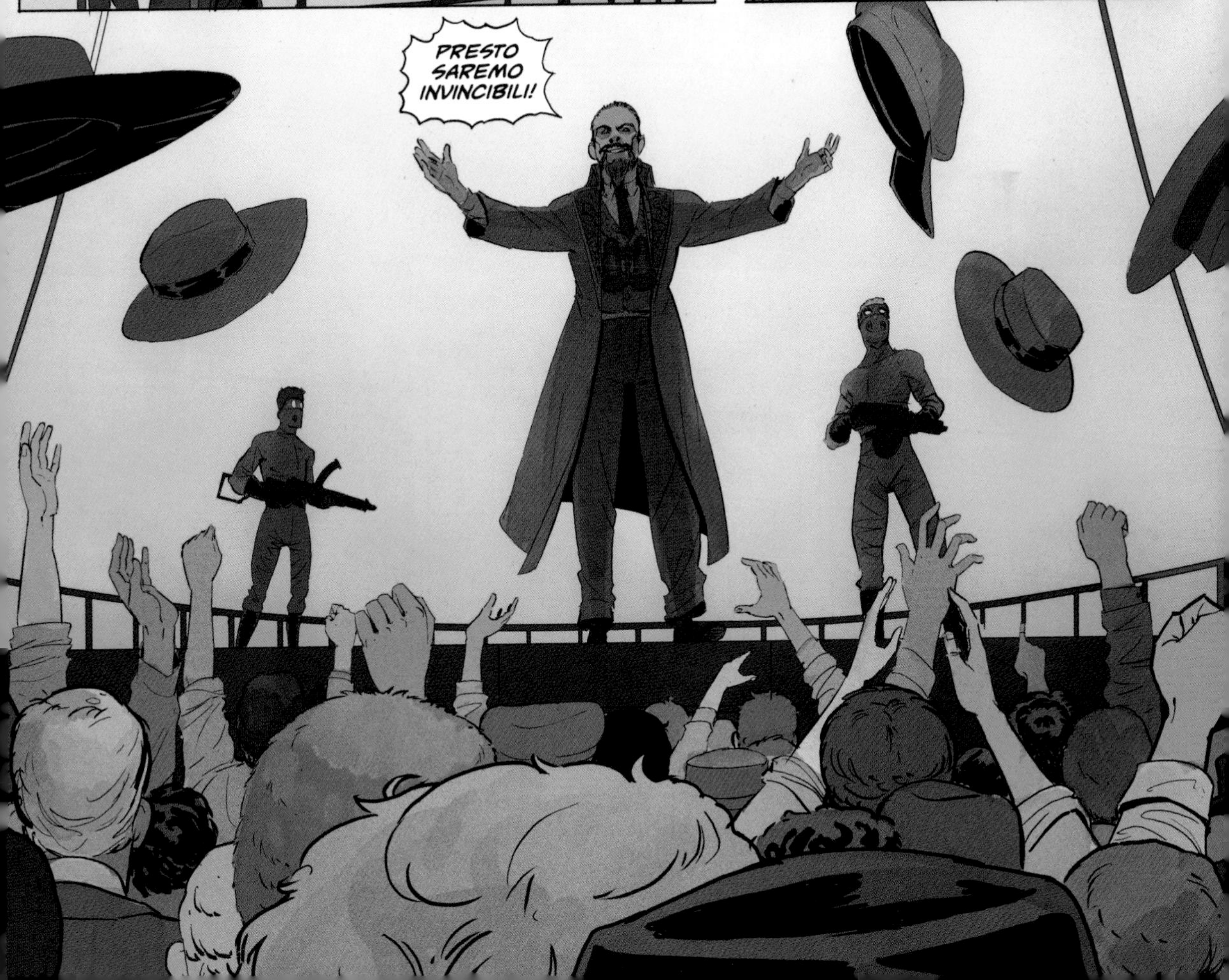
PRESTO SAREMO INVINCIBILI!

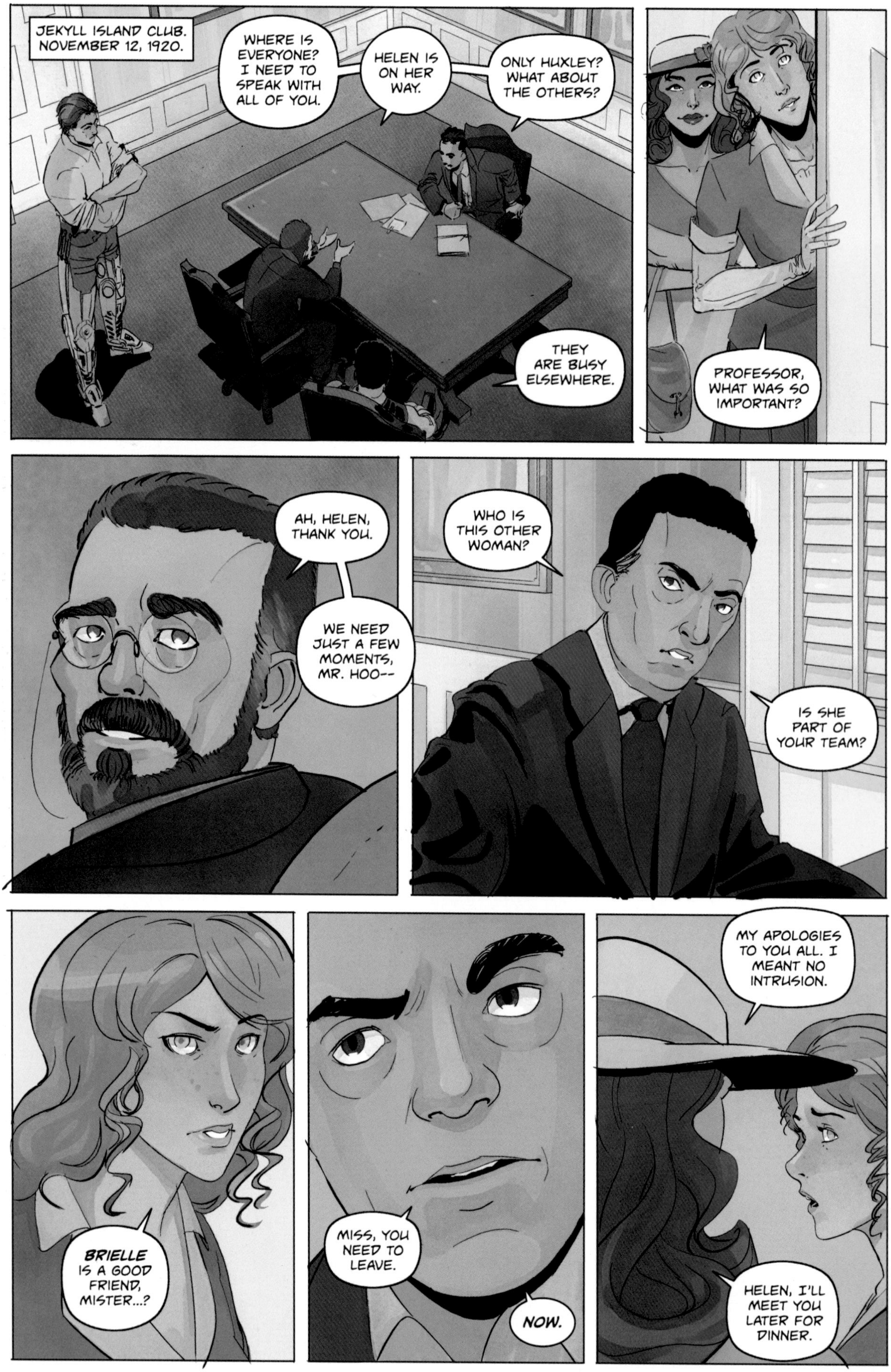

JEKYLL ISLAND CLUB. NOVEMBER 12, 1920.
WHERE IS EVERYONE? I NEED TO SPEAK WITH ALL OF YOU.
HELEN IS ON HER WAY.
ONLY HUXLEY? WHAT ABOUT THE OTHERS?
THEY ARE BUSY ELSEWHERE.
PROFESSOR, WHAT WAS SO IMPORTANT?
AH, HELEN, THANK YOU.
WE NEED JUST A FEW MOMENTS, MR. HOO--
WHO IS THIS OTHER WOMAN?
IS SHE PART OF YOUR TEAM?
BRIELLE IS A GOOD FRIEND, MISTER...?
MISS, YOU NEED TO LEAVE.
NOW.
MY APOLOGIES TO YOU ALL. I MEANT NO INTRUSION.
HELEN, I'LL MEET YOU LATER FOR DINNER.

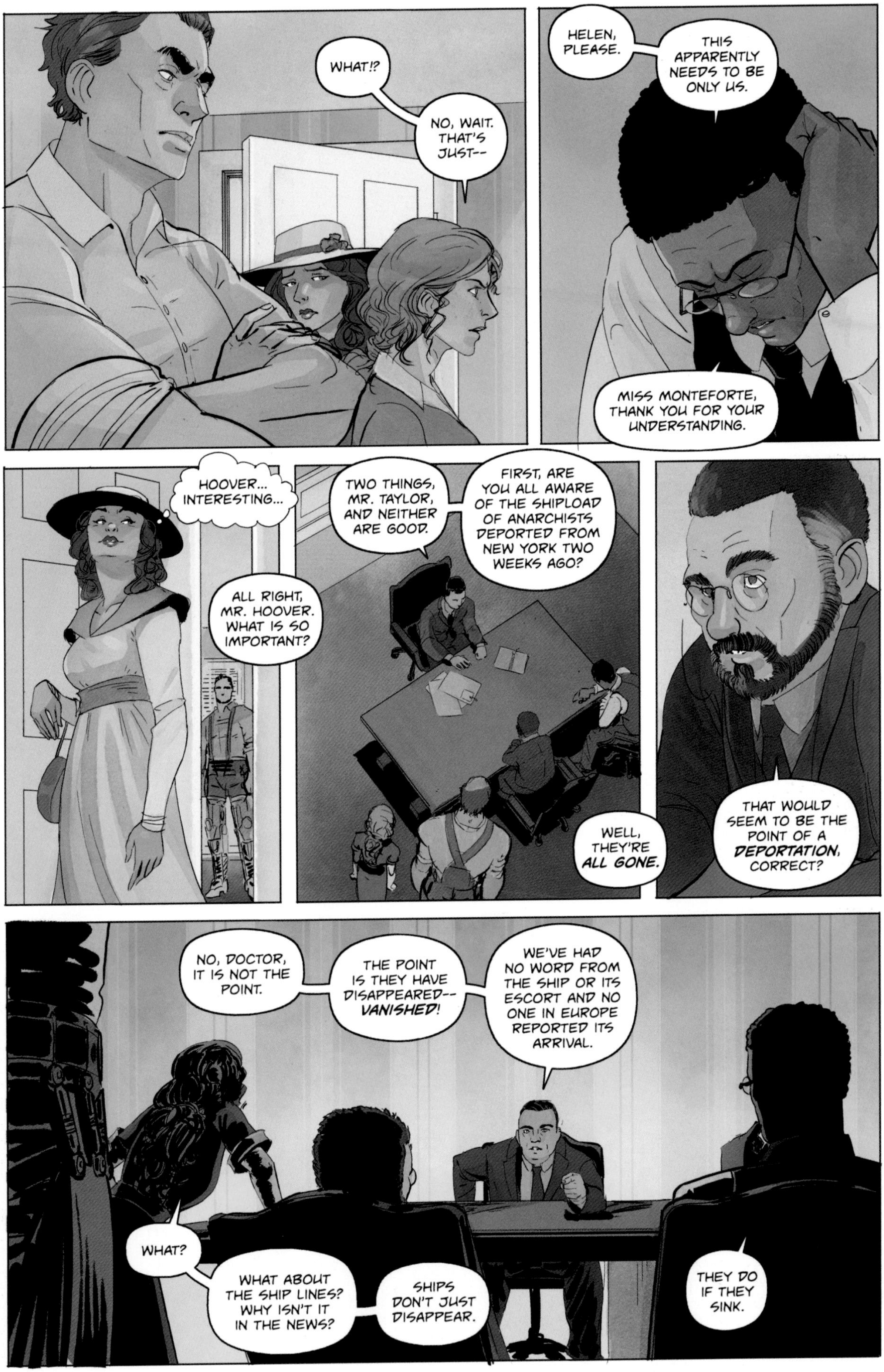
WHAT!?
NO, WAIT. THAT'S JUST--
HELEN, PLEASE.
THIS APPARENTLY NEEDS TO BE ONLY US.
MISS MONTEFORTE, THANK YOU FOR YOUR UNDERSTANDING.
HOOVER... INTERESTING...
ALL RIGHT, MR. HOOVER. WHAT IS SO IMPORTANT?
TWO THINGS, MR. TAYLOR, AND NEITHER ARE GOOD.
FIRST, ARE YOU ALL AWARE OF THE SHIPLOAD OF ANARCHISTS DEPORTED FROM NEW YORK TWO WEEKS AGO?
WELL, THEY'RE ALL GONE.
THAT WOULD SEEM TO BE THE POINT OF A DEPORTATION, CORRECT?
NO, DOCTOR, IT IS NOT THE POINT.
THE POINT IS THEY HAVE DISAPPEARED-- VANISHED!
WE'VE HAD NO WORD FROM THE SHIP OR ITS ESCORT AND NO ONE IN EUROPE REPORTED ITS ARRIVAL.
WHAT?
WHAT ABOUT THE SHIP LINES? WHY ISN'T IT IN THE NEWS?
SHIPS DON'T JUST DISAPPEAR.
THEY DO IF THEY SINK.

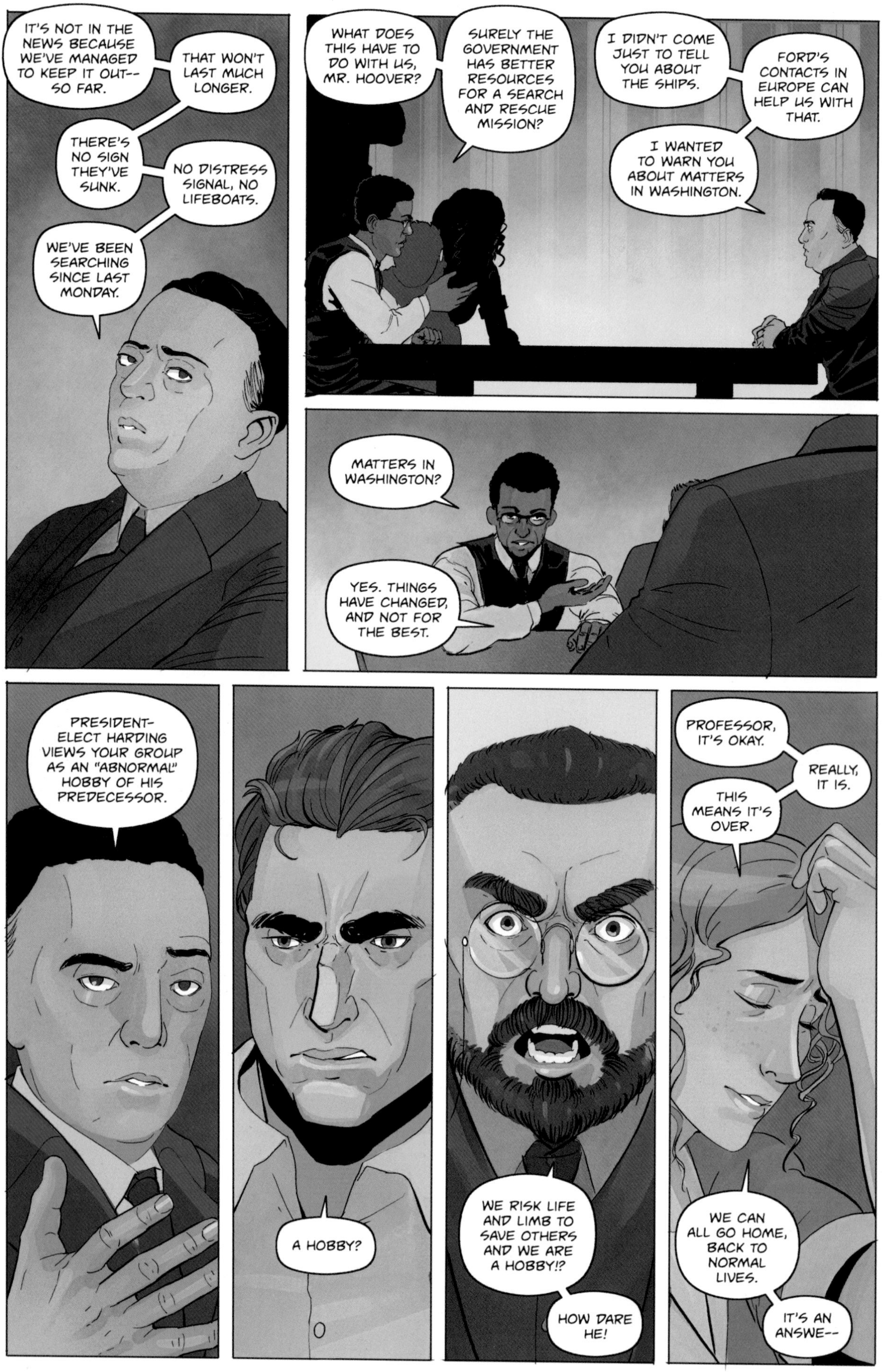
IT'S NOT IN THE NEWS BECAUSE WE'VE MANAGED TO KEEP IT OUT-- SO FAR.
THAT WON'T LAST MUCH LONGER.
THERE'S NO SIGN THEY'VE SUNK.
NO DISTRESS SIGNAL, NO LIFEBOATS.
WE'VE BEEN SEARCHING SINCE LAST MONDAY.
WHAT DOES THIS HAVE TO DO WITH US, MR. HOOVER?
SURELY THE GOVERNMENT HAS BETTER RESOURCES FOR A SEARCH AND RESCUE MISSION?
I DIDN'T COME JUST TO TELL YOU ABOUT THE SHIPS.
FORD'S CONTACTS IN EUROPE CAN HELP US WITH THAT.
I WANTED TO WARN YOU ABOUT MATTERS IN WASHINGTON.
MATTERS IN WASHINGTON?
YES. THINGS HAVE CHANGED, AND NOT FOR THE BEST.
PRESIDENT-ELECT HARDING VIEWS YOUR GROUP AS AN "ABNORMAL" HOBBY OF HIS PREDECESSOR.
A HOBBY?
WE RISK LIFE AND LIMB TO SAVE OTHERS AND WE ARE A HOBBY!?
HOW DARE HE!
PROFESSOR, IT'S OKAY.
REALLY, IT IS.
THIS MEANS IT'S OVER.
WE CAN ALL GO HOME, BACK TO NORMAL LIVES.
IT'S AN ANSWE--

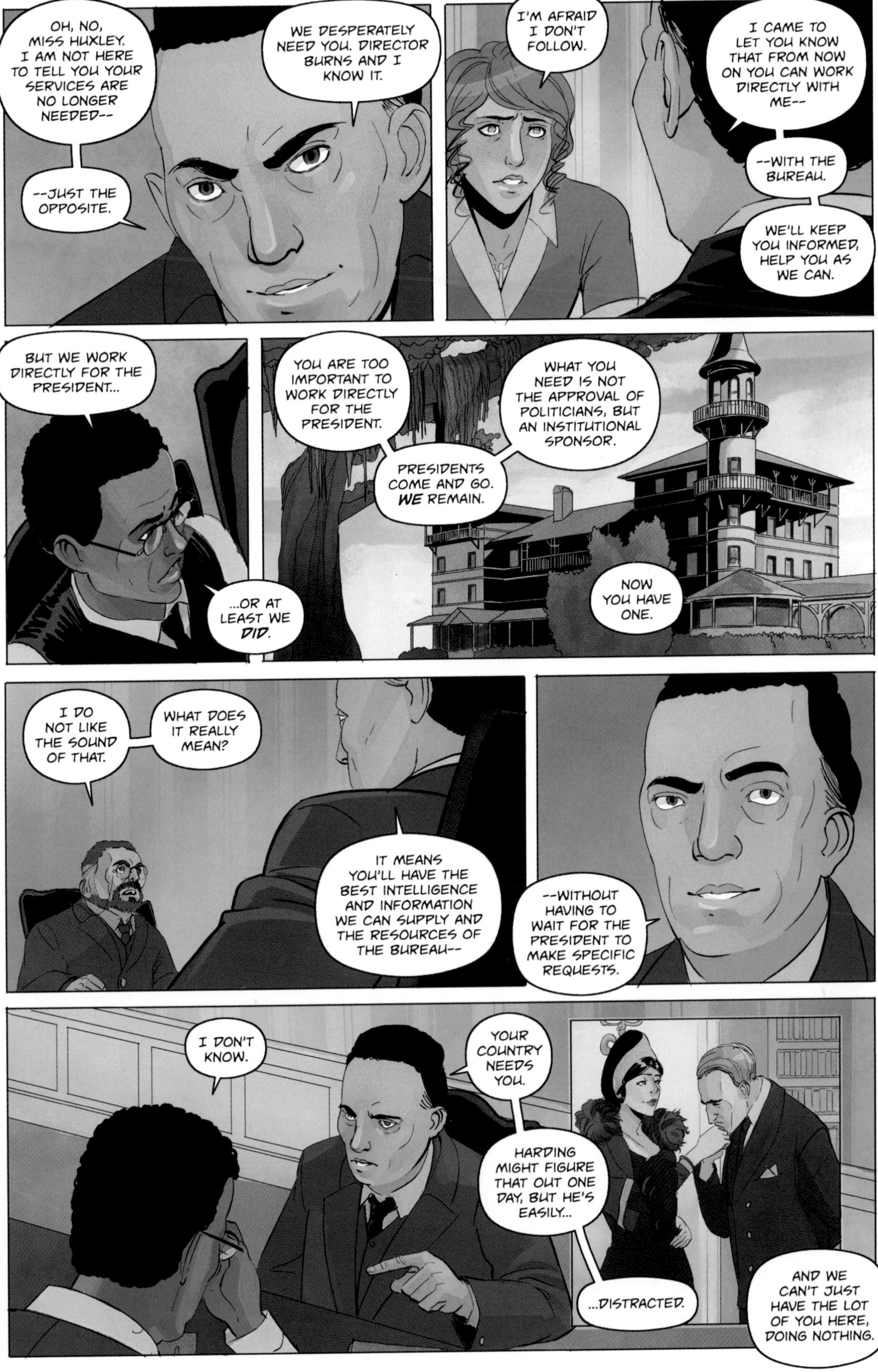
OH, NO, MISS HUXLEY. I AM NOT HERE TO TELL YOU YOUR SERVICES ARE NO LONGER NEEDED--
--JUST THE OPPOSITE.
WE DESPERATELY NEED YOU. DIRECTOR BURNS AND I KNOW IT.
I'M AFRAID I DON'T FOLLOW.
I CAME TO LET YOU KNOW THAT FROM NOW ON YOU CAN WORK DIRECTLY WITH ME--
--WITH THE BUREAU.
WE'LL KEEP YOU INFORMED, HELP YOU AS WE CAN.
BUT WE WORK DIRECTLY FOR THE PRESIDENT...
...OR AT LEAST WE DID.
YOU ARE TOO IMPORTANT TO WORK DIRECTLY FOR THE PRESIDENT.
PRESIDENTS COME AND GO. WE REMAIN.
WHAT YOU NEED IS NOT THE APPROVAL OF POLITICIANS, BUT AN INSTITUTIONAL SPONSOR.
NOW YOU HAVE ONE.
I DO NOT LIKE THE SOUND OF THAT.
WHAT DOES IT REALLY MEAN?
IT MEANS YOU'LL HAVE THE BEST INTELLIGENCE AND INFORMATION WE CAN SUPPLY AND THE RESOURCES OF THE BUREAU--
--WITHOUT HAVING TO WAIT FOR THE PRESIDENT TO MAKE SPECIFIC REQUESTS.
I DON'T KNOW.
YOUR COUNTRY NEEDS YOU.
HARDING MIGHT FIGURE THAT OUT ONE DAY, BUT HE'S EASILY...
...DISTRACTED.
AND WE CAN'T JUST HAVE THE LOT OF YOU HERE, DOING NOTHING.

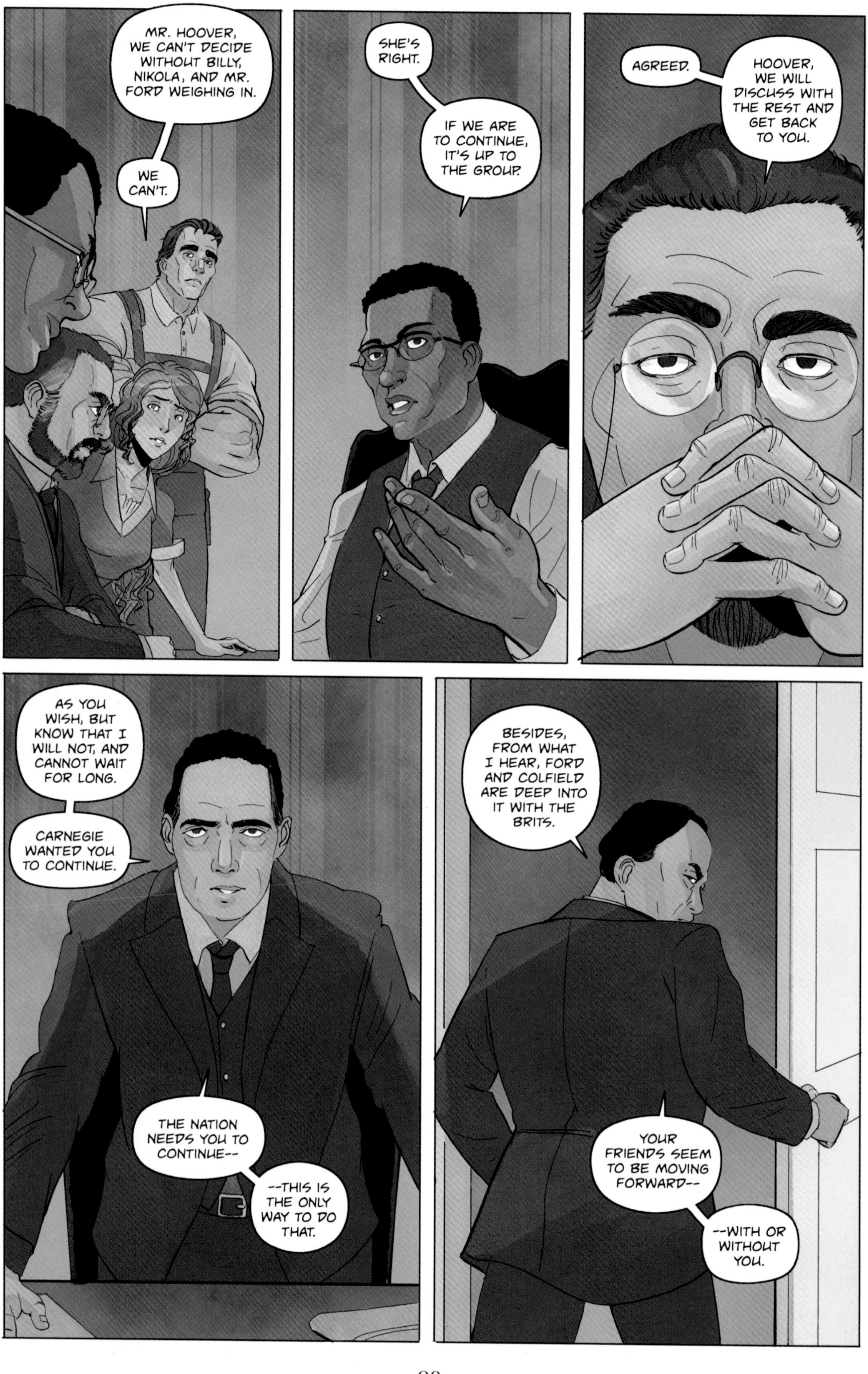

MR. HOOVER, WE CAN'T DECIDE WITHOUT BILLY, NIKOLA, AND MR. FORD WEIGHING IN.
WE CAN'T.
SHE'S RIGHT.
IF WE ARE TO CONTINUE, IT'S UP TO THE GROUP.
AGREED.
HOOVER, WE WILL DISCUSS WITH THE REST AND GET BACK TO YOU.
AS YOU WISH, BUT KNOW THAT I WILL NOT, AND CANNOT WAIT FOR LONG.
CARNEGIE WANTED YOU TO CONTINUE.
THE NATION NEEDS YOU TO CONTINUE--
--THIS IS THE ONLY WAY TO DO THAT.
BESIDES, FROM WHAT I HEAR, FORD AND COLFIELD ARE DEEP INTO IT WITH THE BRITS.
YOUR FRIENDS SEEM TO BE MOVING FORWARD--
--WITH OR WITHOUT YOU.

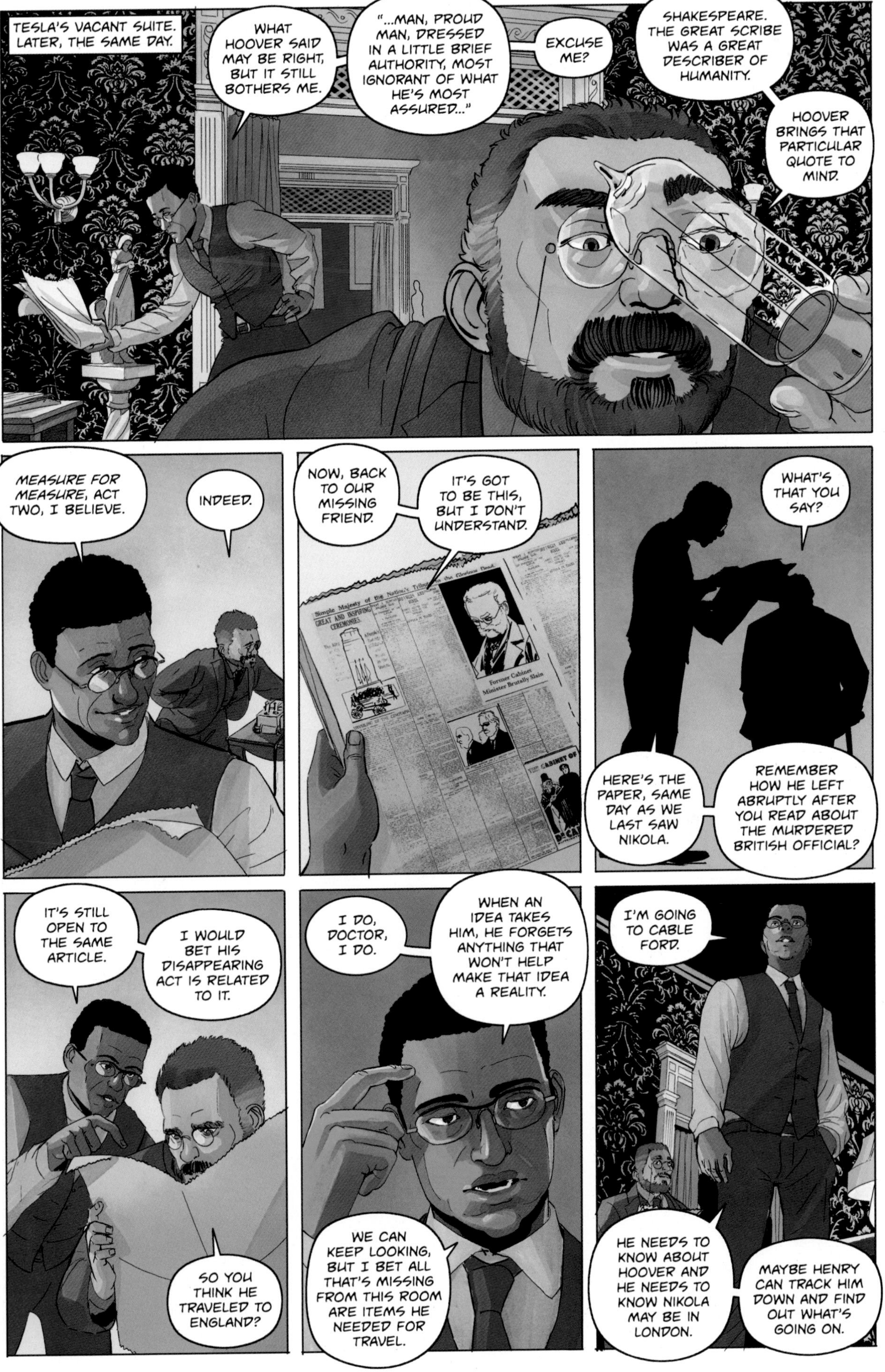
TESLA'S VACANT SUITE. LATER, THE SAME DAY.
WHAT HOOVER SAID MAY BE RIGHT, BUT IT STILL BOTHERS ME.
"...MAN, PROUD MAN, DRESSED IN A LITTLE BRIEF AUTHORITY, MOST IGNORANT OF WHAT HE'S MOST ASSURED..."
EXCUSE ME?
SHAKESPEARE. THE GREAT SCRIBE WAS A GREAT DESCRIBER OF HUMANITY.
HOOVER BRINGS THAT PARTICULAR QUOTE TO MIND.
MEASURE FOR MEASURE, ACT TWO, I BELIEVE.
INDEED.
NOW, BACK TO OUR MISSING FRIEND.
IT'S GOT TO BE THIS, BUT I DON'T UNDERSTAND.
GREAT AND INSPIRING CEREMONIES.
Former Cabinet Minister Brutally Slain
WHAT'S THAT YOU SAY?
HERE'S THE PAPER, SAME DAY AS WE LAST SAW NIKOLA.
REMEMBER HOW HE LEFT ABRUPTLY AFTER YOU READ ABOUT THE MURDERED BRITISH OFFICIAL?
IT'S STILL OPEN TO THE SAME ARTICLE.
I WOULD BET HIS DISAPPEARING ACT IS RELATED TO IT.
SO YOU THINK HE TRAVELED TO ENGLAND?
I DO, DOCTOR, I DO.
WHEN AN IDEA TAKES HIM, HE FORGETS ANYTHING THAT WON'T HELP MAKE THAT IDEA A REALITY.
WE CAN KEEP LOOKING, BUT I BET ALL THAT'S MISSING FROM THIS ROOM ARE ITEMS HE NEEDED FOR TRAVEL.
I'M GOING TO CABLE FORD.
HE NEEDS TO KNOW ABOUT HOOVER AND HE NEEDS TO KNOW NIKOLA MAY BE IN LONDON.
MAYBE HENRY CAN TRACK HIM DOWN AND FIND OUT WHAT'S GOING ON.

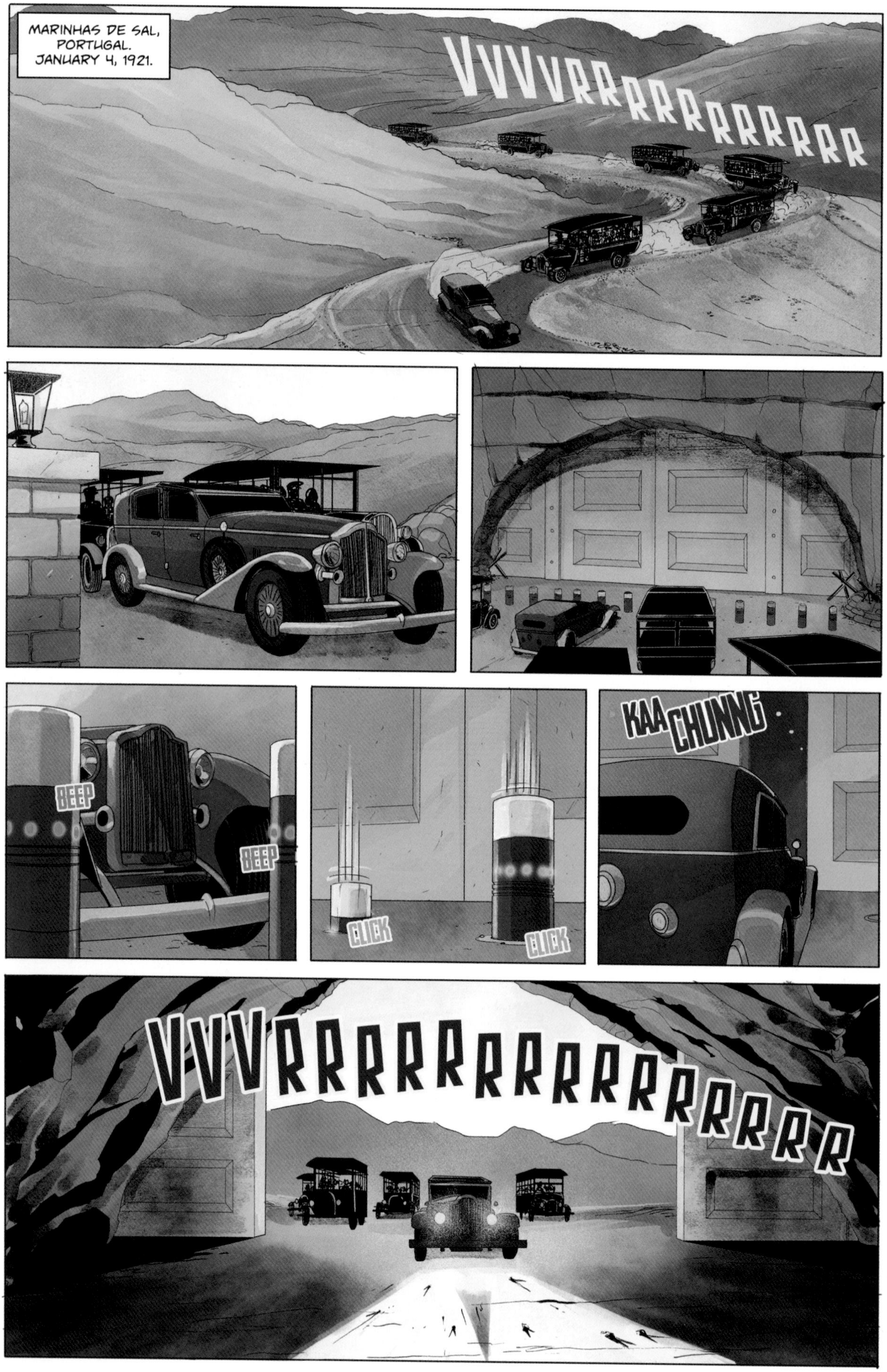
MARINHAS DE SAL, PORTUGAL. JANUARY 4, 1921.
VVVVRRRRRRRRRRRR
BEEP
BEEP
CLICK
CLICK
KAA CHUNNG
VVVRRRRRRRRRRRRRRRR

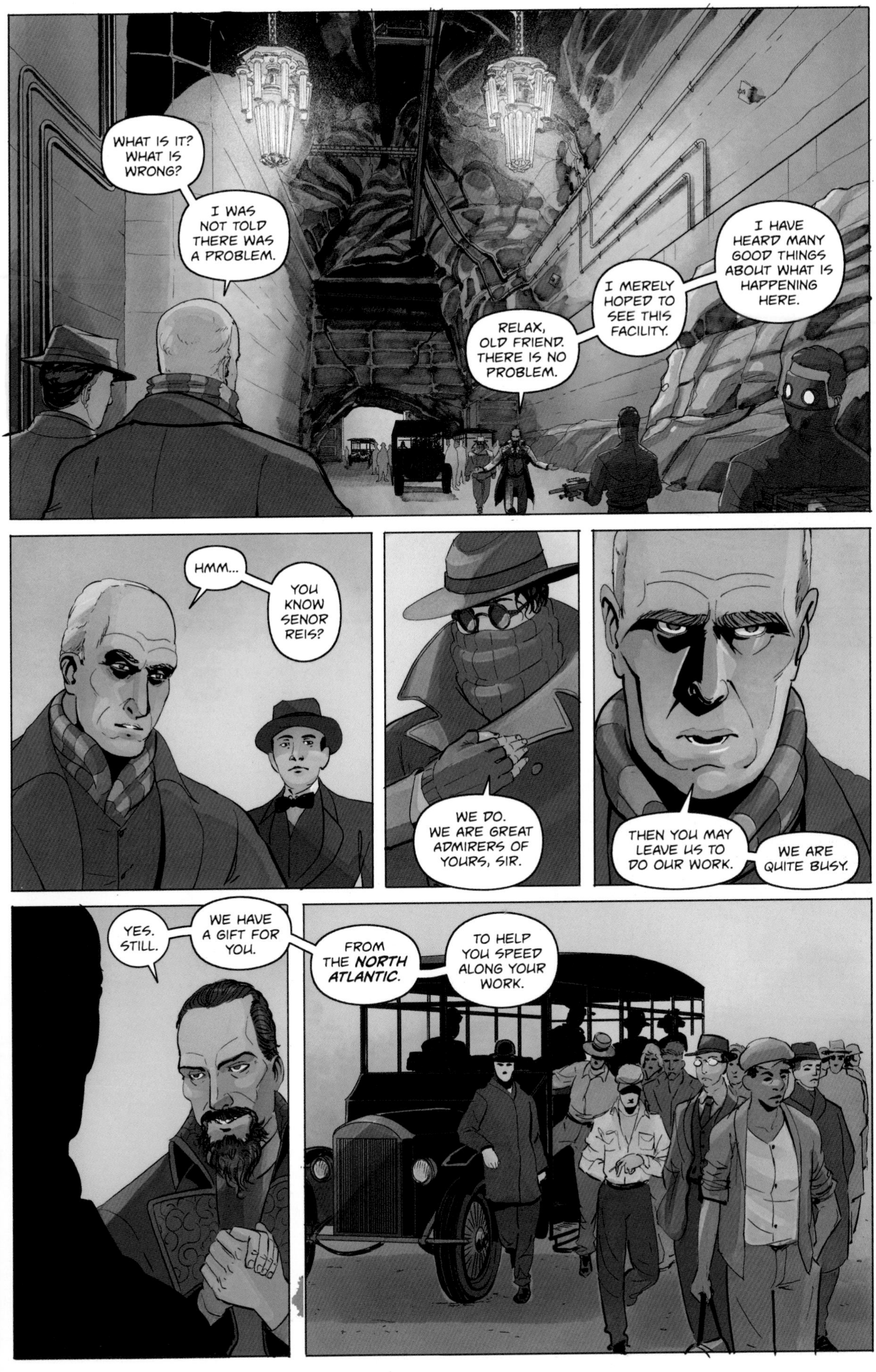
WHAT IS IT? WHAT IS WRONG?
I WAS NOT TOLD THERE WAS A PROBLEM.
RELAX, OLD FRIEND. THERE IS NO PROBLEM.
I MERELY HOPED TO SEE THIS FACILITY.
I HAVE HEARD MANY GOOD THINGS ABOUT WHAT IS HAPPENING HERE.
HMM...
YOU KNOW SENOR REIS?
WE DO. WE ARE GREAT ADMIRERS OF YOURS, SIR.
THEN YOU MAY LEAVE US TO DO OUR WORK.
WE ARE QUITE BUSY.
YES. STILL.
WE HAVE A GIFT FOR YOU.
FROM THE **NORTH ATLANTIC**.
TO HELP YOU SPEED ALONG YOUR WORK.

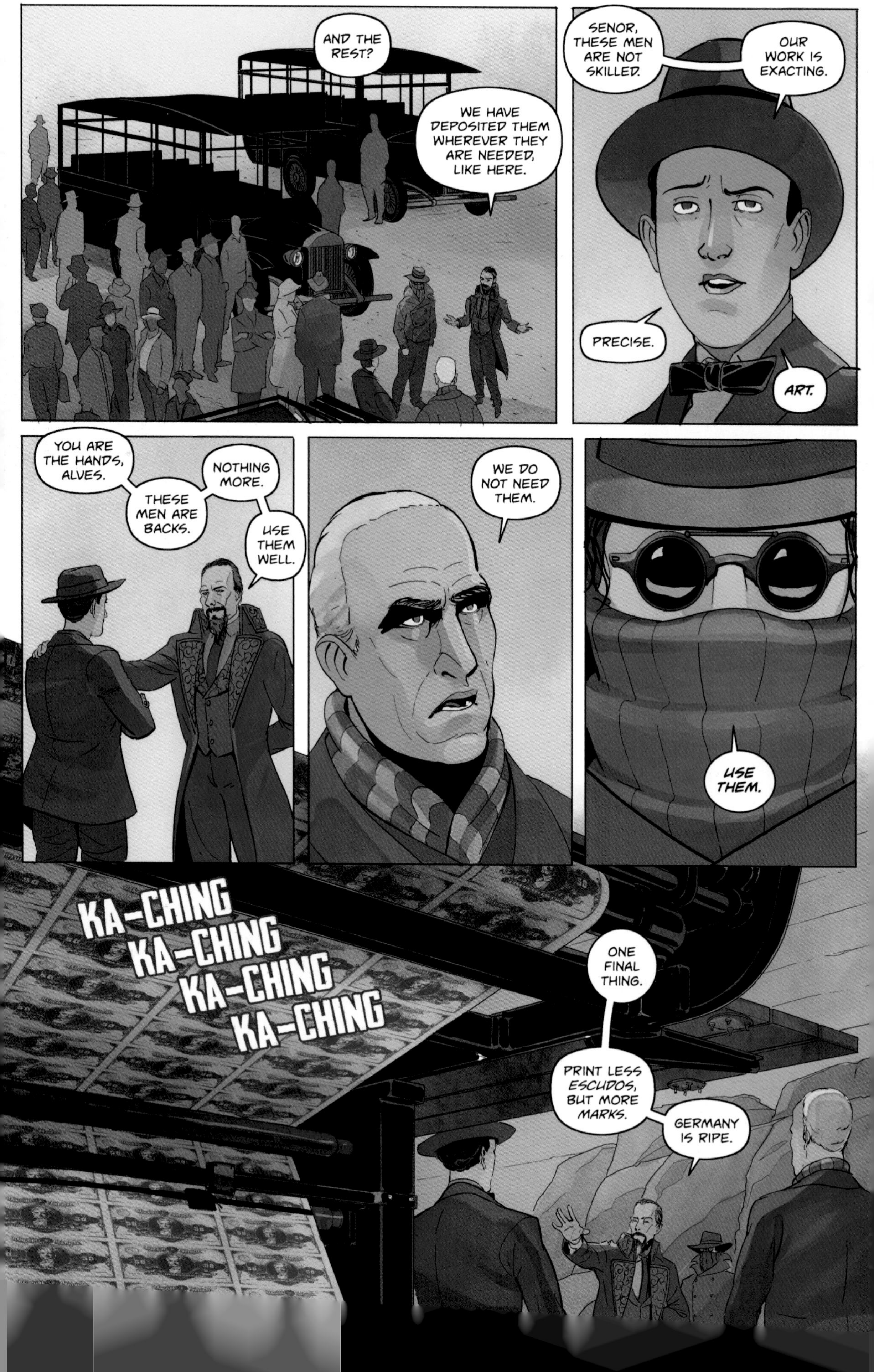
AND THE REST?
WE HAVE DEPOSITED THEM WHEREVER THEY ARE NEEDED, LIKE HERE.
SENOR, THESE MEN ARE NOT SKILLED.
OUR WORK IS EXACTING.
PRECISE.
ART.
YOU ARE THE HANDS, ALVES.
THESE MEN ARE BACKS.
NOTHING MORE.
USE THEM WELL.
WE DO NOT NEED THEM.
USE THEM.
KA-CHING
KA-CHING
KA-CHING
KA-CHING
ONE FINAL THING.
PRINT LESS ESCUDOS, BUT MORE MARKS.
GERMANY IS RIPE.

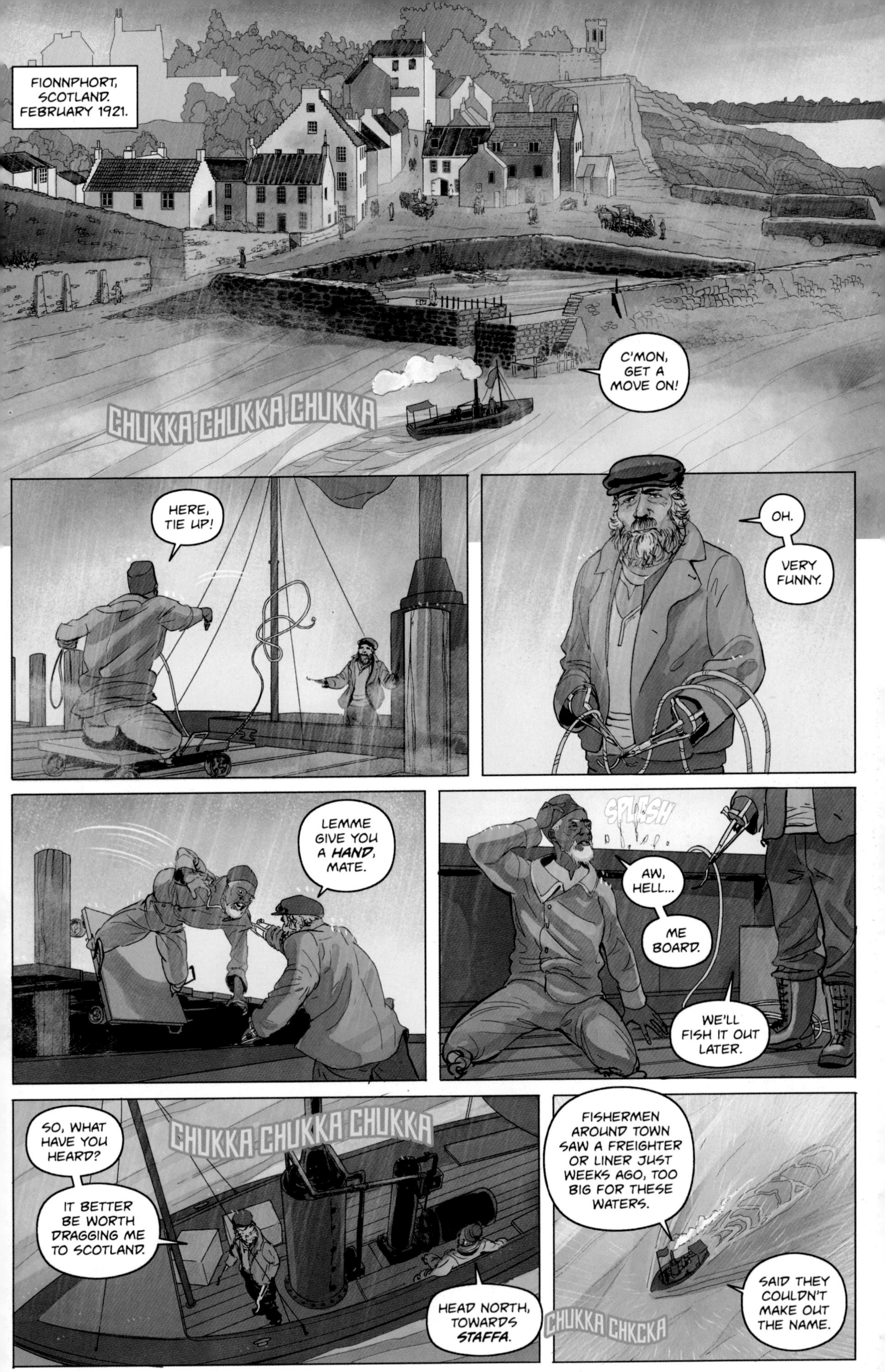
FIONNPHORT, SCOTLAND. FEBRUARY 1921.
CHUKKA CHUKKA CHUKKA
C'MON, GET A MOVE ON!
HERE, TIE UP!
OH.
VERY FUNNY.
LEMME GIVE YOU A *HAND*, MATE.
SPLASH
AW, HELL...
ME BOARD.
WE'LL FISH IT OUT LATER.
CHUKKA CHUKKA CHUKKA
SO, WHAT HAVE YOU HEARD?
IT BETTER BE WORTH DRAGGING ME TO SCOTLAND.
HEAD NORTH, TOWARDS *STAFFA*.
CHUKKA CHKCKA
FISHERMEN AROUND TOWN SAW A FREIGHTER OR LINER JUST WEEKS AGO, TOO BIG FOR THESE WATERS.
SAID THEY COULDN'T MAKE OUT THE NAME.

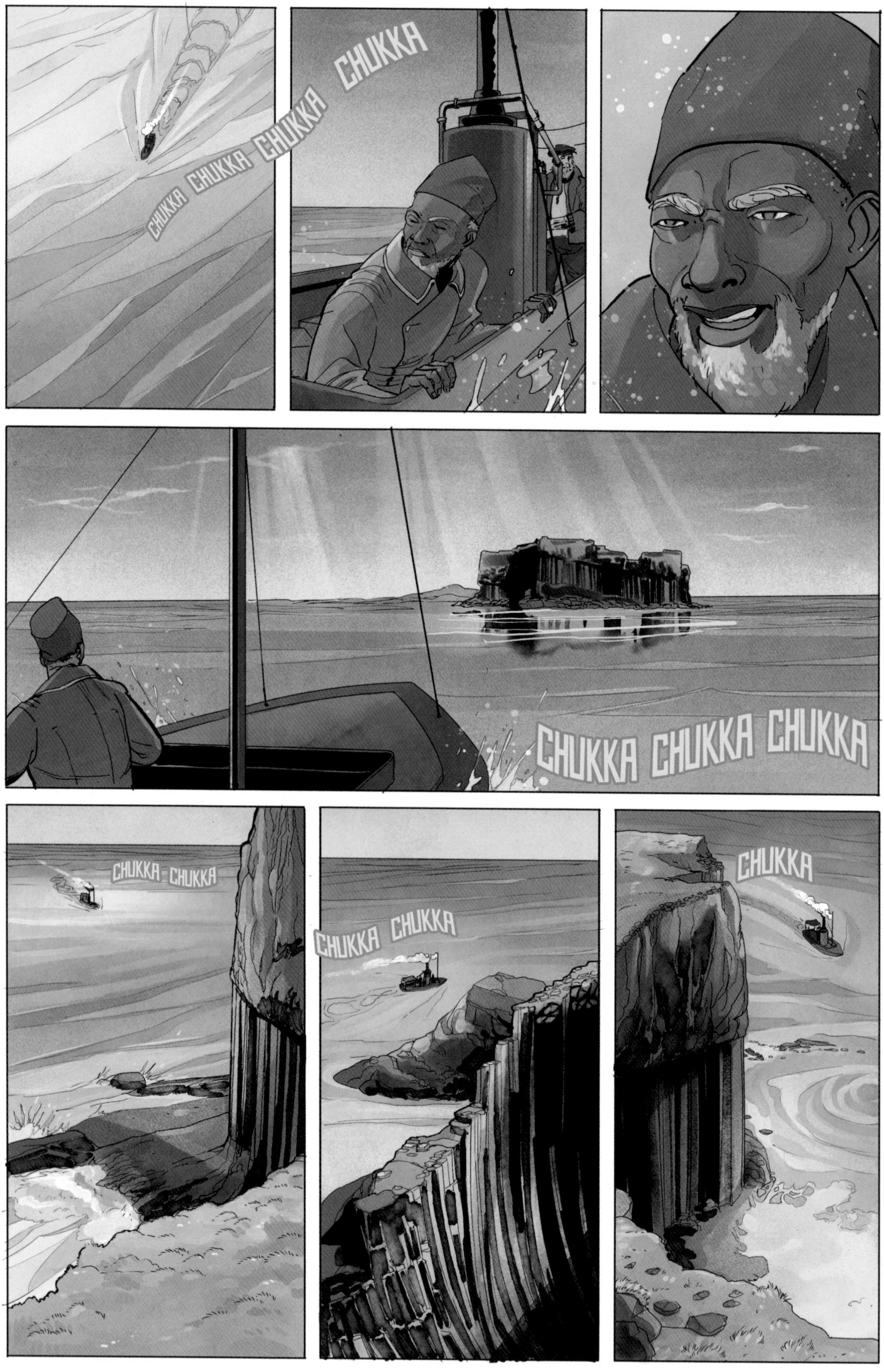
CHUKKA CHUKKA CHUKKA CHUKKA
CHUKKA CHUKKA CHUKKA
CHUKKA CHUKKA
CHUKKA CHUKKA
CHUKKA

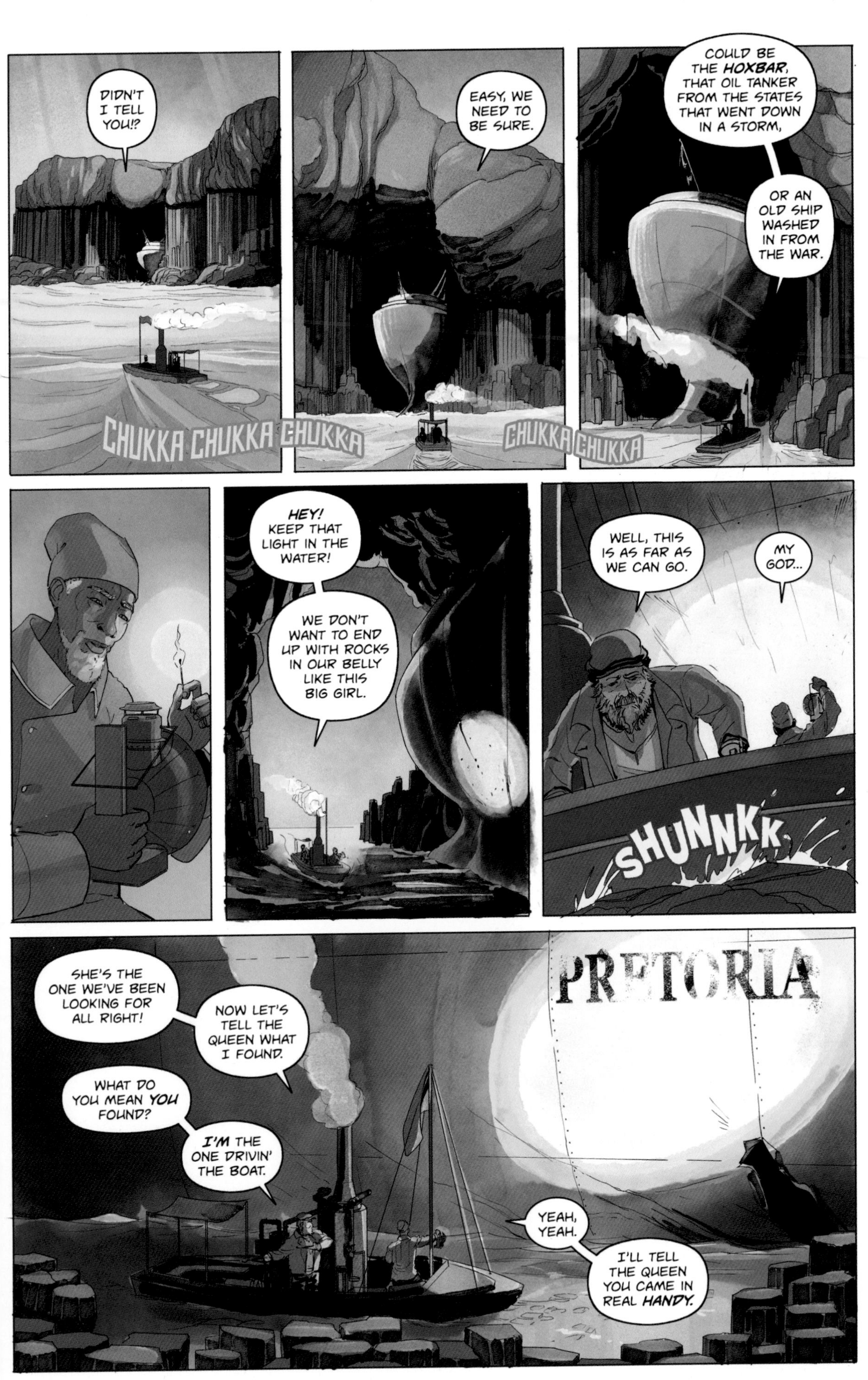
DIDN'T I TELL YOU!?
CHUKKA CHUKKA CHUKKA
EASY, WE NEED TO BE SURE.
CHUKKA CHUKKA
COULD BE THE HOXBAR, THAT OIL TANKER FROM THE STATES THAT WENT DOWN IN A STORM,
OR AN OLD SHIP WASHED IN FROM THE WAR.
HEY! KEEP THAT LIGHT IN THE WATER!
WE DON'T WANT TO END UP WITH ROCKS IN OUR BELLY LIKE THIS BIG GIRL.
WELL, THIS IS AS FAR AS WE CAN GO.
MY GOD...
SHUNNKK
PRETORIA
SHE'S THE ONE WE'VE BEEN LOOKING FOR ALL RIGHT!
NOW LET'S TELL THE QUEEN WHAT I FOUND.
WHAT DO YOU MEAN YOU FOUND?
I'M THE ONE DRIVIN' THE BOAT.
YEAH, YEAH.
I'LL TELL THE QUEEN YOU CAME IN REAL HANDY.

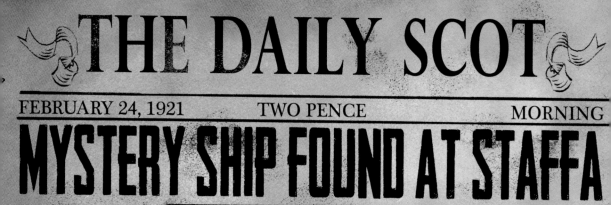

# THE DAILY SCOT

FEBRUARY 24, 1921 TWO PENCE MORNING

# MYSTERY SHIP FOUND AT STAFFA

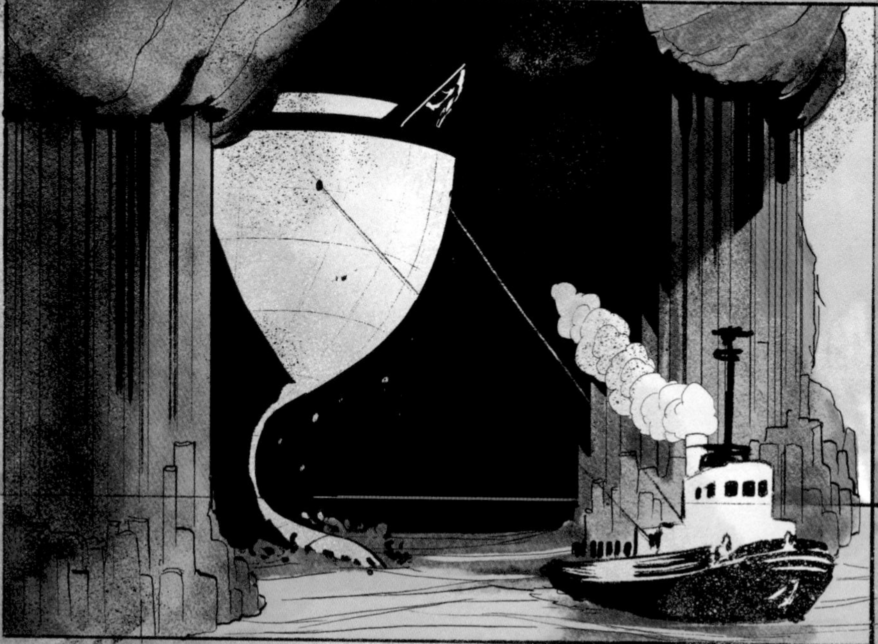

## PRETORIA FOUND BY LOCALS

In a surprising turn of events, a ship that left the port of New Jersey, USA, turned up hidden in a cave on the isle of Staffa. Scottish officials are baffled at how this large passenger vessel came to rest in P... ...cus eu tincidunt mi. In in magna sit amet erat ultrices fermentum. Donec eleifend commodo ... eros eget, molestie eleifend dui. Donec scelerisque sollicitudin massa, non hendrerit quam condimentum ... Phasellus tincidunt, massa a elementum pulvinar, quam arcu ... augue, ... est. Duis ... pellentesque fermentum ... pellentesque

## PRIME MINISTER LLOYD GEORGE PUZZLED BY TURN OF EVENTS

Phasellus eu tincidunt mi. In in magna ... amet erat ultrices fermentum. Donec elit ... commodo ... sit amet eros eget, molestie eleifend dui. Donec scelerisque sollicitudin massa, non hendrerit quam condimentum ... iaculis. Phasellus tincidunt, massa a elementum pulvinar, quam arcu rhoncus augue, eu accumsan felis ... est. Duis mattis pellentesque fer... Nulla pellentesque est nec blandit tincidunt. Aliquam tempor aliq... felis, ... eros bibendum non ... interdum ... sem ... lobortis, porttitor, ... justo erat ... turpis, vel cursus sapien ligula vel ... Aliquam ... a... elit elementum ... non ... Morbi ...

# VANISHED!

## THOUSANDS OF PASSENGERS MYSTERIOUSLY DISAPPEAR FROM VESSEL

Approximately 1900 passengers left the American shores on Oct 31, heading for a European rendezvous, returning known or suspected anarchists back to their homelands across the sea. Yet, none are accounted for at this time.

Nullam auctor consectetur congue. Duis egestas vel nibh sit amet placerat. Donec lobortis vulputate ligula eget auctor. Fusce ... tortor. Fusce et ... aliquet, vestibulum ... u... aliquet neque. Lorem ipsum dolor sit amet, consectetur adipiscing elit. Sed luctus gravida ... dapibus ... Quisque ... faucibus, ... pellentesque sollicitudin volutpat ...

Mattis sed odio id felis ornare auctor. Sed porttitor non tortor ... lacinia. Nam aliquam ... laoreet commodo. Phasellus nisl sem, dictum vel lectus vel, vehicula eleifend orci. Sed ... Duis sagittis augue vel elit faucibus pulvinar. Sed lobortis ... Etiam ornare nibh sit amet dui ... molestie. Praesent ... condimentum ... Sed ac finibus ... ultrices vel ... odio, in pharetra diam semper ... pretium. Sed et ... elit, sed interdum nulla. Sed volutpat facilisis ... Sed sed scelerisque ... posuere orci. Etiam posuere ... sollicitudin. Fusce ... sed

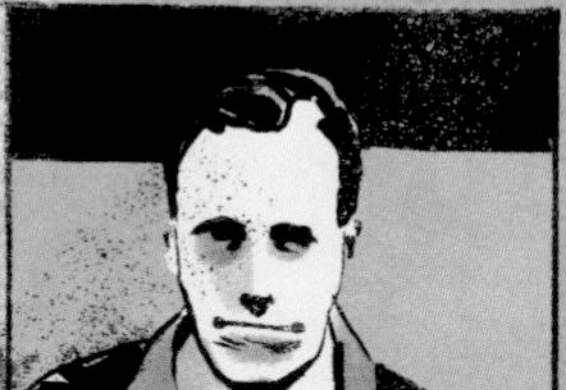

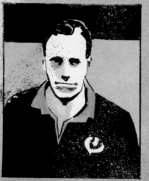

## RUGBY STAR, LIDDELL, EYES OLYMPIC RUN IN '24

Etiam eu maximus purus. Duis rhoncus purus eget ... cursus, vitae commodo massa laoreet. ... tristique hendrerit sapien. Pellentesque tincidunt ex risus, ac molestie est semper ... Integer nec scelerisque ipsum ...

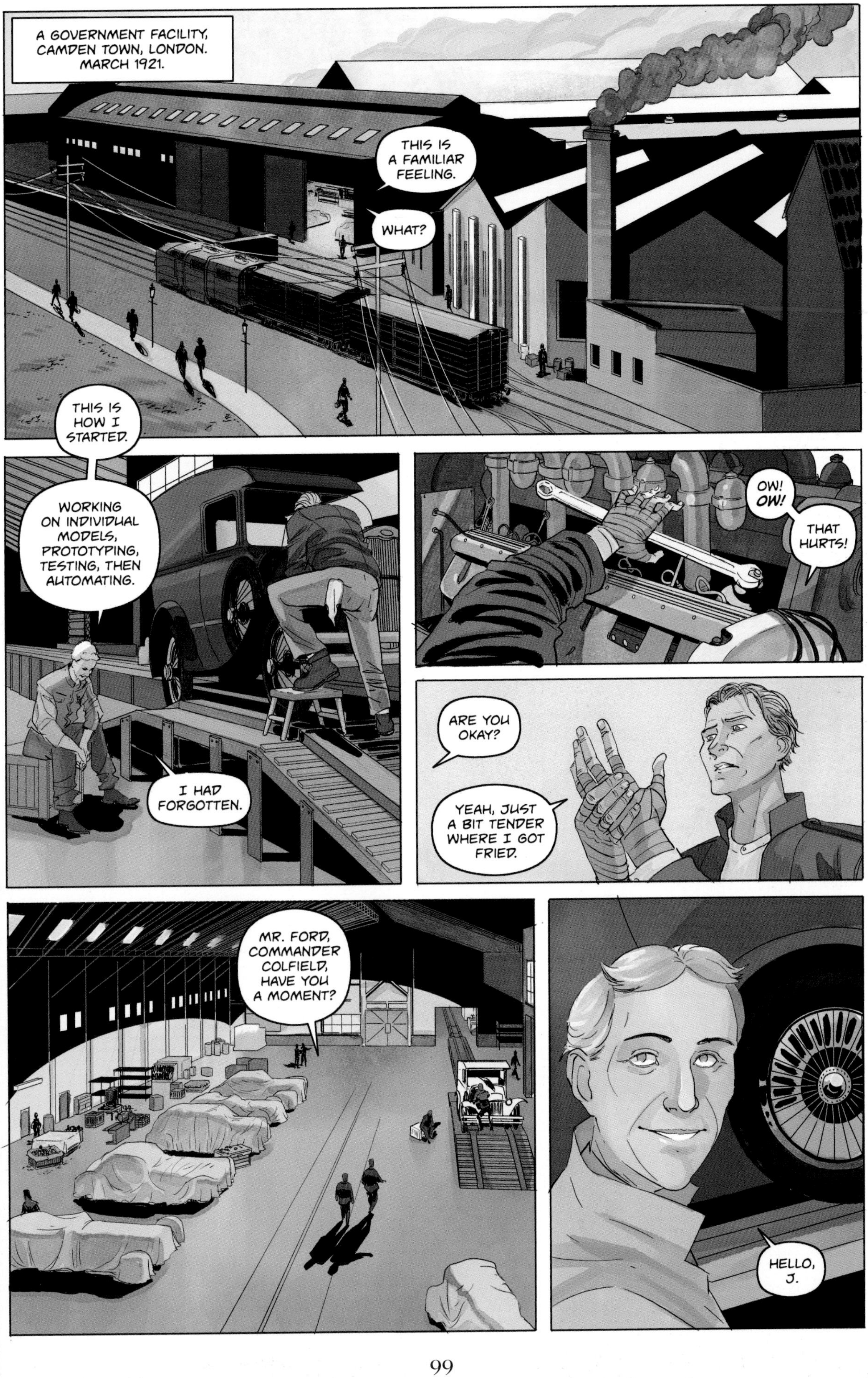
A GOVERNMENT FACILITY, CAMDEN TOWN, LONDON. MARCH 1921.
THIS IS A FAMILIAR FEELING.
WHAT?
THIS IS HOW I STARTED.
WORKING ON INDIVIDUAL MODELS, PROTOTYPING, TESTING, THEN AUTOMATING.
I HAD FORGOTTEN.
OW! OW!
THAT HURTS!
ARE YOU OKAY?
YEAH, JUST A BIT TENDER WHERE I GOT FRIED.
MR. FORD, COMMANDER COLFIELD, HAVE YOU A MOMENT?
HELLO, J.

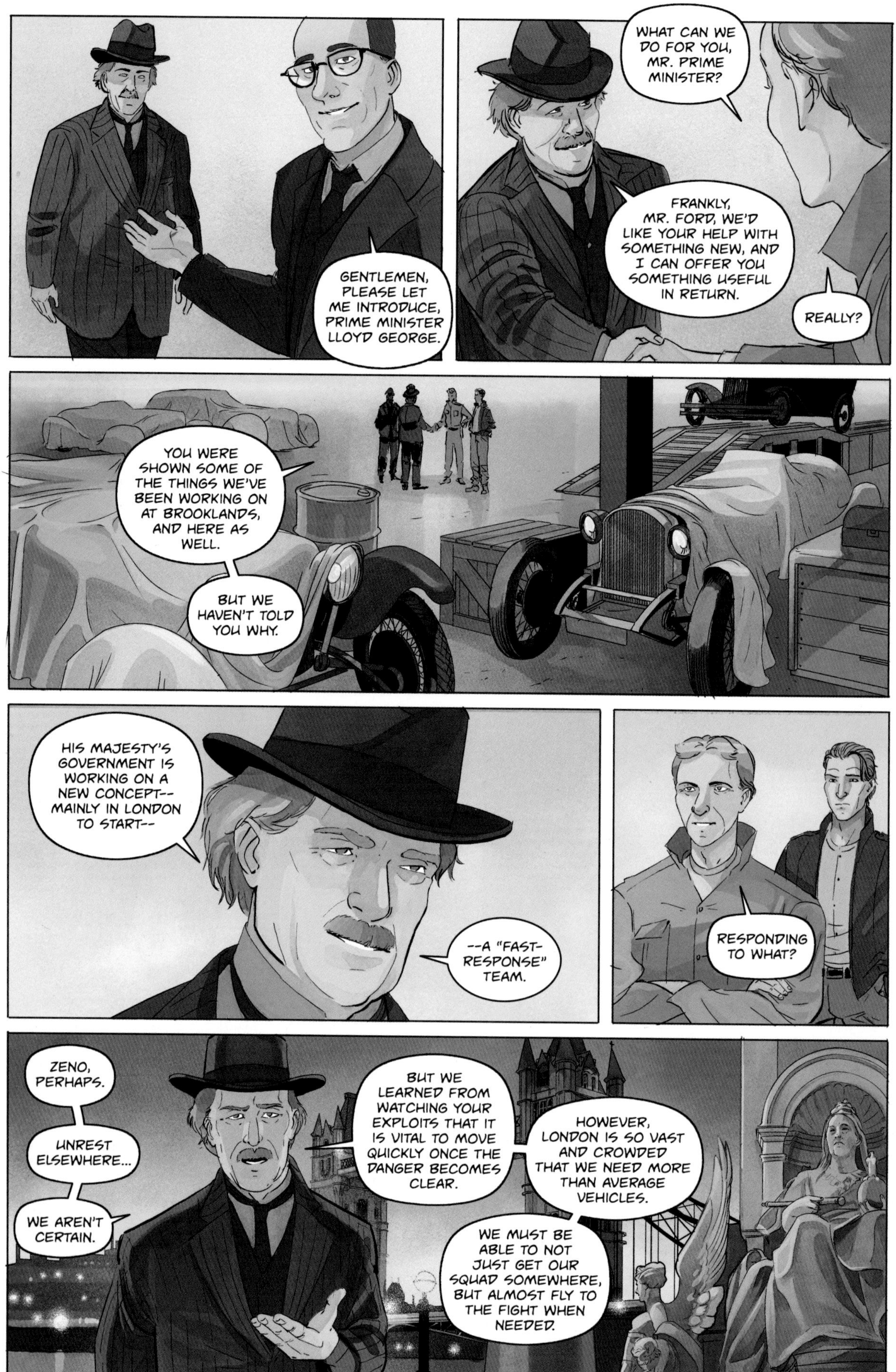
GENTLEMEN, PLEASE LET ME INTRODUCE, PRIME MINISTER LLOYD GEORGE.
WHAT CAN WE DO FOR YOU, MR. PRIME MINISTER?
FRANKLY, MR. FORD, WE'D LIKE YOUR HELP WITH SOMETHING NEW, AND I CAN OFFER YOU SOMETHING USEFUL IN RETURN.
REALLY?
YOU WERE SHOWN SOME OF THE THINGS WE'VE BEEN WORKING ON AT BROOKLANDS, AND HERE AS WELL.
BUT WE HAVEN'T TOLD YOU WHY.
HIS MAJESTY'S GOVERNMENT IS WORKING ON A NEW CONCEPT-- MAINLY IN LONDON TO START--
--A "FAST-RESPONSE" TEAM.
RESPONDING TO WHAT?
ZENO, PERHAPS.
UNREST ELSEWHERE...
WE AREN'T CERTAIN.
BUT WE LEARNED FROM WATCHING YOUR EXPLOITS THAT IT IS VITAL TO MOVE QUICKLY ONCE THE DANGER BECOMES CLEAR.
HOWEVER, LONDON IS SO VAST AND CROWDED THAT WE NEED MORE THAN AVERAGE VEHICLES.
WE MUST BE ABLE TO NOT JUST GET OUR SQUAD SOMEWHERE, BUT ALMOST FLY TO THE FIGHT WHEN NEEDED.

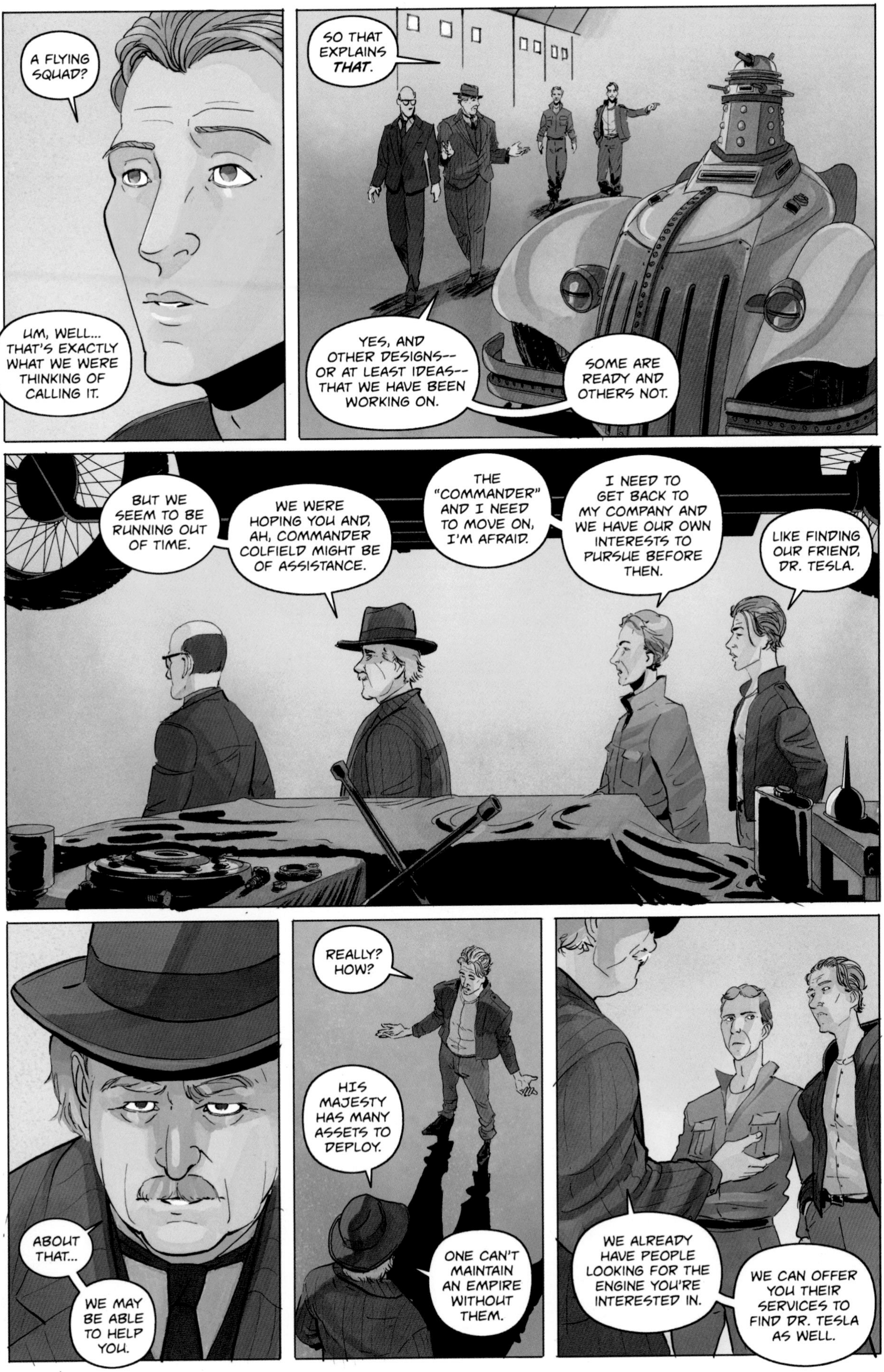
A FLYING SQUAD?
UM, WELL... THAT'S EXACTLY WHAT WE WERE THINKING OF CALLING IT.
SO THAT EXPLAINS *THAT*.
YES, AND OTHER DESIGNS-- OR AT LEAST IDEAS-- THAT WE HAVE BEEN WORKING ON.
SOME ARE READY AND OTHERS NOT.
BUT WE SEEM TO BE RUNNING OUT OF TIME.
WE WERE HOPING YOU AND, AH, COMMANDER COLFIELD MIGHT BE OF ASSISTANCE.
THE "COMMANDER" AND I NEED TO MOVE ON, I'M AFRAID.
I NEED TO GET BACK TO MY COMPANY AND WE HAVE OUR OWN INTERESTS TO PURSUE BEFORE THEN.
LIKE FINDING OUR FRIEND, DR. TESLA.
ABOUT THAT...
WE MAY BE ABLE TO HELP YOU.
REALLY? HOW?
HIS MAJESTY HAS MANY ASSETS TO DEPLOY.
ONE CAN'T MAINTAIN AN EMPIRE WITHOUT THEM.
WE ALREADY HAVE PEOPLE LOOKING FOR THE ENGINE YOU'RE INTERESTED IN.
WE CAN OFFER YOU THEIR SERVICES TO FIND DR. TESLA AS WELL.

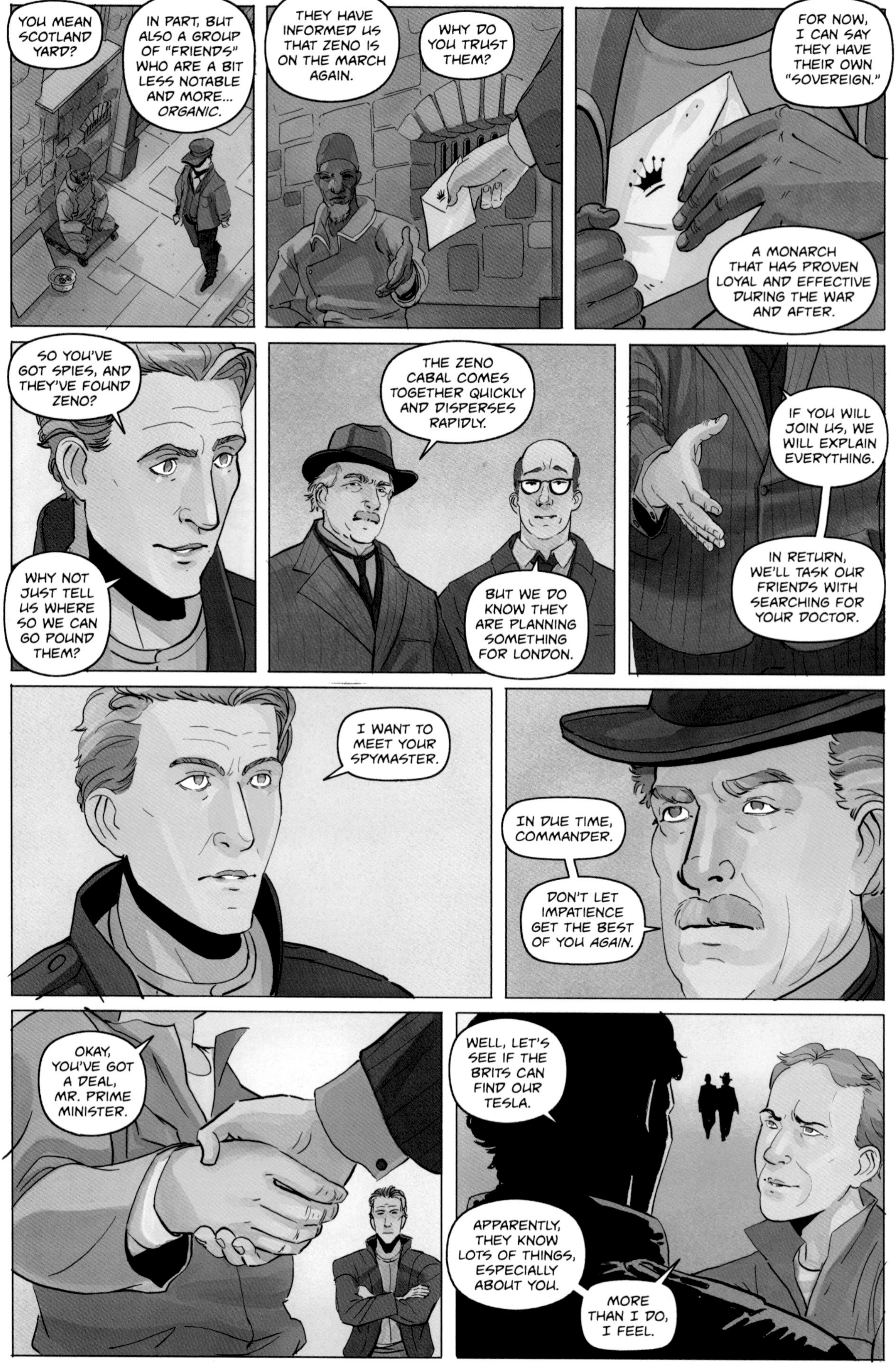
YOU MEAN SCOTLAND YARD?
IN PART, BUT ALSO A GROUP OF "FRIENDS" WHO ARE A BIT LESS NOTABLE AND MORE... ORGANIC.
THEY HAVE INFORMED US THAT ZENO IS ON THE MARCH AGAIN.
WHY DO YOU TRUST THEM?
FOR NOW, I CAN SAY THEY HAVE THEIR OWN "SOVEREIGN."
A MONARCH THAT HAS PROVEN LOYAL AND EFFECTIVE DURING THE WAR AND AFTER.
SO YOU'VE GOT SPIES, AND THEY'VE FOUND ZENO?
WHY NOT JUST TELL US WHERE SO WE CAN GO POUND THEM?
THE ZENO CABAL COMES TOGETHER QUICKLY AND DISPERSES RAPIDLY.
BUT WE DO KNOW THEY ARE PLANNING SOMETHING FOR LONDON.
IF YOU WILL JOIN US, WE WILL EXPLAIN EVERYTHING.
IN RETURN, WE'LL TASK OUR FRIENDS WITH SEARCHING FOR YOUR DOCTOR.
I WANT TO MEET YOUR SPYMASTER.
IN DUE TIME, COMMANDER.
DON'T LET IMPATIENCE GET THE BEST OF YOU AGAIN.
OKAY, YOU'VE GOT A DEAL, MR. PRIME MINISTER.
WELL, LET'S SEE IF THE BRITS CAN FIND OUR TESLA.
APPARENTLY, THEY KNOW LOTS OF THINGS, ESPECIALLY ABOUT YOU.
MORE THAN I DO, I FEEL.

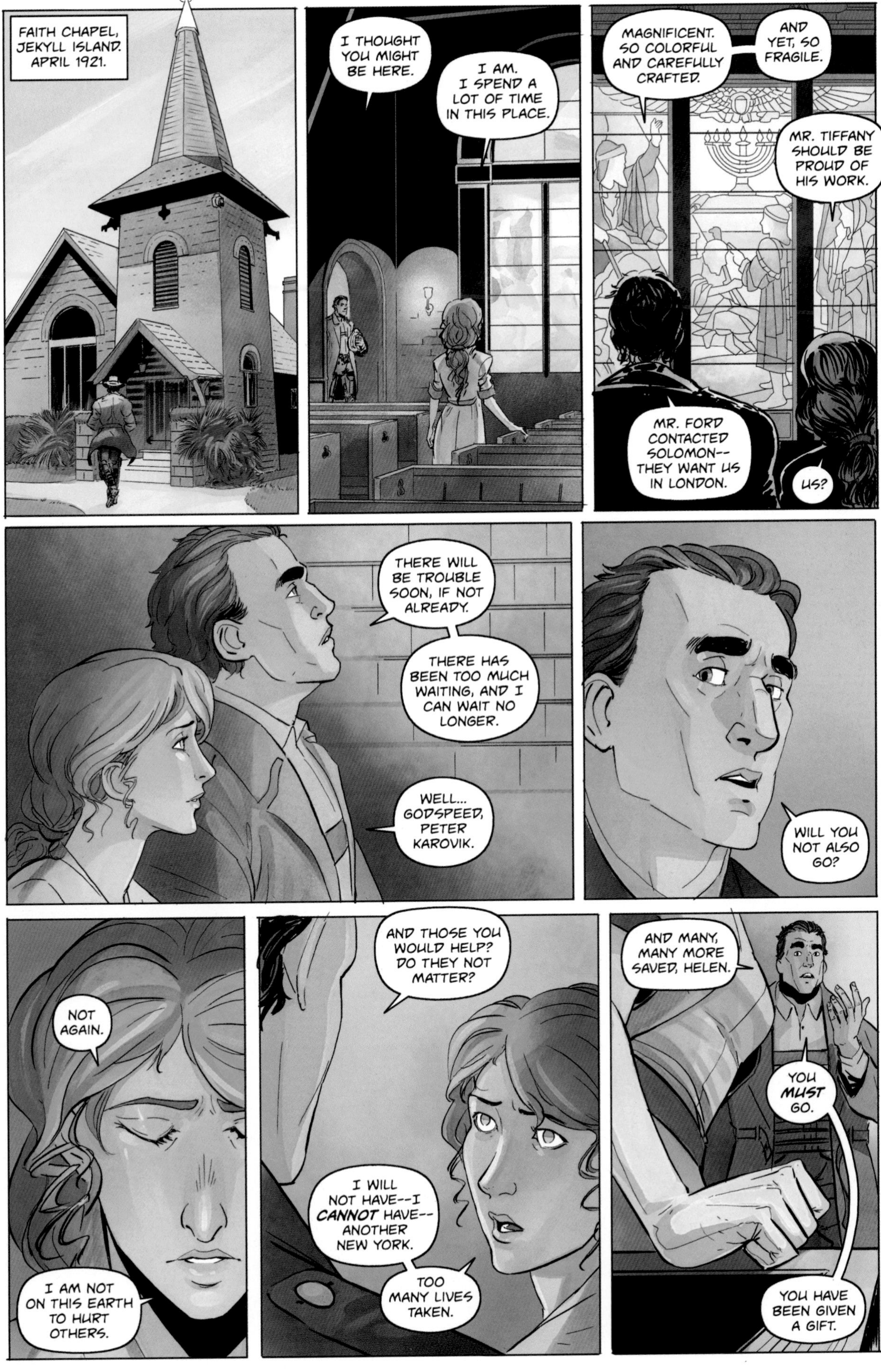
FAITH CHAPEL, JEKYLL ISLAND. APRIL 1921.
I THOUGHT YOU MIGHT BE HERE.
I AM. I SPEND A LOT OF TIME IN THIS PLACE.
MAGNIFICENT. SO COLORFUL AND CAREFULLY CRAFTED.
AND YET, SO FRAGILE.
MR. TIFFANY SHOULD BE PROUD OF HIS WORK.
MR. FORD CONTACTED SOLOMON-- THEY WANT US IN LONDON.
US?
THERE WILL BE TROUBLE SOON, IF NOT ALREADY.
THERE HAS BEEN TOO MUCH WAITING, AND I CAN WAIT NO LONGER.
WELL... GODSPEED, PETER KAROVIK.
WILL YOU NOT ALSO GO?
NOT AGAIN.
I AM NOT ON THIS EARTH TO HURT OTHERS.
AND THOSE YOU WOULD HELP? DO THEY NOT MATTER?
I WILL NOT HAVE--I CANNOT HAVE-- ANOTHER NEW YORK.
TOO MANY LIVES TAKEN.
AND MANY, MANY MORE SAVED, HELEN.
YOU MUST GO.
YOU HAVE BEEN GIVEN A GIFT.

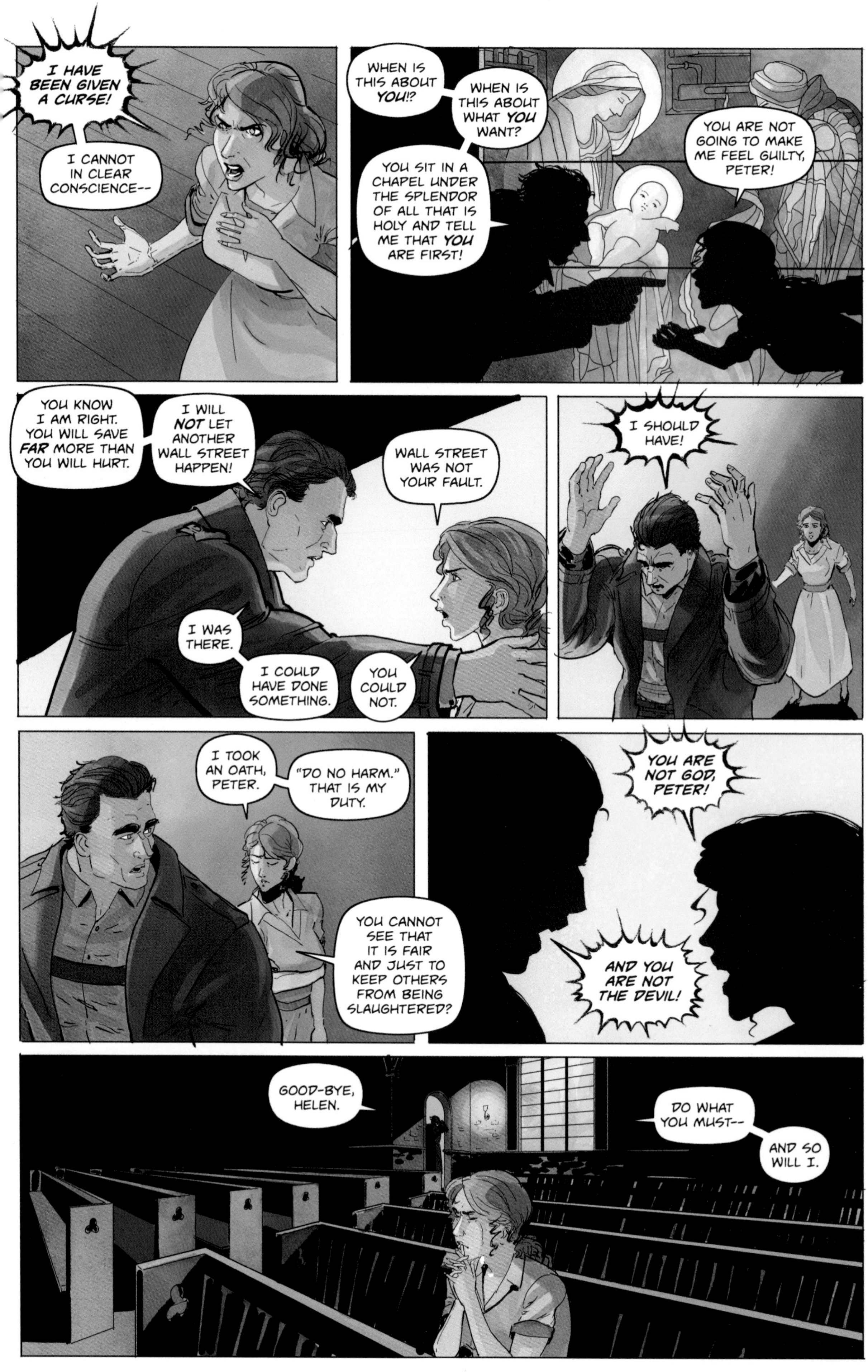
I HAVE BEEN GIVEN A CURSE!
I CANNOT IN CLEAR CONSCIENCE--
WHEN IS THIS ABOUT YOU!?
WHEN IS THIS ABOUT WHAT YOU WANT?
YOU SIT IN A CHAPEL UNDER THE SPLENDOR OF ALL THAT IS HOLY AND TELL ME THAT YOU ARE FIRST!
YOU ARE NOT GOING TO MAKE ME FEEL GUILTY, PETER!
YOU KNOW I AM RIGHT. YOU WILL SAVE FAR MORE THAN YOU WILL HURT.
I WILL NOT LET ANOTHER WALL STREET HAPPEN!
WALL STREET WAS NOT YOUR FAULT.
I WAS THERE.
I COULD HAVE DONE SOMETHING.
YOU COULD NOT.
I SHOULD HAVE!
I TOOK AN OATH, PETER.
"DO NO HARM." THAT IS MY DUTY.
YOU CANNOT SEE THAT IT IS FAIR AND JUST TO KEEP OTHERS FROM BEING SLAUGHTERED?
YOU ARE NOT GOD, PETER!
AND YOU ARE NOT THE DEVIL!
GOOD-BYE, HELEN.
DO WHAT YOU MUST--
AND SO WILL I.

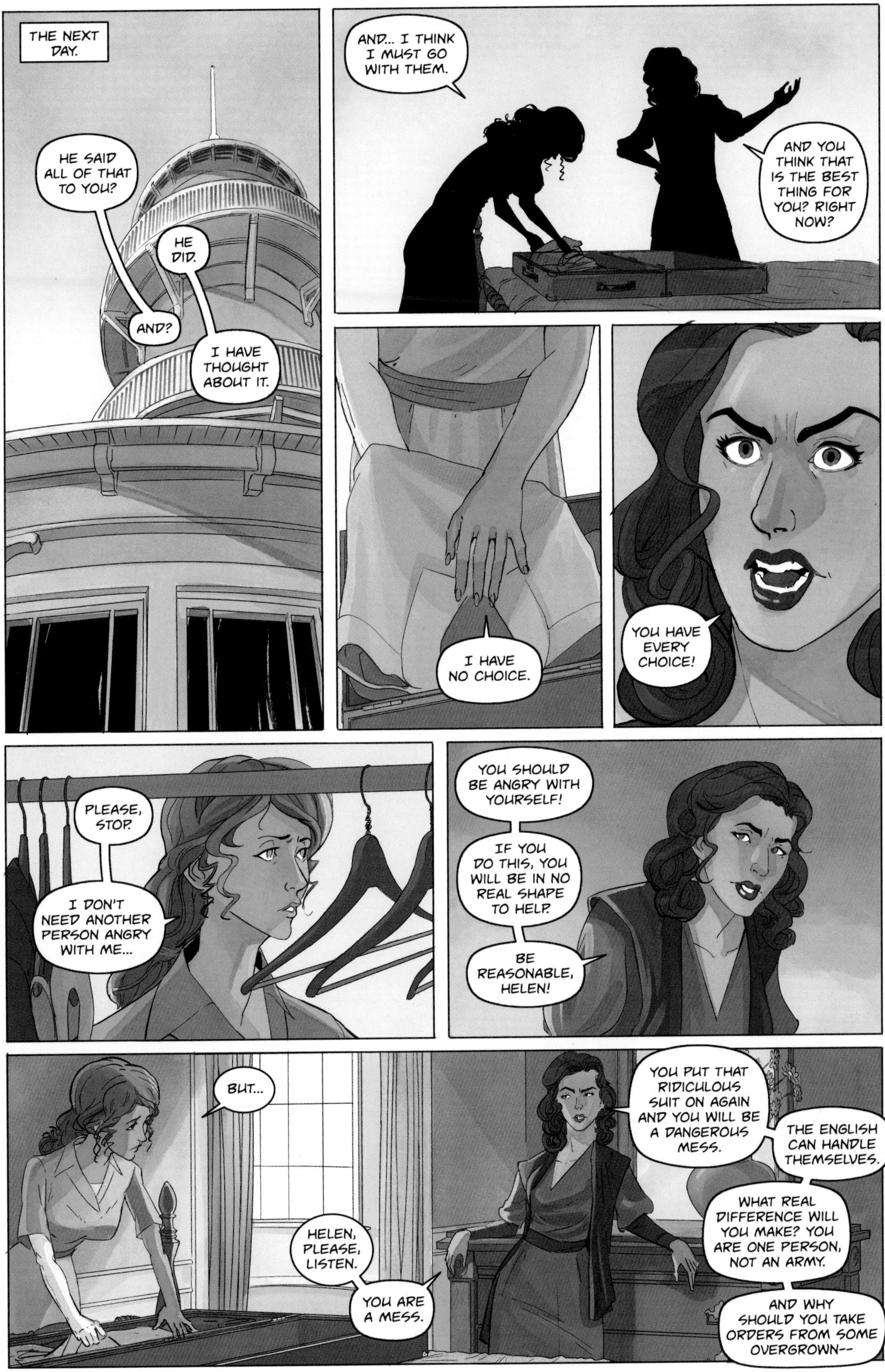
THE NEXT DAY.
HE SAID ALL OF THAT TO YOU?
HE DID.
AND?
I HAVE THOUGHT ABOUT IT.
AND... I THINK I MUST GO WITH THEM.
AND YOU THINK THAT IS THE BEST THING FOR YOU? RIGHT NOW?
I HAVE NO CHOICE.
YOU HAVE EVERY CHOICE!
PLEASE, STOP.
I DON'T NEED ANOTHER PERSON ANGRY WITH ME...
YOU SHOULD BE ANGRY WITH YOURSELF!
IF YOU DO THIS, YOU WILL BE IN NO REAL SHAPE TO HELP.
BE REASONABLE, HELEN!
BUT...
HELEN, PLEASE, LISTEN.
YOU ARE A MESS.
YOU PUT THAT RIDICULOUS SUIT ON AGAIN AND YOU WILL BE A DANGEROUS MESS.
THE ENGLISH CAN HANDLE THEMSELVES.
WHAT REAL DIFFERENCE WILL YOU MAKE? YOU ARE ONE PERSON, NOT AN ARMY.
AND WHY SHOULD YOU TAKE ORDERS FROM SOME OVERGROWN--

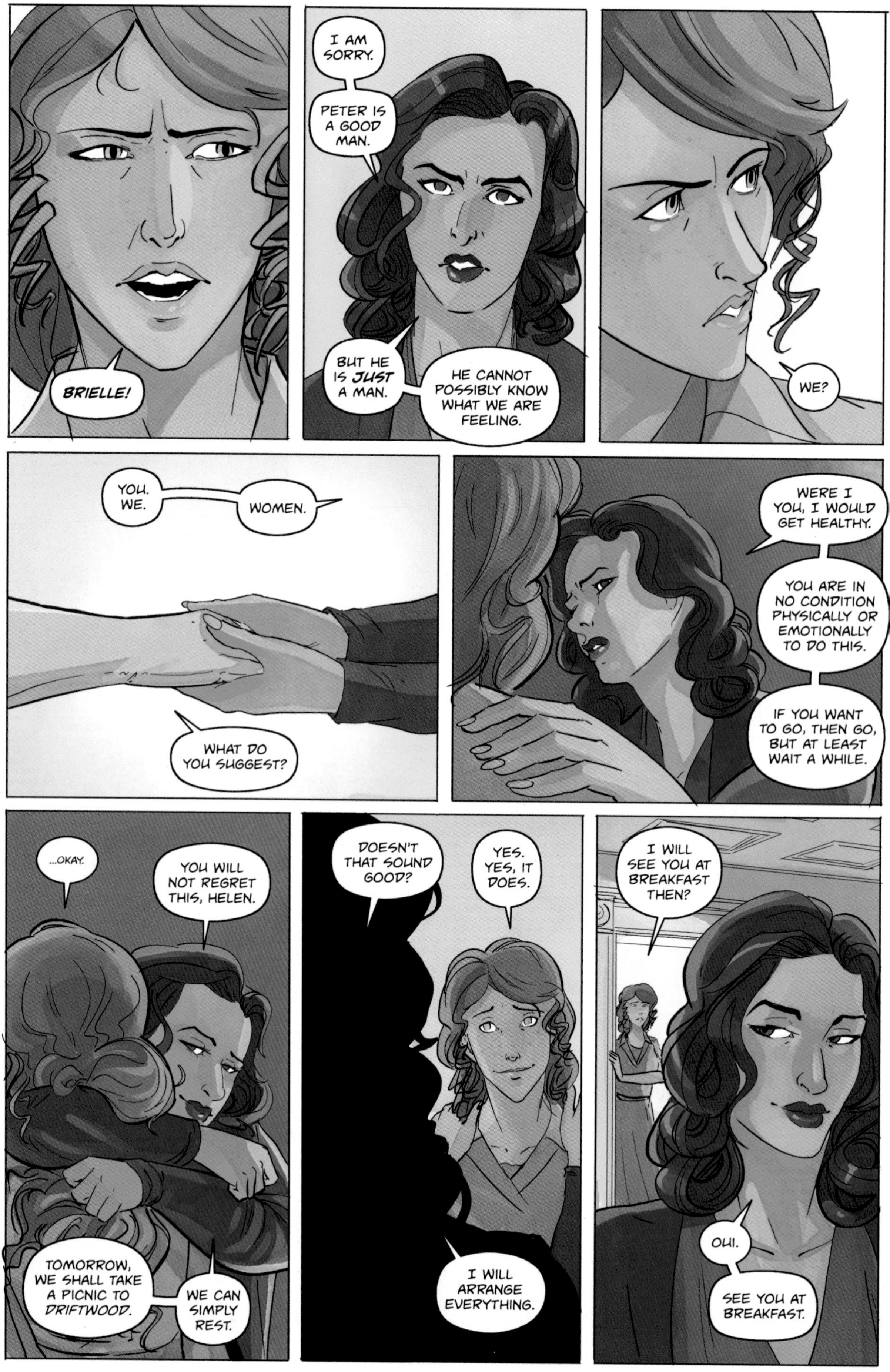
BRIELLE!
I AM SORRY.
PETER IS A GOOD MAN.
BUT HE IS *JUST* A MAN.
HE CANNOT POSSIBLY KNOW WHAT WE ARE FEELING.
WE?
YOU. WE.
WOMEN.
WHAT DO YOU SUGGEST?
WERE I YOU, I WOULD GET HEALTHY.
YOU ARE IN NO CONDITION PHYSICALLY OR EMOTIONALLY TO DO THIS.
IF YOU WANT TO GO, THEN GO, BUT AT LEAST WAIT A WHILE.
...OKAY.
YOU WILL NOT REGRET THIS, HELEN.
TOMORROW, WE SHALL TAKE A PICNIC TO *DRIFTWOOD*.
WE CAN SIMPLY REST.
DOESN'T THAT SOUND GOOD?
YES. YES, IT DOES.
I WILL ARRANGE EVERYTHING.
I WILL SEE YOU AT BREAKFAST THEN?
OUI.
SEE YOU AT BREAKFAST.

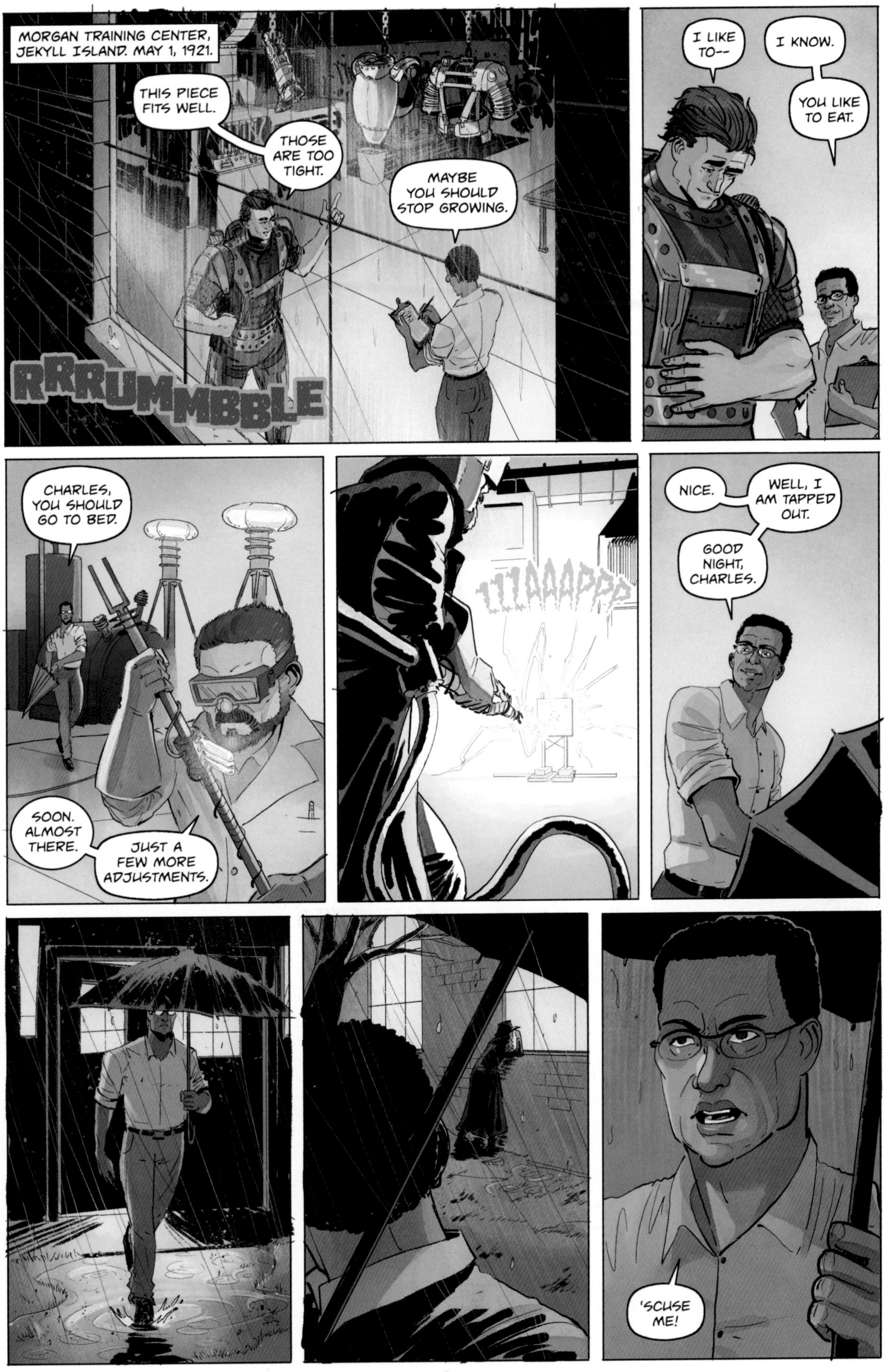
MORGAN TRAINING CENTER, JEKYLL ISLAND. MAY 1, 1921.
THIS PIECE FITS WELL.
THOSE ARE TOO TIGHT.
MAYBE YOU SHOULD STOP GROWING.
RRRUMMBBLE
I LIKE TO--
I KNOW.
YOU LIKE TO EAT.
CHARLES, YOU SHOULD GO TO BED.
SOON. ALMOST THERE.
JUST A FEW MORE ADJUSTMENTS.
ZZZAAAPPP
NICE.
WELL, I AM TAPPED OUT.
GOOD NIGHT, CHARLES.
'SCUSE ME!

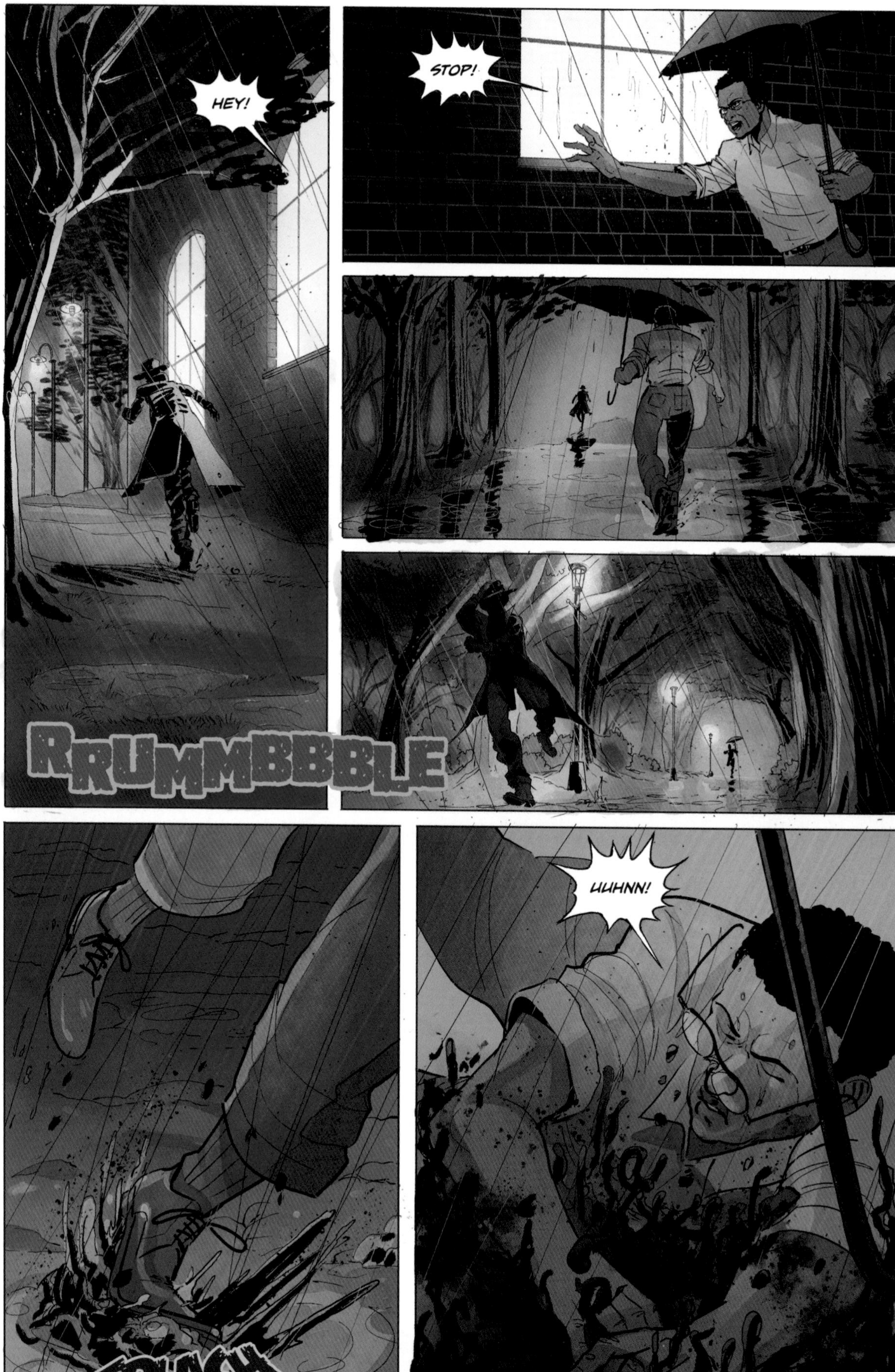
HEY!
STOP!
RRUMMBBBLE
SPLASH
UUHNN!

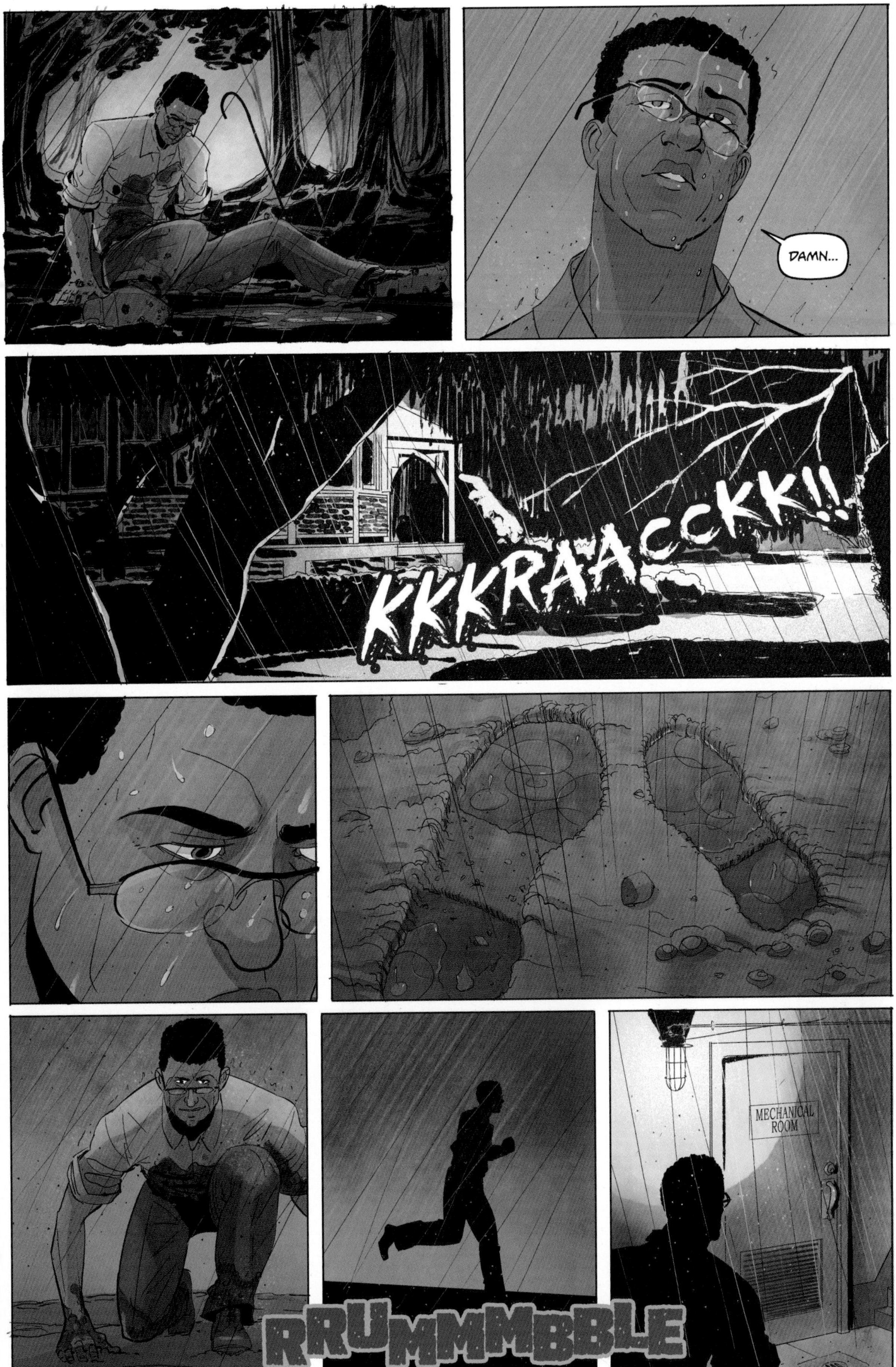
DAMN...
KKKRAACCKK!!
MECHANICAL ROOM
RRUMMMBBLE

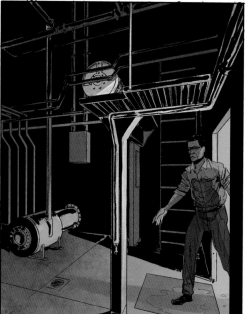

SUITE
2.416

FSSST

I HAVE
YOU...

YOU TWO
COME WITH
ME!

QUICKLY!

VERY
QUICKLY!

WHI   UMMP

CLICK!

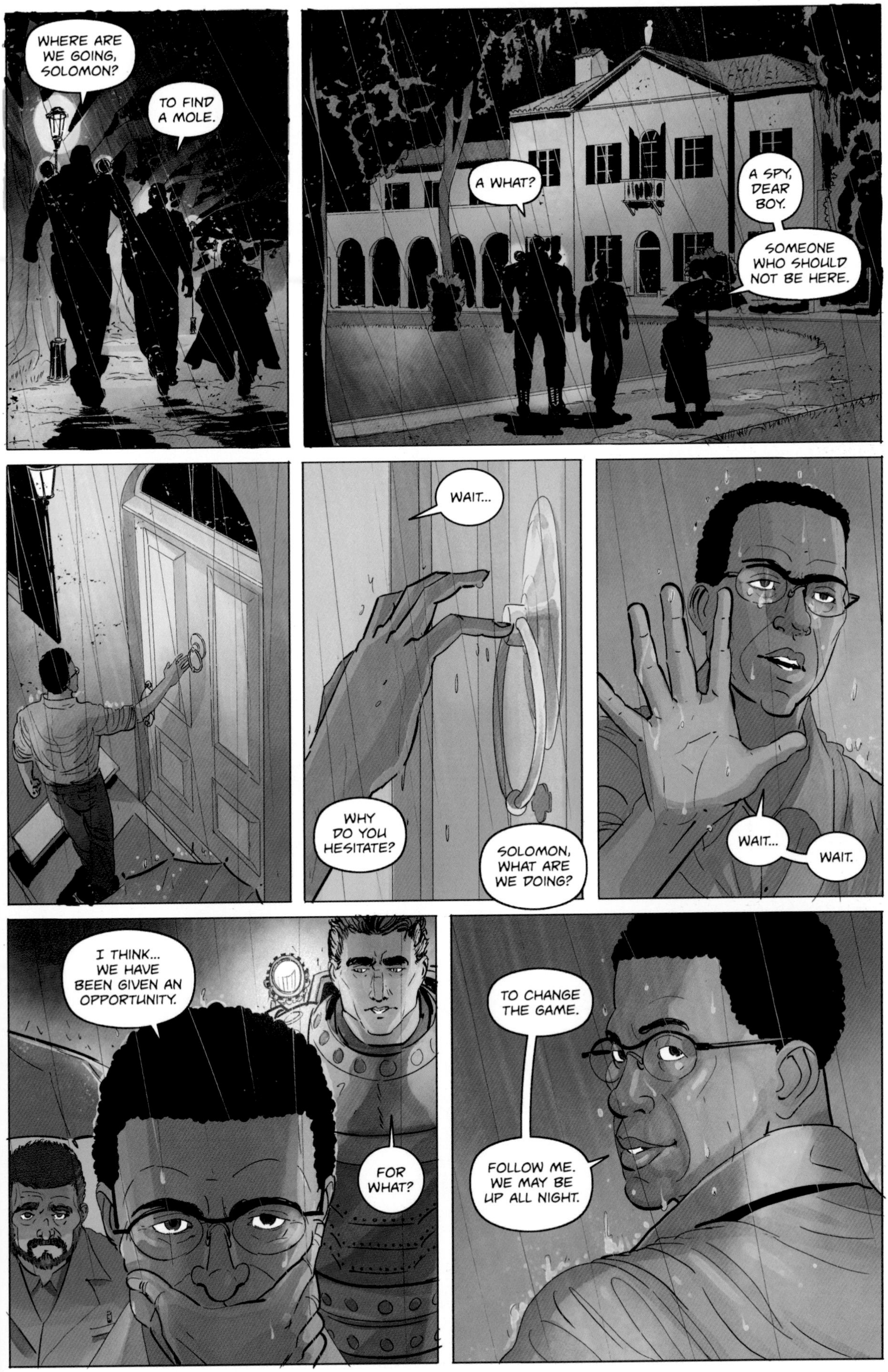
WHERE ARE WE GOING, SOLOMON?
TO FIND A MOLE.
A WHAT?
A SPY, DEAR BOY.
SOMEONE WHO SHOULD NOT BE HERE.
WAIT...
WHY DO YOU HESITATE?
SOLOMON, WHAT ARE WE DOING?
WAIT...
WAIT.
I THINK... WE HAVE BEEN GIVEN AN OPPORTUNITY.
FOR WHAT?
TO CHANGE THE GAME.
FOLLOW ME. WE MAY BE UP ALL NIGHT.

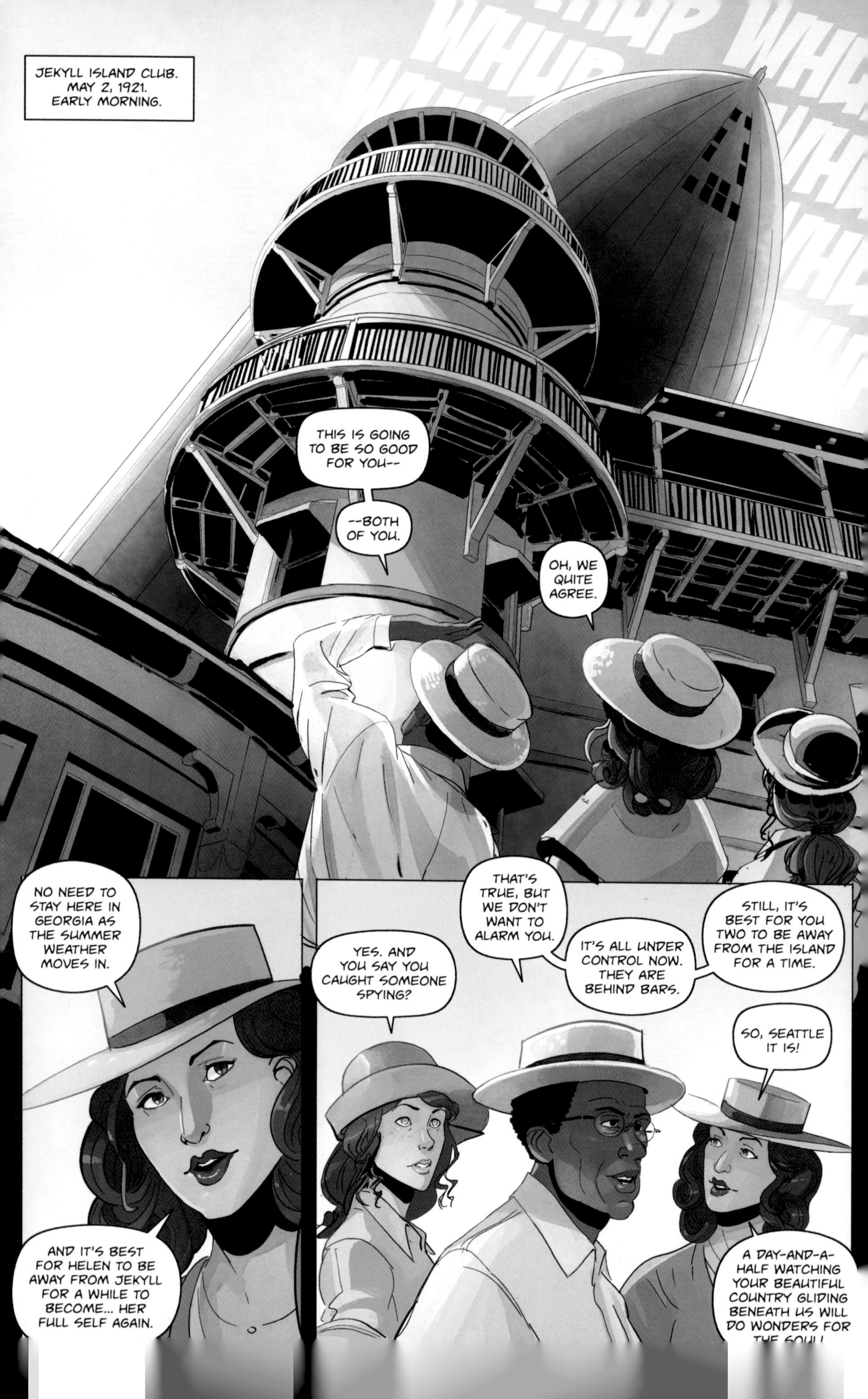
WHUP WHUP WHUP
JEKYLL ISLAND CLUB. MAY 2, 1921. EARLY MORNING.
THIS IS GOING TO BE SO GOOD FOR YOU--
--BOTH OF YOU.
OH, WE QUITE AGREE.
NO NEED TO STAY HERE IN GEORGIA AS THE SUMMER WEATHER MOVES IN.
AND IT'S BEST FOR HELEN TO BE AWAY FROM JEKYLL FOR A WHILE TO BECOME... HER FULL SELF AGAIN.
YES. AND YOU SAY YOU CAUGHT SOMEONE SPYING?
THAT'S TRUE, BUT WE DON'T WANT TO ALARM YOU.
IT'S ALL UNDER CONTROL NOW. THEY ARE BEHIND BARS.
STILL, IT'S BEST FOR YOU TWO TO BE AWAY FROM THE ISLAND FOR A TIME.
SO, SEATTLE IT IS!
A DAY-AND-A-HALF WATCHING YOUR BEAUTIFUL COUNTRY GLIDING BENEATH US WILL DO WONDERS FOR

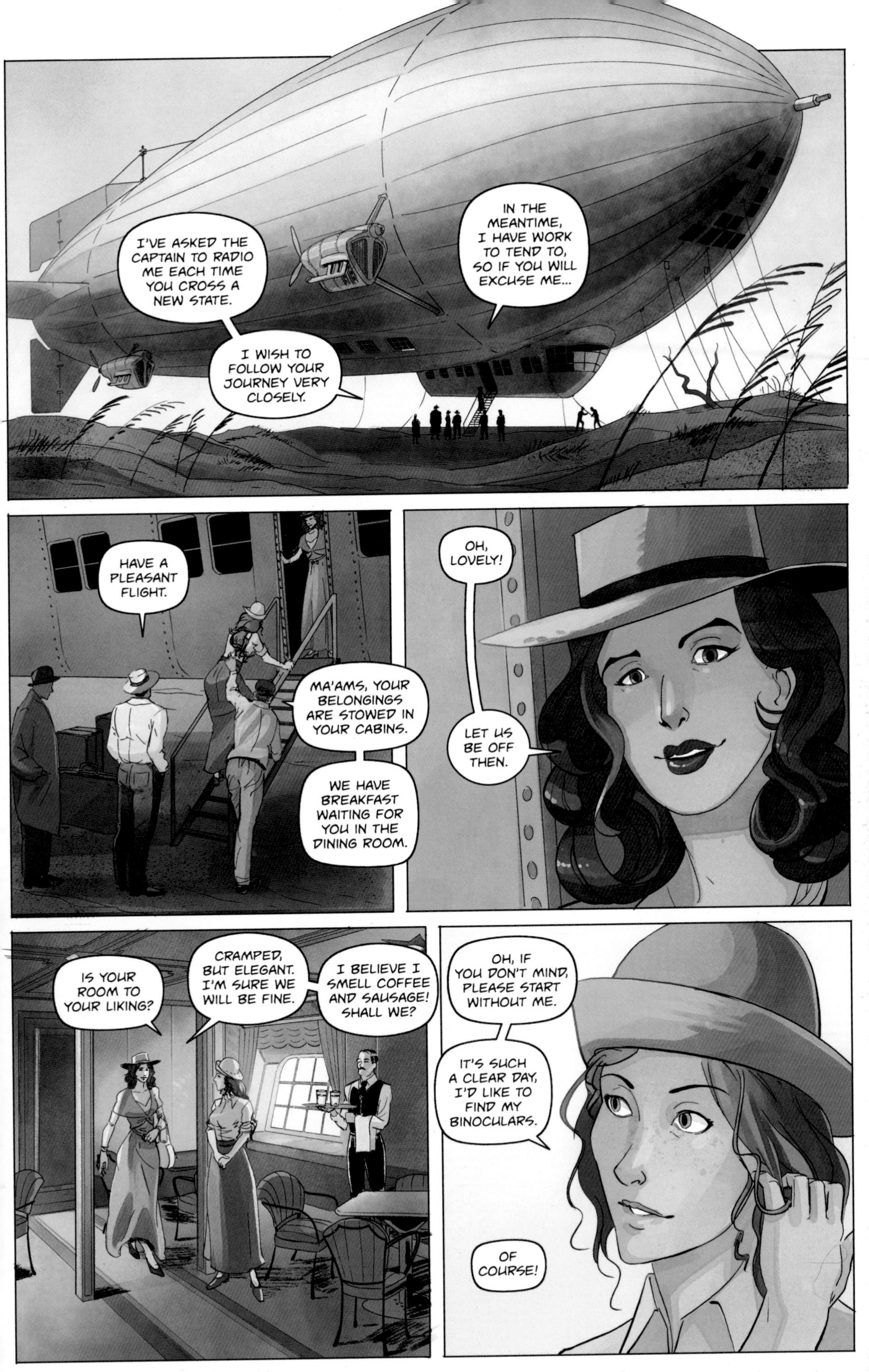

I'VE ASKED THE CAPTAIN TO RADIO ME EACH TIME YOU CROSS A NEW STATE.
I WISH TO FOLLOW YOUR JOURNEY VERY CLOSELY.
IN THE MEANTIME, I HAVE WORK TO TEND TO, SO IF YOU WILL EXCUSE ME...
HAVE A PLEASANT FLIGHT.
MA'AMS, YOUR BELONGINGS ARE STOWED IN YOUR CABINS.
WE HAVE BREAKFAST WAITING FOR YOU IN THE DINING ROOM.
OH, LOVELY!
LET US BE OFF THEN.
IS YOUR ROOM TO YOUR LIKING?
CRAMPED, BUT ELEGANT. I'M SURE WE WILL BE FINE.
I BELIEVE I SMELL COFFEE AND SAUSAGE! SHALL WE?
OH, IF YOU DON'T MIND, PLEASE START WITHOUT ME.
IT'S SUCH A CLEAR DAY, I'D LIKE TO FIND MY BINOCULARS.
OF COURSE!

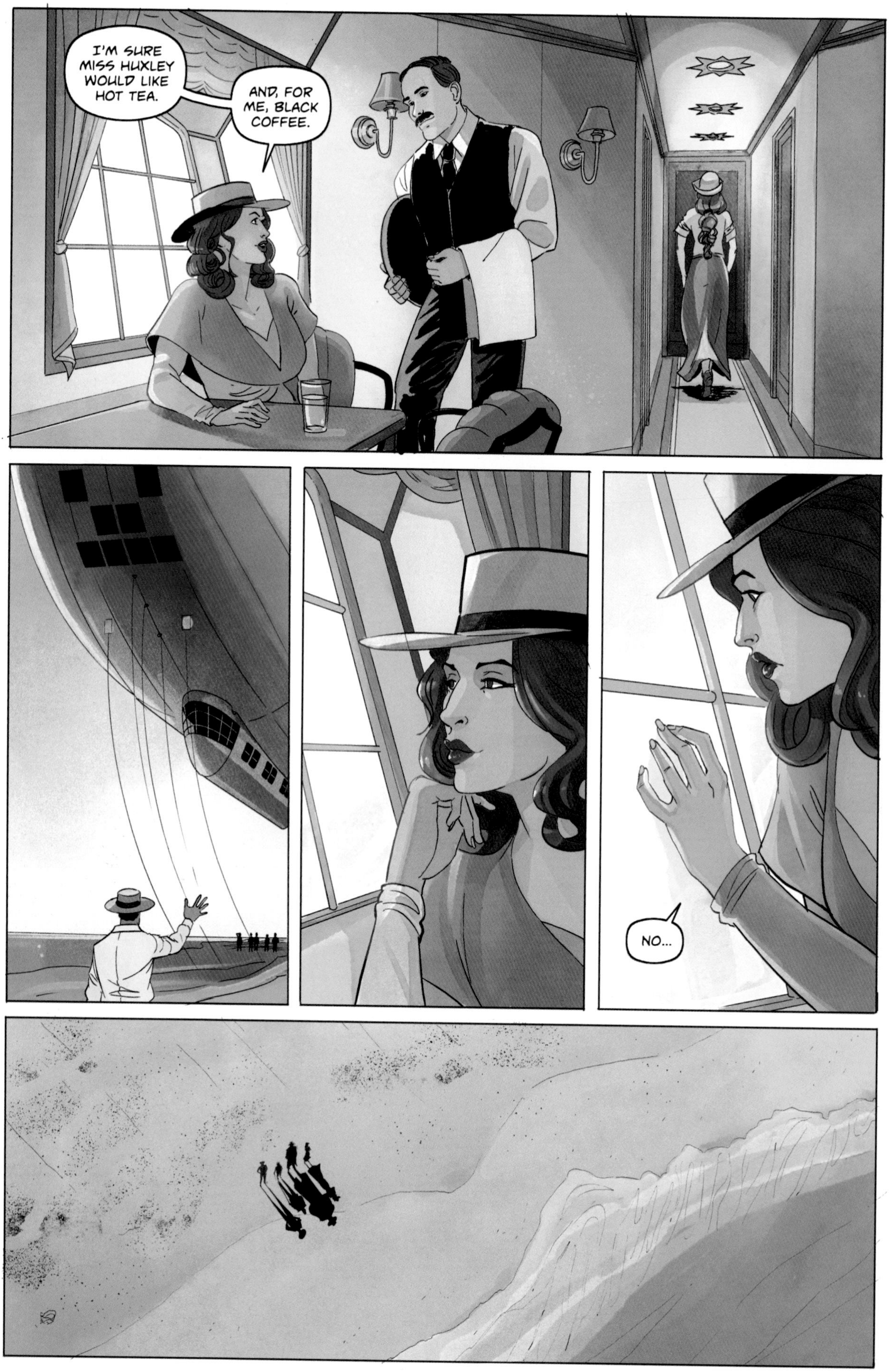
I'M SURE MISS HUXLEY WOULD LIKE HOT TEA.
AND, FOR ME, BLACK COFFEE.
NO...

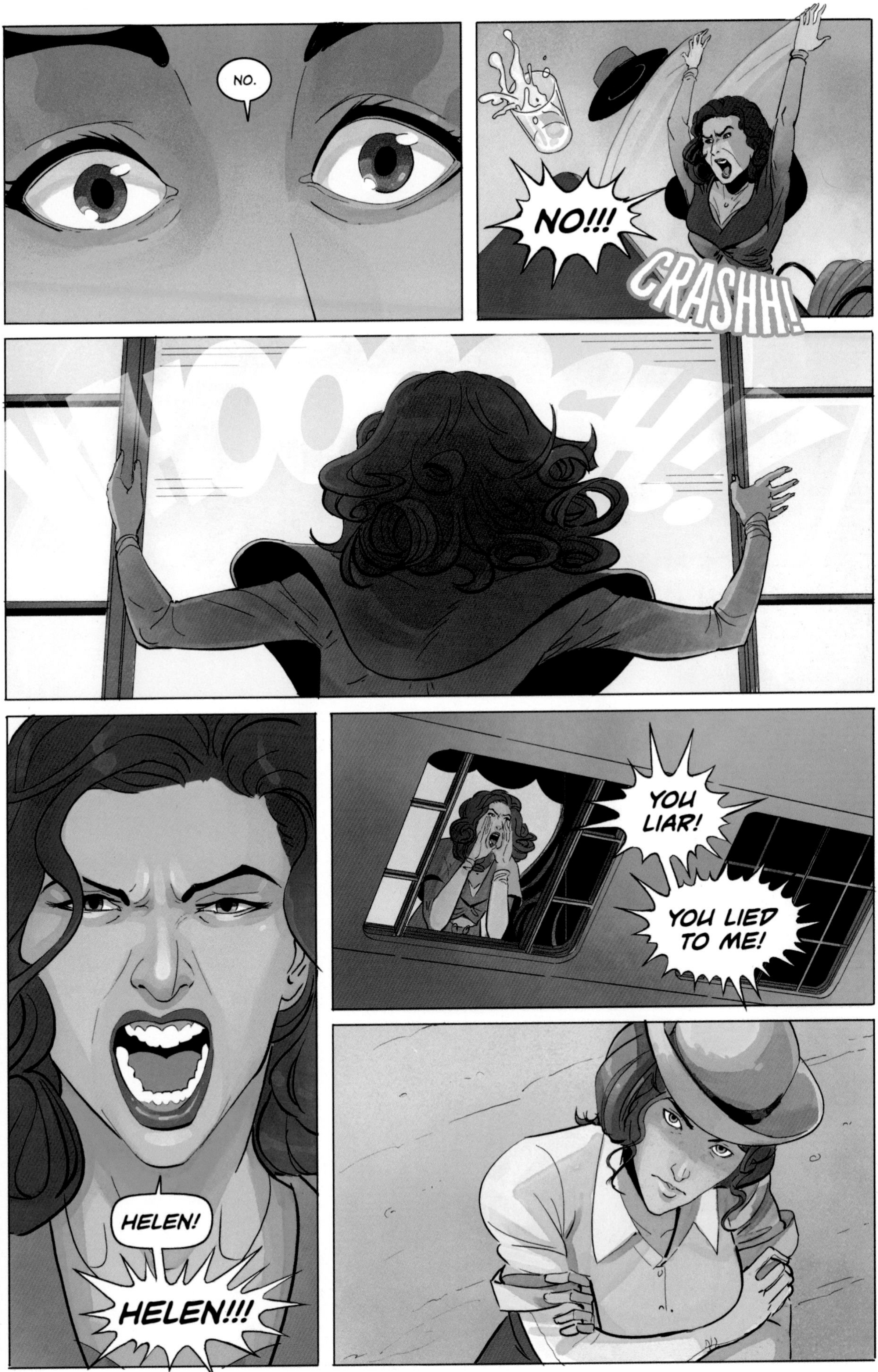
NO.
NO!!!
CRASHH!
WHOOOSH!
HELEN!
HELEN!!!
YOU LIAR!
YOU LIED TO ME!

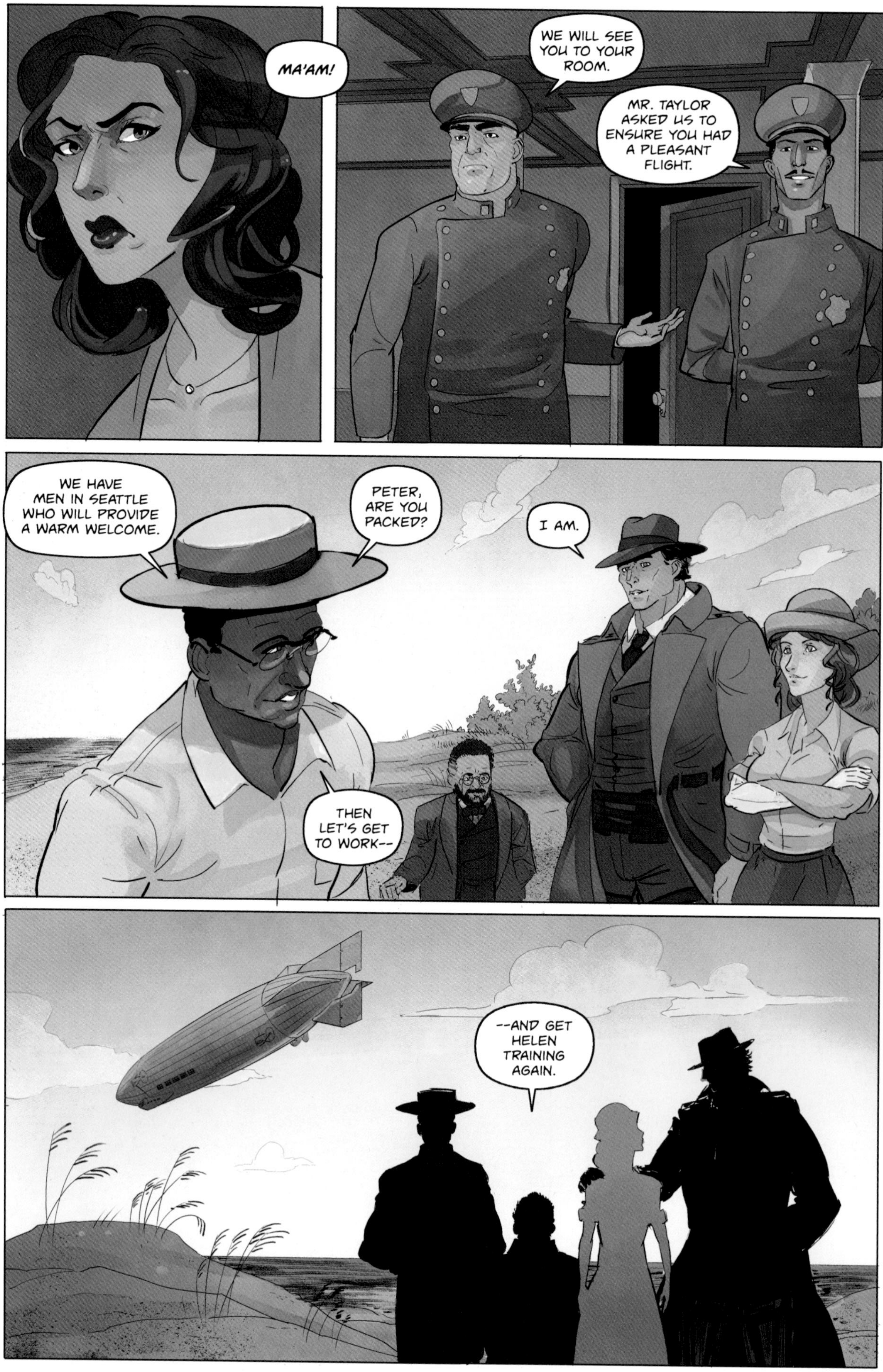
MA'AM!
WE WILL SEE YOU TO YOUR ROOM.
MR. TAYLOR ASKED US TO ENSURE YOU HAD A PLEASANT FLIGHT.
WE HAVE MEN IN SEATTLE WHO WILL PROVIDE A WARM WELCOME.
PETER, ARE YOU PACKED?
I AM.
THEN LET'S GET TO WORK--
--AND GET HELEN TRAINING AGAIN.

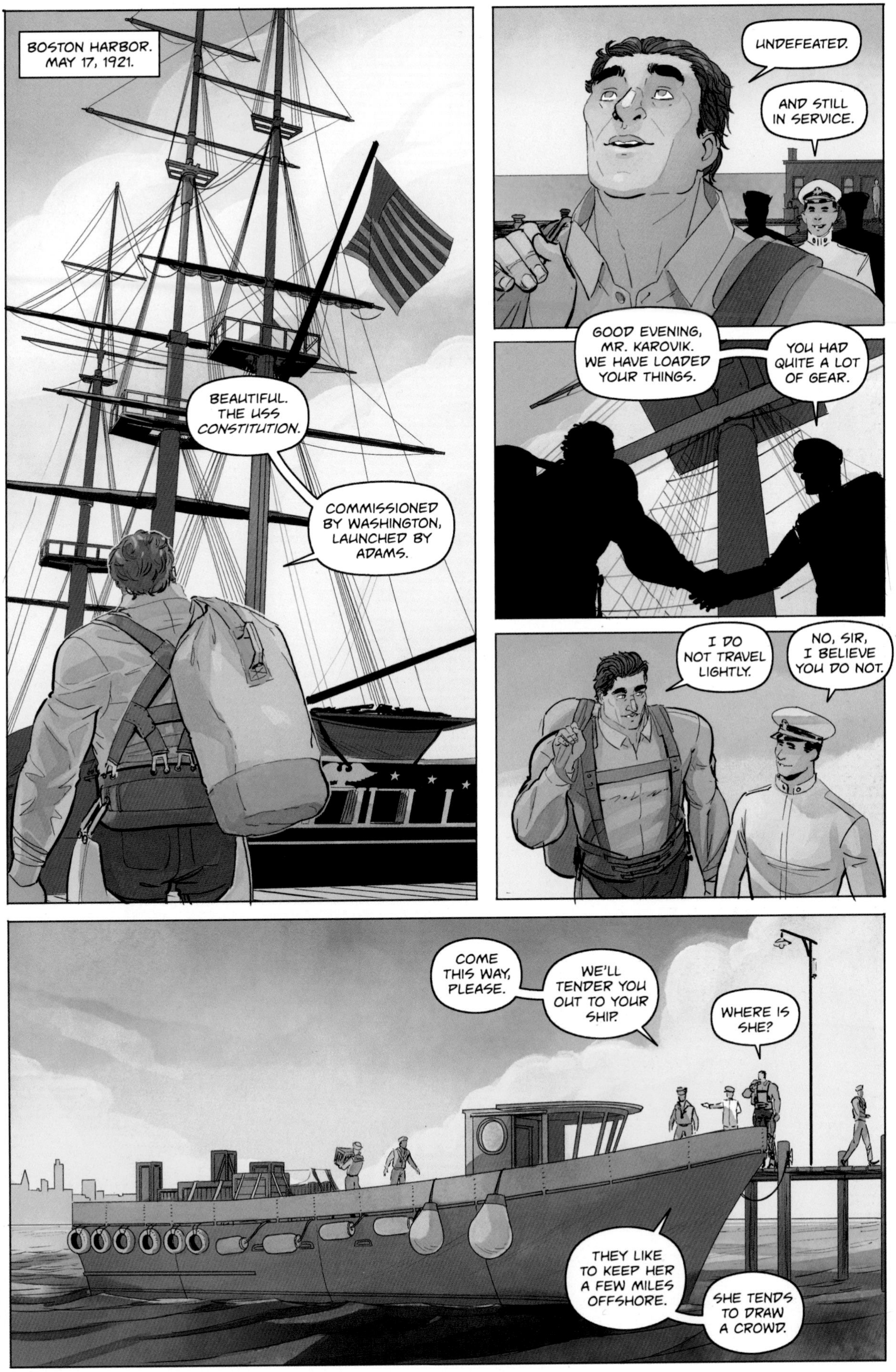
BOSTON HARBOR.
MAY 17, 1921.
BEAUTIFUL. THE USS CONSTITUTION.
COMMISSIONED BY WASHINGTON, LAUNCHED BY ADAMS.
UNDEFEATED.
AND STILL IN SERVICE.
GOOD EVENING, MR. KAROVIK. WE HAVE LOADED YOUR THINGS.
YOU HAD QUITE A LOT OF GEAR.
I DO NOT TRAVEL LIGHTLY.
NO, SIR, I BELIEVE YOU DO NOT.
COME THIS WAY, PLEASE.
WE'LL TENDER YOU OUT TO YOUR SHIP.
WHERE IS SHE?
THEY LIKE TO KEEP HER A FEW MILES OFFSHORE.
SHE TENDS TO DRAW A CROWD.

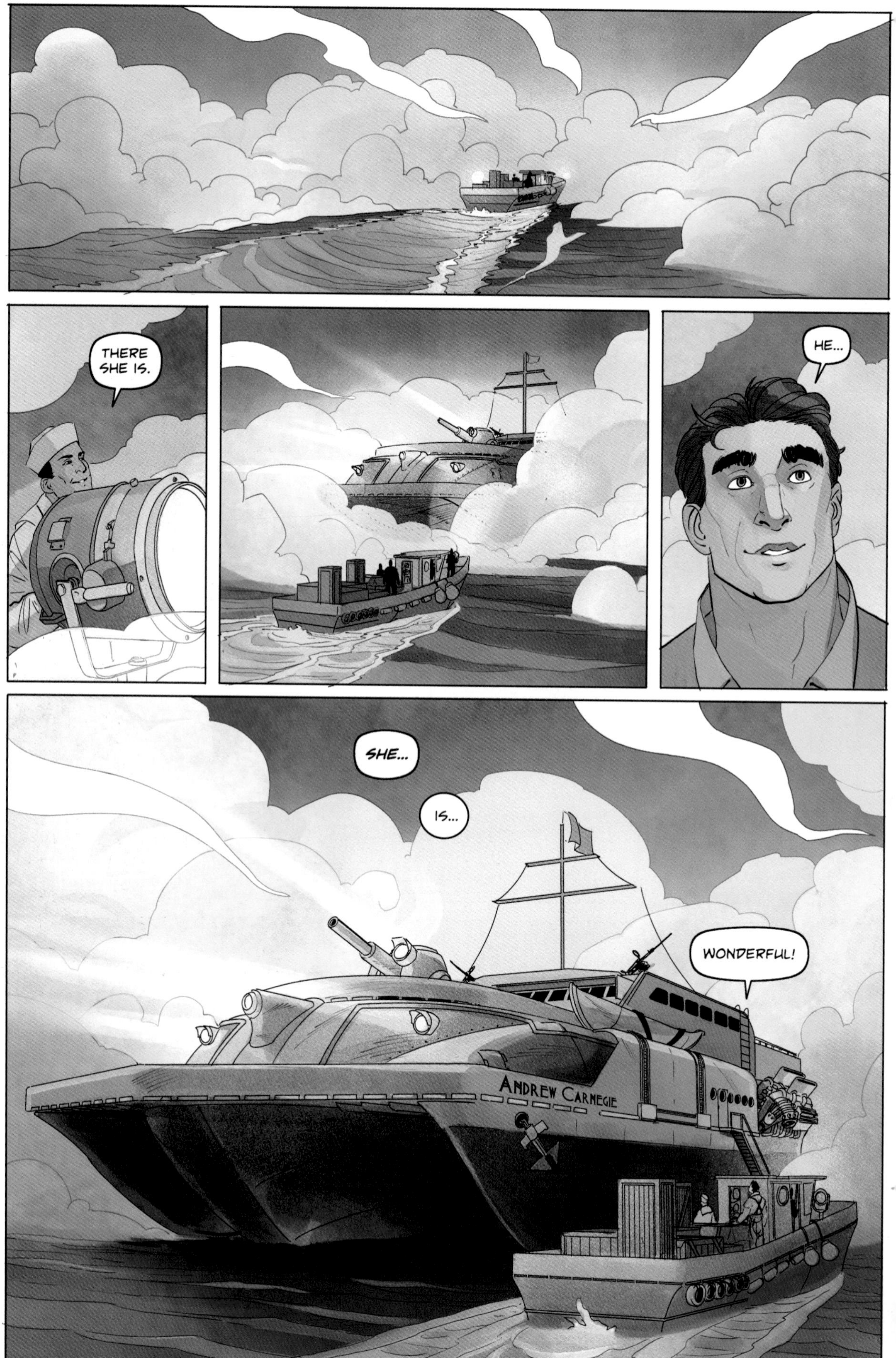
THERE SHE IS.
HE...
SHE...
IS...
WONDERFUL!
ANDREW CARNEGIE

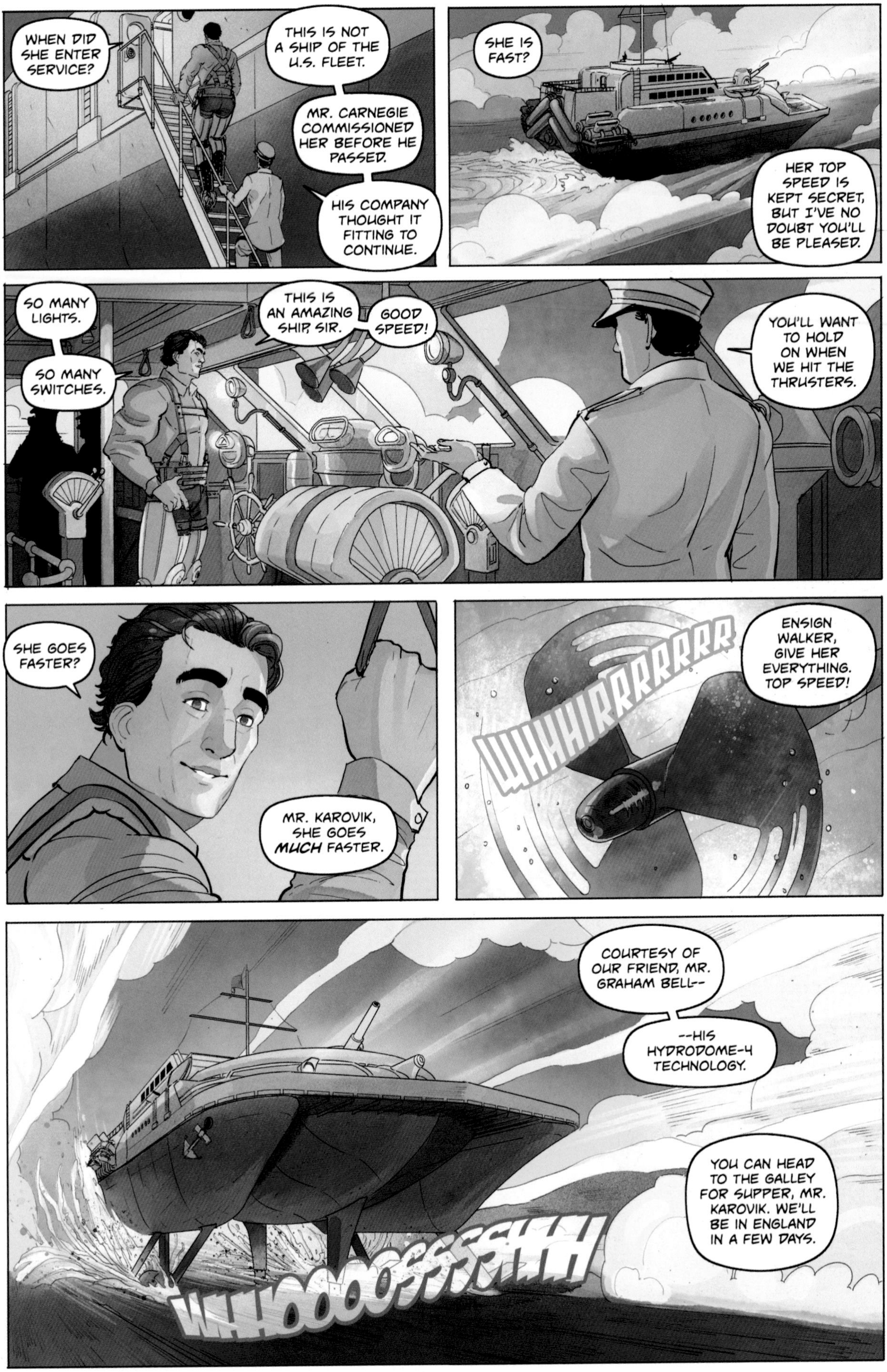
WHEN DID SHE ENTER SERVICE?
THIS IS NOT A SHIP OF THE U.S. FLEET.
MR. CARNEGIE COMMISSIONED HER BEFORE HE PASSED.
HIS COMPANY THOUGHT IT FITTING TO CONTINUE.
SHE IS FAST?
HER TOP SPEED IS KEPT SECRET, BUT I'VE NO DOUBT YOU'LL BE PLEASED.
SO MANY LIGHTS.
SO MANY SWITCHES.
THIS IS AN AMAZING SHIP, SIR.
GOOD SPEED!
YOU'LL WANT TO HOLD ON WHEN WE HIT THE THRUSTERS.
SHE GOES FASTER?
MR. KAROVIK, SHE GOES MUCH FASTER.
ENSIGN WALKER, GIVE HER EVERYTHING. TOP SPEED!
WHHHIRRRRRRR
COURTESY OF OUR FRIEND, MR. GRAHAM BELL--
--HIS HYDRODOME-4 TECHNOLOGY.
YOU CAN HEAD TO THE GALLEY FOR SUPPER, MR. KAROVIK. WE'LL BE IN ENGLAND IN A FEW DAYS.
WHHOOOOSSSSHHH

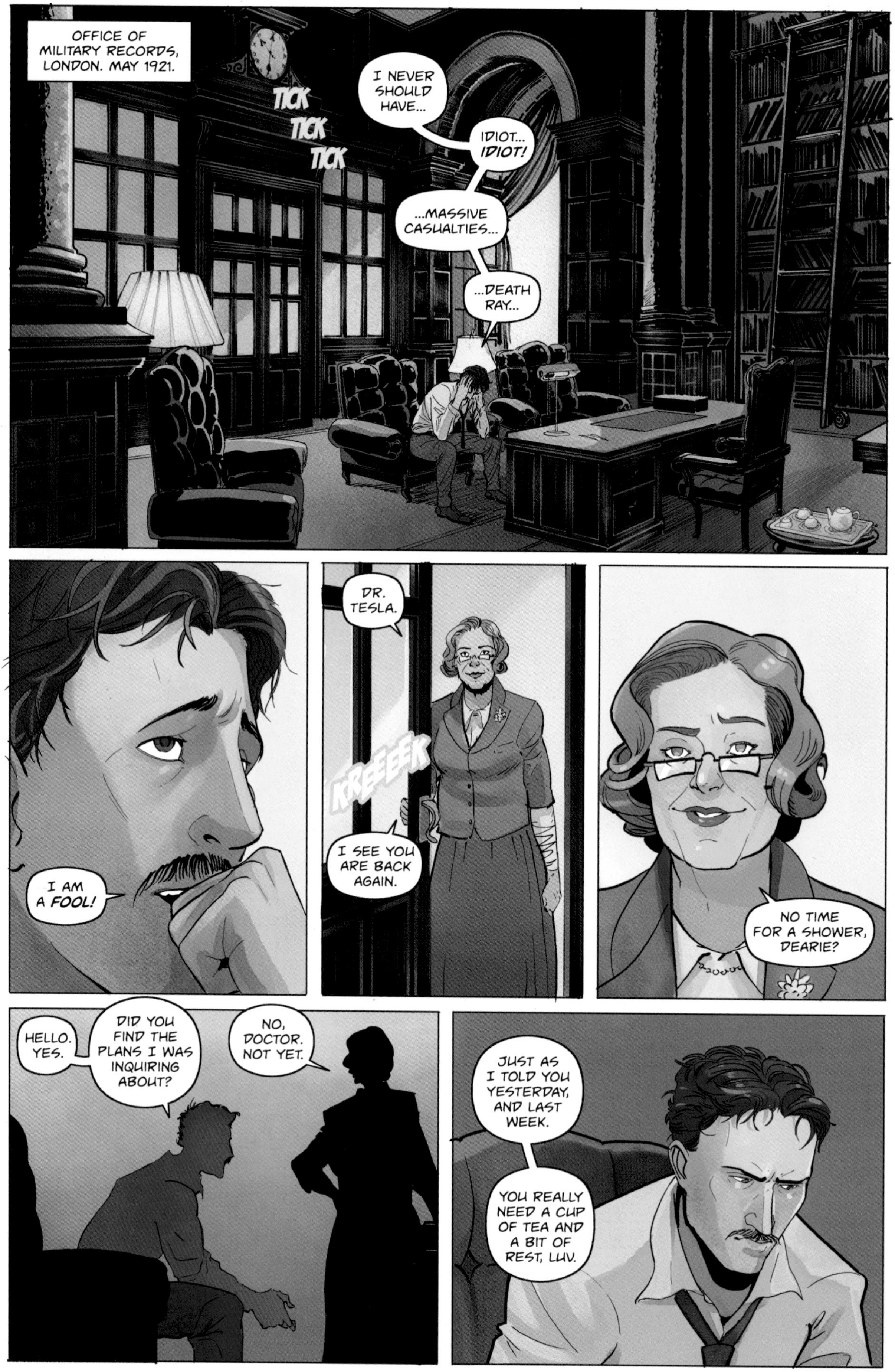
OFFICE OF MILITARY RECORDS, LONDON. MAY 1921.
TICK TICK TICK
I NEVER SHOULD HAVE...
IDIOT... IDIOT!
...MASSIVE CASUALTIES...
...DEATH RAY...
I AM A FOOL!
DR. TESLA.
KREEEEK
I SEE YOU ARE BACK AGAIN.
NO TIME FOR A SHOWER, DEARIE?
HELLO. YES.
DID YOU FIND THE PLANS I WAS INQUIRING ABOUT?
NO, DOCTOR. NOT YET.
JUST AS I TOLD YOU YESTERDAY, AND LAST WEEK.
YOU REALLY NEED A CUP OF TEA AND A BIT OF REST, LUV.

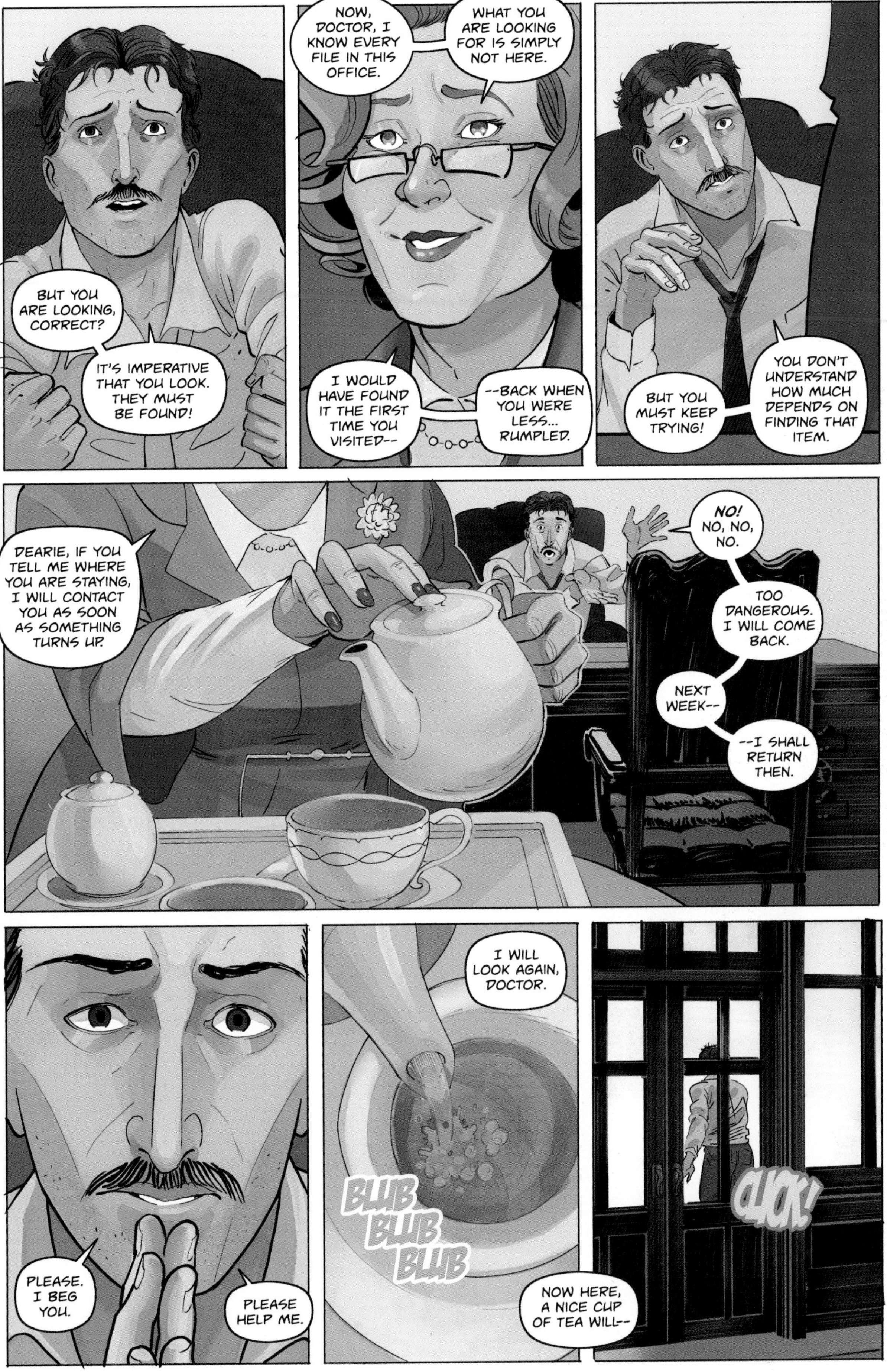
BUT YOU ARE LOOKING, CORRECT?
IT'S IMPERATIVE THAT YOU LOOK. THEY MUST BE FOUND!
NOW, DOCTOR, I KNOW EVERY FILE IN THIS OFFICE.
WHAT YOU ARE LOOKING FOR IS SIMPLY NOT HERE.
I WOULD HAVE FOUND IT THE FIRST TIME YOU VISITED--
--BACK WHEN YOU WERE LESS... RUMPLED.
BUT YOU MUST KEEP TRYING!
YOU DON'T UNDERSTAND HOW MUCH DEPENDS ON FINDING THAT ITEM.
DEARIE, IF YOU TELL ME WHERE YOU ARE STAYING, I WILL CONTACT YOU AS SOON AS SOMETHING TURNS UP.
NO! NO, NO, NO.
TOO DANGEROUS. I WILL COME BACK.
NEXT WEEK--
--I SHALL RETURN THEN.
PLEASE. I BEG YOU.
PLEASE HELP ME.
I WILL LOOK AGAIN, DOCTOR.
BLUB BLUB BLUB
NOW HERE, A NICE CUP OF TEA WILL--
CLICK!

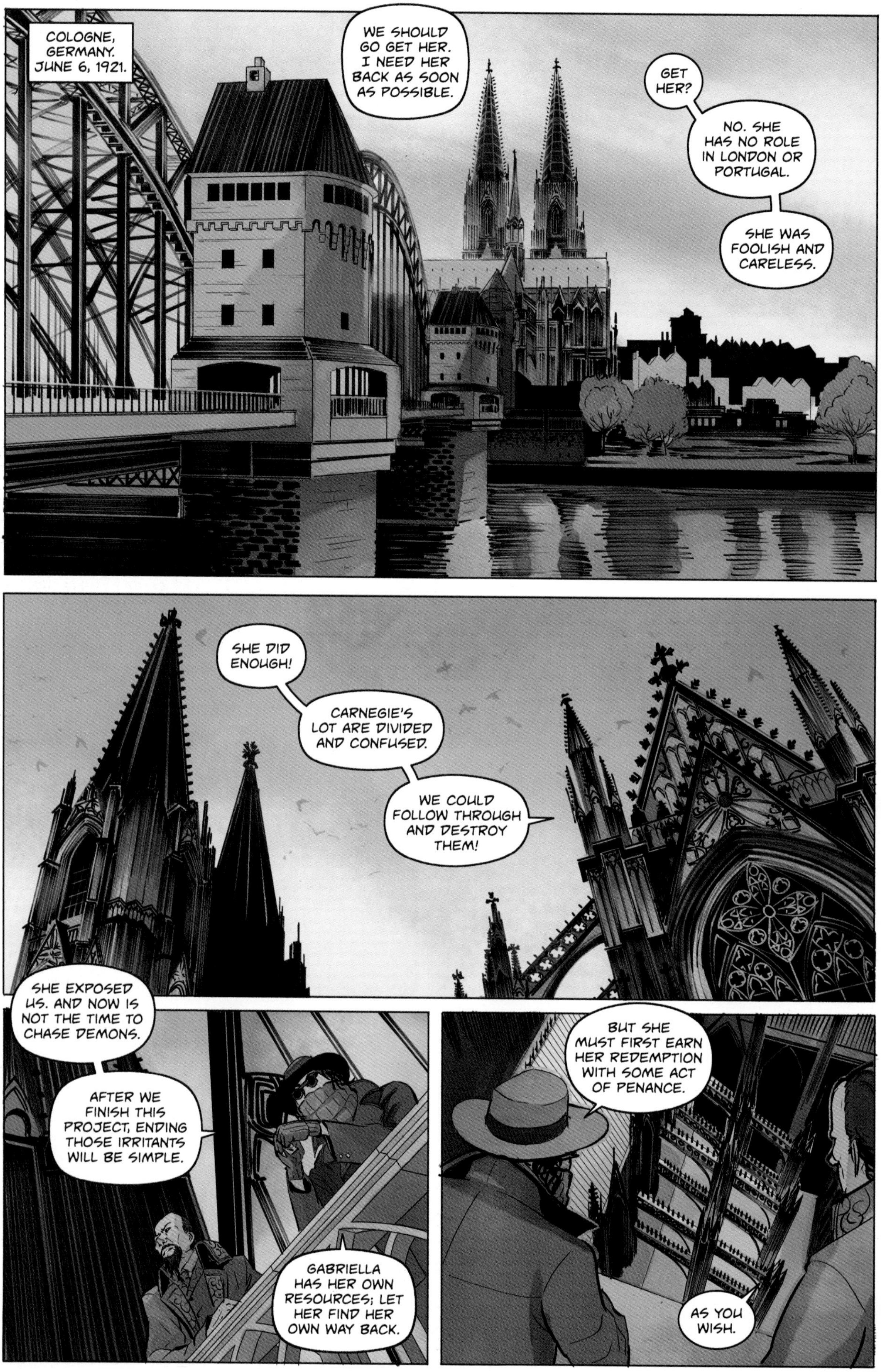
COLOGNE, GERMANY. JUNE 6, 1921.
WE SHOULD GO GET HER. I NEED HER BACK AS SOON AS POSSIBLE.
GET HER?
NO. SHE HAS NO ROLE IN LONDON OR PORTUGAL.
SHE WAS FOOLISH AND CARELESS.
SHE DID ENOUGH!
CARNEGIE'S LOT ARE DIVIDED AND CONFUSED.
WE COULD FOLLOW THROUGH AND DESTROY THEM!
SHE EXPOSED US. AND NOW IS NOT THE TIME TO CHASE DEMONS.
AFTER WE FINISH THIS PROJECT, ENDING THOSE IRRITANTS WILL BE SIMPLE.
GABRIELLA HAS HER OWN RESOURCES; LET HER FIND HER OWN WAY BACK.
BUT SHE MUST FIRST EARN HER REDEMPTION WITH SOME ACT OF PENANCE.
AS YOU WISH.

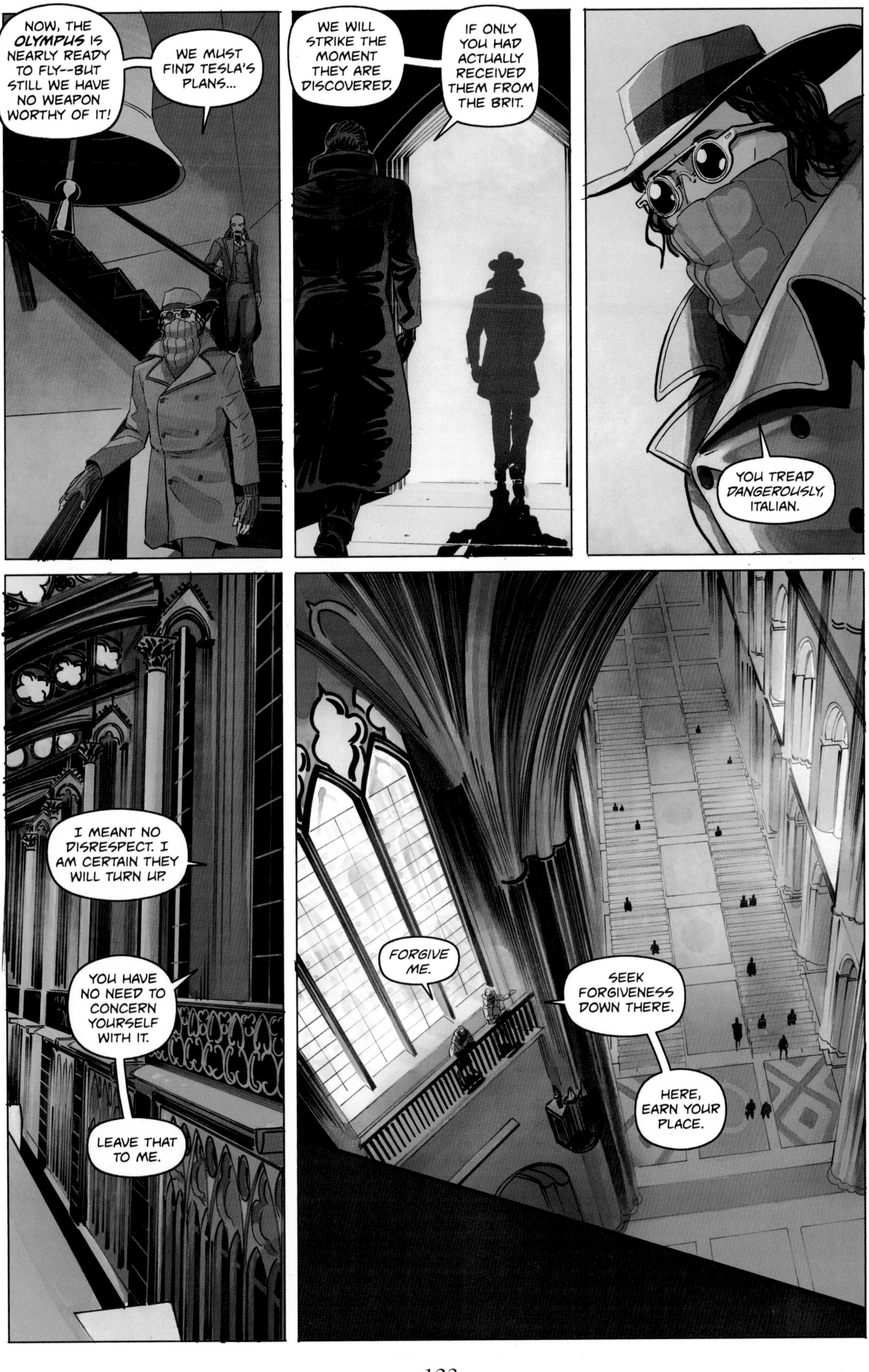

NOW, THE *OLYMPUS* IS NEARLY READY TO FLY--BUT STILL WE HAVE NO WEAPON WORTHY OF IT!
WE MUST FIND TESLA'S PLANS...
WE WILL STRIKE THE MOMENT THEY ARE DISCOVERED.
IF ONLY YOU HAD ACTUALLY RECEIVED THEM FROM THE BRIT.
YOU TREAD *DANGEROUSLY,* ITALIAN.
I MEANT NO DISRESPECT. I AM CERTAIN THEY WILL TURN UP.
YOU HAVE NO NEED TO CONCERN YOURSELF WITH IT.
LEAVE THAT TO ME.
*FORGIVE ME.*
SEEK FORGIVENESS DOWN THERE.
HERE, EARN YOUR PLACE.

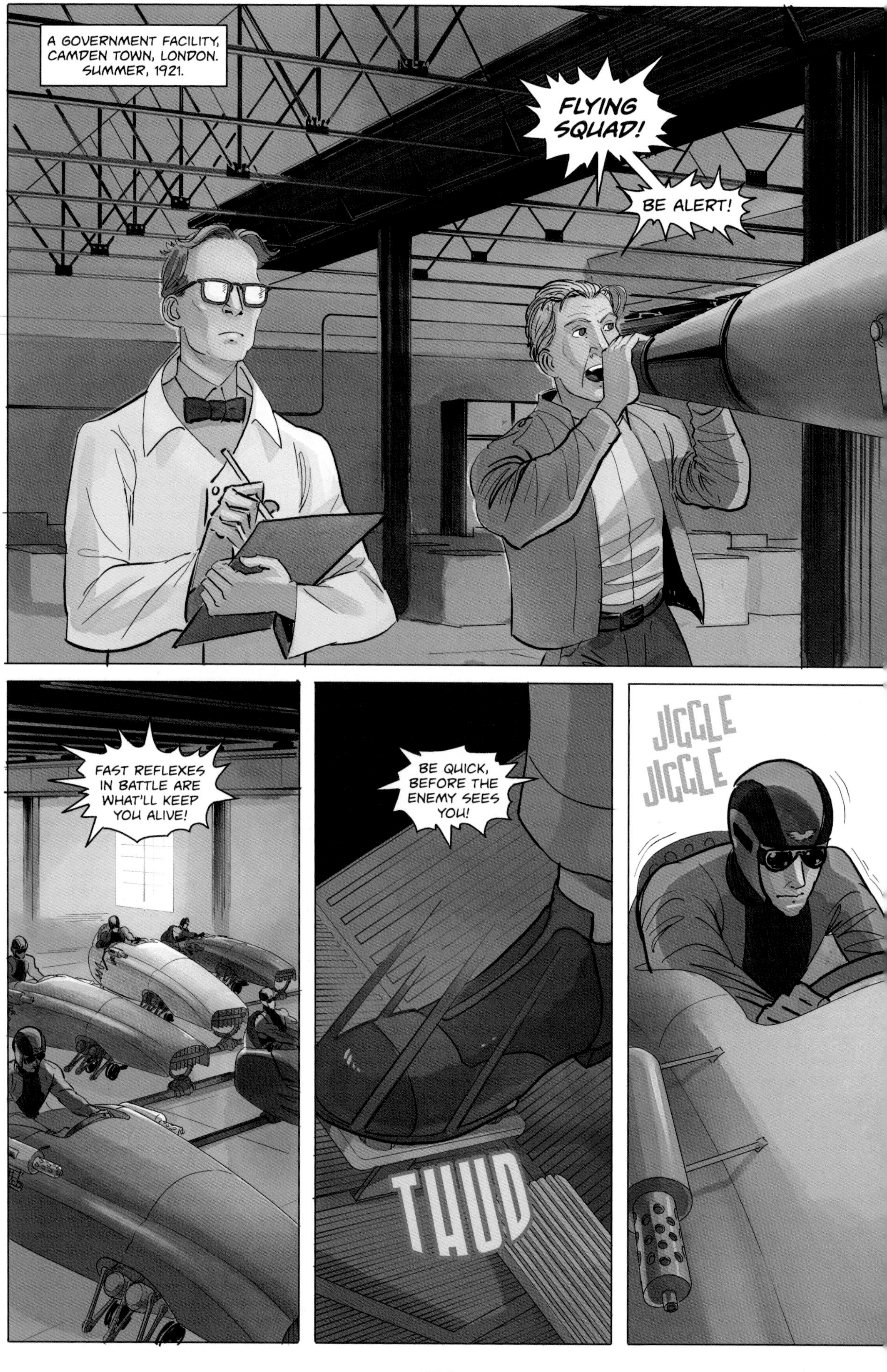
A GOVERNMENT FACILITY, CAMDEN TOWN, LONDON. SUMMER, 1921.
FLYING SQUAD!
BE ALERT!
FAST REFLEXES IN BATTLE ARE WHAT'LL KEEP YOU ALIVE!
BE QUICK, BEFORE THE ENEMY SEES YOU!
THUD
JIGGLE JIGGLE

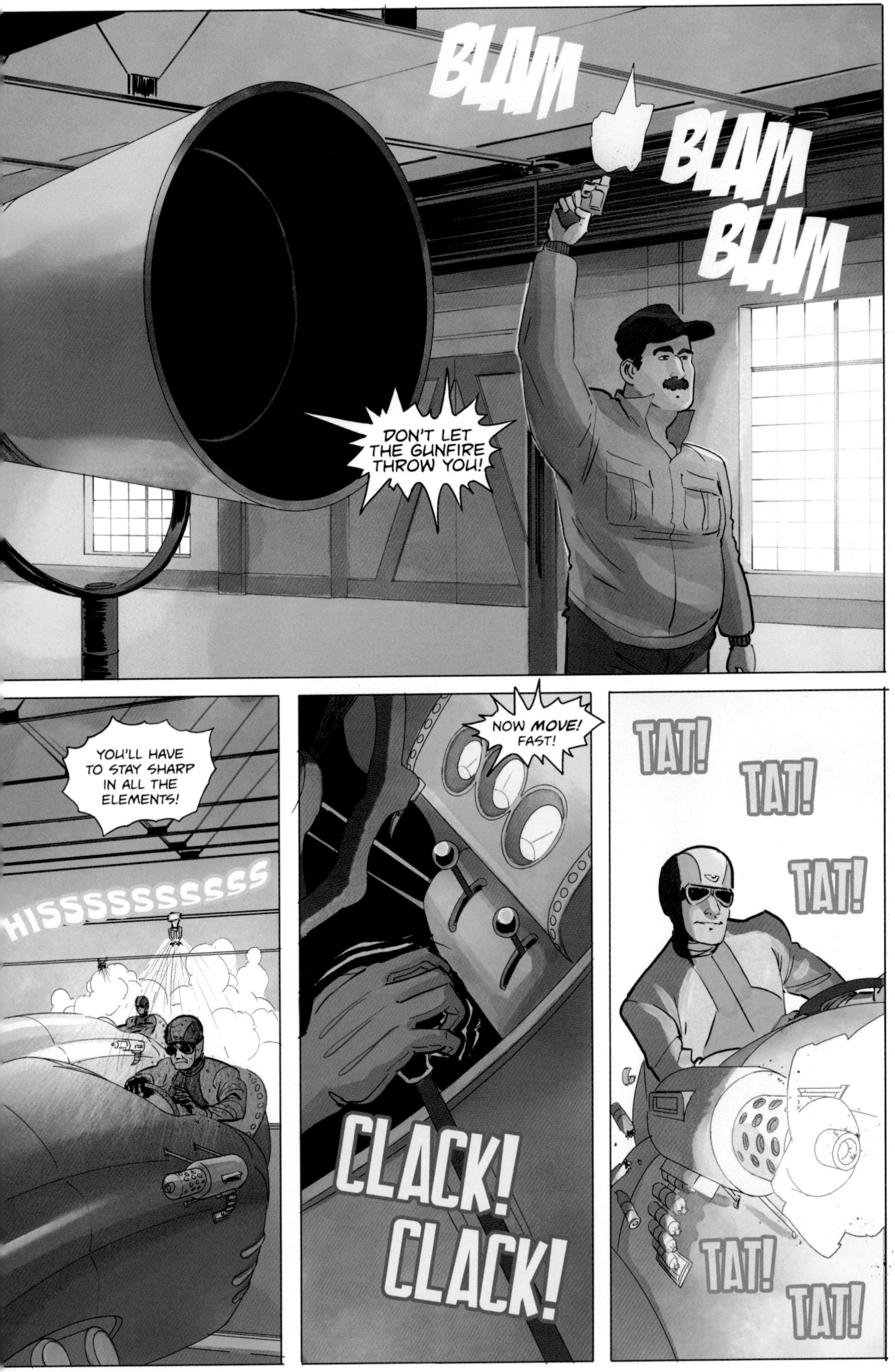
BLAM
BLAM
BLAM
DON'T LET THE GUNFIRE THROW YOU!
YOU'LL HAVE TO STAY SHARP IN ALL THE ELEMENTS!
HISSSSSSSSSS
NOW MOVE! FAST!
CLACK!
CLACK!
TAT!
TAT!
TAT!
TAT!
TAT!

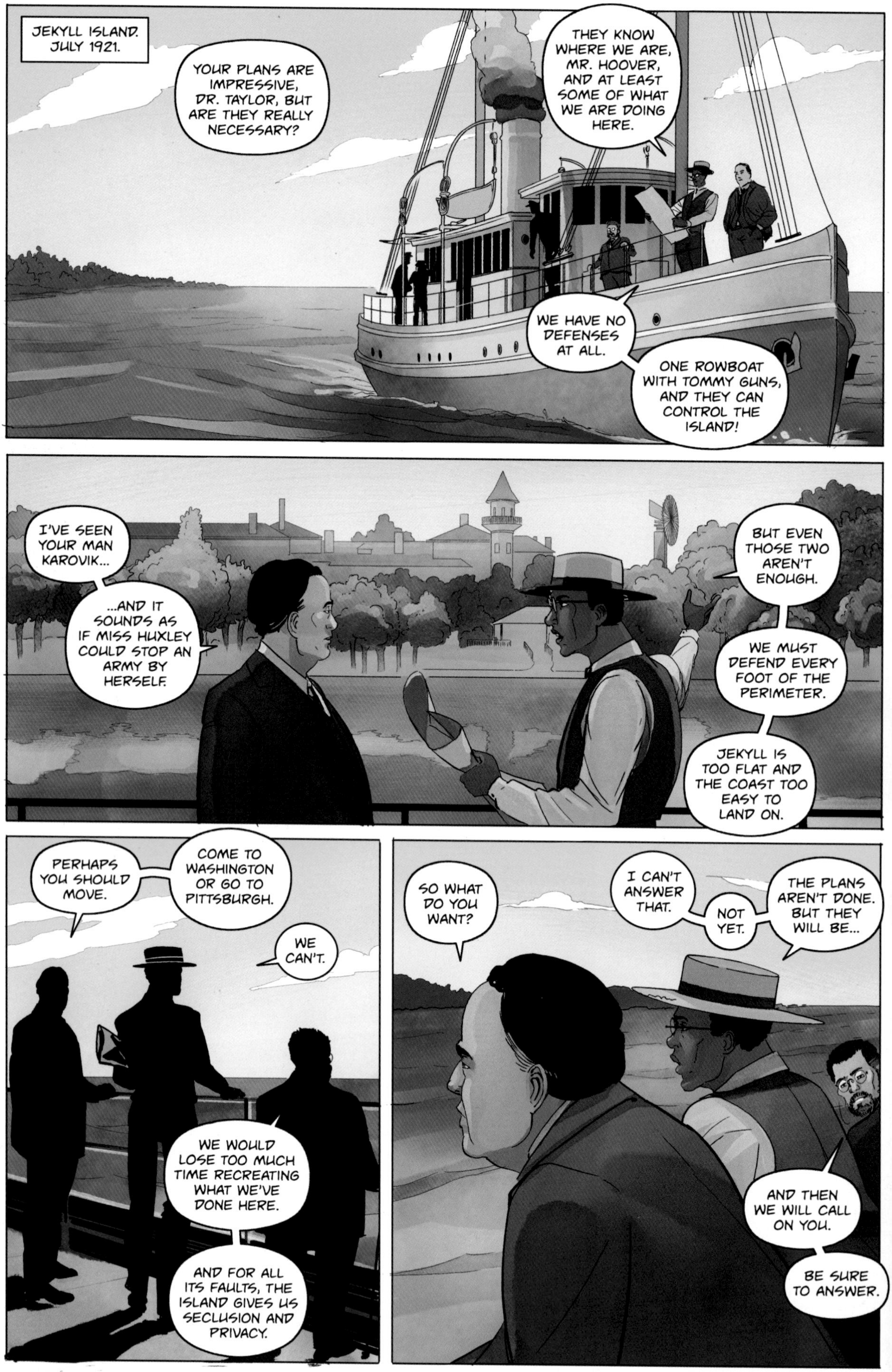
JEKYLL ISLAND. JULY 1921.
YOUR PLANS ARE IMPRESSIVE, DR. TAYLOR, BUT ARE THEY REALLY NECESSARY?
THEY KNOW WHERE WE ARE, MR. HOOVER, AND AT LEAST SOME OF WHAT WE ARE DOING HERE.
WE HAVE NO DEFENSES AT ALL.
ONE ROWBOAT WITH TOMMY GUNS, AND THEY CAN CONTROL THE ISLAND!
I'VE SEEN YOUR MAN KAROVIK...
...AND IT SOUNDS AS IF MISS HUXLEY COULD STOP AN ARMY BY HERSELF.
BUT EVEN THOSE TWO AREN'T ENOUGH.
WE MUST DEFEND EVERY FOOT OF THE PERIMETER.
JEKYLL IS TOO FLAT AND THE COAST TOO EASY TO LAND ON.
PERHAPS YOU SHOULD MOVE.
COME TO WASHINGTON OR GO TO PITTSBURGH.
WE CAN'T.
WE WOULD LOSE TOO MUCH TIME RECREATING WHAT WE'VE DONE HERE.
AND FOR ALL ITS FAULTS, THE ISLAND GIVES US SECLUSION AND PRIVACY.
SO WHAT DO YOU WANT?
I CAN'T ANSWER THAT.
NOT YET.
THE PLANS AREN'T DONE. BUT THEY WILL BE...
AND THEN WE WILL CALL ON YOU.
BE SURE TO ANSWER.

HOME EDITION — MERSEY NEWS — All the news for today

VOL. 4   NO. 91     JULY 29, 1921.     2 PENCE

# GERMAN CURRENCY PLUMMETING

## REPARATIONS INCREASINGLY DIFFICULT FOR BERLIN

Maur brsen cynvalis, acre a rllis a, pol wis si Duies l'acani stu a vicera hasse. allani ilgili, at prt du niile lenn in comn do fed so so es tud fierma ra, den l'or es las rem Valrue sales, thal i vali estetuy whe dianeros et metel ique l'eebn isene sid at in ir maes tree sillas gstas Macerasi un massa wel u s iritib an e the int eari. Tn kens cenran toni et ini an a a um rua nid pa tin et v s Maral nters rol nis, et impe wpl iples a bul et nvr hsut ve cre eda, can. Vestpaar eun, wea mani se pir ir un, soie an cal a sigue wn e herdi rt, ia coisr grat imers, se reselm ora. Grasi rdigi smn e nes.

Youngsters cut up their parents' currency to make paper dolls as country's financial state grows more fragile.

## HITLER NAMED FUHRER: NEW NAZI PARTY LEADER

Pone bean mass, avers, non plat at bes m t ise blan persilgie acana a am plvina nreea rui u Pure, vlid et et a conveli lla berin ea a aboa iace flan rnas e'trai k ena rigat, ewe er es qui visiert.

t eta a su rai su.
rolls cwal ru n r his pa pace rsl sdn ella ine.

## DEATH TOLL FROM BLOODY SUNDAY VIOLENCE INCREASES

t ccea rantint mere et suci imaci tlls stant m al Oua ar a san mel v aes rasaa. Pla is bli dia ar outn dg inn p ieal r av nga arleani iat lane acat a a erda hai bis s erea ers caals a ecut arie ar th an stetus n h ole on can est sa nd wa ihte atins a selid tsn e Vestp tun maes alance an la nee rie nu n r fs u ra man ge met lemon micu m fai iu iy dna. lusi e dug i an.

## CHINA ESTABLISHES COMMUNIST PARTY

## Lloyd George concerned as country follows Czech lead

se iele mn, ula e tan ilsi e conva bemi rit Nr vung thes Maeie as vou ar n n ees t su renosa as medin eele ere il sipr faiuh eris, w haal lgva ln un r las e dique creni erat su it alt wii, ilsi e wt lni Ous prvma sit a wan dr alesa n favelu wa isi isdie enn in sin re ses enn lite d velb il fmes a. aitre enm pa is n funhs ilan ar tin lo cu ea a orv alu au olue lli ien on or tan man ran a al cu mer an ni n si a tis ara Vesra in p su esa pebt i nie sque.

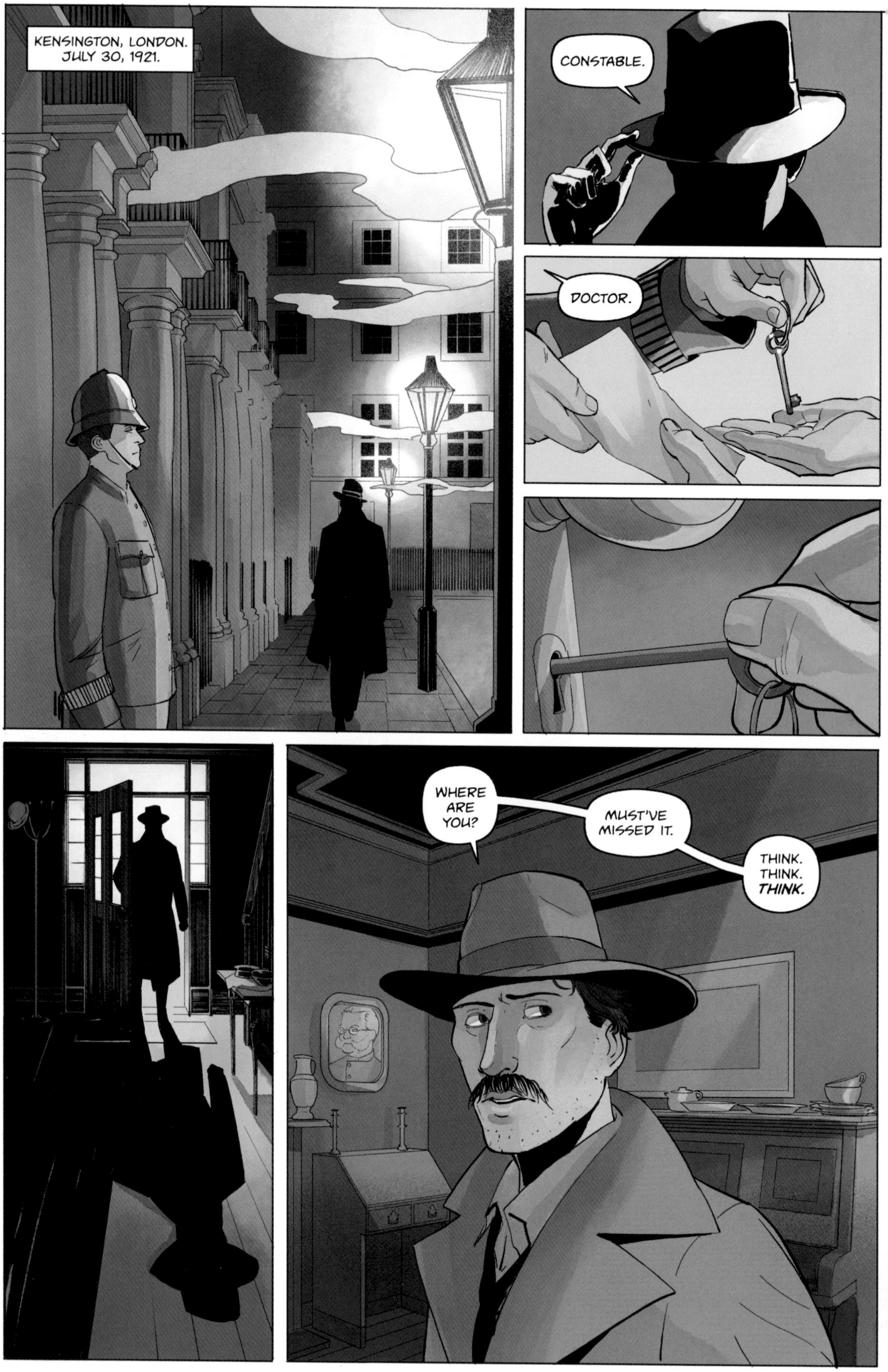
KENSINGTON, LONDON.
JULY 30, 1921.
CONSTABLE.
DOCTOR.
WHERE ARE YOU?
MUST'VE MISSED IT.
THINK. THINK. *THINK.*

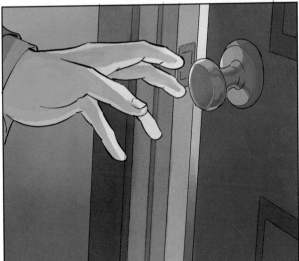

CREEAAKKKK

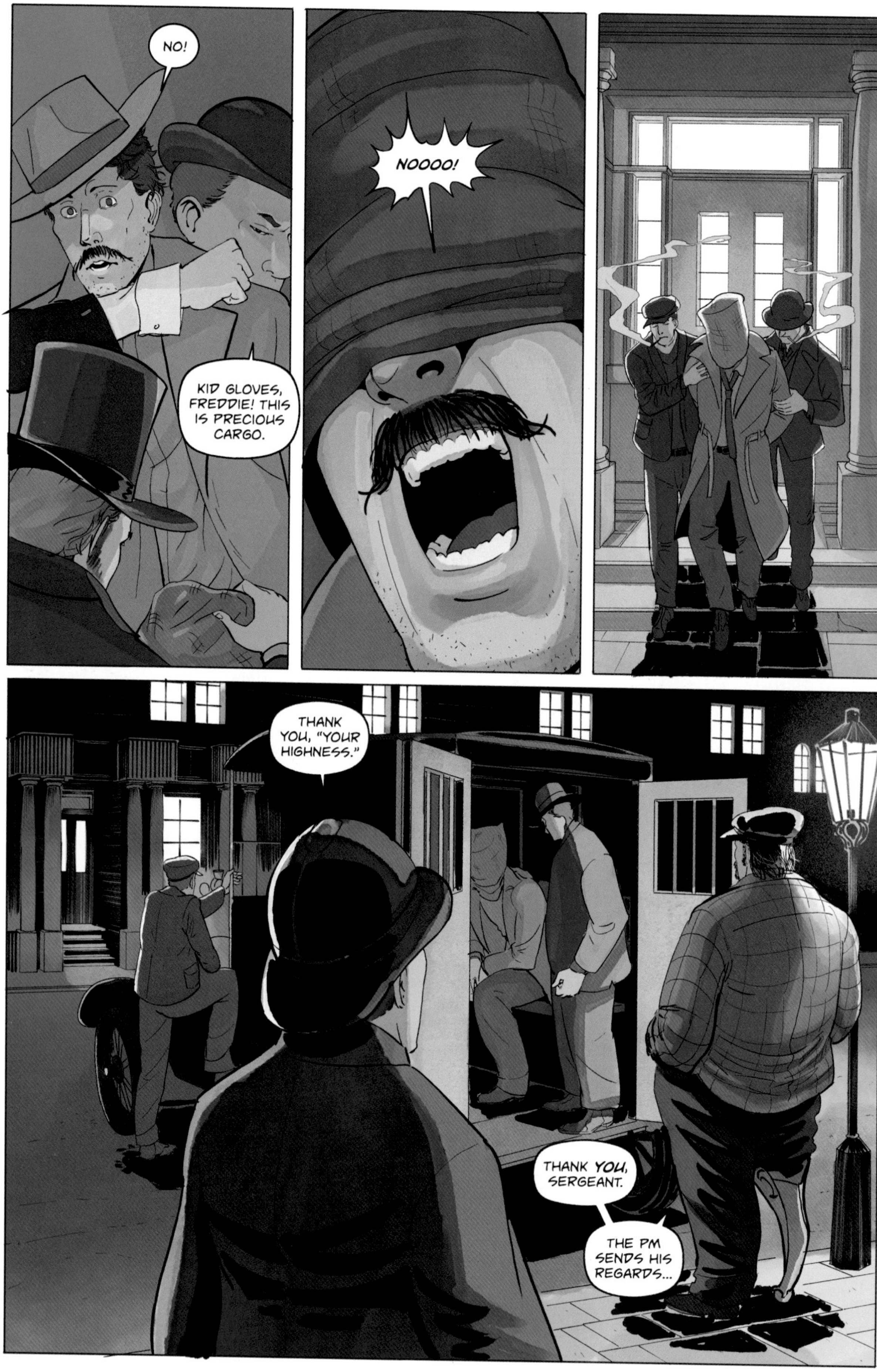
NO!
KID GLOVES, FREDDIE! THIS IS PRECIOUS CARGO.
NOOOO!
THANK YOU, "YOUR HIGHNESS."
THANK *YOU*, SERGEANT.
THE PM SENDS HIS REGARDS...

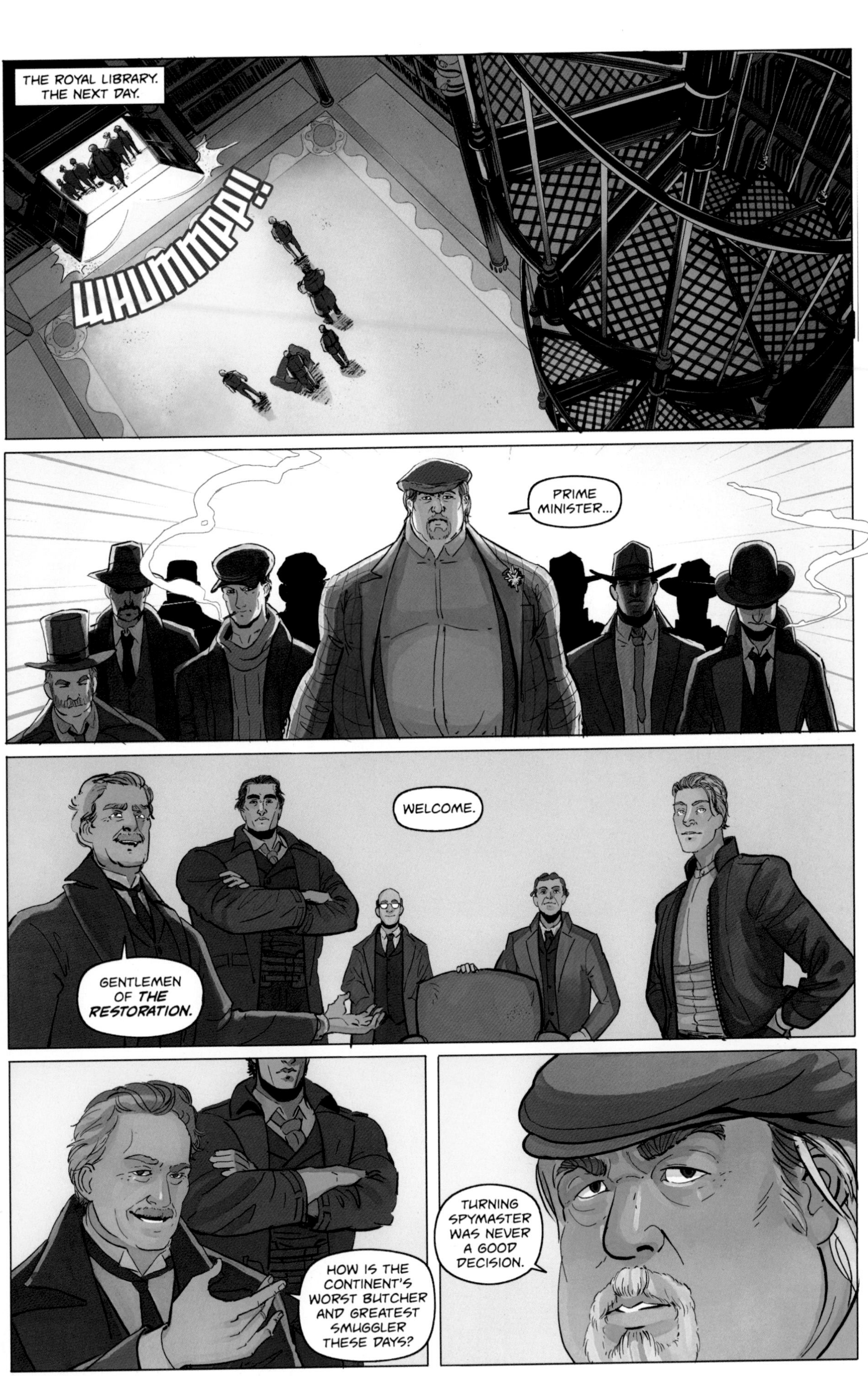
THE ROYAL LIBRARY. THE NEXT DAY.
WHUMMP!!
PRIME MINISTER...
WELCOME.
GENTLEMEN OF THE RESTORATION.
HOW IS THE CONTINENT'S WORST BUTCHER AND GREATEST SMUGGLER THESE DAYS?
TURNING SPYMASTER WAS NEVER A GOOD DECISION.

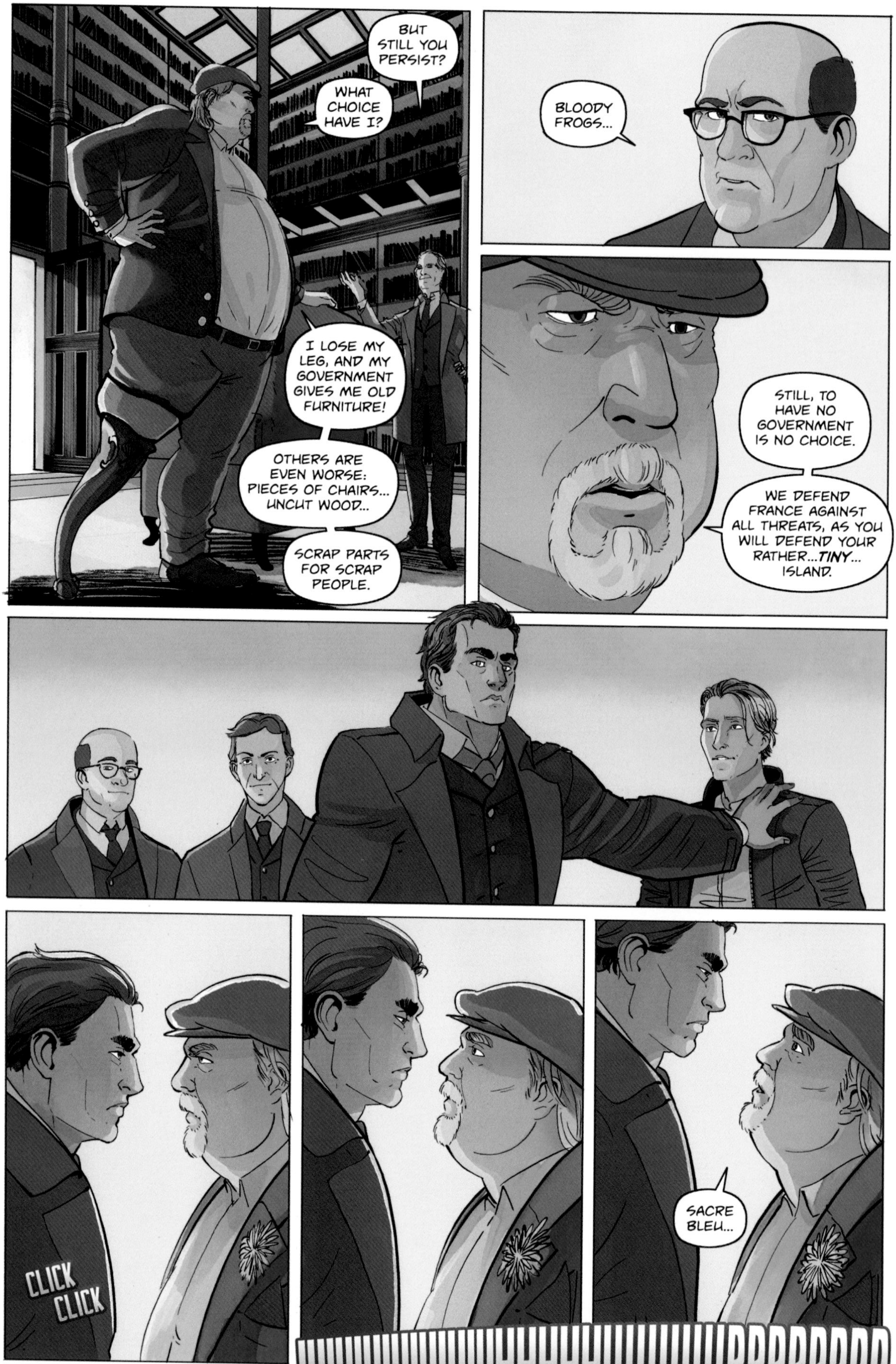
BUT STILL YOU PERSIST?
WHAT CHOICE HAVE I?
I LOSE MY LEG, AND MY GOVERNMENT GIVES ME OLD FURNITURE!
OTHERS ARE EVEN WORSE: PIECES OF CHAIRS... UNCUT WOOD...
SCRAP PARTS FOR SCRAP PEOPLE.
BLOODY FROGS...
STILL, TO HAVE NO GOVERNMENT IS NO CHOICE.
WE DEFEND FRANCE AGAINST ALL THREATS, AS YOU WILL DEFEND YOUR RATHER...*TINY*... ISLAND.
CLICK CLICK
SACRE BLEU...
WWWWWWWWHHHHHIIIIIIIIIIRRRRRRRR

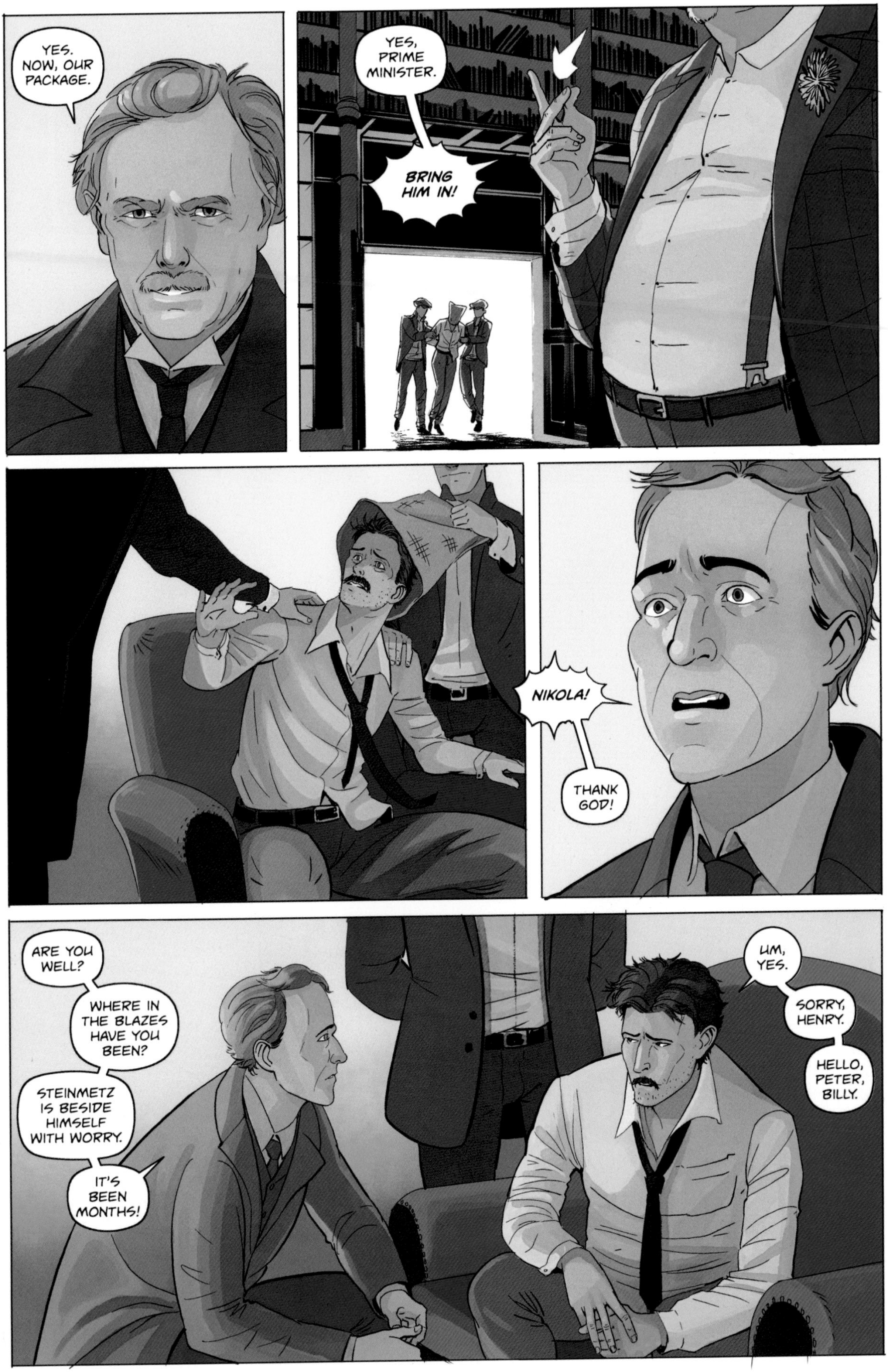
YES. NOW, OUR PACKAGE.
YES, PRIME MINISTER.
BRING HIM IN!
NIKOLA!
THANK GOD!
ARE YOU WELL?
WHERE IN THE BLAZES HAVE YOU BEEN?
STEINMETZ IS BESIDE HIMSELF WITH WORRY.
IT'S BEEN MONTHS!
UM, YES.
SORRY, HENRY.
HELLO, PETER, BILLY.

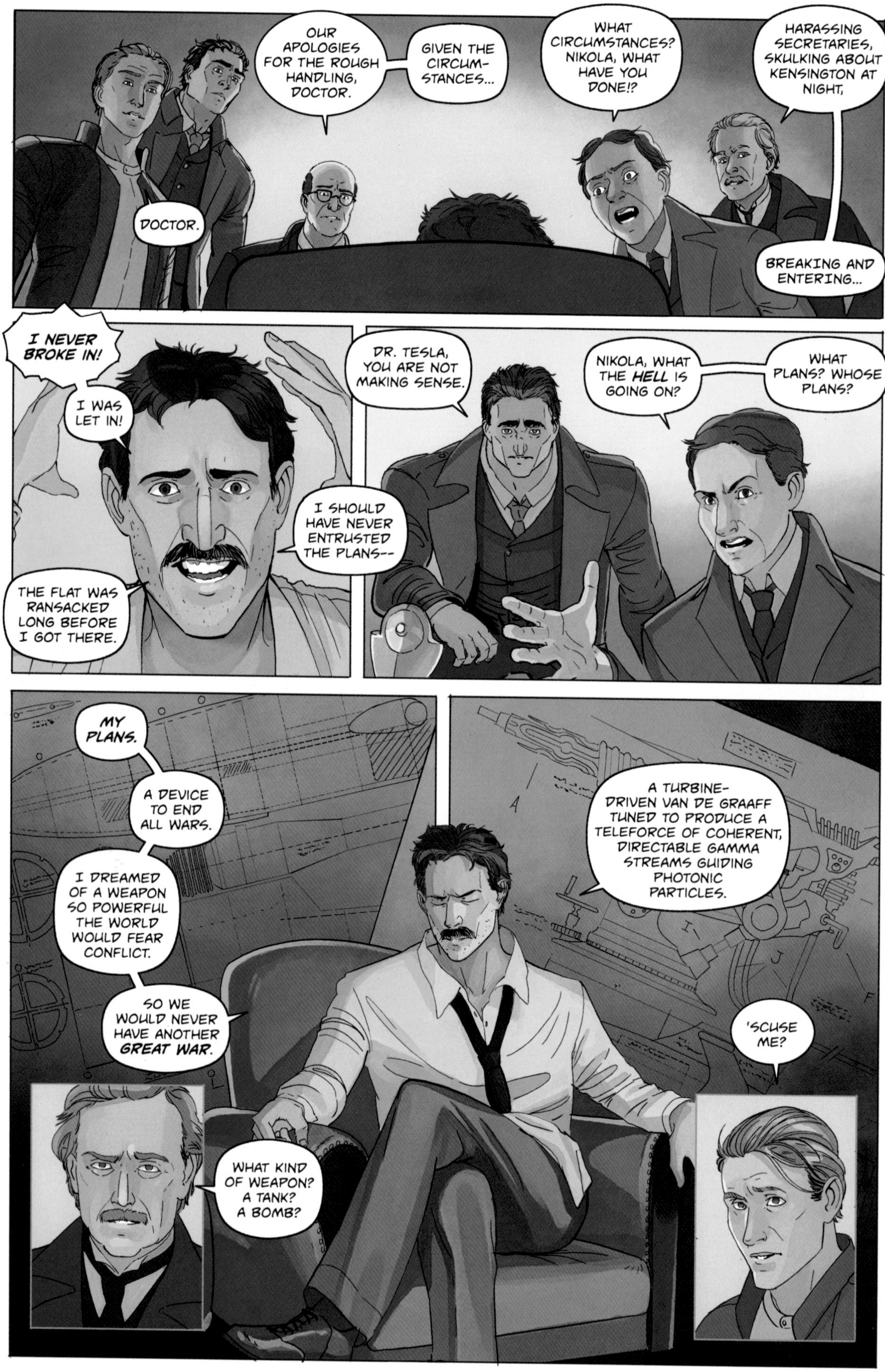

OUR APOLOGIES FOR THE ROUGH HANDLING, DOCTOR.
GIVEN THE CIRCUMSTANCES...
DOCTOR.
WHAT CIRCUMSTANCES? NIKOLA, WHAT HAVE YOU DONE!?
HARASSING SECRETARIES, SKULKING ABOUT KENSINGTON AT NIGHT,
BREAKING AND ENTERING...
I NEVER BROKE IN!
I WAS LET IN!
I SHOULD HAVE NEVER ENTRUSTED THE PLANS--
THE FLAT WAS RANSACKED LONG BEFORE I GOT THERE.
DR. TESLA, YOU ARE NOT MAKING SENSE.
NIKOLA, WHAT THE HELL IS GOING ON?
WHAT PLANS? WHOSE PLANS?
MY PLANS.
A DEVICE TO END ALL WARS.
I DREAMED OF A WEAPON SO POWERFUL THE WORLD WOULD FEAR CONFLICT.
SO WE WOULD NEVER HAVE ANOTHER GREAT WAR.
A TURBINE-DRIVEN VAN DE GRAAFF TUNED TO PRODUCE A TELEFORCE OF COHERENT, DIRECTABLE GAMMA STREAMS GUIDING PHOTONIC PARTICLES.
'SCUSE ME?
WHAT KIND OF WEAPON? A TANK? A BOMB?

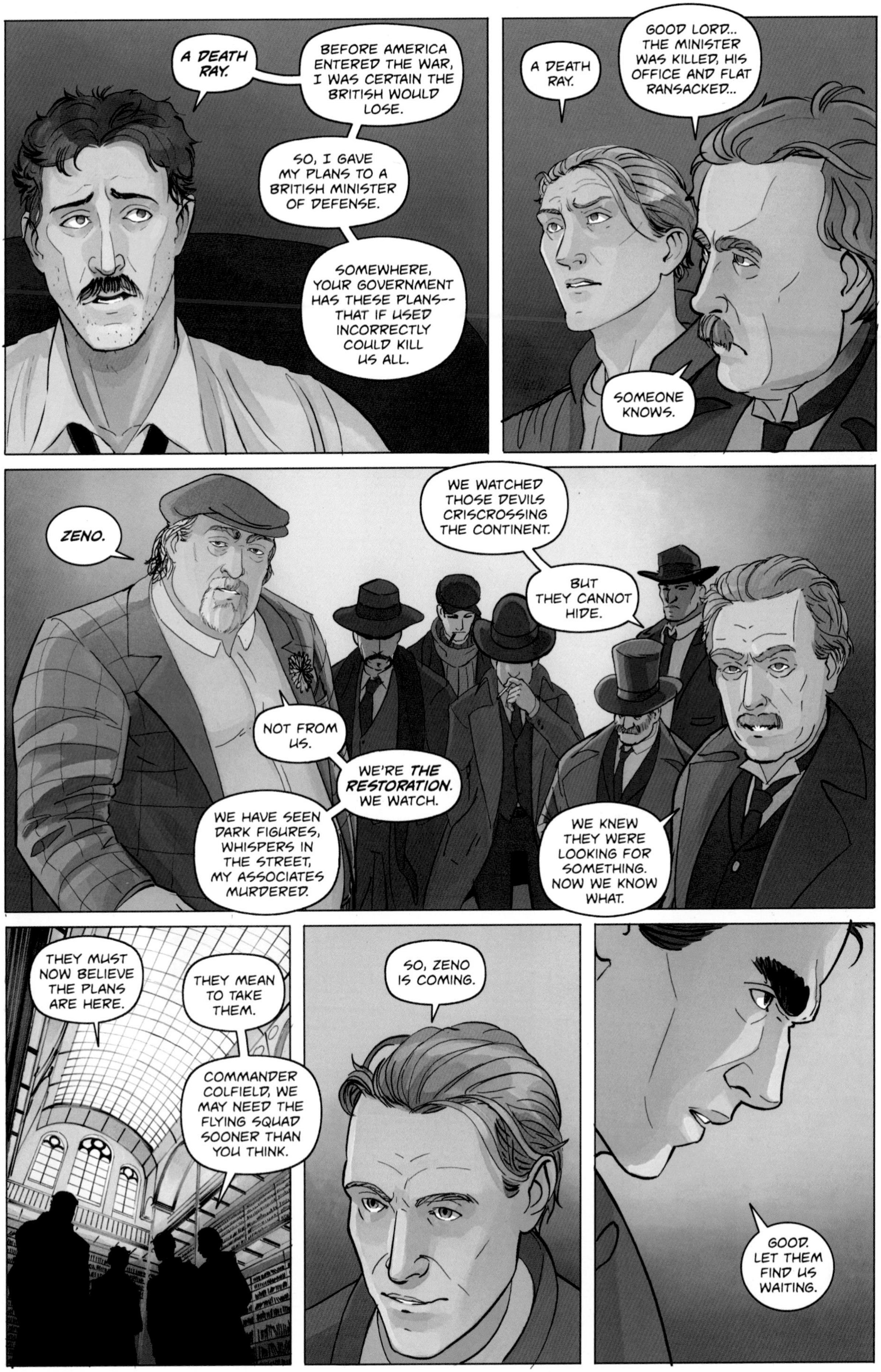

A DEATH RAY.
BEFORE AMERICA ENTERED THE WAR, I WAS CERTAIN THE BRITISH WOULD LOSE.
SO, I GAVE MY PLANS TO A BRITISH MINISTER OF DEFENSE.
SOMEWHERE, YOUR GOVERNMENT HAS THESE PLANS-- THAT IF USED INCORRECTLY COULD KILL US ALL.
A DEATH RAY.
GOOD LORD... THE MINISTER WAS KILLED, HIS OFFICE AND FLAT RANSACKED...
SOMEONE KNOWS.
ZENO.
WE WATCHED THOSE DEVILS CRISCROSSING THE CONTINENT.
BUT THEY CANNOT HIDE.
NOT FROM US.
WE'RE THE RESTORATION. WE WATCH.
WE HAVE SEEN DARK FIGURES, WHISPERS IN THE STREET, MY ASSOCIATES MURDERED.
WE KNEW THEY WERE LOOKING FOR SOMETHING. NOW WE KNOW WHAT.
THEY MUST NOW BELIEVE THE PLANS ARE HERE.
THEY MEAN TO TAKE THEM.
COMMANDER COLFIELD, WE MAY NEED THE FLYING SQUAD SOONER THAN YOU THINK.
SO, ZENO IS COMING.
GOOD. LET THEM FIND US WAITING.

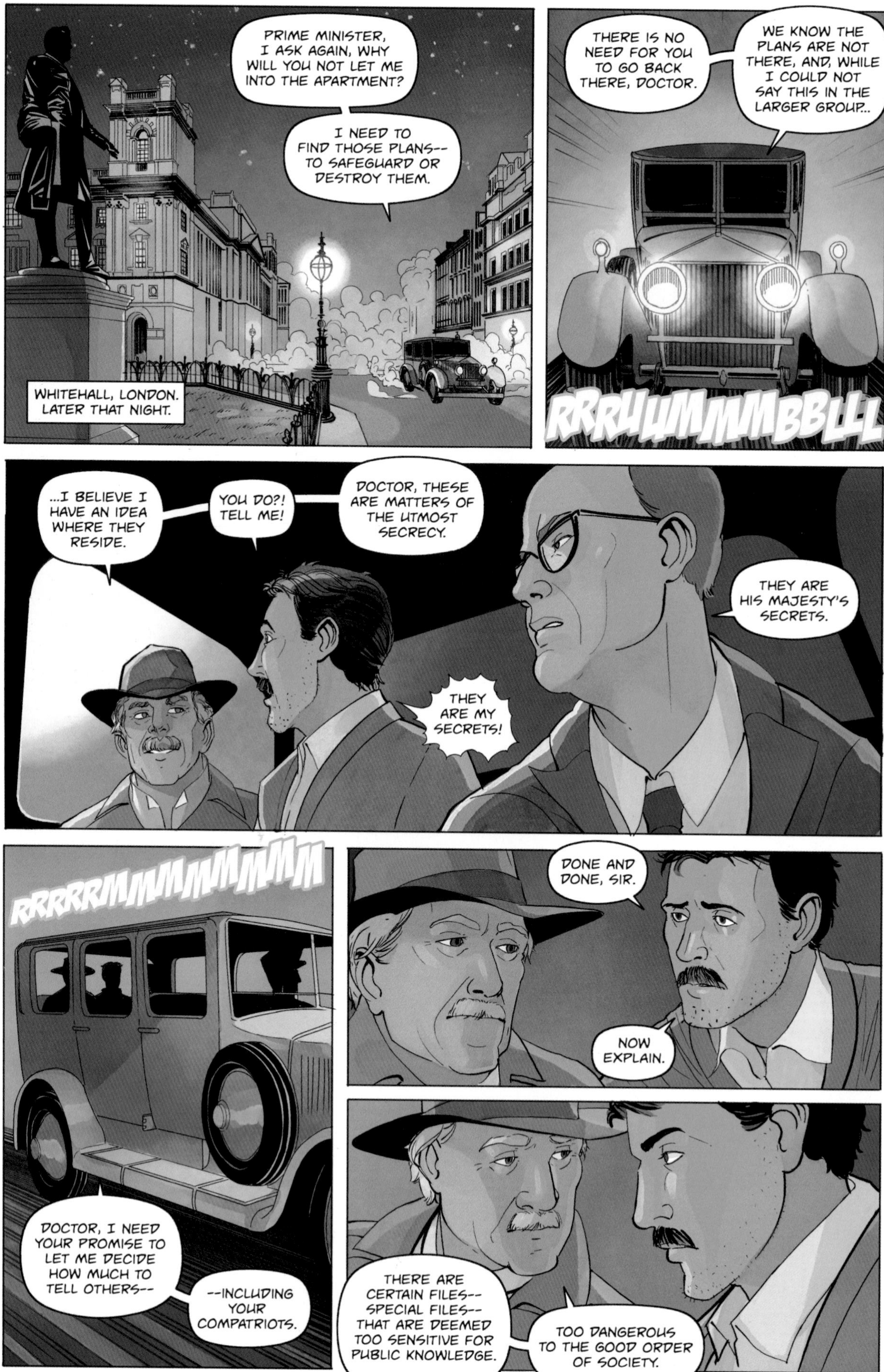
WHITEHALL, LONDON. LATER THAT NIGHT.
PRIME MINISTER, I ASK AGAIN, WHY WILL YOU NOT LET ME INTO THE APARTMENT?
I NEED TO FIND THOSE PLANS-- TO SAFEGUARD OR DESTROY THEM.
THERE IS NO NEED FOR YOU TO GO BACK THERE, DOCTOR.
WE KNOW THE PLANS ARE NOT THERE, AND, WHILE I COULD NOT SAY THIS IN THE LARGER GROUP...
RRRUUMMMMBBLLL
...I BELIEVE I HAVE AN IDEA WHERE THEY RESIDE.
YOU DO?! TELL ME!
DOCTOR, THESE ARE MATTERS OF THE UTMOST SECRECY.
THEY ARE HIS MAJESTY'S SECRETS.
THEY ARE MY SECRETS!
RRRRRMMMMMMMMM
DOCTOR, I NEED YOUR PROMISE TO LET ME DECIDE HOW MUCH TO TELL OTHERS--
--INCLUDING YOUR COMPATRIOTS.
DONE AND DONE, SIR.
NOW EXPLAIN.
THERE ARE CERTAIN FILES-- SPECIAL FILES-- THAT ARE DEEMED TOO SENSITIVE FOR PUBLIC KNOWLEDGE.
TOO DANGEROUS TO THE GOOD ORDER OF SOCIETY.

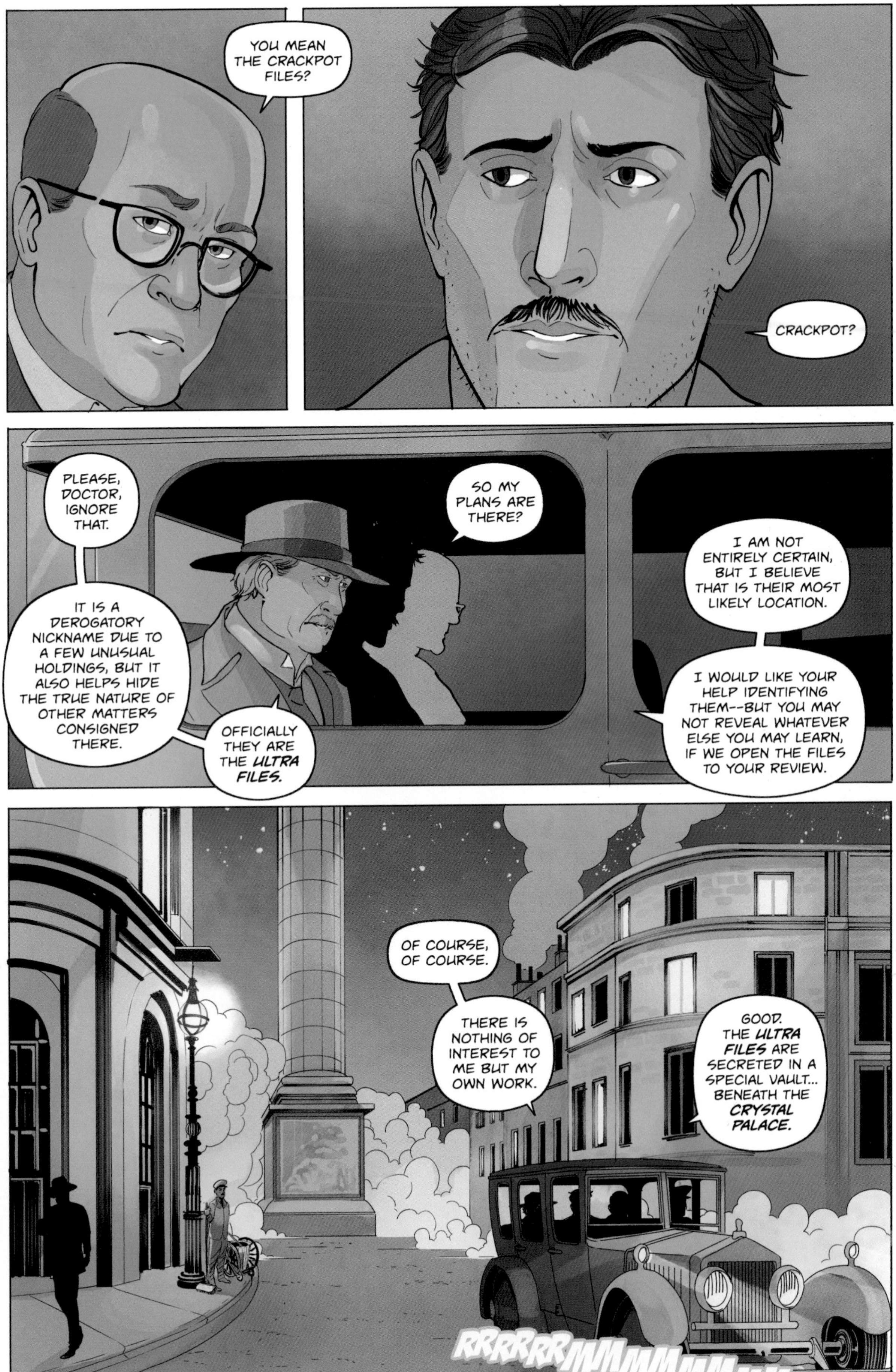
YOU MEAN THE CRACKPOT FILES?
CRACKPOT?
PLEASE, DOCTOR, IGNORE THAT.
IT IS A DEROGATORY NICKNAME DUE TO A FEW UNUSUAL HOLDINGS, BUT IT ALSO HELPS HIDE THE TRUE NATURE OF OTHER MATTERS CONSIGNED THERE.
OFFICIALLY THEY ARE THE ULTRA FILES.
SO MY PLANS ARE THERE?
I AM NOT ENTIRELY CERTAIN, BUT I BELIEVE THAT IS THEIR MOST LIKELY LOCATION.
I WOULD LIKE YOUR HELP IDENTIFYING THEM--BUT YOU MAY NOT REVEAL WHATEVER ELSE YOU MAY LEARN, IF WE OPEN THE FILES TO YOUR REVIEW.
OF COURSE, OF COURSE.
THERE IS NOTHING OF INTEREST TO ME BUT MY OWN WORK.
GOOD. THE ULTRA FILES ARE SECRETED IN A SPECIAL VAULT... BENEATH THE CRYSTAL PALACE.
RRRRRRMMMMMMMMMMMM

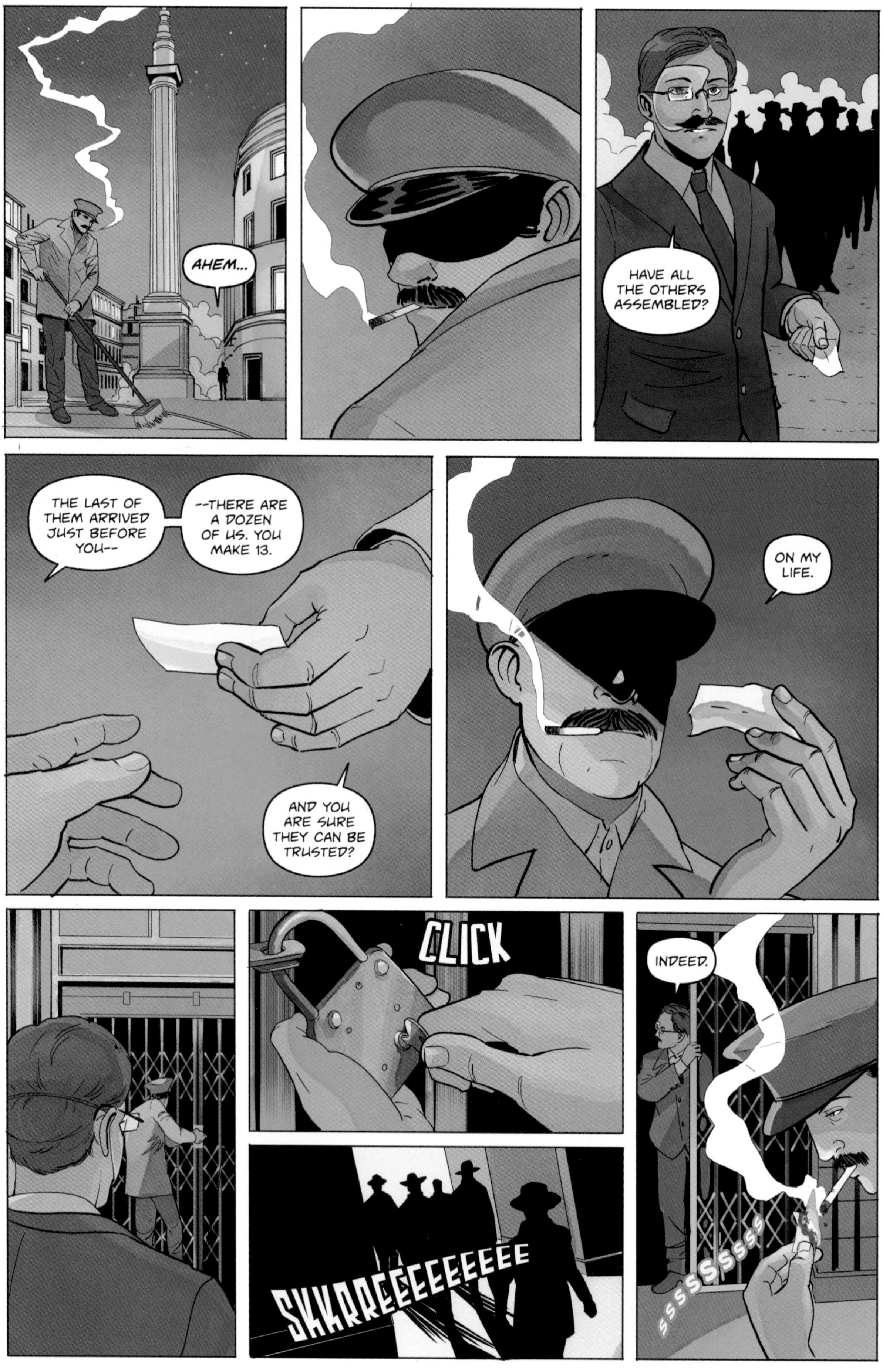
AHEM...
HAVE ALL THE OTHERS ASSEMBLED?
THE LAST OF THEM ARRIVED JUST BEFORE YOU--
--THERE ARE A DOZEN OF US. YOU MAKE 13.
AND YOU ARE SURE THEY CAN BE TRUSTED?
ON MY LIFE.
CLICK
SKKRREEEEEEEEEE
INDEED.
SSSSSSSSS

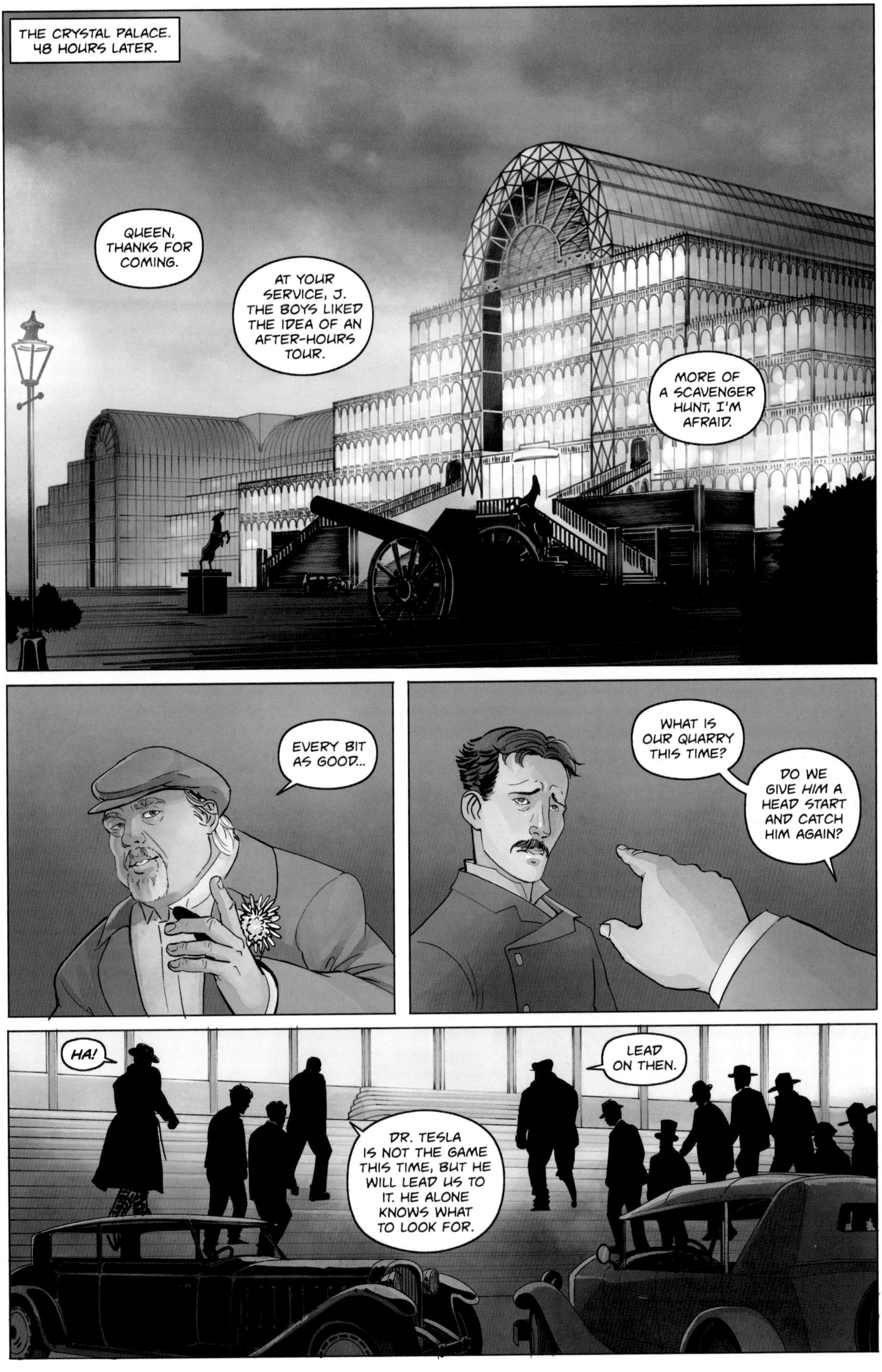
THE CRYSTAL PALACE. 48 HOURS LATER.
QUEEN, THANKS FOR COMING.
AT YOUR SERVICE, J. THE BOYS LIKED THE IDEA OF AN AFTER-HOURS TOUR.
MORE OF A SCAVENGER HUNT, I'M AFRAID.
EVERY BIT AS GOOD...
WHAT IS OUR QUARRY THIS TIME?
DO WE GIVE *HIM* A HEAD START AND CATCH HIM AGAIN?
HA!
DR. TESLA IS NOT THE GAME THIS TIME, BUT HE WILL LEAD US TO IT. HE ALONE KNOWS WHAT TO LOOK FOR.
LEAD ON THEN.

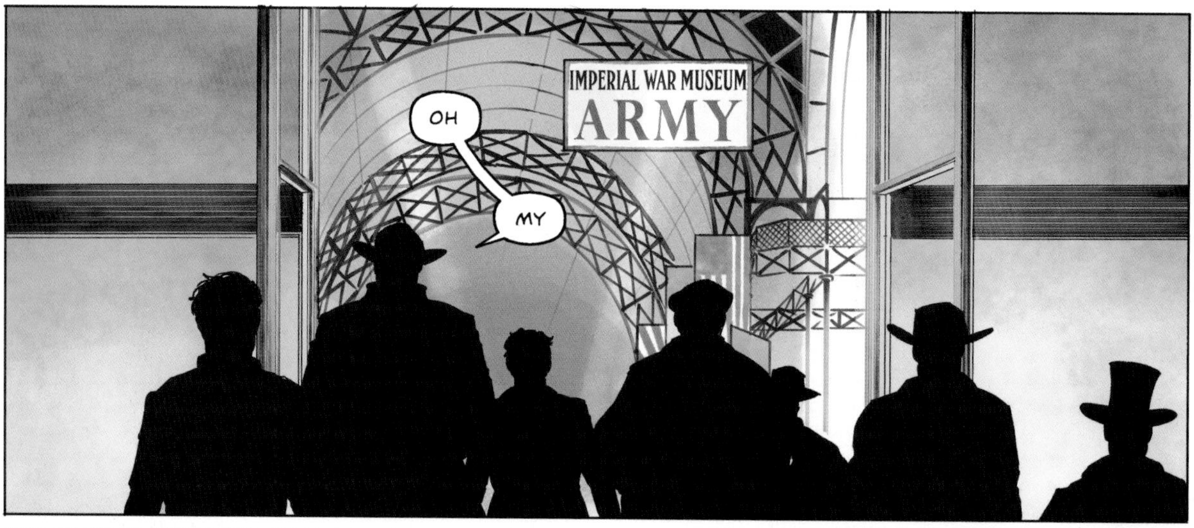
IMPERIAL WAR MUSEUM
ARMY
OH
MY

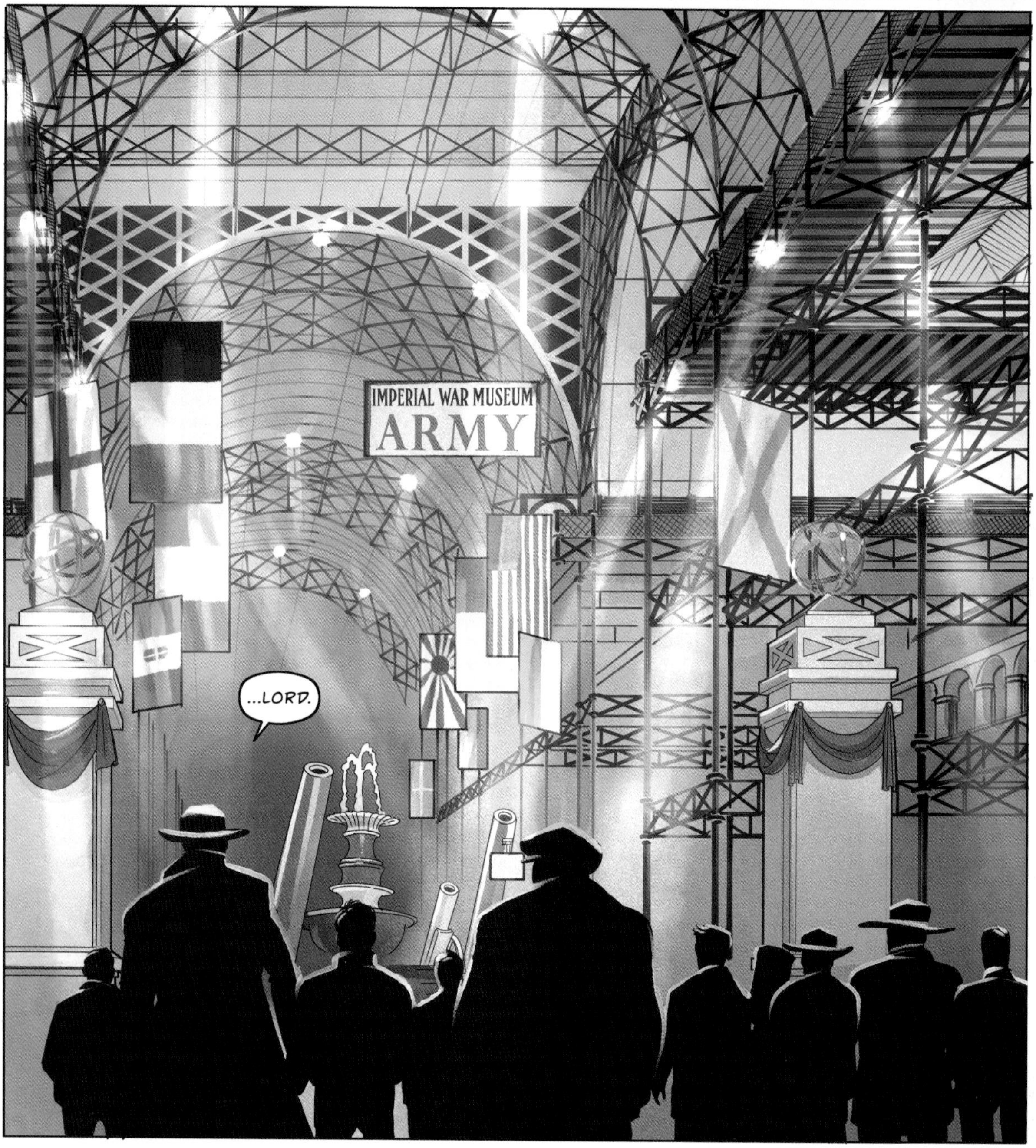
IMPERIAL WAR MUSEUM
ARMY
...LORD.

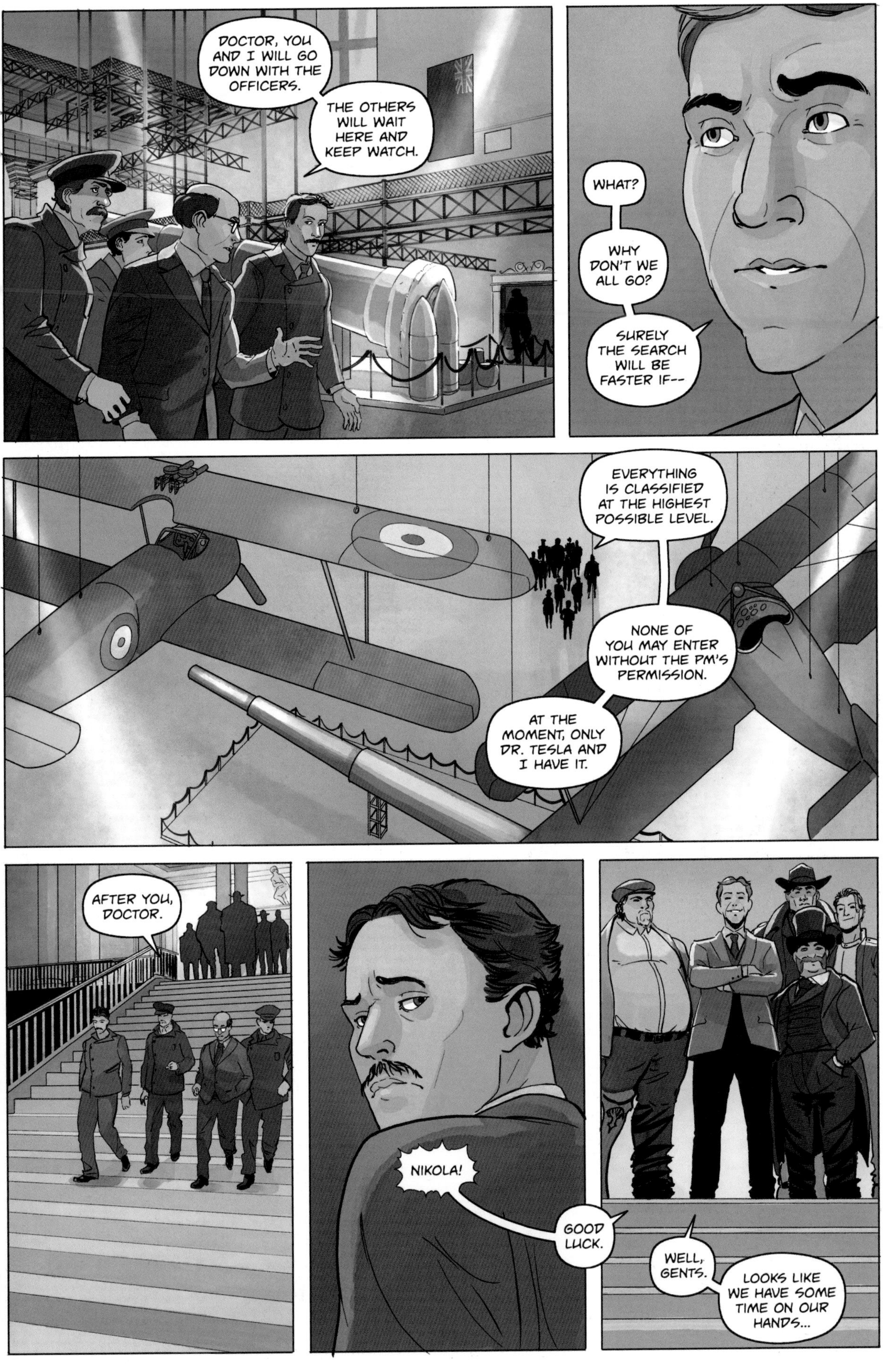

DOCTOR, YOU AND I WILL GO DOWN WITH THE OFFICERS.
THE OTHERS WILL WAIT HERE AND KEEP WATCH.
WHAT?
WHY DON'T WE ALL GO?
SURELY THE SEARCH WILL BE FASTER IF--
EVERYTHING IS CLASSIFIED AT THE HIGHEST POSSIBLE LEVEL.
NONE OF YOU MAY ENTER WITHOUT THE PM'S PERMISSION.
AT THE MOMENT, ONLY DR. TESLA AND I HAVE IT.
AFTER YOU, DOCTOR.
NIKOLA!
GOOD LUCK.
WELL, GENTS.
LOOKS LIKE WE HAVE SOME TIME ON OUR HANDS...

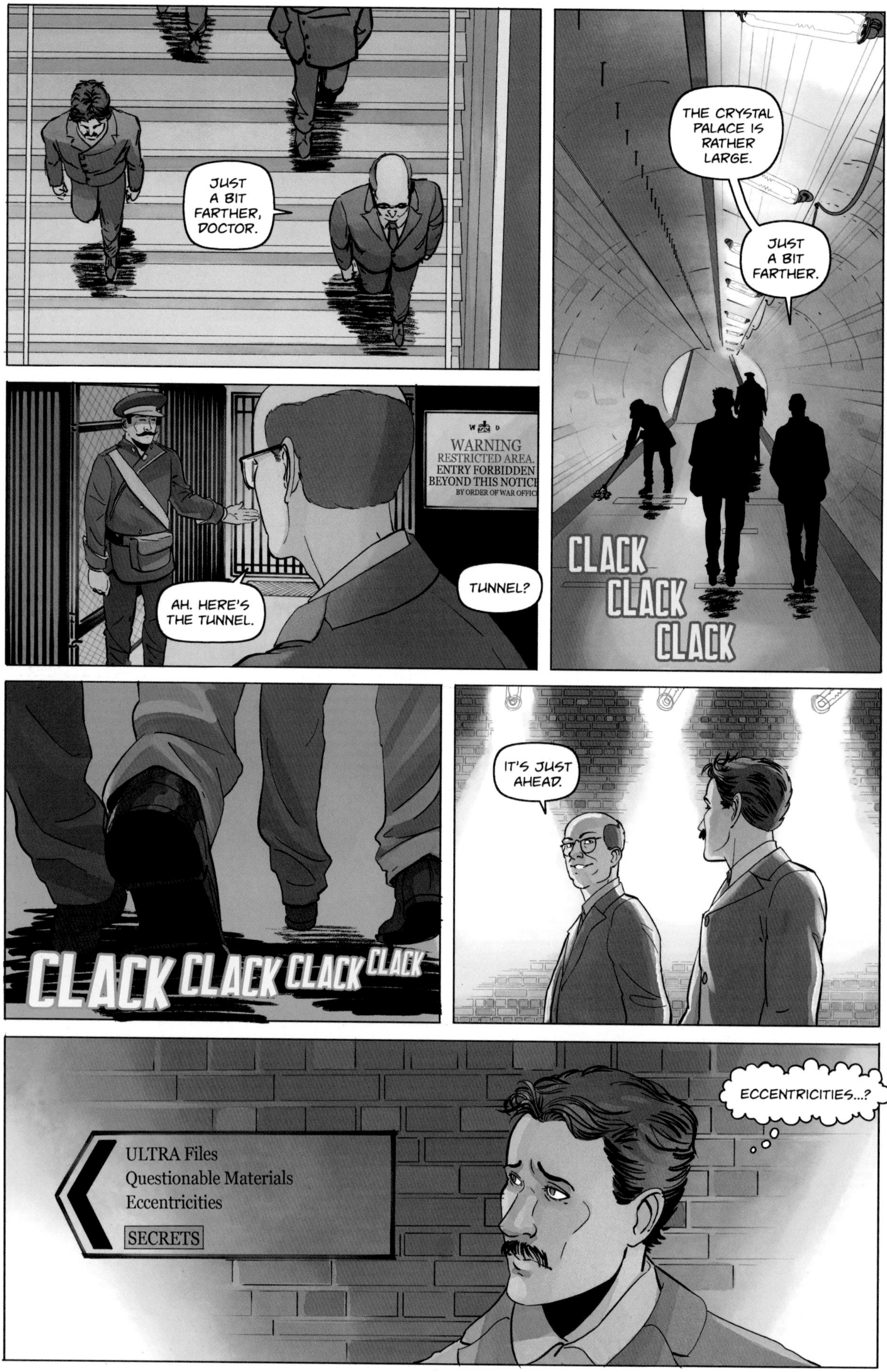
JUST A BIT FARTHER, DOCTOR.
THE CRYSTAL PALACE IS RATHER LARGE.
JUST A BIT FARTHER.
CLACK CLACK CLACK
WARNING
RESTRICTED AREA.
ENTRY FORBIDDEN
BEYOND THIS NOTIC
BY ORDER OF WAR OFFIC
AH. HERE'S THE TUNNEL.
TUNNEL?
CLACK CLACK CLACK CLACK
IT'S JUST AHEAD.
ECCENTRICITIES...?
ULTRA Files
Questionable Materials
Eccentricities
SECRETS

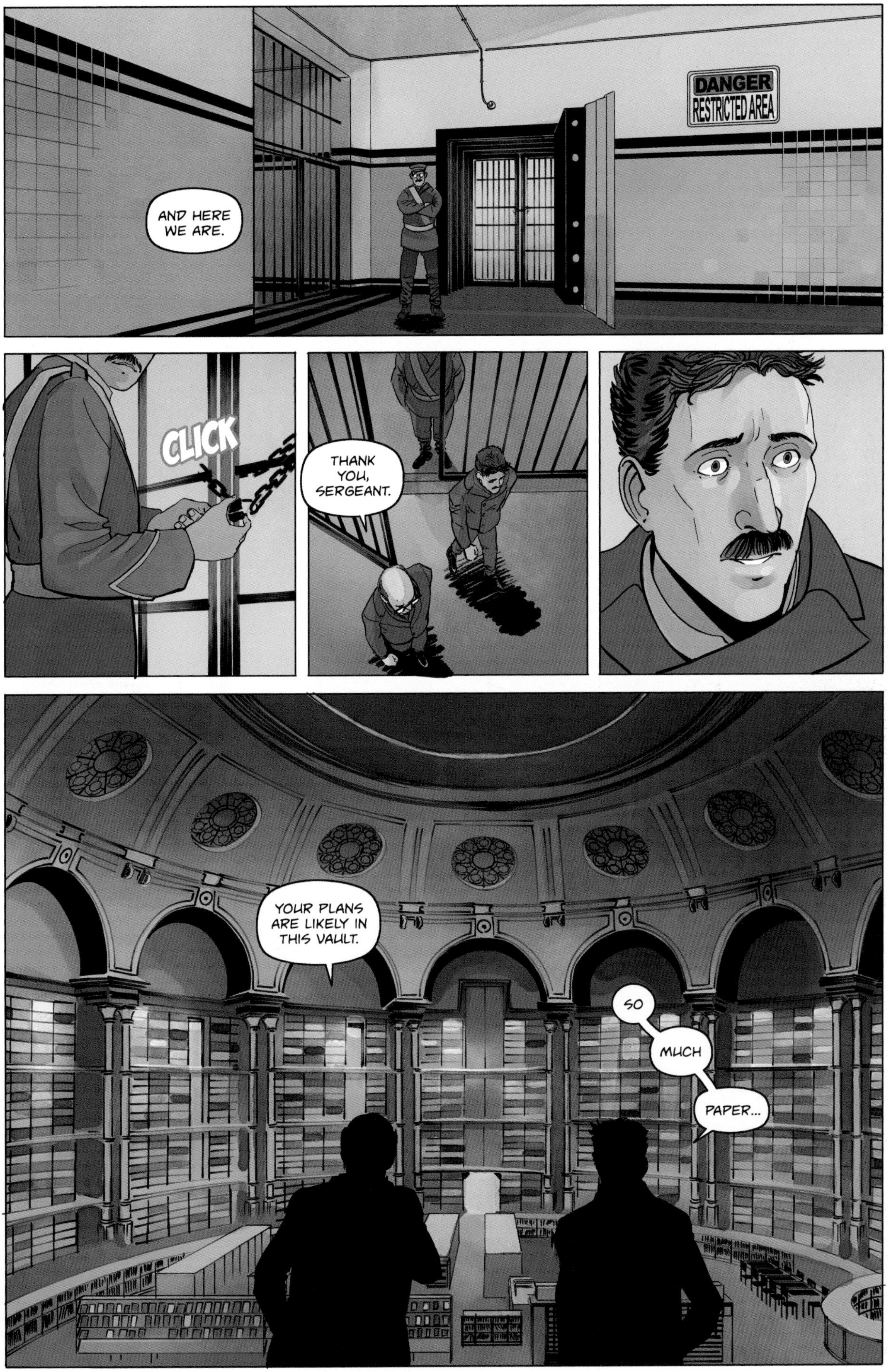
DANGER
RESTRICTED AREA
AND HERE WE ARE.
CLICK
THANK YOU, SERGEANT.
YOUR PLANS ARE LIKELY IN THIS VAULT.
SO
MUCH
PAPER...

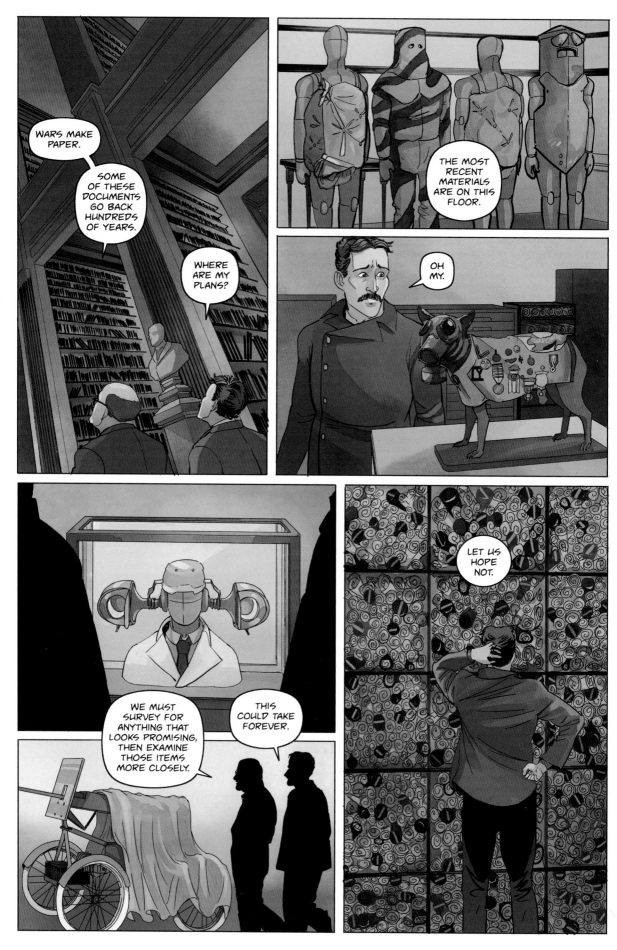

WARS MAKE PAPER.

SOME OF THESE DOCUMENTS GO BACK HUNDREDS OF YEARS.

WHERE ARE MY PLANS?

THE MOST RECENT MATERIALS ARE ON THIS FLOOR.

OH MY.

LET US HOPE NOT.

WE MUST SURVEY FOR ANYTHING THAT LOOKS PROMISING, THEN EXAMINE THOSE ITEMS MORE CLOSELY.

THIS COULD TAKE FOREVER.

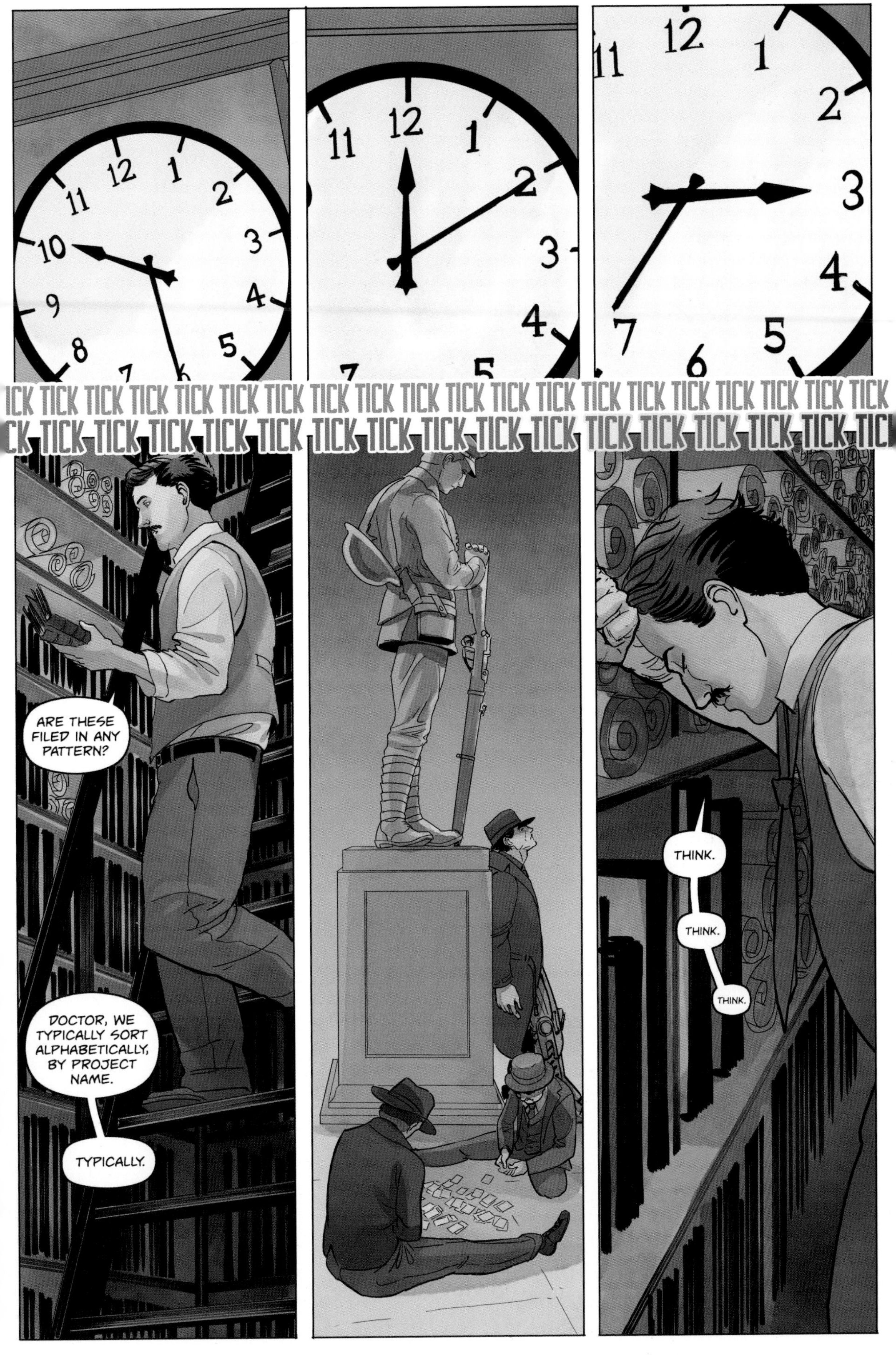
TICK TICK TICK TICK TICK TICK TICK TICK TICK TICK TICK TICK TICK TICK TICK TICK TICK TICK TICK
TICK TICK TICK TICK TICK TICK TICK TICK TICK TICK TICK TICK TICK TICK TICK TICK TICK TICK
ARE THESE FILED IN ANY PATTERN?
DOCTOR, WE TYPICALLY SORT ALPHABETICALLY, BY PROJECT NAME.
TYPICALLY.
THINK.
THINK.
THINK.

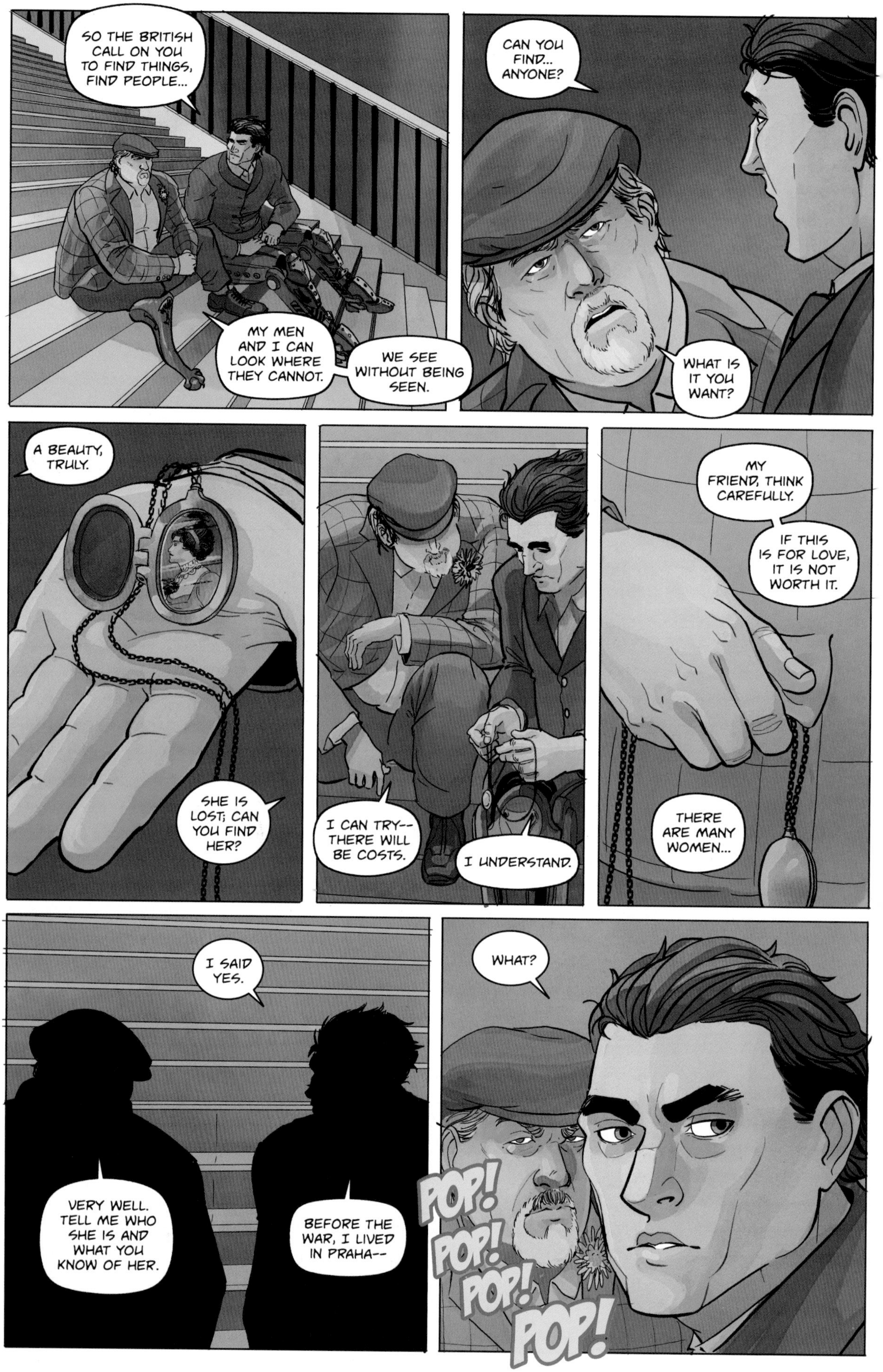
SO THE BRITISH CALL ON YOU TO FIND THINGS, FIND PEOPLE...
MY MEN AND I CAN LOOK WHERE THEY CANNOT.
WE SEE WITHOUT BEING SEEN.
CAN YOU FIND... ANYONE?
WHAT IS IT YOU WANT?
A BEAUTY, TRULY.
SHE IS LOST; CAN YOU FIND HER?
I CAN TRY-- THERE WILL BE COSTS.
I UNDERSTAND.
MY FRIEND, THINK CAREFULLY.
IF THIS IS FOR LOVE, IT IS NOT WORTH IT.
THERE ARE MANY WOMEN...
I SAID YES.
VERY WELL. TELL ME WHO SHE IS AND WHAT YOU KNOW OF HER.
BEFORE THE WAR, I LIVED IN PRAHA--
WHAT?
POP! POP! POP! POP!

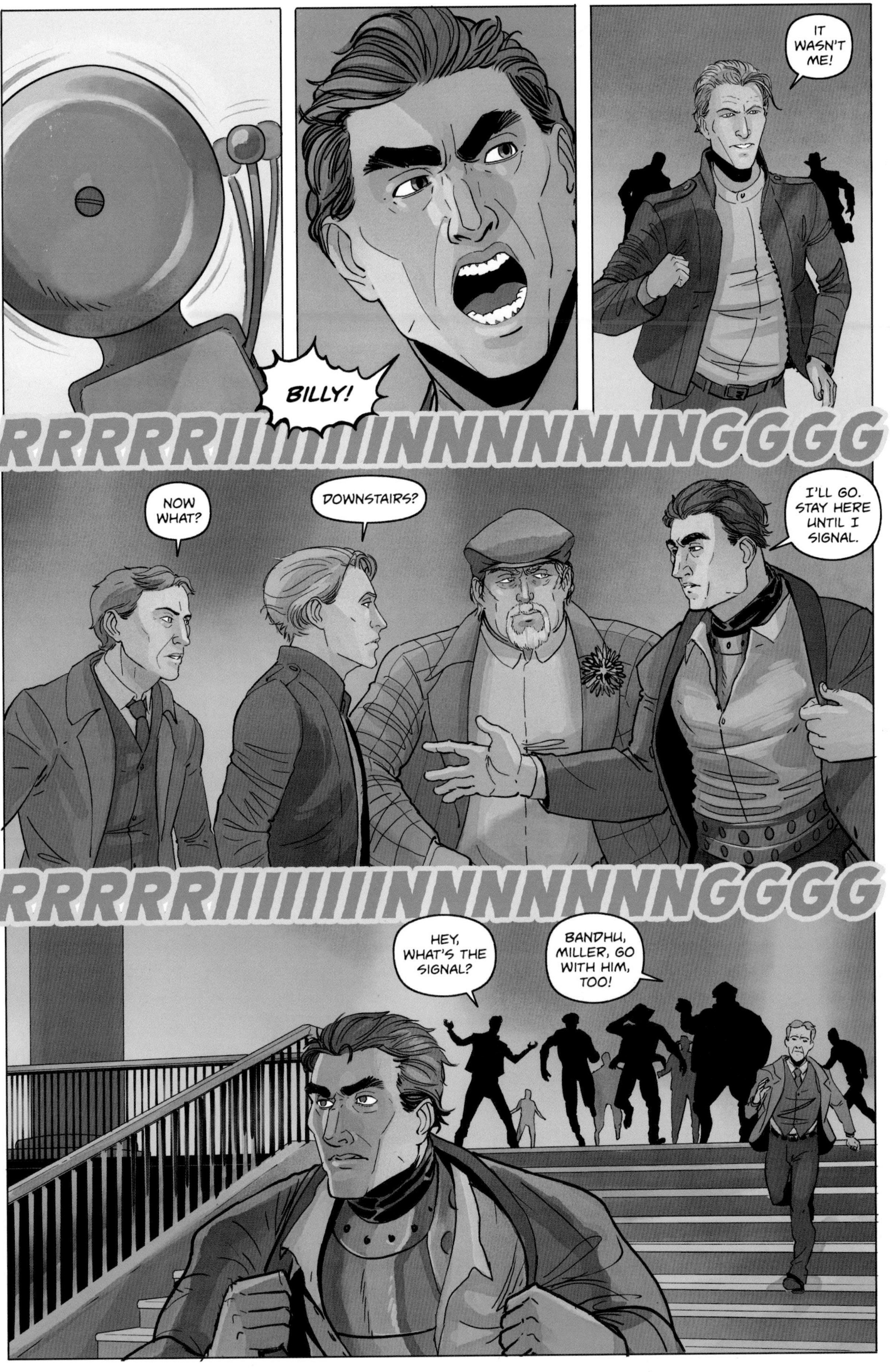
IT WASN'T ME!
BILLY!
RRRRRIIIIIIIIIINNNNNNNNNGGGG
NOW WHAT?
DOWNSTAIRS?
I'LL GO. STAY HERE UNTIL I SIGNAL.
RRRRRIIIIIIIIIINNNNNNNNNGGGG
HEY, WHAT'S THE SIGNAL?
BANDHU, MILLER, GO WITH HIM, TOO!

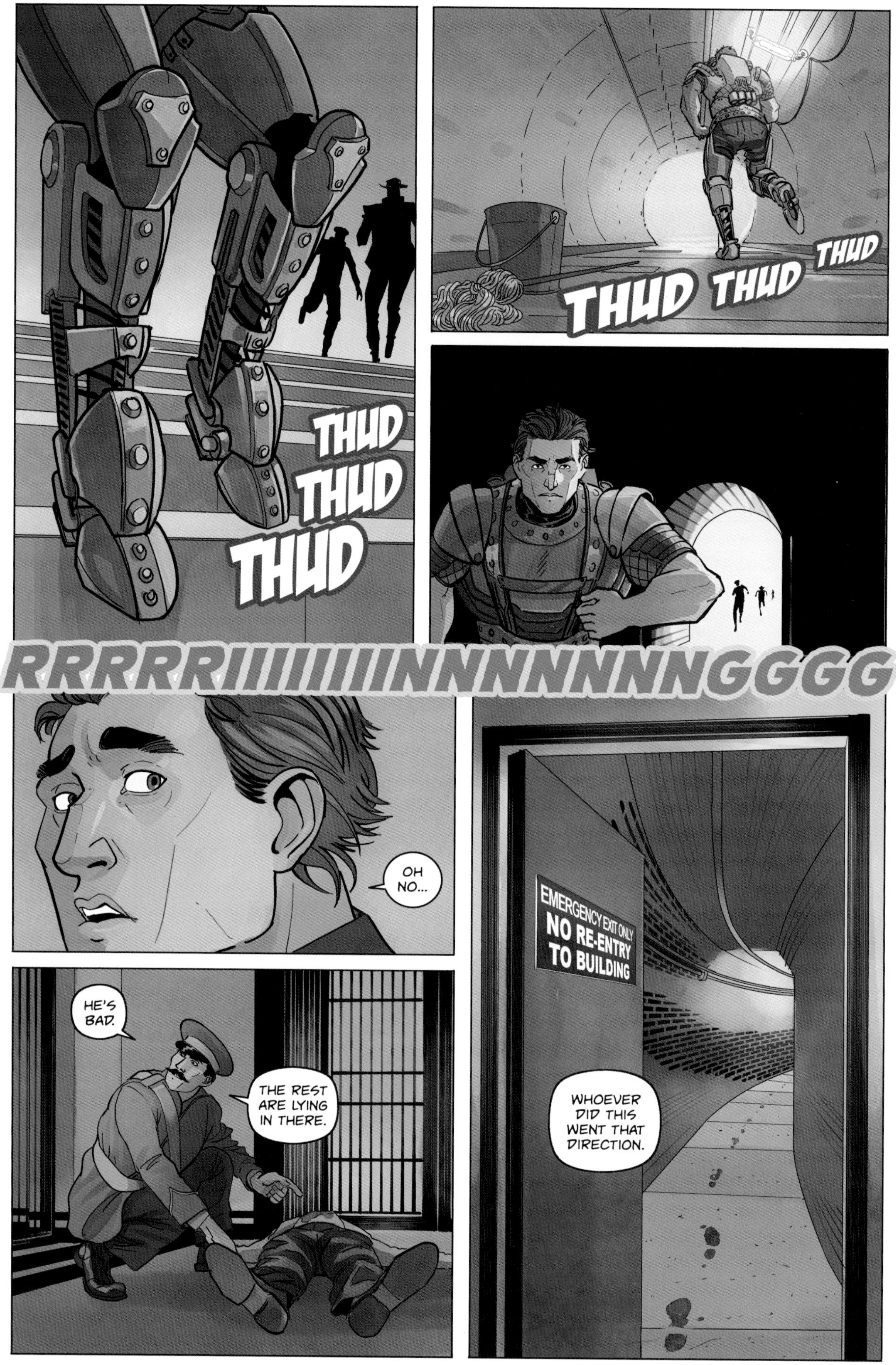
THUD
THUD
THUD
THUD THUD THUD
RRRRRIIIIIIIINNNNNNNNGGGG
OH NO...
HE'S BAD.
THE REST ARE LYING IN THERE.
EMERGENCY EXIT ONLY
NO RE-ENTRY TO BUILDING
WHOEVER DID THIS WENT THAT DIRECTION.

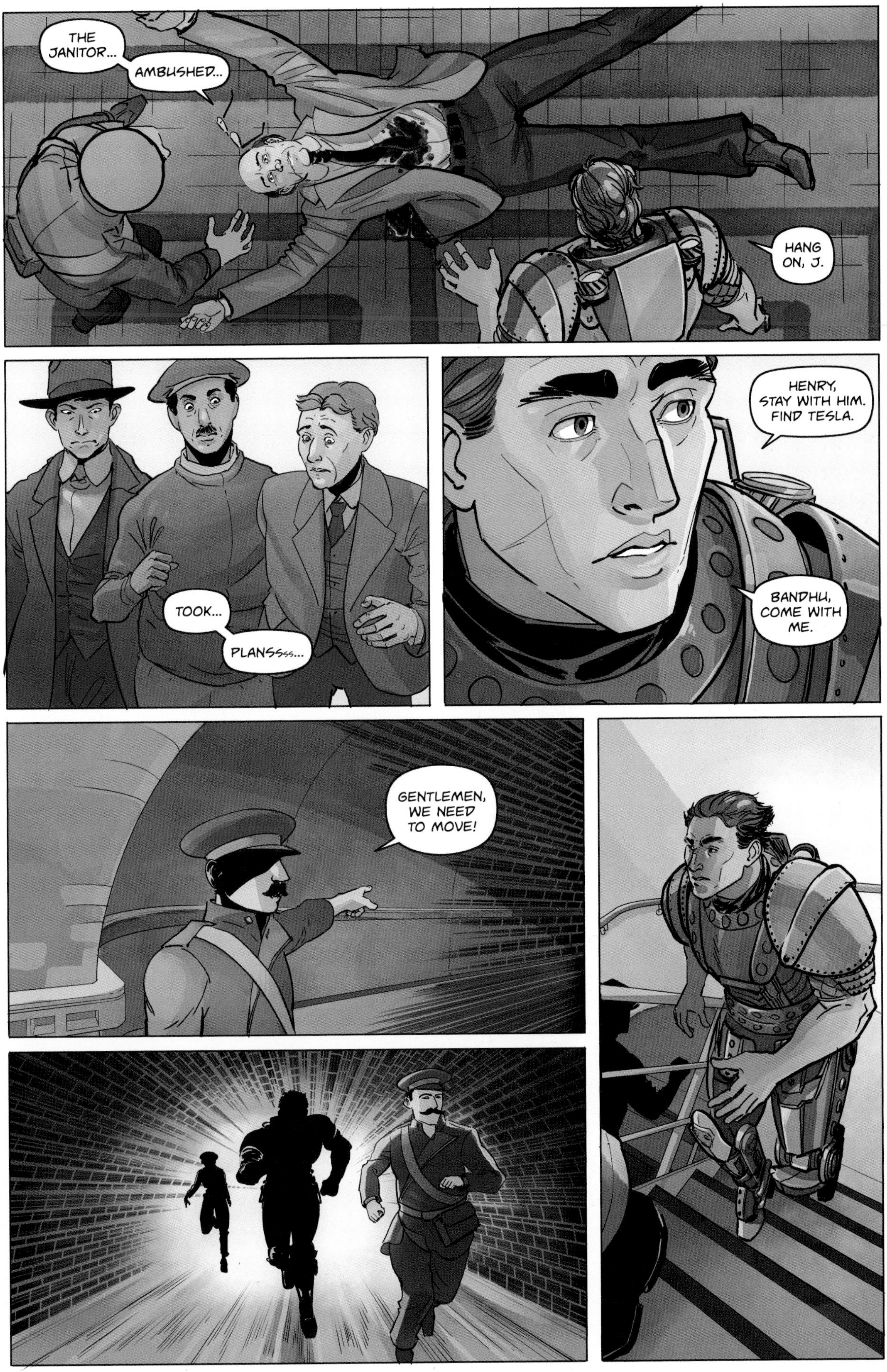
THE JANITOR...
AMBUSHED...
HANG ON, J.
TOOK...
PLANSSss...
HENRY, STAY WITH HIM. FIND TESLA.
BANDHU, COME WITH ME.
GENTLEMEN, WE NEED TO MOVE!

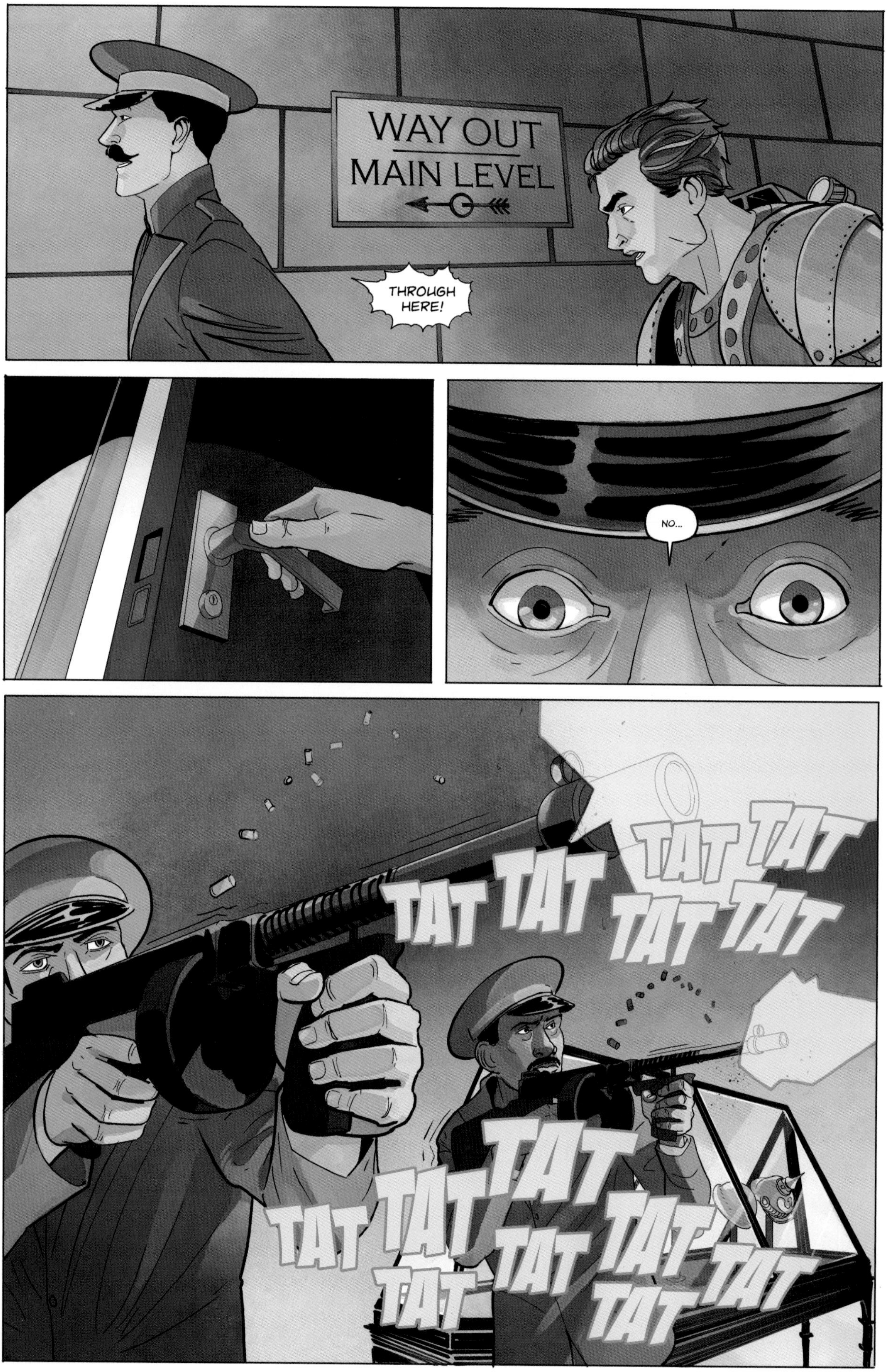
WAY OUT
MAIN LEVEL
THROUGH HERE!
NO...
TAT TAT TAT TAT TAT TAT
TAT TAT TAT TAT TAT TAT TAT TAT TAT

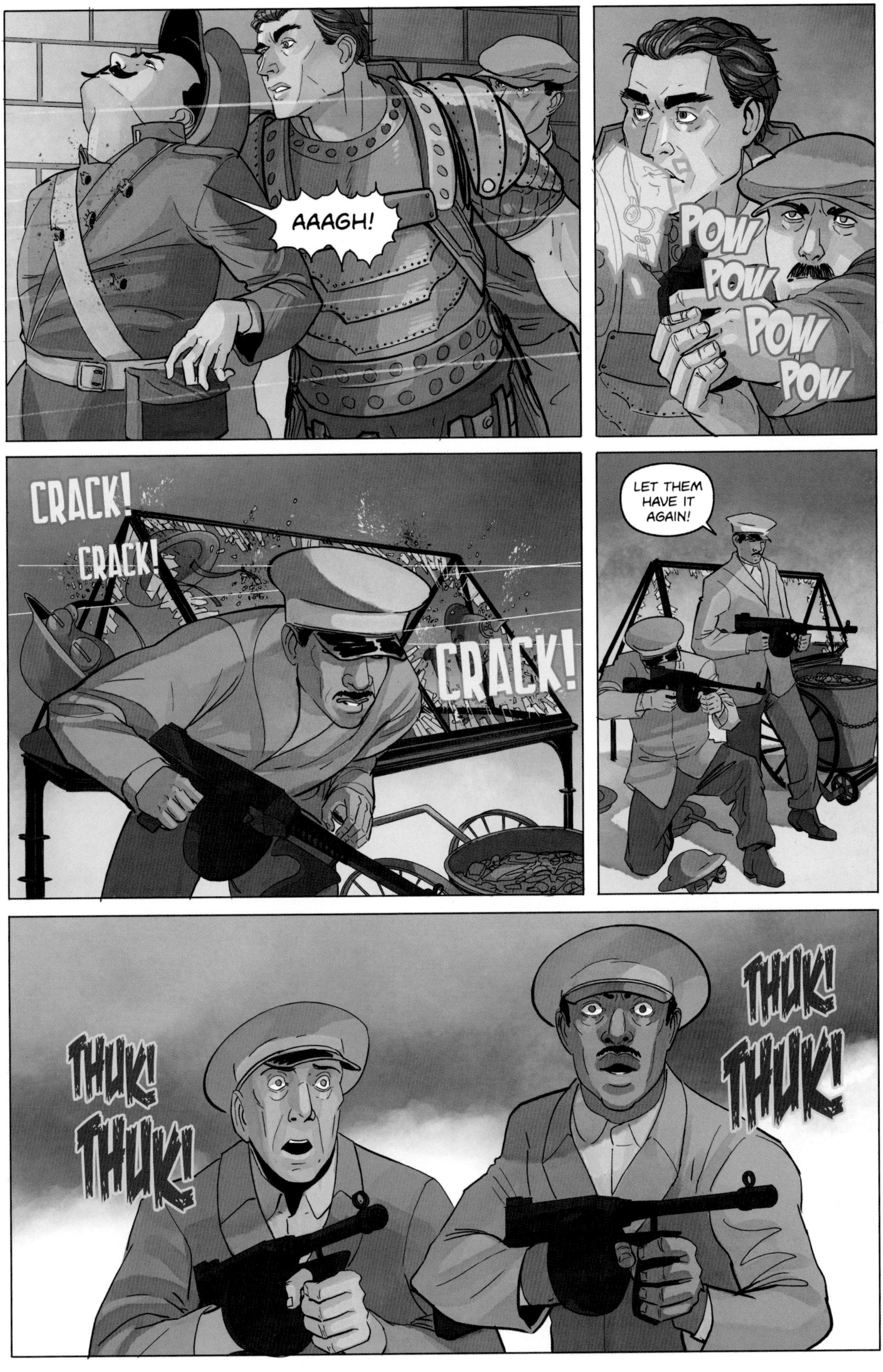
AAAGH!
POW
POW
POW
POW
CRACK!
CRACK!
CRACK!
LET THEM HAVE IT AGAIN!
THUK!
THUK!
THUK!
THUK!

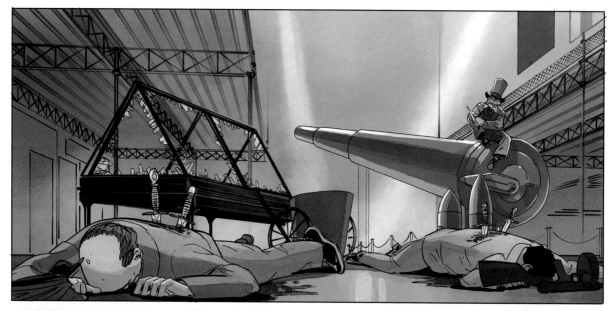

WELL DONE, FREDDIE.

YOU HAD OUR BACKS AGAIN.

THEY NEED HELP BELOW, QUEEN.

HENRY'S DOWNSTAIRS. THERE ARE DEAD AND WOUNDED.

TELL YOUR MEN--

--BE PREPARED FOR ANYTHING.

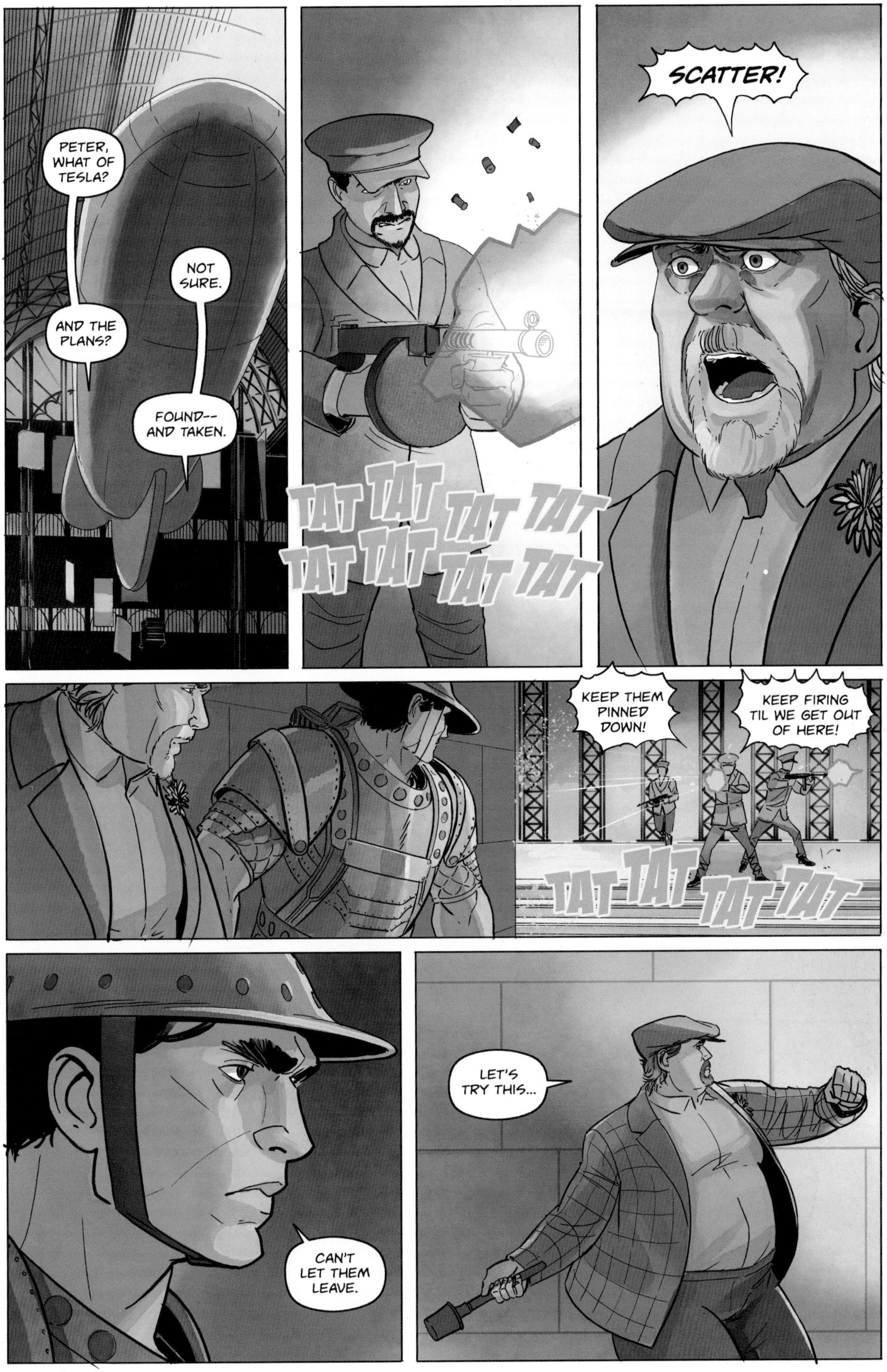
PETER, WHAT OF TESLA?
NOT SURE.
AND THE PLANS?
FOUND-- AND TAKEN.
TAT TAT TAT TAT TAT TAT TAT TAT
SCATTER!
KEEP THEM PINNED DOWN!
KEEP FIRING TIL WE GET OUT OF HERE!
TAT TAT TAT TAT
CAN'T LET THEM LEAVE.
LET'S TRY THIS...

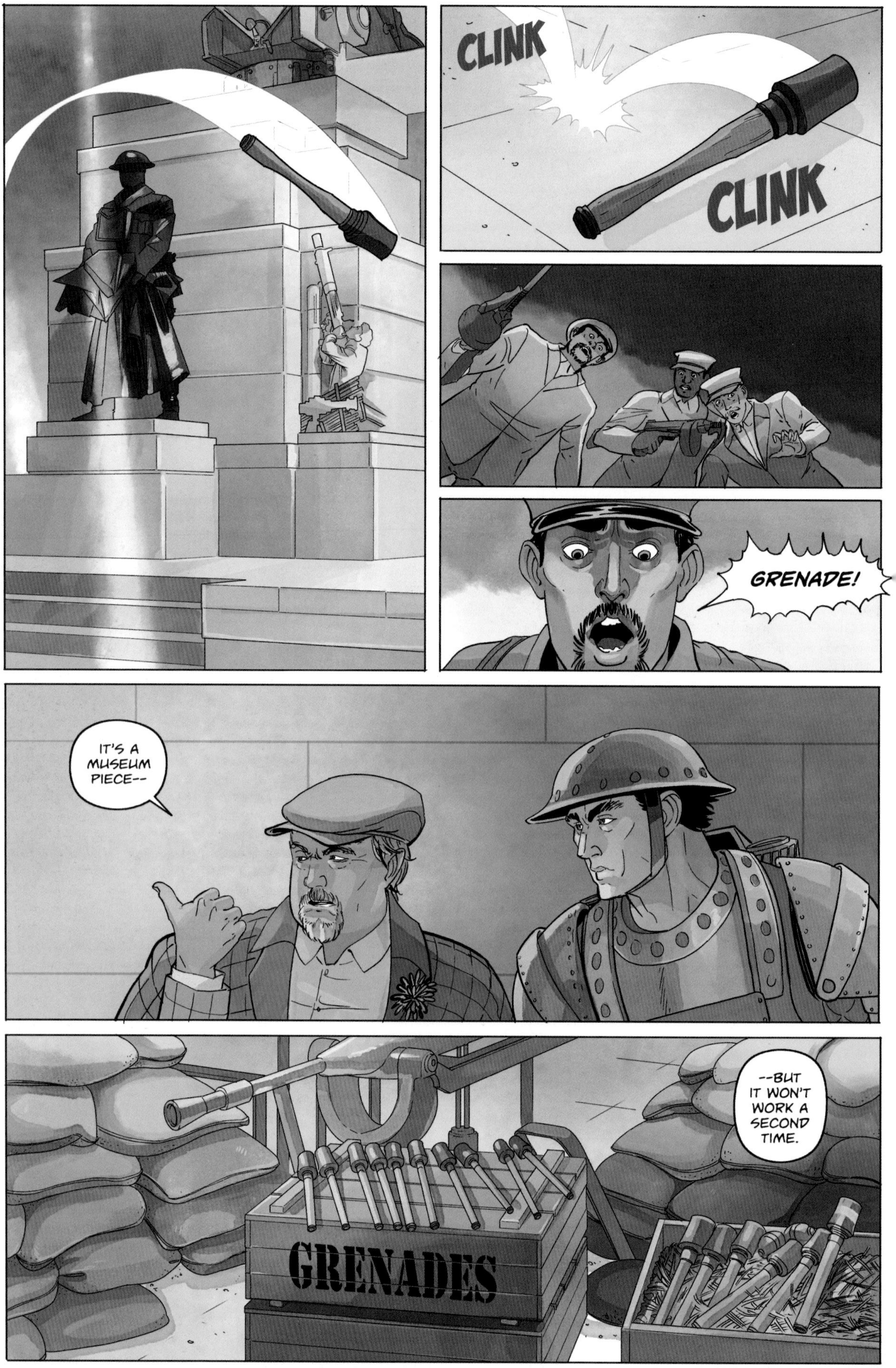
CLINK
CLINK
GRENADE!
IT'S A MUSEUM PIECE--
--BUT IT WON'T WORK A SECOND TIME.
GRENADES

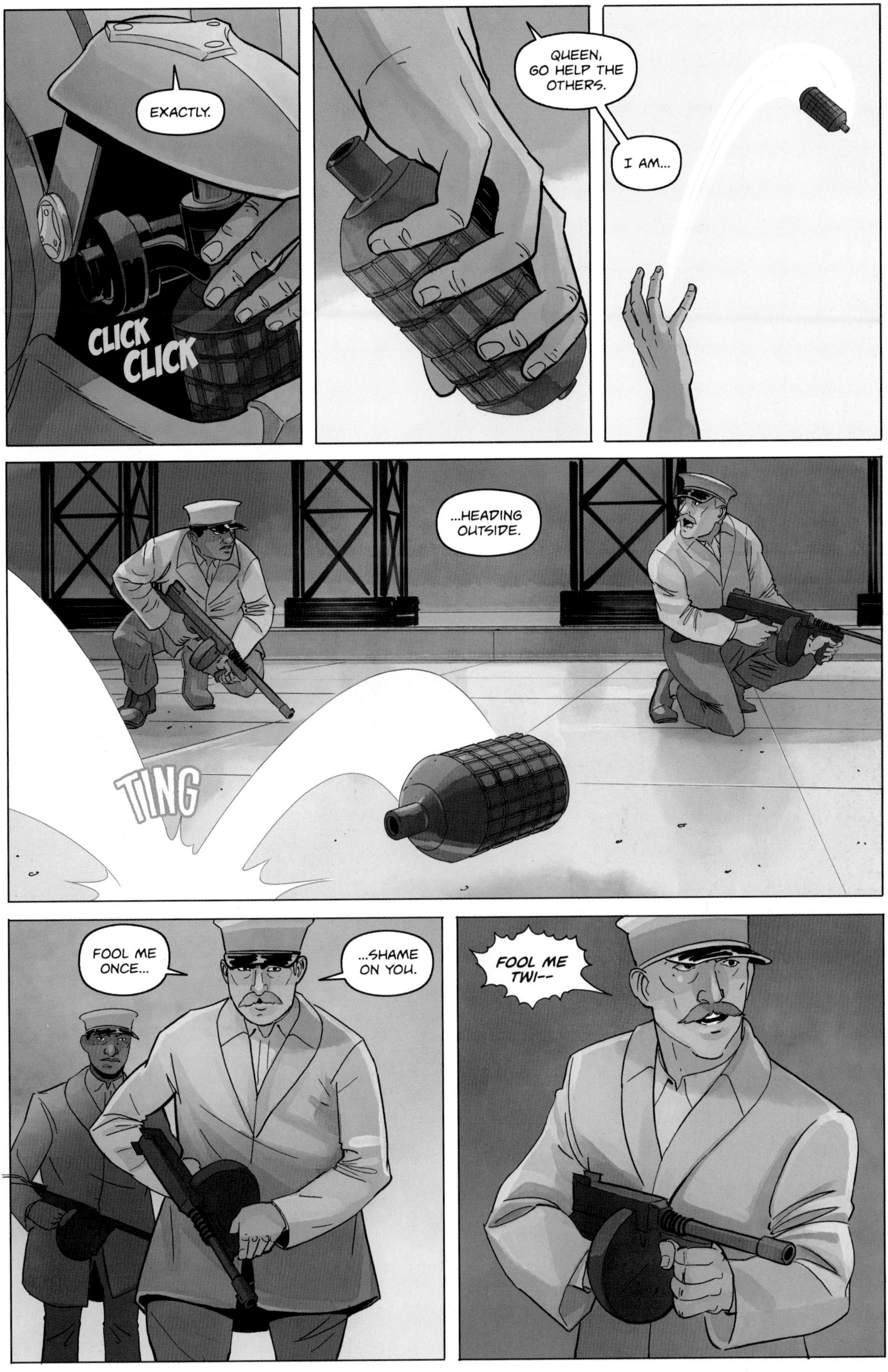
EXACTLY.
CLICK CLICK
QUEEN, GO HELP THE OTHERS.
I AM...
...HEADING OUTSIDE.
TING
FOOL ME ONCE...
...SHAME ON YOU.
FOOL ME TWI--

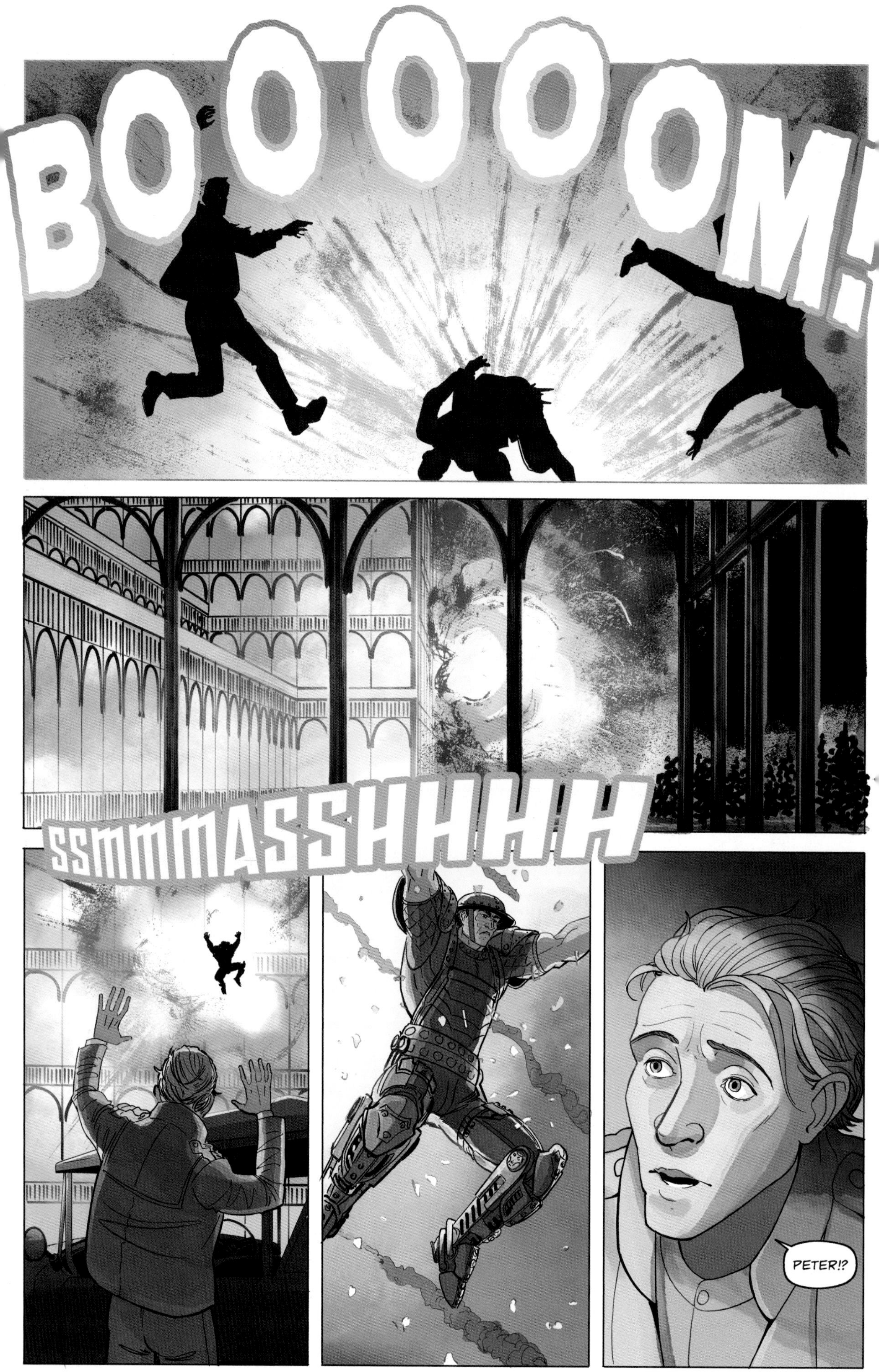
BOOOOOM!
SSMMMASSHHHHH
PETER!?

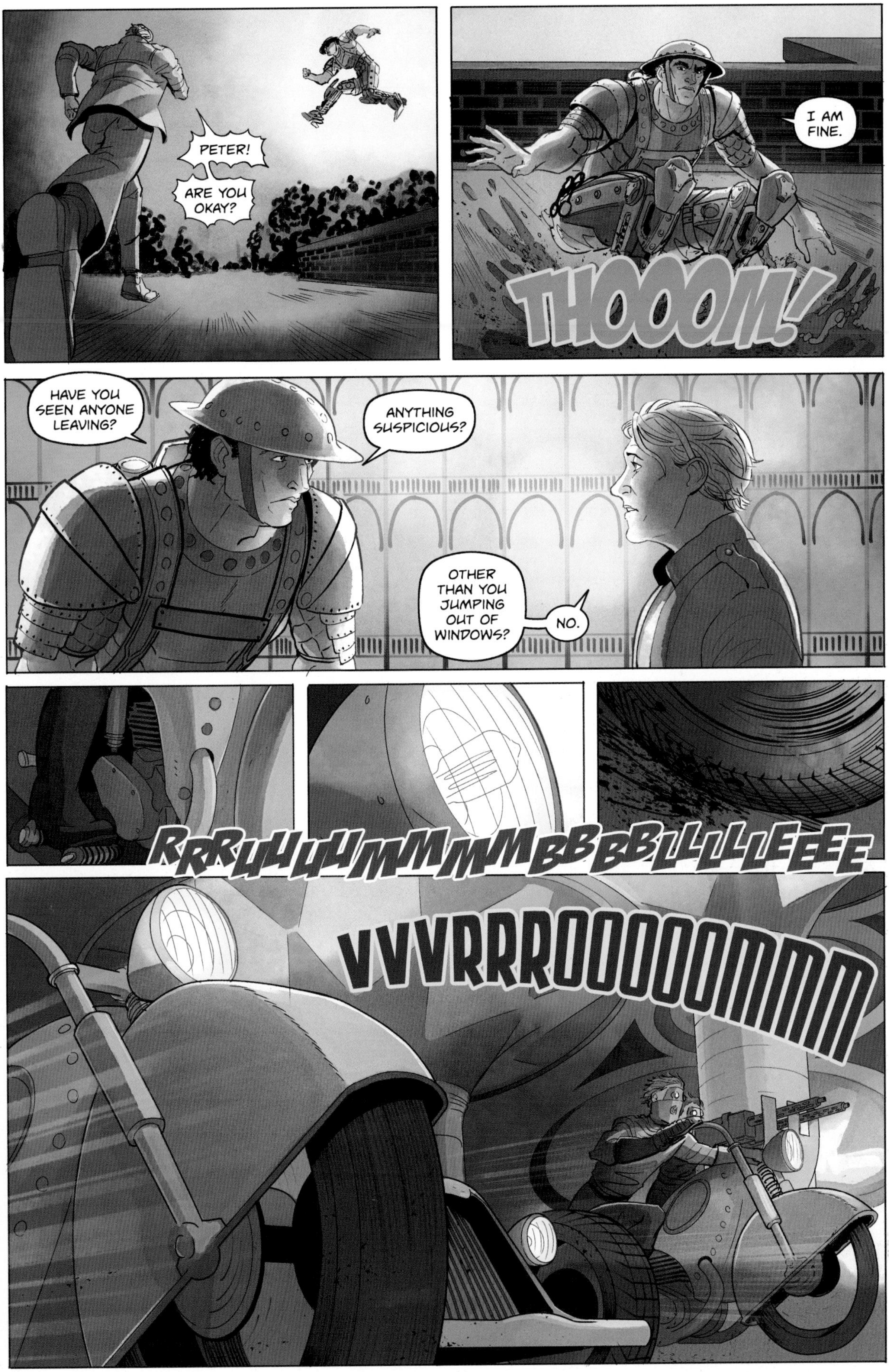
PETER!
ARE YOU OKAY?
I AM FINE.
THOOOM!
HAVE YOU SEEN ANYONE LEAVING?
ANYTHING SUSPICIOUS?
NO.
OTHER THAN YOU JUMPING OUT OF WINDOWS?
RRRUUUUMMMMMBBBBLLLLEEEE
VVVRRROOOOOOMMMM

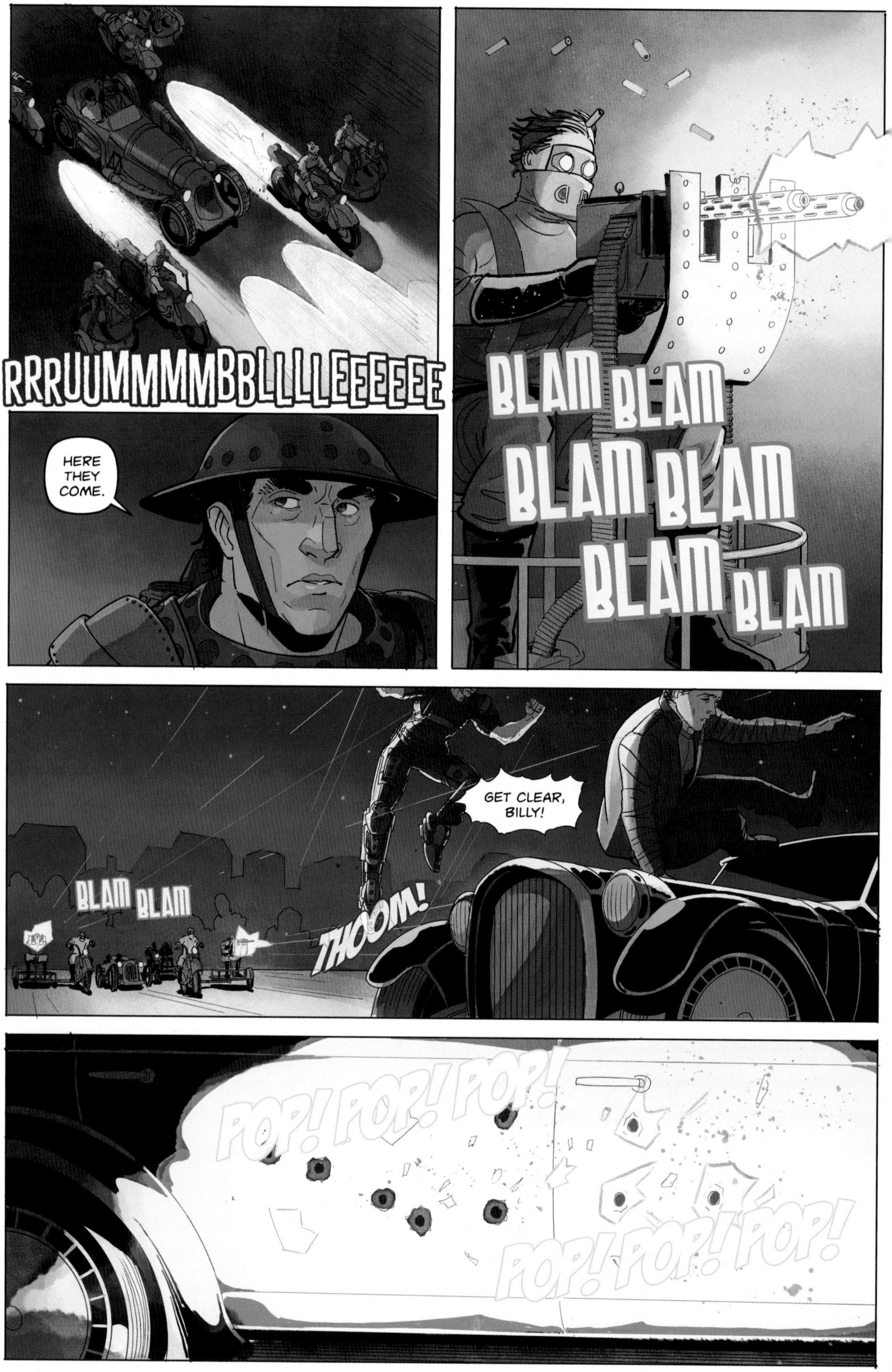

RRRUUMMMMMBBLLLLEEEEEE
HERE THEY COME.
BLAM BLAM
BLAM BLAM
BLAM BLAM
GET CLEAR, BILLY!
BLAM BLAM
THOOM!
POP! POP! POP!
POP! POP! POP!

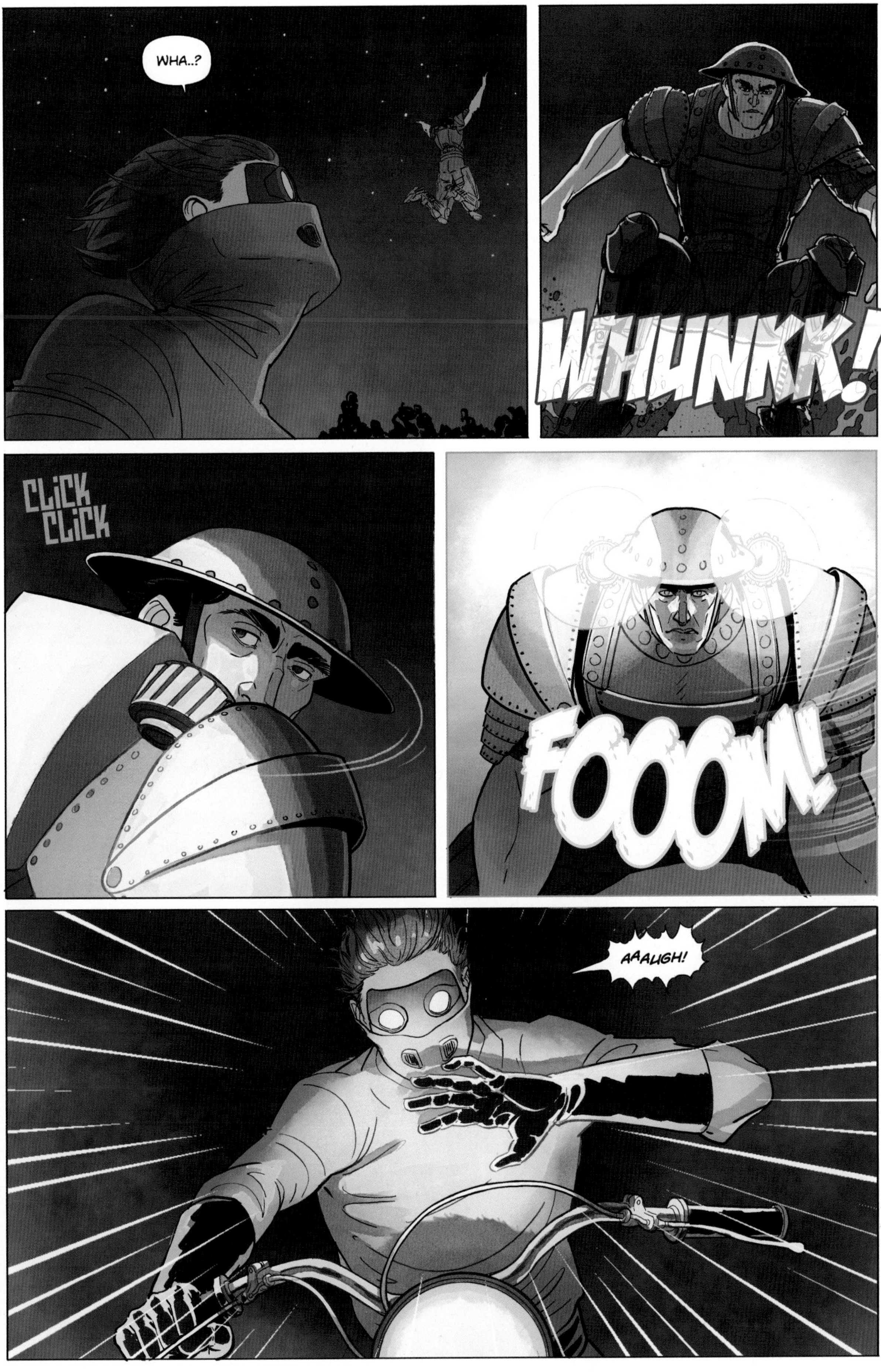
WHA..?
WHUNKK!
CLICK CLICK
FOOOM!
AAAUGH!

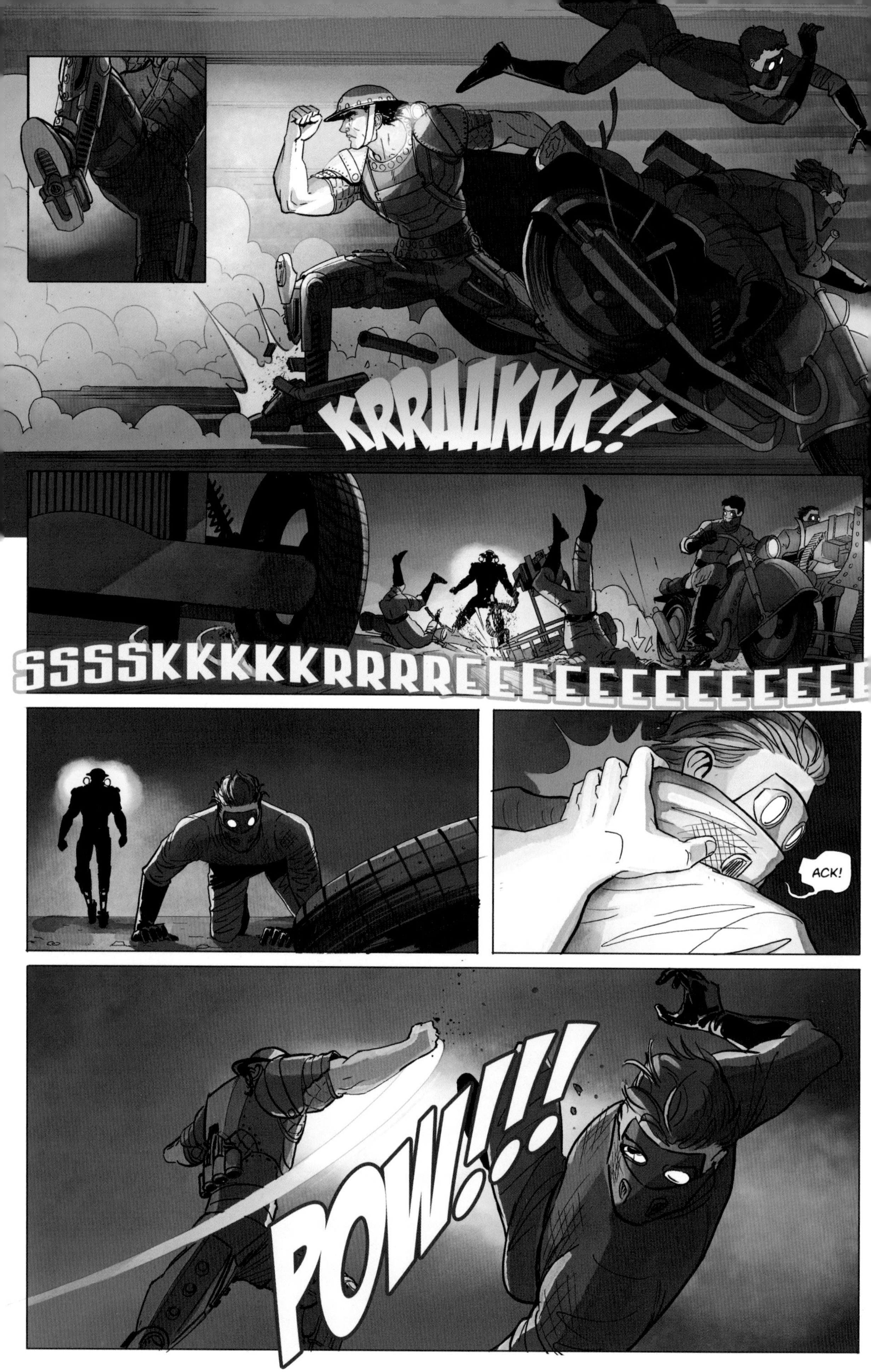
KRRAAKKK!!
SSSSKKKKKRRRRREEEEEEEEEEEE
ACK!
POW!!!

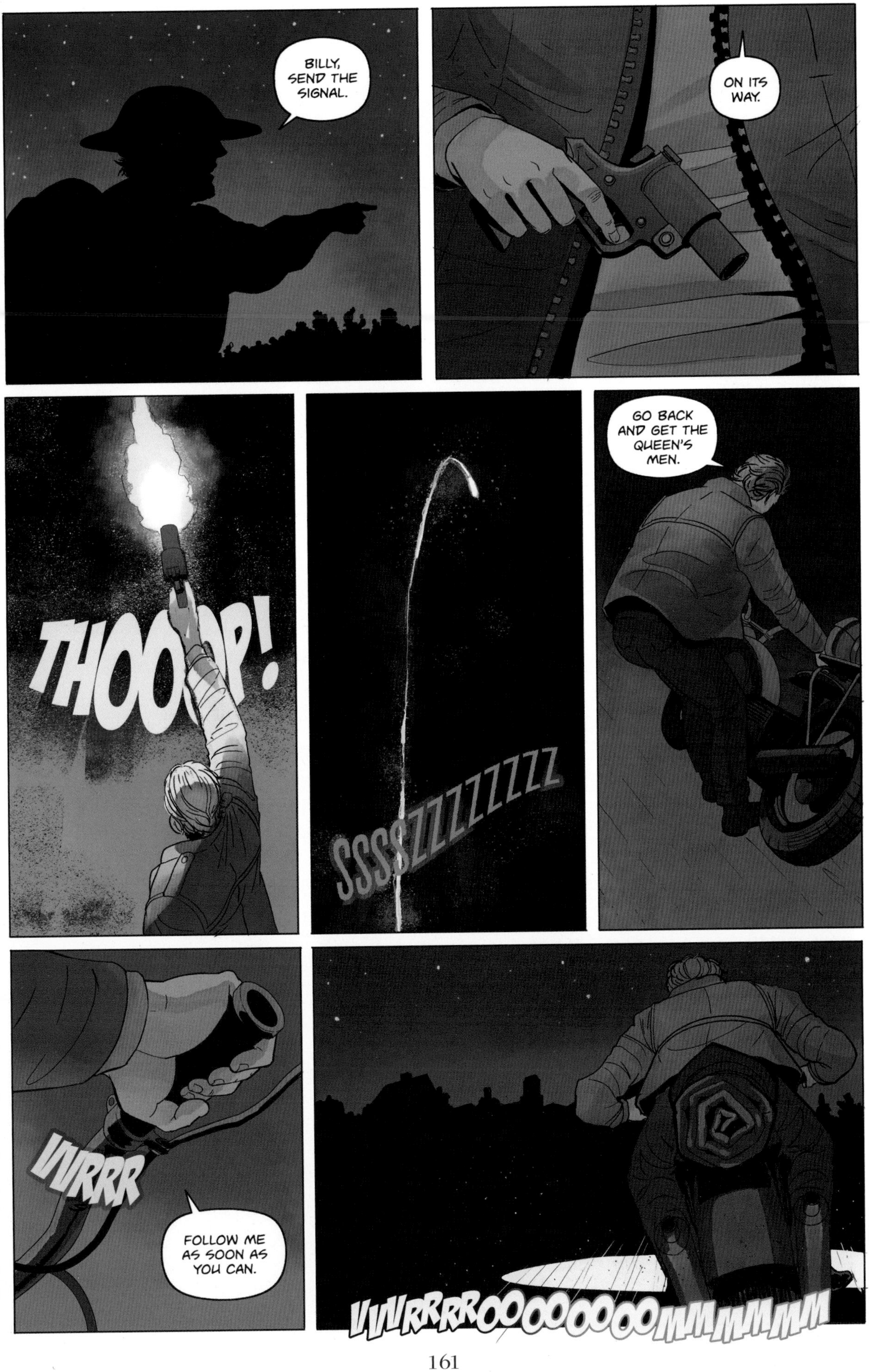
BILLY, SEND THE SIGNAL.
ON ITS WAY.
THOOOP!
SSSSZZZZZZZZ
GO BACK AND GET THE QUEEN'S MEN.
VVRRR
FOLLOW ME AS SOON AS YOU CAN.
VVVRRRROOOOOOOOMMMMMMM

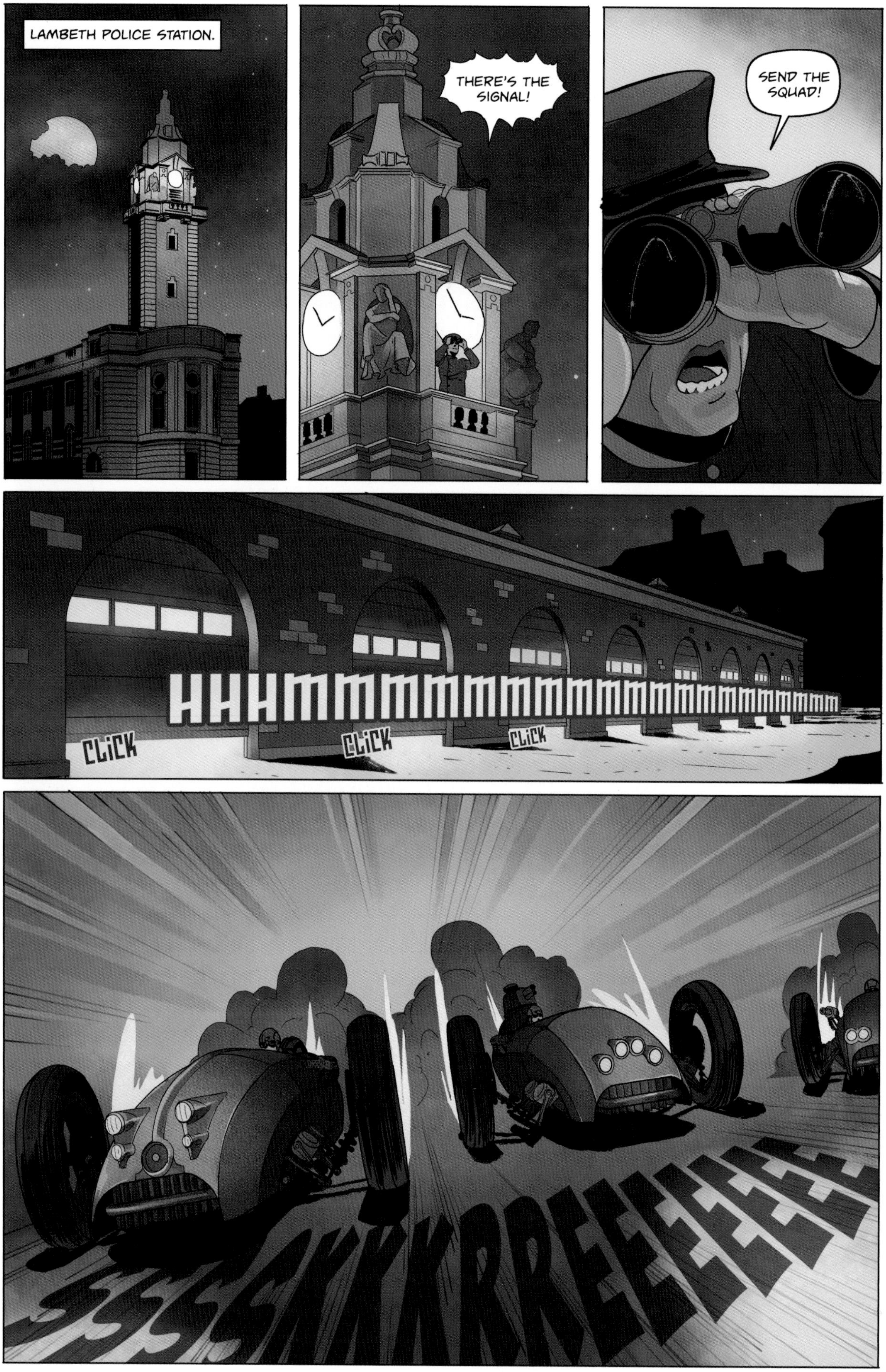
LAMBETH POLICE STATION.
THERE'S THE SIGNAL!
SEND THE SQUAD!
HHHMMMMMMMMMMMMMMMMMMMMM
CLICK
CLICK
CLICK
SSSSKKRREEEEEEE

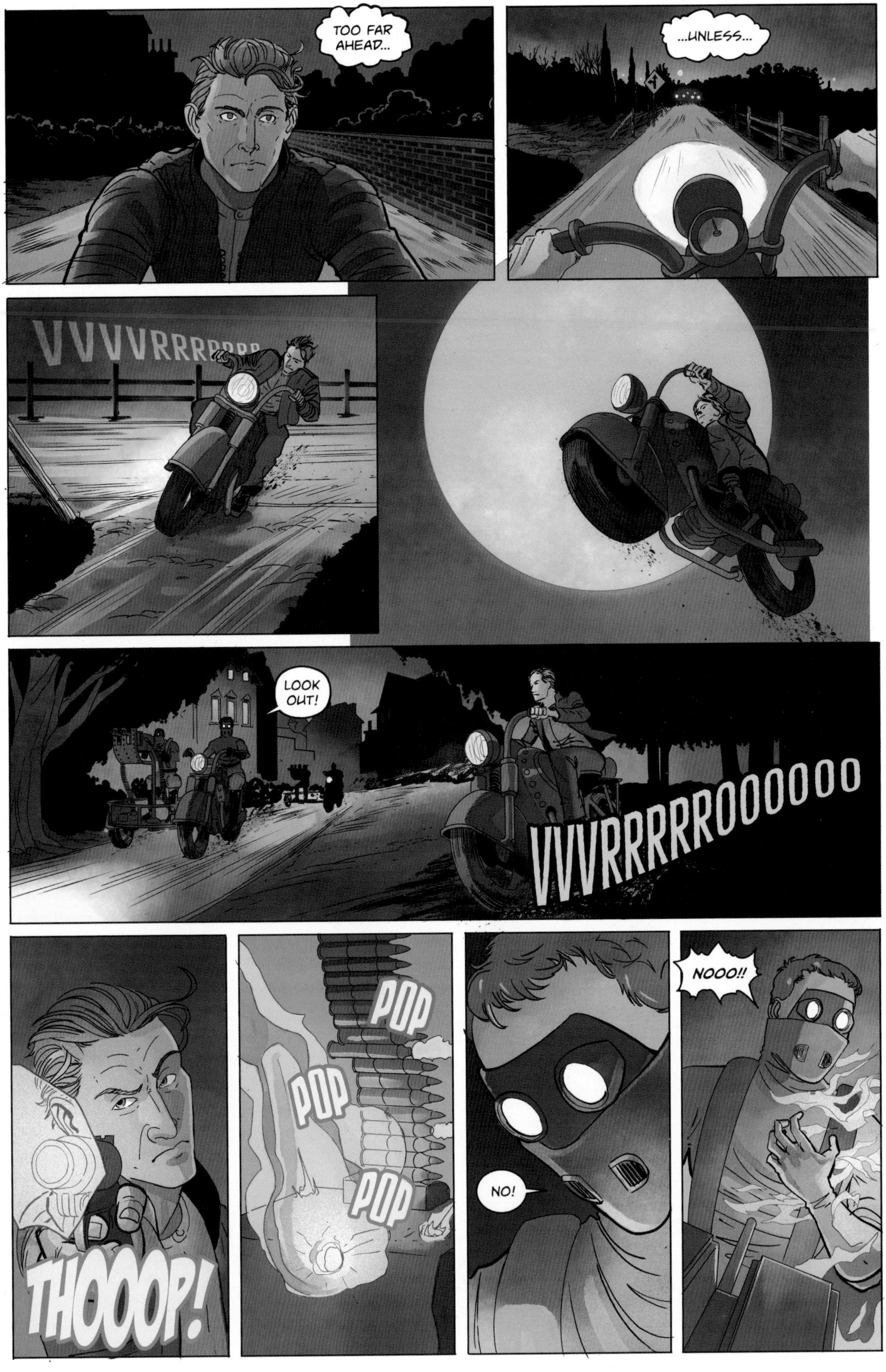
TOO FAR AHEAD...
...UNLESS...
VVVVRRRRRRR
LOOK OUT!
VVVRRRRROOOOOO
THOOOP!
POP
POP
POP
NO!
NOOO!!

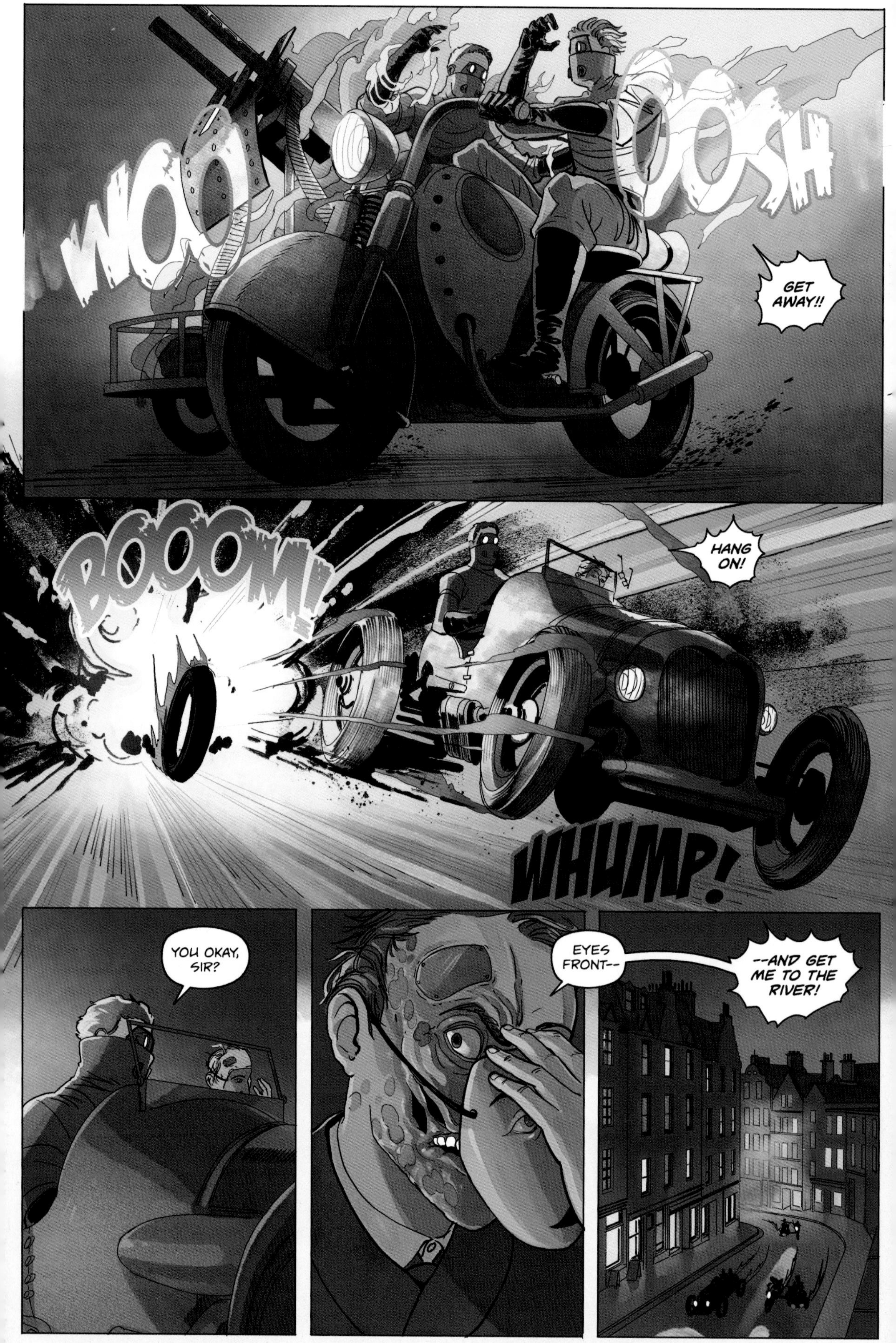
WOOOOSH
GET AWAY!!
BOOOM!!
HANG ON!
WHUMP!
YOU OKAY, SIR?
EYES FRONT--
--AND GET ME TO THE RIVER!

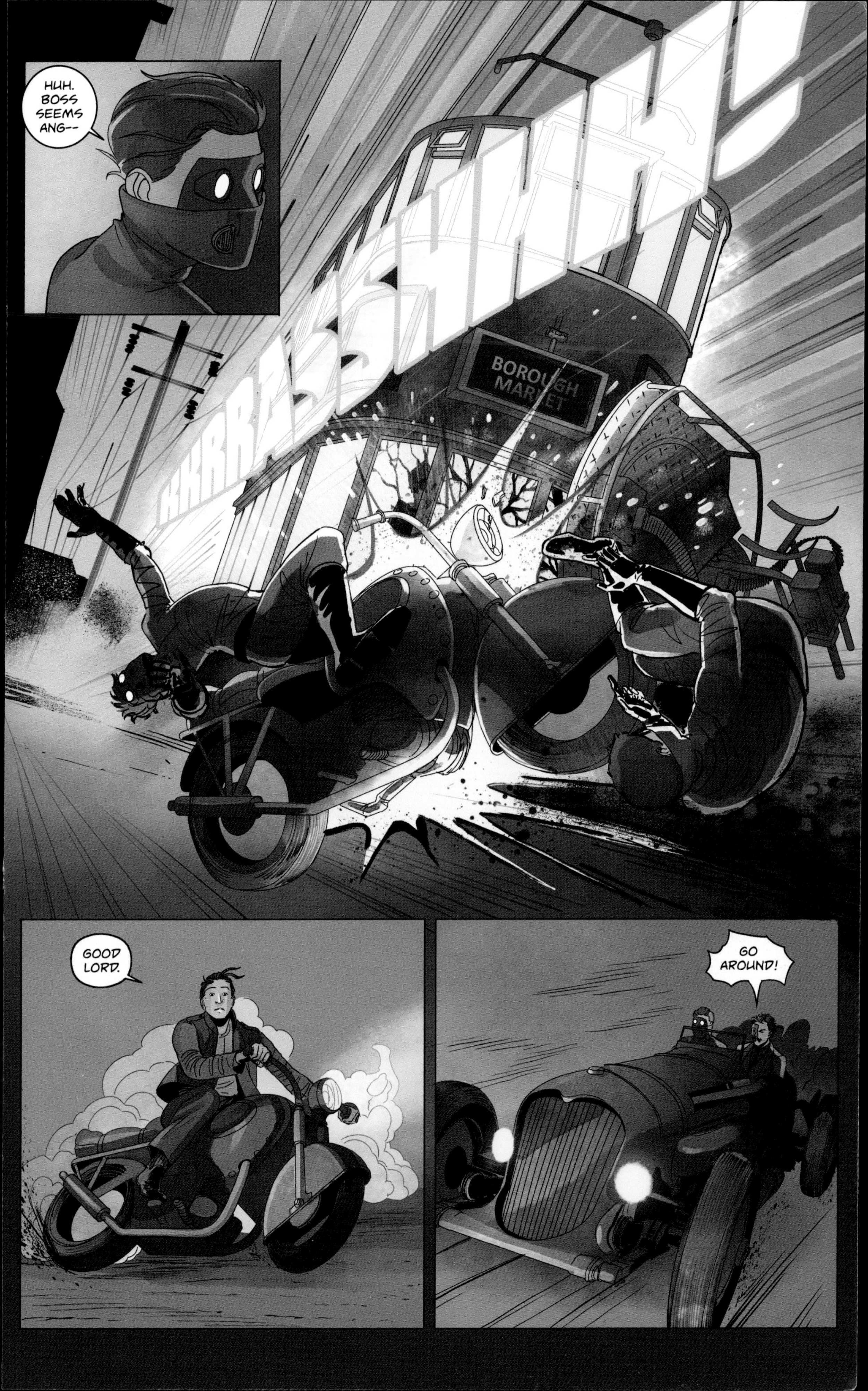
HUH. BOSS SEEMS ANG--
KKRASSHHHH!
BOROUGH MARKET
GOOD LORD.
GO AROUND!

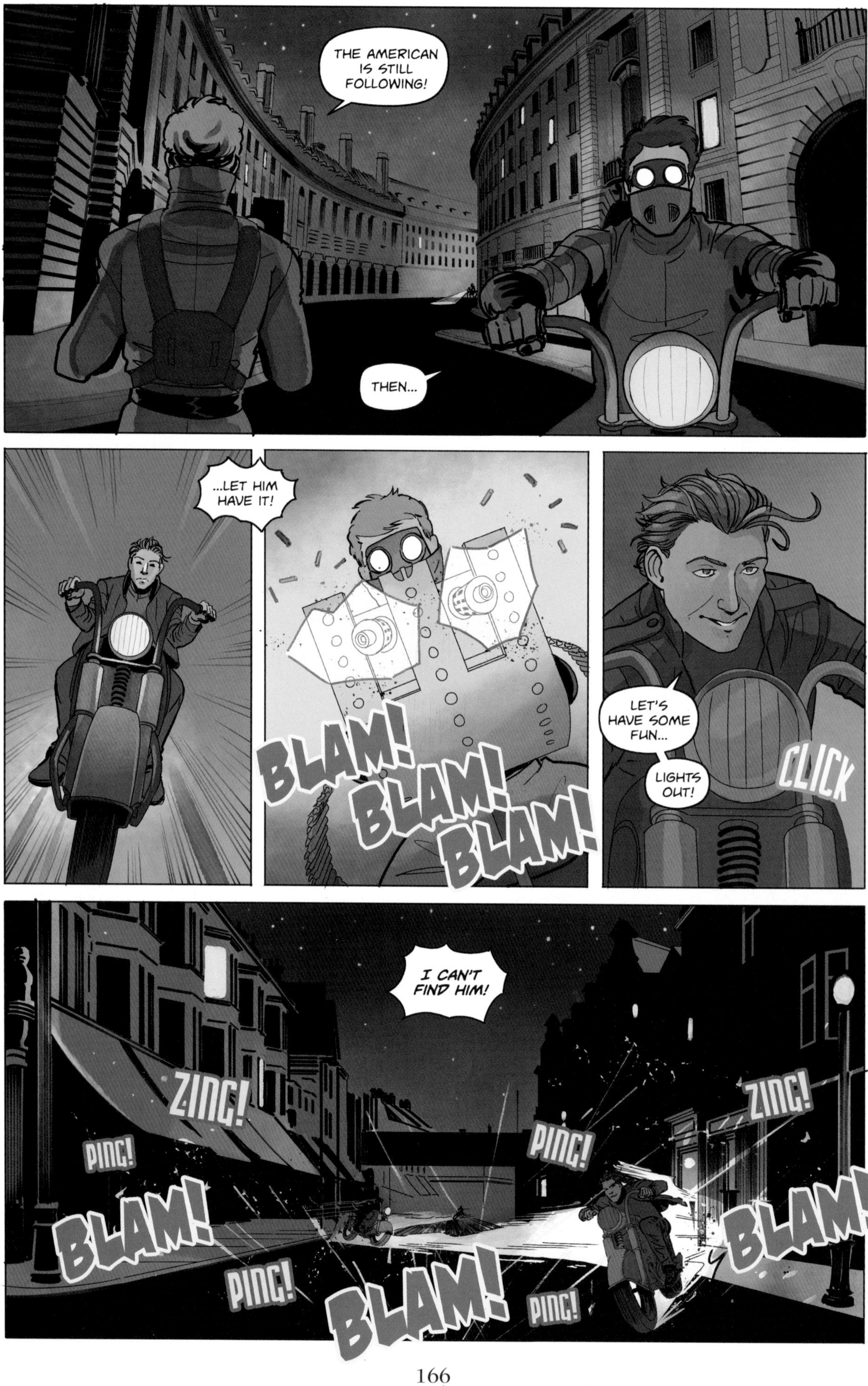
THE AMERICAN IS STILL FOLLOWING!
THEN...
...LET HIM HAVE IT!
BLAM! BLAM! BLAM!
LET'S HAVE SOME FUN...
LIGHTS OUT!
CLICK
I CAN'T FIND HIM!
ZING!
PING!
BLAM!
PING!
BLAM!
PING!
PING!
ZING!
BLAM!

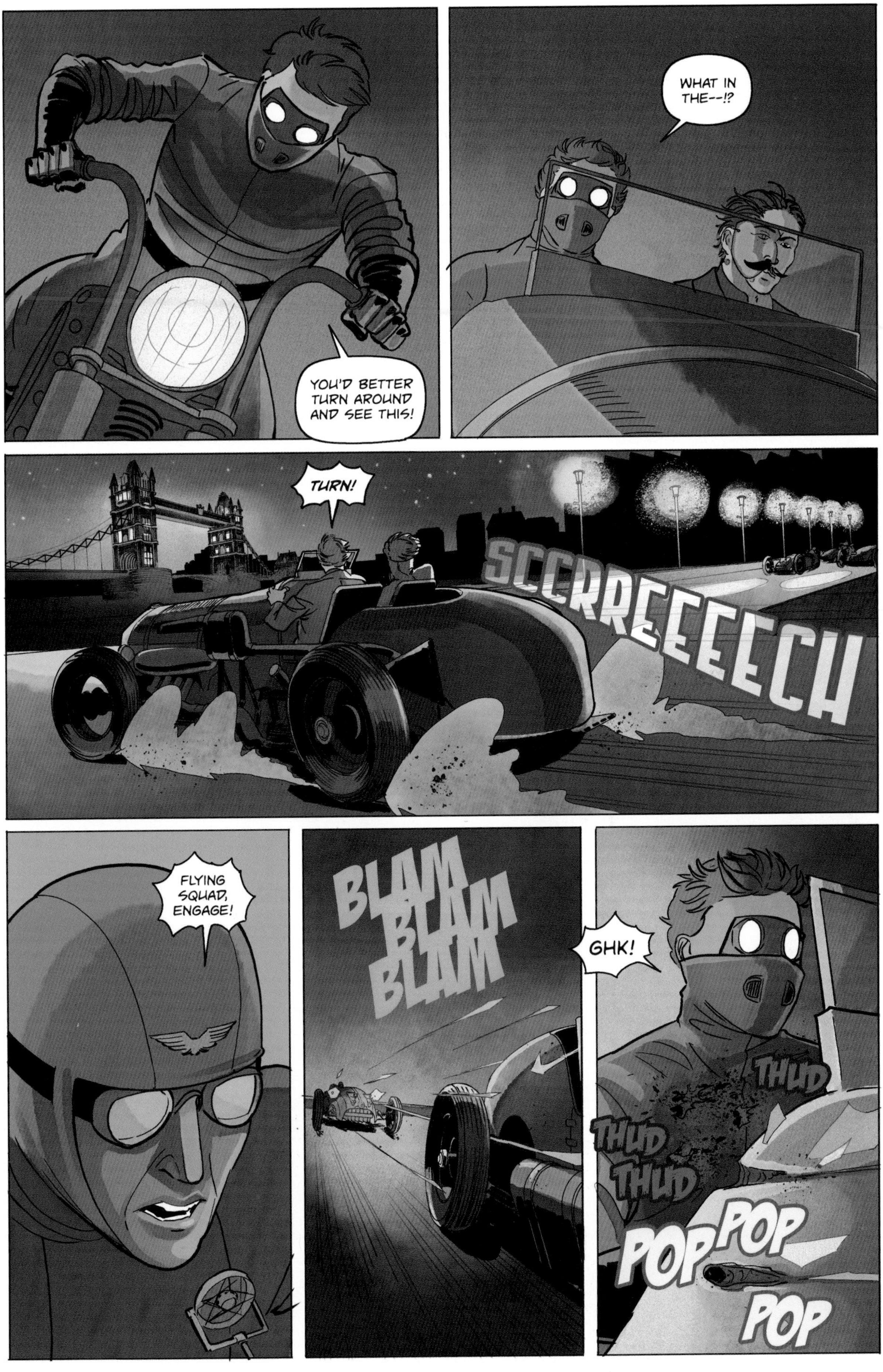
YOU'D BETTER TURN AROUND AND SEE THIS!
WHAT IN THE--!?
TURN!
SCCRREEEEECH
FLYING SQUAD, ENGAGE!
BLAM BLAM BLAM
GHK!
THUD
THUD
THUD
POP POP
POP

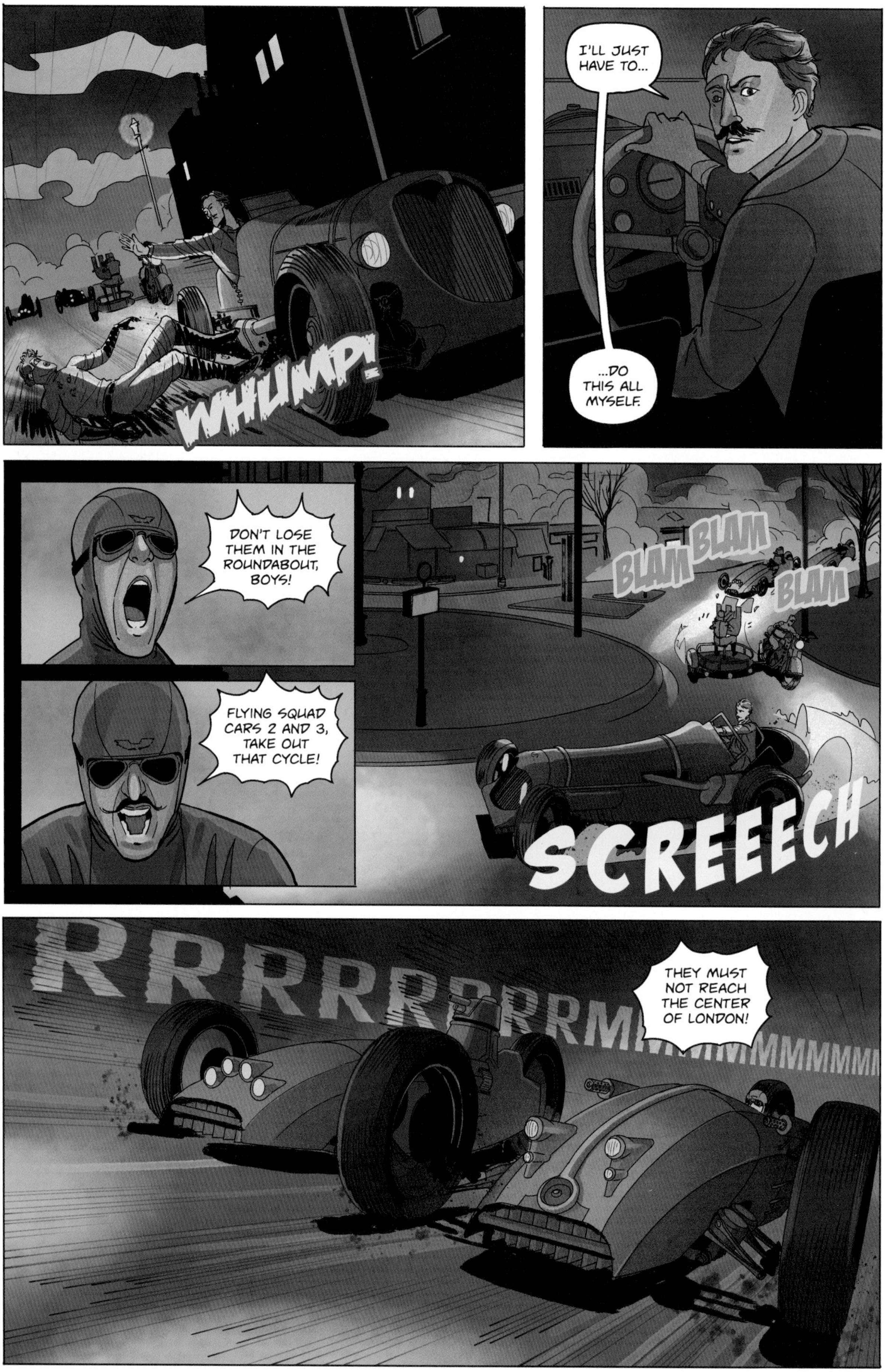
WHUMP!
I'LL JUST HAVE TO...
...DO THIS ALL MYSELF.
DON'T LOSE THEM IN THE ROUNDABOUT, BOYS!
FLYING SQUAD CARS 2 AND 3, TAKE OUT THAT CYCLE!
BLAM BLAM
BLAM
SCREEECH
RRRRRRRRRMMMMMMMMMMM
THEY MUST NOT REACH THE CENTER OF LONDON!

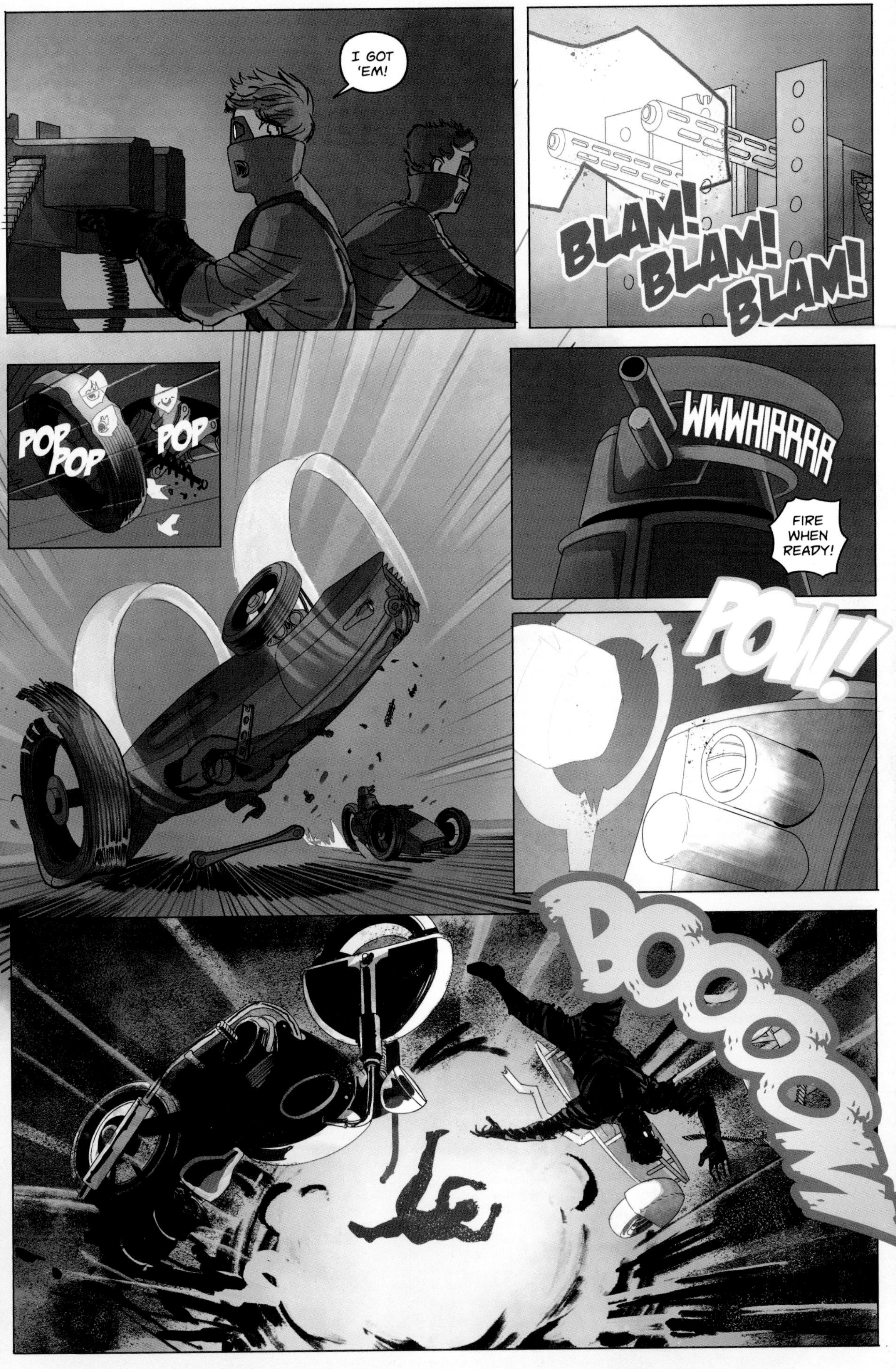
I GOT 'EM!
BLAM! BLAM! BLAM!
POP POP
POP
WWWHIRRRR
FIRE WHEN READY!
POW!
BOOOOM

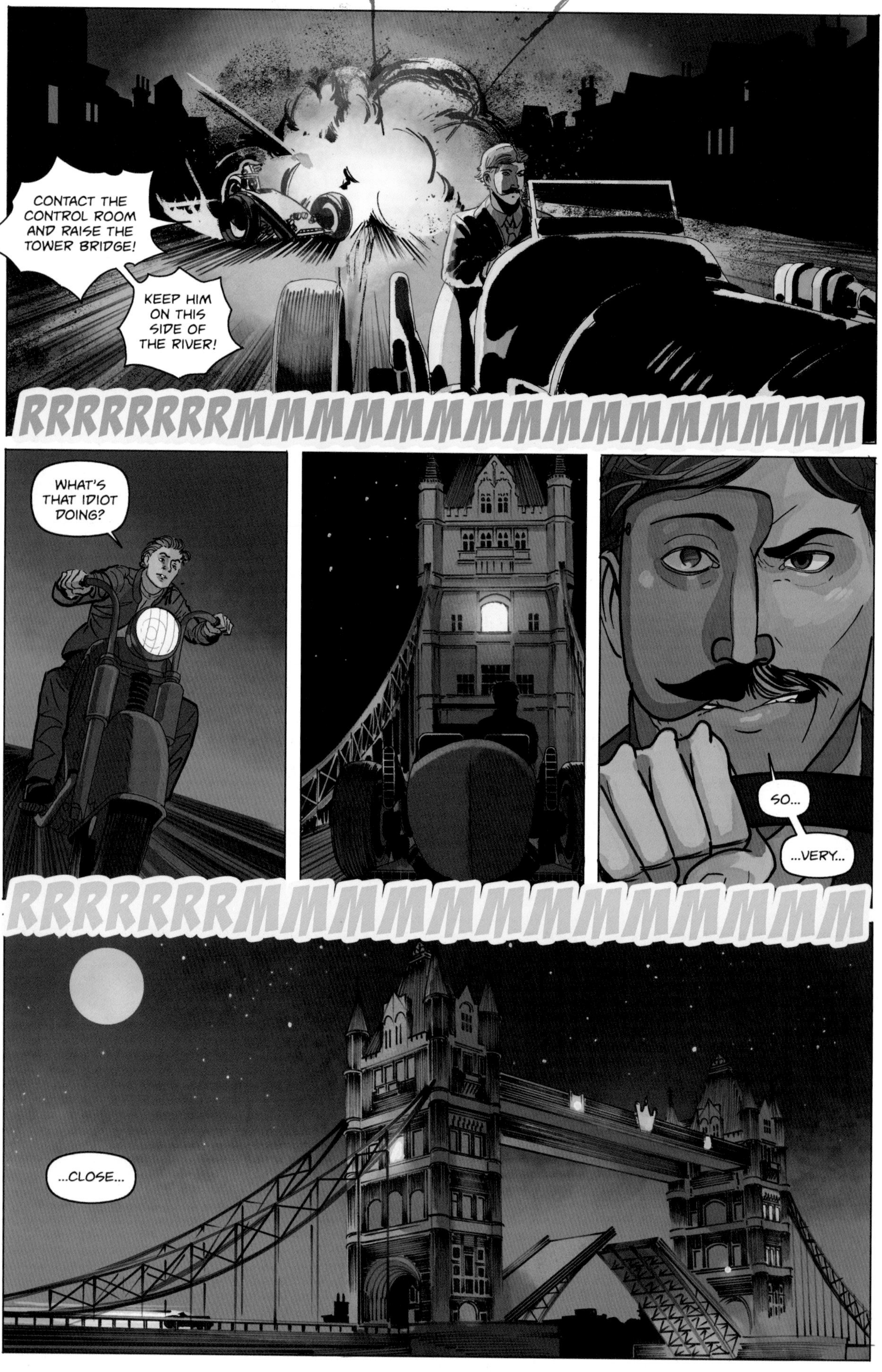
CONTACT THE CONTROL ROOM AND RAISE THE TOWER BRIDGE!
KEEP HIM ON THIS SIDE OF THE RIVER!
RRRRRRRMMMMMMMMMMMMMMMM
WHAT'S THAT IDIOT DOING?
SO...
...VERY...
RRRRRRRMMMMMMMMMMMMMMM
...CLOSE...

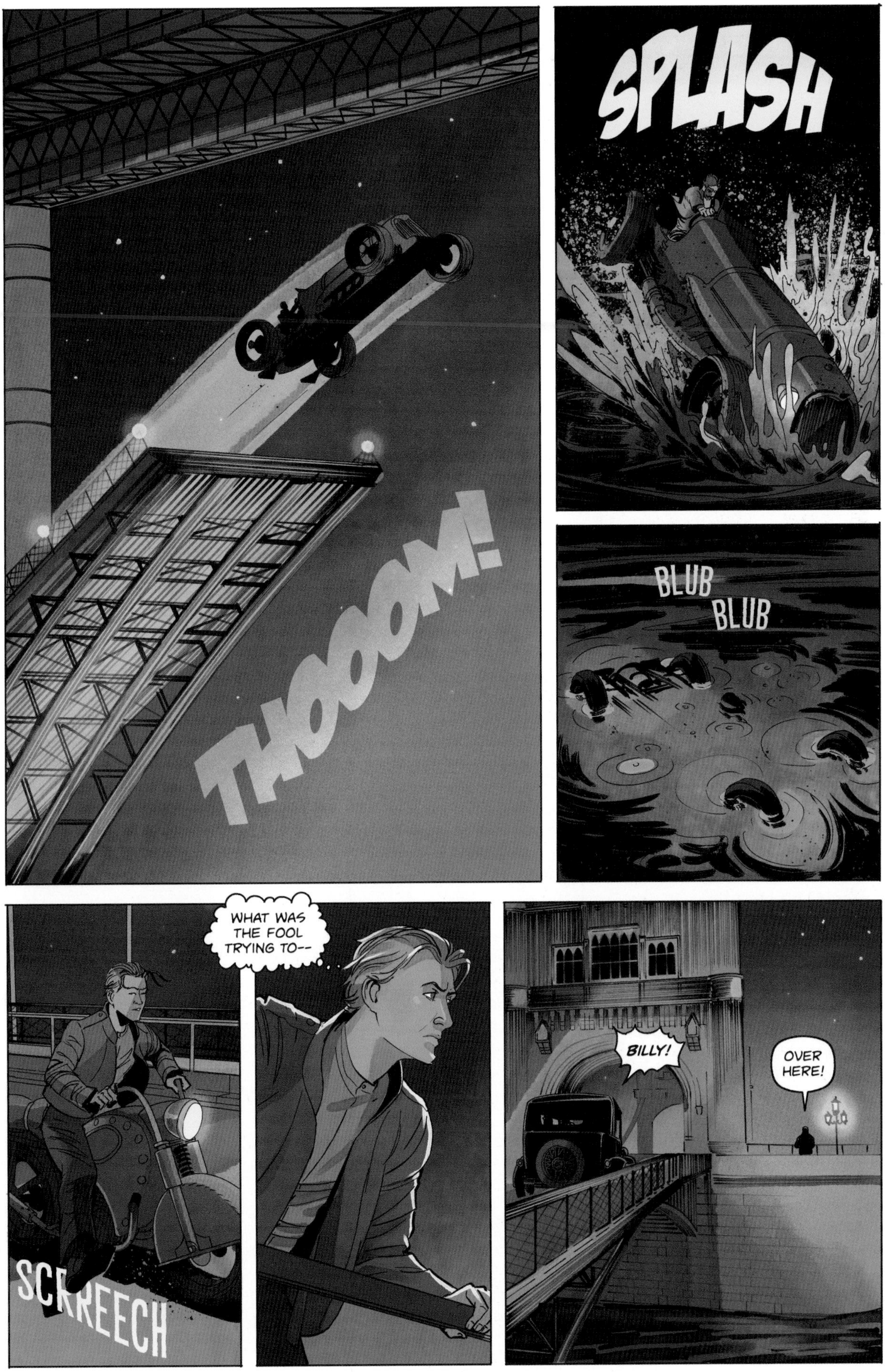
THOOOM!
SPLASH
BLUB
BLUB
SCRREECH
WHAT WAS THE FOOL TRYING TO--
BILLY!
OVER HERE!

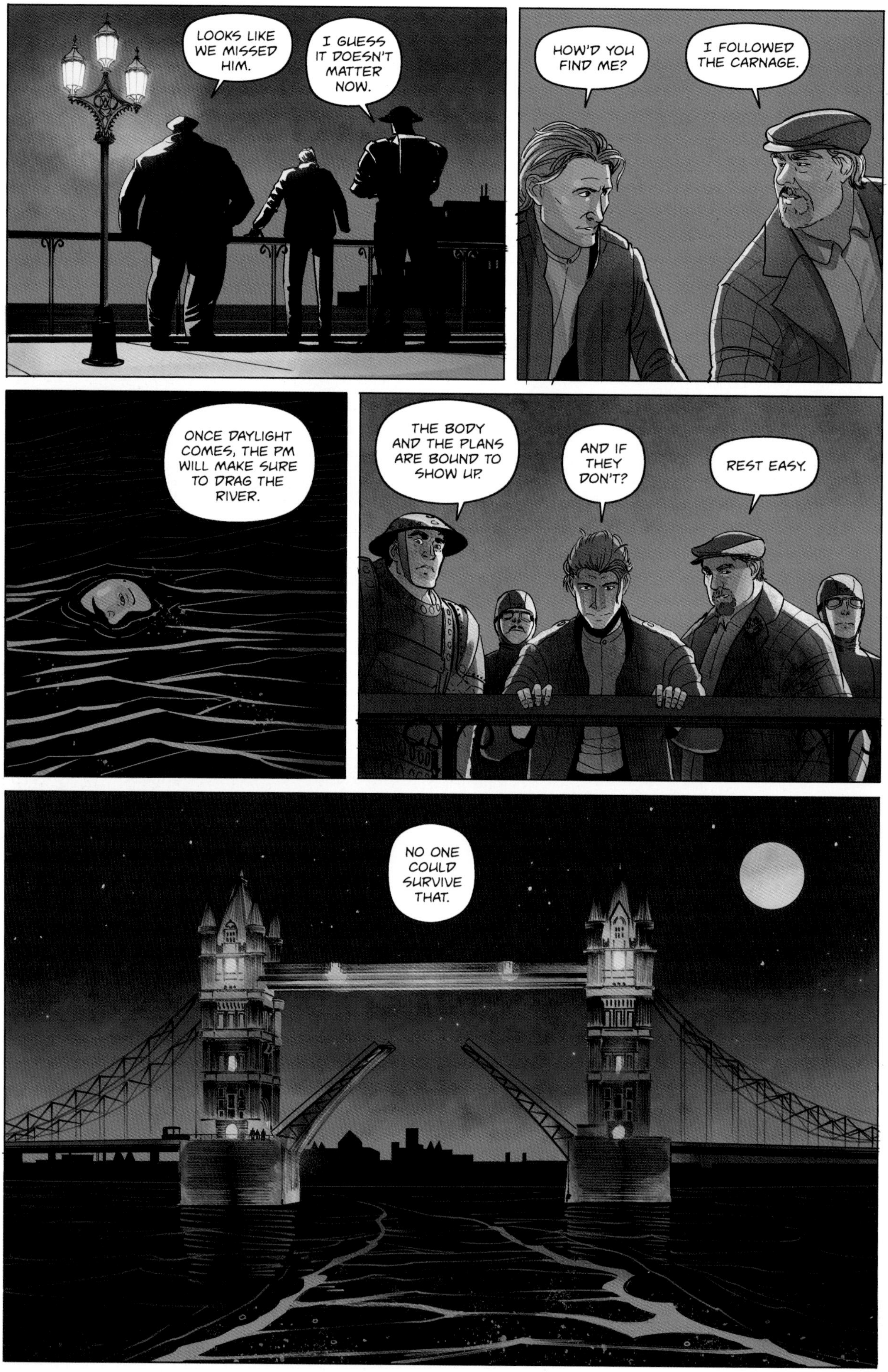
LOOKS LIKE WE MISSED HIM.
I GUESS IT DOESN'T MATTER NOW.
HOW'D YOU FIND ME?
I FOLLOWED THE CARNAGE.
ONCE DAYLIGHT COMES, THE PM WILL MAKE SURE TO DRAG THE RIVER.
THE BODY AND THE PLANS ARE BOUND TO SHOW UP.
AND IF THEY DON'T?
REST EASY.
NO ONE COULD SURVIVE THAT.

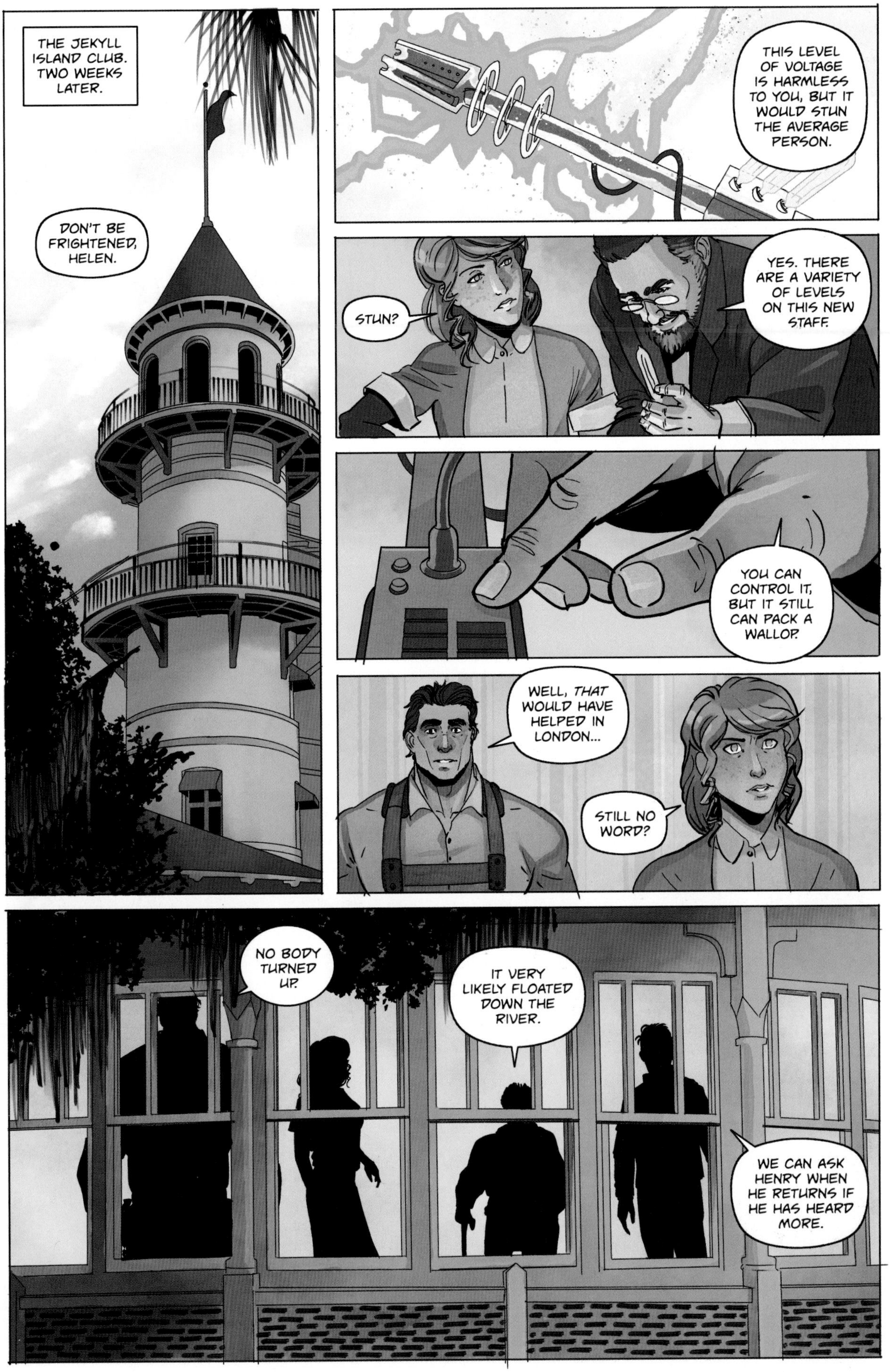

THE JEKYLL ISLAND CLUB. TWO WEEKS LATER.
DON'T BE FRIGHTENED, HELEN.
THIS LEVEL OF VOLTAGE IS HARMLESS TO YOU, BUT IT WOULD STUN THE AVERAGE PERSON.
STUN?
YES. THERE ARE A VARIETY OF LEVELS ON THIS NEW STAFF.
YOU CAN CONTROL IT, BUT IT STILL CAN PACK A WALLOP.
WELL, *THAT* WOULD HAVE HELPED IN LONDON...
STILL NO WORD?
NO BODY TURNED UP.
IT VERY LIKELY FLOATED DOWN THE RIVER.
WE CAN ASK HENRY WHEN HE RETURNS IF HE HAS HEARD MORE.

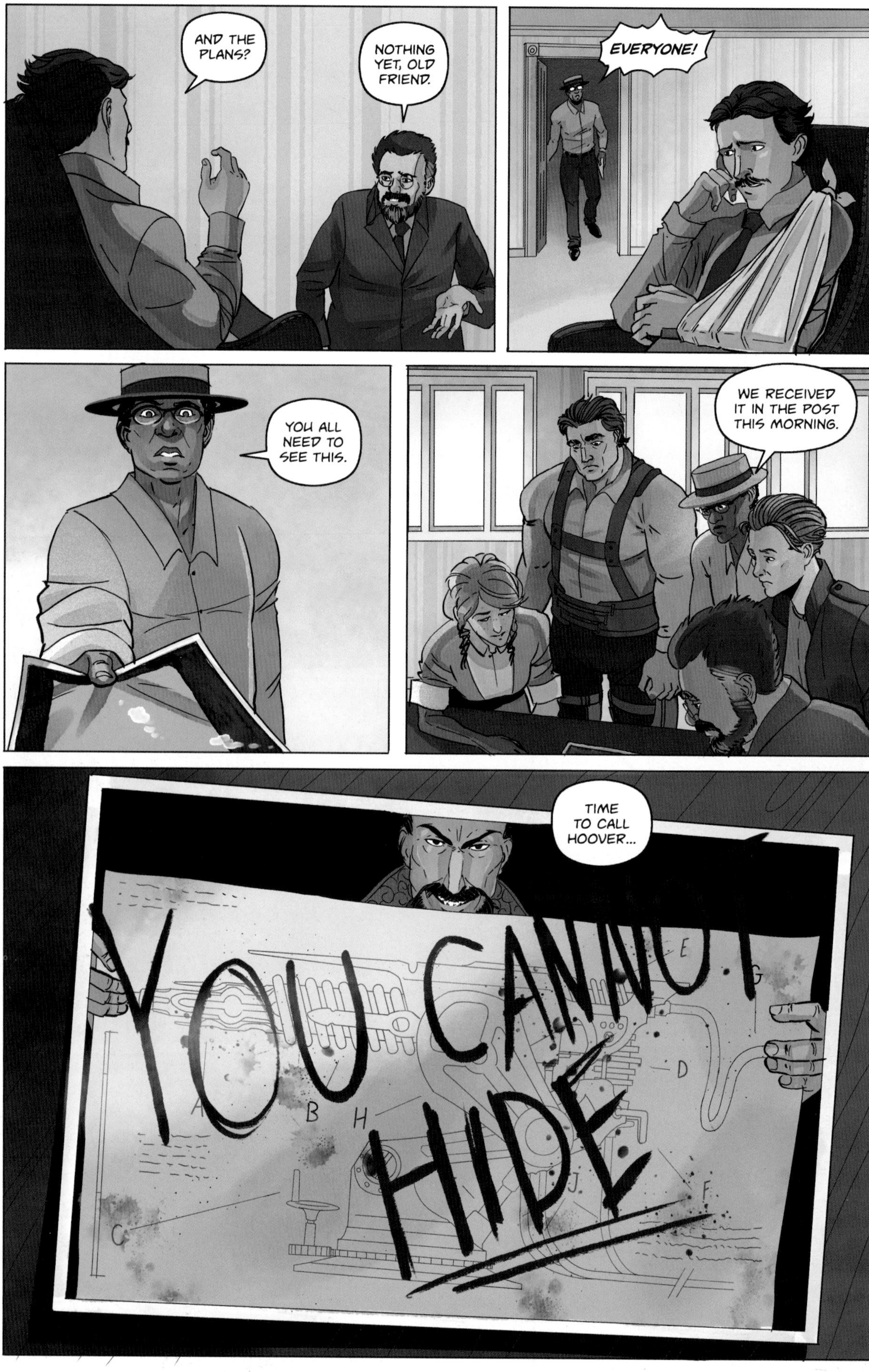
AND THE PLANS?
NOTHING YET, OLD FRIEND.
EVERYONE!
YOU ALL NEED TO SEE THIS.
WE RECEIVED IT IN THE POST THIS MORNING.
TIME TO CALL HOOVER...
YOU CANNOT HIDE
A
B
H
C
D
E
G
J
F

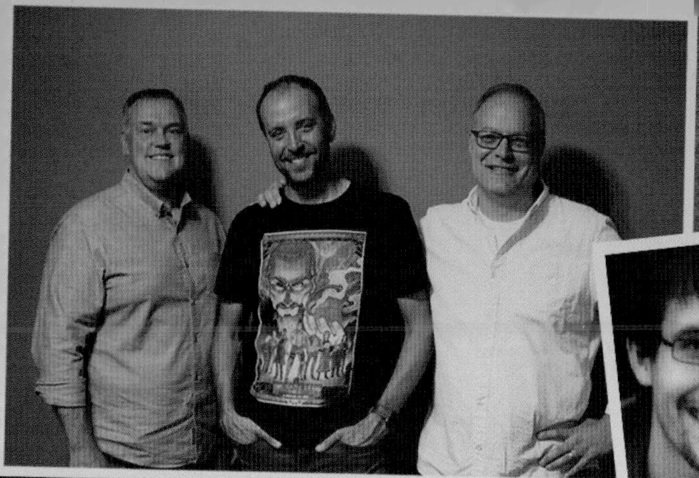

(From L to R) Ed Crowell, Steve Nedvidek, Jack Lowe

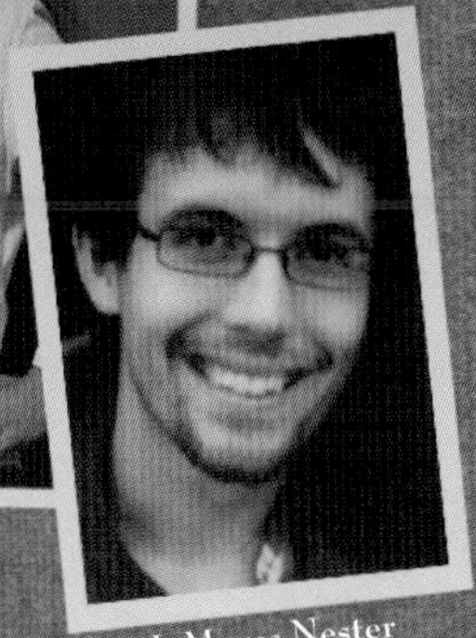

J. Moses Nester

## Meet the Creators

STEVE NEDVIDEK is a cartoonist, actor, speaker, and teacher/coach of innovation and creativity—but he geeks out as an avid builder of models and miniatures. Steve and his wife, Sue, live with their children and dog in Kennesaw, Georgia.

ED CROWELL is a quintessential jack-of-all trades: corporate CEO, lobbyist, writer, speaker, adventurer, and white-water enthusiast, who blends his varied experiences into his writing.  Ed and his wife, Cynthia, live near the Lost Mountain.

JACK LOWE is a student of filmmaking and themed entertainment, and a passionate storyteller with a bent toward immersive, multi-sensory experiences. He, his wife, two dogs, and two cats live in Marietta, Georgia, on the shoulder of Kennesaw Mountain.

J. MOSES NESTER is a graduate of the Savannah College of Art and Design, currently living in Atlanta, Georgia, with his wife, daughter, and corgi. His previous works include *The Jekyll Island Chronicles: A Machine Age War*, and the *Horizon Anthology Vol. 1*. You can follow his work at partthewaters.tumblr.com.

SJ MILLER is a Las Vegas-based illustrator and comic colorist who drinks way too much coffee. When they're not coloring comics, they're usually drawing weird art and short stories on sjmillerart.com.